Stanisław Ignacy Witkiewicz

SEVEN PLAYS

T0160711

Stanisław Ignacy Witkiewicz
circa 1930

Stanisław Ignacy Witkiewicz

SEVEN PLAYS

Translated and Edited
by
DANIEL GEROULD

Martin E. Segal Theatre Center Publications
New York
© 2004

LIBRARY OF CONGRESS CATALOGING-IN-PUBLICATION DATA
Witkiewicz, Stanislaw Ignacy, 1885-1939
    [Plays. English. Selections]
    Seven plays / Stanislaw Ignacy Witkiewicz ; translated and edited by Daniel Gerould.
        p. cm.
    Includes bibliographical references.
    Contents: The pragmatists -- Tumor Brainiowicz -- Gyubal Wahazar, or, Along the cliffs of the absurd -- The anonymous work -- A few words about the role of the actor in the theatre of pure form -- The cuttlefish, or, The Hyrcanian world view -- Dainty shapes and hairy apes, or, The green pill -- The Beelzebub sonata, or, What really happened in Mordovar.
    ISBN 0-9666152-6-3
    I. Gerould, Daniel Charles, 1928- II. Title.

PG7158.W52A24 2004
891.8'5272--dc22

                    2004059220

Copy-editing, typography, design, and graphics by Kurt Taroff

TABLE OF CONTENTS

Stanisław Ignacy Witkiewicz
Self-portrait
1912

INTRODUCTION

by

Daniel Gerould

Stanisław Ignacy Witkiewicz

Witkacy is by birth, by race, to the very marrow of his bones an artist. He lives exclusively by and for art. And his relationship to art is profoundly dramatic; he is one of those tormented spirits who in art seek the solution not to problems of success, but to the problem of their own being.

Tadeusz Boy Żeleński   (1921)

Polish theatre has a long history going back to late medieval mystery plays and Renaissance court spectacles. During Poland's prolonged domination by foreign powers, drama has played a special role in the cultural life of the country by serving to maintain a sense of national identity. But, although Polish dramatic literature is one of the most original in all of Europe, its very Polishness, closely tied to the vicissitudes of history, has made it largely inaccessible to audiences abroad, and only in the second half of the twentieth century have Polish plays become part of the international repertory.

Stanisław Ignacy Witkiewicz, seven of whose dramas are presented in this volume, is one of the first Polish dramatists to surmount the cultural barrier and become known to general readers and theatre-goers world-wide. The story of how this breakthrough happened is all the more noteworthy because Witkiewicz was an outsider within his own culture, existing on the margins of the theatrical life of his era and seemingly doomed to lasting failure. An account of the playwright's confrontation with the Polish theatre in his own lifetime, his defeat at the hands of an uncomprehending public and hostile critical establishment, and his posthumous triumph is the subject of my prefatory essay which serves as a general introduction to his work and provides the context for the plays, each of which has a separate foreword.

Painter, playwright, novelist, aesthetician, philosopher, photographer, and expert on narcotics, Witkiewicz—or Witkacy, his artistic persona and the pen name by which he was known—is now recognized as a major avant-gardist of the twentieth century. A rebel who could not be assimilated to any school or movement, the multitalented Witkacy brought to playwriting an extraordinary breadth of interests and depth of vision, as well as an abiding hostility to the commercial theatre of his own age. The distinctive qualities of Witkacy's work are a powerful visual imagination evoking dream states by means of hallucinatory images, colors, and shapes, a deeply felt philosophy of man's tragic isolation in an alien universe, and an acute sense of the grotesque and absurd that generates subversive self-mockery and parody.

An Embryo Complex: The Formative Years

Witkacy's story begins in the nineteenth century, when Poland did not exist as a nation, having been divided among its more powerful predatory neighbors, Prussia, Russia, and Austria, The Witkiewiczes were a large, well connected land-owning family from Polish Lithuania, related to Marshall Józef Piłsudski, Poland's future strongman in the interwar years, and to the Gielguds, of whom the British actor, Sir John, would become the celebrated offspring. As was the case with many Poles at the time, the Witkiewicz family suffered major losses of status and property because of their patriotic zeal, which involved them in opposition to the occupying forces.

The playwright's great uncle, Jan Witkiewicz (1808-1839), after being arrested at the age of fifteen and condemned to death for purported anti-Czarist activities (as a founder member of a patriotic student organization), was then sent as a conscript to Central Asia, where he eventually became a highly regarded Russian secret agent, prized for his mastery of Middle-Eastern languages and disguises, and engaged in conspiratorial missions against the British in the struggle between the two empires for dominance over Persia and Afghanistan. Of divided loyalties and troubled conscience, this enigmatic adventurer committed suicide or perhaps was murdered at the age of thirty-one.

The writer's father, Stanisław Witkiewicz (1851-1915), as an adolescent spent four years in Siberia with his father, who had been exiled and deprived of his property for taking part in the Uprising of 1863 against Russia. Stanisław subsequently became a charismatic turn-of-the-century artist and cultural critic, who achieved the status of national sage, preaching a gospel of creative independence for Poles through a return to native arts and crafts, while they awaited inevitable political liberation.

Born on February 24, 1885 in Czarist-ruled Warsaw—and thus a Russian subject in his partitioned homeland—young Staś (the diminutive of Stanisław) grew up and spent most of his life in Zakopane in the Polish Tatras Mountains—then a part of the Austro-Hungarian Empire—where his father had moved in 1890 because of failing health brought on by tuberculosis.

At first a small artists' colony and picturesque resort rich in spectacular mountains, dramatic seasonal changes and weather, colorful highlanders, and regional folklore, Zakopane soon grew into a major tourist attraction for skiers, hikers, and vacationers. From 4500 inhabitants in 1900, the population reached 17,000 in 1937—figures which were doubled or tripled during the summer season. Poland's international stars in the arts often visited Zakopane, where many built homes in the local architectural style promoted by the elder Witkiewicz. Although it had no permanent theatre of its own, Zakopane was in the cultural orbit of Cracow, the ancient Polish capital fifty miles to the north, which at the turn of the century became the center of a progressive new movement in the arts known as Young Poland.

Throughout the nineteenth century Polish theatre had flourished as an art of the performer, but shackled by censorship and the constraints of partition and occupation, drama for the most part stagnated. The great poet-playwrights of the romantic era had written in exile or for the drawer, and their works extolling freedom were forbidden in consequence of the uprisings and bloody reprisals.

In the 1890s the situation gradually began to change as the old imperial structures showed signs of approaching decline and disintegration. Because in the relatively tolerant Austrian sector government control of the arts was less stringent, writers and artists inspired by the new modernist trends from Western Europe—naturalism and symbolism—made Cracow their headquarters. A new municipal theatre, built in 1893, introduced the modern repertory of Ibsen, Hauptmann, Strindberg, and Wedekind. The old city itself was a kind of stage upon which a small band of writers, artists, and bourgeois bohemians lived theatricalized lives. Back from art studies and theatre-going in Paris, the painter-playwright Stanisław Wyspiański developed a uniquely Polish form of poetic drama, based on a synthesis of the arts. Using a powerful theatrical language of metaphors and images capable of embodying complex social and political issues, Polish modernist theatre was in Wyspiański's hands nationalist and liberationist in ideology.

Zakopane was quick to adopt the new currents with which Cracow was astir. The Witkiewicz household, although modest in means, became a major center for Polish intellectual life; the talk that young Staś heard as a child was of Nietzsche, Maeterlinck, Wilde, and the latest premieres in Cracow. Taught entirely at home by tutors (prestigious friends of the family from the world of the arts and sciences), according to his father's radically nonconformist educational principles, Staś was encouraged to develop his talents freely in many directions. The aim was to transform the boy into an independent spirit capable of standing above the herd, but dedicated to public service and the national cause.

By the age of five Staś was painting and playing the piano, at seven he wrote his first play, *Cockroaches*, which he printed himself on his own press. In his *Comedies of Family Life*, the child playwright is the self-reflexive hero around whom the action revolves; when a character in the play—an admiring lady visitor reading one of Staś's comedies—exclaims, "It's exactly like Maeterlinck!" the young author's creativity becomes the subject of his own drama.

Other visitors to the Witkiewicz household included his godmother, the Polish-American actress Helena Modjeska, and the young Yiddish writer, Sholem Asch. Due to his father's position of eminence, the boy associated with the most famous and talented people of the time. The painter-mathematician Leon Chwistek, the composer, Karol Szymanowski, the anthropologist, Bronisław Malinowski, and a little later the pianist Artur Rubinstein were among Witkacy close friends in these formative years.

Defying his father's opposition to all formal schooling, he enrolled off and on again for three years (from 1906 to 1909) at the Cracow Academy of Fine Arts, where he studied drawing and painting with the Polish modernist Józef Mehoffer. There he developed a facility at reproducing the modes and mannerisms of "Young Poland."

Modernism had found a congenial setting in *fin-de-siècle* Zakopane, where a penchant for histrionic role-playing, artistic poses, and perverse eroticism fostered the performance aspects of life and the wearing of masks. As a precocious child and then as a psychologically riven young man, Witkacy absorbed the modernist ethos of his elders and played its abstruse games without truly being able to believe in them or in himself. The young would-be artist exhibited his paintings at local museums and galleries, had a torrid love affair with a celebrated modernist actress, Irena Solska, eight-years his elder, and wrote an autobiographical *roman à clef* about the affair, *The 622 Downfalls of Bungo, or The Demonic Woman*, which remained unpublished until 1972 because of its too gamy sexuality (which included a homoerotic episode with Malinowski, alias Duke of Nevermore).

With his pen, his brush and crayons, and his camera, Witkacy parodied the Zakopane sensibility and life style in a manner that both celebrated and mocked modernism and himself as its exponent. If we can call Witkacy's mature work postmodern—and I think we can—here then is the storehouse of modernist props and attitudes that he will hereafter pillage and subject to deforming irony and sarcasm.

Artistically, at this early point in his career, Witkacy is most innovative in his photography. With the camera—introduced to him by his father when he was still a child—he produces hundreds of photographic portraits of himself (and his many playful or sinister alter egos and doubles), as well as of his family and friends. In pictures cropped to show only the full face, Witkacy creates brooding psychic studies that reveal the metaphysical anxiety behind the social mask and highlight the terror of existence caught in the subject's eyes. A compulsory self-portraitist constantly asking himself who he is, Witkacy tries to establish an identity through endless self-interrogation. The artist made a lifetime study of his own face; he was obsessed with what he called "mugs" and would eventually establish a portrait painting firm and earn his living by turning out pastel portraits in one or two sittings.

"As the proprietor of a large 'mugs-made-to-order' firm, or in other words, being a psychological portrait painter, I have the foible of being uncommonly interested in the human mug," Witkacy declared. "Our country does abound in mugs: profoundly mendacious, intriguingly masked and bizarre, complicated and ravaged by life—one must give Poland credit for that." The playwright was struck by how people stare at one another and drain and suck one another with their obsessive looks and glances, and in his dramas ocular attraction and repulsion constitutes an essential element in the dynamic tension among the characters.

Under the influence of *The Isle of the Dead* and other fantastic canvases by the Swiss-painter Arnold Böcklin, which he saw on visits abroad, Witkacy definitively abandoned faithful reproduction of nature in landscapes in favor of the macabre and grotesque. At this period he did a long series of bizarre charcoal drawings (affectionately dubbed "monsters" by his father), with titles such as *The Prince of Darkness Tempts Saint Theresa with the Aid of a Waiter from Budapest*, *Suicide-to-be Five Seconds Before Pulling the Trigger*, *A Family of Pimps*, and *Introduction to Cruel Perversions*. These cryptic mini-dramas with narrative titles, condensed casts of characters, and submerged plots reveal, in a humorous cartoon-like style, the horrors of domestic life, of sexuality, and of existence itself.

Witkacy was destined by his father to be a high-minded artist with a noble mission, but he was unsure of his vocation and consumed by ironic doubts about himself. Because he could not conquer his demons, he underwent a severe crisis of identity in his mid-twenties.

Through parody and playfulness he called into question the grandiose mission accorded to the artist in Poland and challenged his own artistic importance by constantly clowning before the camera, making faces, and staging hundreds of partially costumed "auto-Witkacies"—his own version of performance art. This aspect of Witkacy—the artist as prankster, displaying a fondness for jokes, tricks, and exhibitionist games—kept his contemporaries from treating him seriously.

Fearing a breakdown or incipient madness, Witkacy was analyzed in 1912 for several months by Dr. Beaurain, an artistically inclined psychiatrist living in Zakopane who had taken up Freud's theories. The doctor told him he was suffering from an embryo complex—in other words, he felt himself to be in competition with his father as an artist. Psychoanalysis fascinated Witkacy as a theory that located the sources of human creativity in the sublimation of erotic feelings, but it failed him as a therapy, and he discontinued his sessions with Beaurain.

At the beginning of 1913 the troubled young man became engaged to Jadwiga Janczewska, whom he decided he must marry in order to salvage his wasted life. Then on February 21, 1914, Witkacy's fiancee committed suicide, shooting herself at the foot of a cliff, after placing a bouquet of flowers nearby in a modernist gesture linking Eros and Thanatos.

If it were not for this unexpected tragic event, Witkacy might have spent the rest of his life in provincial Zakopane as a local prodigy laboring under the oppressive shadow cast by his father's national glory. Instead he was thrust out into the larger world of social and political realities, forcing him to transform himself. Janczewska's death—probably the result of some staged scenario or mystification involving Szymanowski—plunged the guilt-ridden Witkacy into a state of suicidal despair. Throughout his life he was gripped by self-destructive impulses, which he feared would finally overpower him. Suicide and the corpse occupy a central position in his work.

At this moment of crisis, his closest friend Malinowski (already gaining fame as an anthropologist, lecturing at the London School of Economics, and publishing in English), came to the rescue with an invitation for Witkacy to accompany him to Australia to attend the Congress of the British Association for the Advancement of Science.

The journey to the East, via the Indian Ocean with a two-week stopover in Ceylon for a change of ships, opened the painter's eyes to the vivid colors of nature and the different hues of human skin and offered him a glimpse of a non-Western culture that was home to a ritual theatre of metaphysical dimensions. Exposure to the colonial world of the British empire with its inferior subject peoples had a profound impact on Witkacy's understanding of power structures and the nature of otherness, leading him to write a group of plays set in the tropics that drew upon his own travel experiences conflated with his reading of Joseph Conrad, another former Pole turned Anglo like Malinowski. For Witkacy the imperialist system of domination found its microcosm in the paternalistic family where the father constantly browbeat his offspring in the name of their own self-improvement.

Upon the outbreak of World War I, two weeks after arriving in Australia, Witkacy volunteered for military service in the Russian Army, despite the fact that as an only son he was exempt from conscription. Even though Witkacy felt that he was defending Poland against the Germans, his decision to fight in support of the Czarist empire was deeply upsetting to his father, who died in 1915, without ever seeing his son again.

Witkacy underwent a metamorphosis as the result of his experiences in Russia, where after completing officers training school he was commissioned second lieutenant. "Calm, almost joyful, he holds himself straight with his head raised high," an aunt in Petrograd wrote to his mother; "he has completely shaken off the despairing state of apathy in which we first saw him when he arrived." Sent with his regiment to the Eastern front, Witkacy was seriously wounded in 1916 and decorated for bravery. On convalescent leave for the rest of the war, he experienced the final days of the Russian Empire in Petrograd and witnessed both the February and October Revolutions at close hand. All the while he painted actively and was introduced to narcotics, orgies, and other decadent pastimes by the white Russian aristocracy in its death throes. At one point Witkacy thought of joining the Polish Legions that were then being formed in Russia after the fall of the Romanovs in anticipation of Poland's gaining its independence.

Before returning to independent Poland in July 1918 with a heavy load of his paintings and portraits, he spent eight uneasy months in post-revolutionary Russia. This was a period of his life about which the playwright talked only enigmatically. As a former Czarist officer, his life was constantly at risk, and he lived in fear of the Bolsheviks from then on.

Plans for the Theatre

From 1918 until his death in 1939, Witkacy lived in Zakopane, at first painting compositions in oils as a member of the vanguard group of artists called "Formists," while earning his living as a portraitist (in pastels) and writing prolifically in many genres. He traveled throughout Poland by train pursuing commissions for portraits, but never went abroad again. His life was largely consumed by a routine of hard work both as the "old portrait-painting prostitute" (his own words) and as a highly disciplined creative artist and thinker.

The impetus for Witkacy's torrential creative outpouring in the 1920s was concentrated in the adventures and traumas of the previous decade. In short order he had been exposed to Freudian psychoanalysis, imperialism and colonialism, cultural anthropology, non-Western civilization, war, revolution, and communism—fundamental twentieth-century ideologies, viewpoints, and experiences that soon became woven into the texture of his dramas.

Paradoxically, Witkacy's theory of the theatre—Pure Form—asserts that the experiential, discursive content of drama is of only incidental significance and that the sole element of enduring value is the formal, which alone creates the metaphysical feelings that are the goal of art. Artistic practice, he felt, should find its basis in theoretical principles.

Strongly drawn to philosophy and aesthetics since adolescence, the former officer had returned from Russia not only with a bundle of paintings, but also with a completed treatise, *New Forms in Painting*, which he published in 1919. In it he maintains that religion, philosophy, and art have traditionally attempted to ease the pain of existence, but that art now is the sole means of confronting the horror and absurdity of contemporary life, since religion has long since ceased to be a living force and philosophy is in the process of committing suicide through overspecialization. But by the end of the 1920s the playwright had lost belief in the efficacy of art as an antidote to the "atrociousness of our existence," and turned to philosophy, to which he devoted the remaining years of his life.

In philosophy a biological monadist (with an affinity for Leibnitz), Witkacy recognized the Individual Existence of each and every monad, including those of animals (to whom he was particularly attached), and even of trees and plants. From his point of view, the central philosophical issue was ontological. The problem of the one and the many (or unity in plurality in Witkacy's formulation) took its characteristic shape from the directly given feeling of the unity of the personality on the part of each Individual Being (the "I" or self) as it confronts the plurality of all that lies outside (the "non-I" or other).

These existential premises lead to a tragic sense of life, comprised of feelings of loneliness, consciousness of the accidental character of everything, recognition of the menace of nothingness, and bewilderment vis-à-vis an alien universe. Each of us is assailed by unanswerable questions, such as: "Why am I precisely this being and not some other? In this place in infinite space and at this instant in infinite time? In precisely this group of beings, on this planet? And why do I exist? I could just as well not exist. Why does anything exist?" These are the ultimate philosophical dilemmas posed in Witkacy's dramas, which portray what he calls "the experiences of a group of degenerate ex-people in the face of the growing mechanization of life," who suffer from loss of "the metaphysical feeling of the strangeness of existence."

In the course of eight years—from 1918 to 1926—Witkacy wrote over thirty plays, but many remained unpublished and unperformed. Of the seven plays in this volume four were not performed in Witkacy's lifetime, and three were not published.

The launching of Witkacy's career as a playwright coincided with the reconstitution of Poland as a nation. Although his family name may at first have been an asset, Witkacy remained a lonely and misunderstood figure whose flamboyant individuality created an adverse legend. In the course of a few years he aggressively attempted to impose a radical new concept of the theatre and to put his own dramas on stage as illustrations of his theory of Pure Form. He sent his plays to directors, visited companies, corresponded with theatre artists, and wrote provocative articles for the press. His campaign was vigorous, and in the early 20s the playwright did achieve a certain notoriety as an eccentric outsider. But the obstacles that Witkacy faced were immense, the result of social, political, and cultural conditions that arose in the aftermath of the war.

When in 1918, as a result of the Treaty of Versailles, Poland regained its independence, the country and its arts were no longer under foreign domination for the first time in 123 years. Once the occupying forces were withdrawn and the country recovered its identity as a self-determining nation, Poland became post-colonial and, in the abstract, was free to develop its culture as it wished.

The Czarist bureaucracy, which had maintained and controlled all the theatres in the largest sector of the partitioned country (including Warsaw), suddenly dissolved overnight. During twenty years of precarious existence before disaster struck in 1939, Polish theatre enjoyed a brief but unstable interlude in which it was allowed to stand on its own and survive as best as it could. Since the government was too poor to subsidize theatres, the burden of financing fell on the municipalities, but after the world-wide crisis of 1929, the situation grew desperate. The 1920s was a period of instability, financial crisis, and mounting danger and menace from political extremism.

The brief war with the Soviet Union in 1919-20, successfully waged by the strongman Marshall Józef Piłsudski, intensified Polish fears of Russian Bolshevism. Censorship and government interference in the arts, previously wielded by foreign oppressors against an occupied nation, were now directed by Poles against other Poles, who could be accused of being Bolshevik or anarchist for simply engaging in any form of artistic experimentation. As the government grew increasingly authoritarian, perceived leftist writers were harassed, magazines confiscated, and theatres raided.

Despite the general hostility to innovation in the arts, there were serious attempts to break the mold of a conventional theatre of entertainment. The leading director of the period, Leon Schiller created a "monumental theatre," using Shakespeare, the Polish romantics and neo-romantics, and Brecht, to create large scale works, composed in dynamic images, with huge crowds, choruses, choirs, music, song, and rhythmic movement. Soviet-style proletarian theatre, promoted by Bruno Jasieński and Witold Wandurski, was not tolerated, and both writers went in exile to the USSR where they were eventually liquidated.

Juliusz Osterwa, an actor who had spent the war years in Moscow where he became acquainted with Stanislavsky's work, founded an actors' studio in 1919 which he called the Reduta (Redoubt), an outpost in the battle against falsity and conventionality. Monastic dedication to truth in art was the company's credo, which Osterwa felt could be implemented by scrupulous psychological realism and selfless communal acting.

Witkacy accepted none of these models, but it was particularly in reaction to the psychological realism of Stanislavsky and the Reduta that he formulated his theory of *Pure Form in the Theatre*, which he published in 1920. *Pure Form* is a radical theory of non-realistic drama, according to which the performers and their words, gestures, and actions should serve as sounds, colors, and shapes in a total composition rather than as a depiction of the outside "real" world. Witkacy wished to free drama from conventional psychology and storytelling and give it the formal possibilities of modern art and music.

Through the purely formal arrangement of component elements, which would reflect the structure of the universe, he hoped to arouse in the spectator the metaphysical feeling of the strangeness of existence which would be lost forever in the mechanized routine of the perfect ant hill society of the future. Art, for Witkacy, meant the creation of form, and theatre should be not a means of expression, but a construct in which the actor could function as a pure instrument rather than as a register of "experiences," as was the aim of Stanislavsky and his disciples

Both the conservative critical establishment and the left-leaning Futurists (the largest Polish avant-garde formation) refused to accept either Witkacy's plays or his theories. The theatre critics claimed that his plays made no sense at all, while the Futurists found, on the contrary, that they made far too much sense.

Witkacy maintained that the wrong people were writing for the stage; not professional men of the theatre, but children and painters should become playwrights, he argued. Through the theory and practice of

Pure Form, Witkacy hoped to restore to the overly rationalized stage of realism the magical perceptions of childhood and the modern painter's sense of color and shape. The theatre would thus become an autonomous art with a scenic language of its own.

For the materials of his dramas, Witkacy was wildly eclectic in his borrowings and appropriations. He constantly blurred the borders separating popular culture and high art and had recourse to the low genres of melodrama, farce, and science fiction, and he utilized the materials of popular entertainments, such as adventure stories, pulp romances, spy thrillers, and "yellow peril" tales of horror. He frequently turned to the classics—Shakespeare—as well as to modernist literature—Conrad—and also showed a fondness for children's literature—Stevenson's *Kidnapped* and *Treasure Island*. His favorite dramaturgical device was the "risen corpse," which sabotaged the rules of drama by allowing the dead to return to life nonchalantly, as though nothing had happened. He treated theatre, including his own irreverently, and he self-parodied the shibboleths of modernism on which he had been nurtured.

In 1923 Witkacy entered into marriage with the aristocratic Jadwiga Unrug according to a pre-arranged plan guaranteeing each complete freedom. Although they lived apart—she in her Waraw apartment, he with his mother in Zakopane—Jadwiga proved a good friend and intelligent helper. During the sixteen years that they were married, Witkacy wrote to her three or for times a week and was totally dependent on her for the organization of his literary career.

The year 1924 was a turning point in Witkacy's career. After having spent more than six years attempting to provide models for Pure Form in painting and theatre without having any impact on the artistic community, he now abandoned painting as a pure art and devoted himself exclusively to portraits as a commercial or applied art. In 1925 he established "The Witkiewicz Portrait-Painting Firm," a mock capitalist enterprise designed to distance the artist from the demeaning hack work he was compelled to do for money, and he published *The Rules of the S.I. Witkiewicz Portrait-Painting Firm* in 1928. The Firm's motto, "The customer must be satisfied. Misunderstandings are ruled out," indicates the proprietor's ironic attitude toward the public. Prices varied according the degree of deformation requested and the kinds of drugs the artist had taken. Witkacy was a pioneer in his experimentation with drugs and their effect on the creative process; he indicated on the canvas the dosages of narcotics and alcohol that he had used. His most interesting—and most distorted portraits—were of friends done at private parties he called "orgies."

At the same time that his playwriting slackened off in the mid-

1920s, Witkacy embarked on a new career as a novelist, and in literature he turned to impure genres and activities in which he could express his ideas directly. He wrote two long dystopian novels, *Farewell to Autumn* (1927) and *Insatiability* (1930), and in 1932 he published his book on drugs, *Narcotics: Nicotine, Alcohol Cocaine, Morphine, and Ether.*

A lonely and misunderstood figure out of step with his age, Witkacy rejected abstraction and maintained an ironically skeptical attitude toward Polish Futurism inspired by Mayakovsky. Having experienced the Revolution of 1917 in Petrograd as a Polish officer in the Czarist army, he was under no illusion that the political and artistic revolutions were working to achieve the same goals. He could not partake of the utopian belief in the future characteristic of the 1920s avant-gardes; his own views of what awaited humanity were profoundly pessimistic.

At a period in European history when writers and artists were enrolling under various political banners and joining parties, Witkacy resisted all ideologies of either right or left. He saw the danger of mass movements fueled by slogans, and the picture of modern totalitarian regimes and demented dictators in his dystopian fantasies proved prophetic.

The critical incomprehension and animosity that greeted his work lured Witkacy into endless polemics, in which he strove to refute the objections of his enemies, but finally tired and discouraged, he abandoned playwriting and devoted the last ten years of his life to philosophy, attending philosophical congresses, corresponding with professional philosophers and writing philosophical articles and treatises.

Death and Resurrection

Witkacy's last years were full of apprehensions of disaster. In 1937 he saw the coming world catastrophe and predicted his own death at fifty-four during the war. He knew the end was near, and that fascism and communism meant the demise of art. "I live in the half-shadow between life and death," he wrote to his friend and mentor, the German philosopher Hans Cornelius in 1938. In poor health and horrified at the fate of civilization, killing himself now seemed inevitable.

After the Nazis invaded Poland on September 1, 1939, Witkacy fled to the east with Czesława Korzeniowska, a much younger woman who was the great love of the last decade of his life. They had reached the little village of Jeziory (now in Ukraine) when word came on September 17 that the Soviets had attacked and the Red Army would soon arrive. There was no way out. During the night of September 18, 1939, Witkacy killed himself by slashing his wrists and cutting his throat after first taking pills to make the blood flow faster.   Czesława, who tried unsuccessfully to kill herself, described how she found Witkacy's corpse.

> When I woke up again it was already morning. His jacket was under my head, he must have put it there. He was lying beside me on his back, with his left leg drawn up, he had his arm bent at the elbow and pulled up. His eyes and mouth were open. . . . On his face there was a look of relief. A relaxing after great fatigue. I started to yell, to say something to Staś. We both were wet from the morning mist, acorns from the oak had fallen on top of us. I tried to bury him by raking dirt over him with my hands. With water from the mug for the luminal I washed his face and covered it with ferns. I felt frightfully weak. I saw double. Then there were two Stasés . . . and I crawled away from him on my hands and knees to get some manuscripts that had to be saved, but I didn't know how; then I returned and sat helplessly on the ground. It was Tuesday, September 19, 1939.

Throughout the war and during the immediate post-war communist take-over of Poland, there was no hope of reviving Witkacy's work. For nearly six years of Nazi occupation, no open theatre existed, except for collaborationist light entertainment. An underground home production of *The Madman and the Nun* by students at the Clandestine Warsaw University went into final rehearsals in the spring of 1942, but was never actually realized.

In January 1949, socialist realism was proclaimed the only acceptable style in the arts, and later that year a Festival of Russian and Soviet Drama was instituted to teach Polish playwrights how to write in the Moscow-approved style. All theatres were put under centralized bureaucratic control, Polish romantic dramas were banned, and for the next five years of Stalinism, an extreme individualist like Witkacy seemed doomed to oblivion in the triumphant ant hill society against which he had warned.

But the playwright demonstrated uncanny skill in predicting his own posthumous rediscovery. On a striking portrait all in dark red, done in 1931, there is the inscription: "For the posthumous exhibition in 1955." It was in 1956 that Tadeusz Kantor opened his theatre Cricot II in Cracow with *The Cuttlefish*, the first postwar production of Witkacy's work.

With the bloodless October revolution of 1956 following Khrushchev's speech denouncing Stalin, Poland acquired an autonomous policy in the arts. Socialist realism was quickly scuttled; formally the arts were now free, but censorship of content continued, ruling out truthful presentation of everyday social reality or any criticism of the USSR or the communist party,

The liberalization of 1956 made possible the gradual recovery of Witkacy, although there were constant battles with the censor over publication and performance of his plays. His flamboyant life and uncompromising suicide in 1939—to evade Nazis and Bolsheviks—made him a hero to artists and intellectuals, and his work became a major influence on the formation of the new postwar theatre. His bizarre, colorful plays and anti-ideological theory of Pure Form were the perfect antidote to five dreary years of enforced socialist realism, and his sardonic humor and prophetic insights into the workings of history made him, posthumously, a truly subversive and untamable author who attracted the most daring and imaginative directors and designers. The rediscovery of Witkacy—producing a long series of premieres of previously unknown and unproduced plays and frequent clashes with the censor—was one of the most exciting aspects of Polish cultural life from the later 1950s to the 1970s.

First discovered by the theatrical elite in their battle against Soviet-imposed socialist realism, Witkacy's "non-Euclidean dramas," his novels, and even his doggerel verse gradually became accessible to the broad public and was assimilated into popular culture in jazz, cabaret performance, songs, and rock musicals. With the fall of communism, he has become a classic avant-gardist and the most important Polish playwright-theorist of the twentieth century. No longer forced into an anti-regime mold, Witkacy—with his self-referential parody of modernism, pastiche of different styles, blending of theory and practice, and mixture of high and low genres—now can be regarded as one of the first postmodern playwrights. Although a product and victim of the historical forces that shaped his life, he is a writer more for our time than for his own. In his plays, novels, and essays, he dealt not only with politics and the totalitarian menace, but also in new and daring ways with sexuality and gender, human cloning, identity theft, drugs, pills, and narcotics, colonialism, science and the arts, and many other aspects of the postmodern world

Witkacy slowly won fame and acceptance in the sort of leveling mass society that he had said would mean the death of art. Like one of his own dramatic heroes, Witkacy rose from the dead to enjoy a triumphant second life in communist Poland, where he successfully battled censors and commissars. The year 1985, the one hundredth anniversary of his birth, was declared the "Year of Witkacy" by UNESCO, and the Polish People's

Republic issued commemorative postage stamps bearing his self-portraits. Was this official recognition the long overdue vindication of his embattled life as an artist, or the ultimate realization of his worst fears?

An ironic answer to this question came in 1988 when the Polish Ministry of Culture decided to act on the repeatedly deferred plan to bring Witkacy's "mortal remains" back to Zakopane. There, it was decreed, the playwright would be given a state funeral accorded only to Poland's greatest writers.

In 1939 Witkacy had been hastily buried in the old Orthodox cemetery of Jeziory. A pine cross bore the writer's name carved with a penknife. Neglected for many years, the grave and marker had become effaced. In the 1970s a tombstone and plaque were secretly placed on the site by a former Polish resident of Jeziory whose parents had sheltered Witkacy for several days in that distant September and who returned illegally to pay tribute to the playwright. Before *glasnost*, the USSR would not permit Poles to travel to their former lands.

All that had radically changed by April 11, 1988 when the body of the revered author was publicly exhumed at Jeziory before the assembled Ukrainian and Polish party dignitaries. After the panegyric speeches by the bureaucrats, the sealed coffin was officially handed over to the Polish delegation along with an x-ray photograph of its contents. When a Witkacy scholar traveling with the Polish delegation took a look at the x-ray, he immediately pointed out that the skull contained a full set of teeth, whereas the playwright had had many extractions. The photograph mysteriously disappeared, and the ceremony proceeded as scheduled.

When the body of the "false Witkacy" arrived in Zakopane on April 13, a week of festivities began that included eulogies, lectures, concerts, films, and theatrical performances throughout Poland. On April 14 "Witkacy's remains," draped in national colors and decked with mounds of flowers, were publicly displayed. An honor guard composed of leading Zakopane citizens, actors, and relatives led the funeral procession. The coffin was transported to the cemetery on a local peasant wagon drawn by horses caparisoned in black, followed by a huge crowd of fifty thousand. The Minster of Culture spoke at the grave, as did the Deputy Minister of Culture from Ukraine, and a solemn funeral mass was celebrated. The body of the "false Witkacy" was placed in his mother's tomb, a few steps from where his wife is buried (his father's grave is at the other end of the cemetery). A large tombstone proclaims the return of the author to his native land.

The fraud was exposed almost immediately, and the ensuing scandal led to accusations and recriminations as to who was responsible for the grotesque farce.   All true admirers of Witkacy rejoiced that the playwright—famous for his "risen corpses"—had succeeded in evading the authorities once again.   The author had staged yet another posthumous triumph.   The communist hierarchy, which for years had suppressed his work, censored his books, and tried to keep his plays off the stage, could seize possession of neither his body nor his spirit.   The officials and bureaucrats who honored the author by burying an anonymous skeleton (which turned out to be that of an unidentified young woman) in his mother's grave have now faded into oblivion.   Witkacy's corpse enjoys its lonely freedom no one knows precisely where.

Fascinated by the strange fate of his friend, the poet and playwright Tadeusz Miciński, who had been killed in Ukraine in 1918 without leaving behind a trace, Witkacy often said that he too would like to have no grave. How splendid, he exclaimed, that all the world knows a writer and finds him everywhere, even though there are no material remains.

Witkacy's death—his last hours, suicide, burial, and then his rebirth, reburial, and final escape—has become a legend that is now the subject of many novels, plays, and films dealing with these events in either a documentary or fictional mode.   As a young man, the thought of experiencing, or watching, one's own death had fascinated Witkacy, and throughout his career he talked of "taking a posthumous look at oneself." He was self-haunted, observed by his own ghost.   New generations continue to be fascinated by Witkacy's elusive specter and attempt to find him in his plays, novels, paintings, and photographs.

Stanisław Ignacy Witkiewicz
Self-portrait
1930

THEORETICAL PREFACE

by

S.I. Witkiewicz
(1921)

THEORETICAL PREFACE
(1921)

It is a well-established fact that the theatre had its origins in the religious mysteries. This is how it happened in ancient Greece, and the beginnings of modern theatre at the waning of the Middle Ages correspond to the process of the birth of Greek tragedy. However, artistic effect does not necessarily have to be connected to the expression of religious feelings *per se*. It can be the result of contemplating the form alone, independent of whether or not the real-life content of a given work has any direct connection to metaphysical experiences. Since the elements of theatre are the actions of living beings, the theatre gradually lost its religious character, and the essential, formal content became reduced to an auxiliary role in the service of a heightened representation of life, symbolic or real, and the problems associated with it.

The essence of art in general is the directly given unity of personality, or what we call metaphysical feeling, expressed in a construction of whatever the elements may be: i. e. colors, sounds, words or actions. Painting and music possess homogenous elements. In addition to its sound values and possibilities for evoking visual images, poetry also makes use of concepts, the meanings of which are, in our opinion, just as good artistic material as any of the pure qualities. However, the theatre has the additional element of actions, whoever the Individual Beings who act may be. Thus poetry and theatre are complex arts as opposed to the simple arts, painting and music. In painting each work has, besides its purely formal values—composition, harmony of colors and conception of form—its objective content, which derives from the fact that metaphysical feeling, generally the same for all Individual Beings, becomes polarized in the psyche of a given person, creating a unique form, which is more abstract as pure construction, the more condensed the personality of the individual creating it. Hence a certain intrinsic contradiction is at the heart of artistic creation.

What the world of objects and representations is to painting, so the world of emotions is to music, and conceptual meaning is to poetry and the sense of actions is to theatre. If we agree that the formal content, i. e. the construction in itself of the work of art is its essence, then we are no longer obliged to be concerned with the inessential, but still indispensable elements of the process of creation, which have only an indirect connection to the completed work. Seen in this light, deformation of the external world in painting, violation of emotional logic in music, real-life and logical absurdity in poetry and on the stage need not outrage us. In our opinion, the breaking of certain inessential bad habits touching the real-life aspect of works of art opens new horizons for formal possibilities, mainly having to do with the question of composition. In the theatre what can give new formal possibilities is a certain fantastic quality of the psychology and actions as opposed to an external fantastic quality: dragons, sorcerers, and other such creatures appropriate to the deformation of the external world. Of course, aims of this kind must be essential, and not schematic. Schematic distortion of normal shapes, schematic absurdity in poetry or in the theatre, is a very sad phenomenon. Deformation for deformation's sake, absurdity for absurdity's sake, not justified in purely formal dimensions, deserves the most severe condemnation. Whether some of the departures from the beaten path evident in the plays that this volume contains are justified in this fashion remains to be tested in practice. Theoretically this is possible, and we suppose that if not these plays, then perhaps other plays by other authors, will someday prove the validity of these propositions.

Of course, it may seem ridiculous to some and outrageous to others. If any one is genuinely amused by this, in a way that we consider totally unimportant, we would be delighted, given the scarcity of laughter in our gloomy times. If, on the other hand, some one is deeply outraged, but without flying into a perfect rage—well, so be it—it's absolutely impossible to please every one. There are fewer and fewer people who split their sides with laughter at the sight of square ankles in Picasso's paintings or who cover their ears in indignation upon hearing a Stravinsky ballet score. Without prejudging in the least the formal values of the plays presented here, we assume that in principle one may with good will totally accept a "subject" which is purely external and, from a real-life point of view, even grotesque and monstrous.

One thing more: besides erotic matters, the contents of the plays are certain fantasies, on the theme of the revolution in mathematics and physics in *Tumor Brainiowicz* and on the theme of psychiatry in *Pentemychos*. The experiences of a band of degenerate former people confronting the mechanization of life is the content of *Maciej Korbowa*. Philosophical divagations and the problems arising from the absolute insatiability for life are interwoven in the following plays: *Multiflakopulo*; *The Pragmatists* (published, unfortunately without the proof corrections, in the third issue of *Zdrój*, 1920); *The New Deliverance*; *Tropical Madness* (written in collaboration with Eugenia Borkowska); *They*; *Crumplette, or in The Snares of INSOUCIANCE; Philosophers and Martyrs, or The Harlot from Ecbatana*; *Country House*; *The Independence of Triangles*; *The Terrible*

Tutor; and *Metaphysics of a Two-headed Calf*.

By our fantasies on mathematics and psychiatry we have not intended to offend any particular scientists or scholars, just as by our opinions on "love," social issues, and supernatural phenomena we meant no offense to sex fiends, social activists, or spiritualists. These fantasies are only pretexts for certain formal combinations. To use a term analogous to the concept of "directional tension," introduced by us into the theory of painting, what we are now attempting is to impart to certain masses of events in time a kind of "dynamic tension." This is the formal significance of the so-called "content" of poems and plays. Please note that we do not attribute any objective significance to the "opinions" expressed by the characters in these plays.

Stanisław Ignacy Witkiewicz
*The Man Afflicted with Dropsy
Lying in Wait for His Wife's Lover*
circa 1910

THE PRAGMATISTS

A Play in Three Acts
(1919)

Foreword

Written in 1919, *The Pragmatists* was Witkacy's first play to be published, appearing in 1920 in a Poznań Expressionist magazine. It was also his first play to exemplify his theory of Pure Form, whereby color, sound, and movement assume equal importance to the spoken dialogue, and the actor, freed from the imitation of reality, acquires an autonomous creative role. The extensive stage directions, which constitute one-third of the play, indicate how the actors are to implement the play's emphasis on the physical expression of psychic states and abstract qualities.

Performed on December 29, 1921 at a recently organized avant-garde theatre in Warsaw as the opening production, *The Pragmatists* gave rise to a stormy controversy between Witkacy and the critics in which the playwright defended the play and elaborated his ideas on non-representational dramaturgy in the essay "Theoretical Preface," which was later attached to *Tumor*.   Three more performances followed before the theatre closed its doors without ever presenting any other work. At the amateur Formist Theatre which Witkacy and a circle of friends established in Zakopane there was a performance of the play in 1925, with scenery and costumes designed by the author.

Pragmatists can be viewed as a chamber work in several senses. It is written for a small number of players, to be performed on an intimate stage before a select audience. Its single setting is at the same time torture chamber, chamber of the heart, and chamber for virtuoso recital. Witkacy tips his hat repeatedly to Strindberg's most famous chamber play, *The Ghost Sonata*, which provided him with various threads and pieces of fabric: struggle for domination, battle of the sexes, interplay of humans with mysterious higher powers, and fatal web of circumstances binding characters together, as well as a mummy and hidden secret from the past.

More starkly and tersely than Witkacy's later plays, *Pragmatists* lays bare within a narrow frame the underlying theme of all his work: the crisis of the self at times of historical dislocation. The characters, who come from Witkacy's decadent museum of "former people," cultivate the sensibility of crisis to the point of hysteria. These ex-people, who have lost their bearings, are insistently confronted by questions of identity: "Who am I?" and "Who are They?"

Classifications by old-fashioned notions of profession, station, race, class, and gender have grown unstable. In Witkacy, the classic social classes—as defined by Marx—have lost their functions and are being displaced by different non-class formations, such as bureaucracy and technology. Ex-people are quick change artists, always ready to adopt a new mask. The aristocratic Count von Telek is now a technocrat, a former drug-taker who has become a drug regulator and an entrepreneur, dabbling in the arts (making up new musical instruments) and exploiting others, namely, his protoplasmic friend Plasfodor and Plasfodor's mute medium and lover Mammalia, whose unspeakable angst the impresario will turn into a profitable cabaret act and take on tour. Mammalia's muteness makes her into something of a silent film star and introduces into the drama a cinematographic aesthetic.

The boyish servant, Masculette, and racial outsider, Chinese Mummy (formerly the beautiful Princess Tsui), assert their independence and refuse to play the minor roles usually assigned such characters. Each voices her own perceptions of the goings-on. Masculette sneers at her mistress and tries to steal von Telek (who rebuffs her advances and smashes her skull with an upholstery hammer). Although she is cast in a traditional female stage role as maid or soubrette, the borders between genders have eroded. Masculette is sexually active as a woman, but androgynous in appearance. Princess Tsui, a mummy's voice from another world, critiques the nature of theatrical reality and the characters who people it, when she observes that "White people say so many useless things both in life and on the stage." At the penultimate moment of the drama the Chinese Mummy leads the trio of Masculette-Plasfodor-Mammalia to an encounter with the frightening mystery of eternal recurrence: the afterlife will be nothing more than a repetition of this life.

Pragmatists is tinged by colonial fantasies about the Orient, but these are unreliable pseudo-memories or figments of an overheated dramatic imagination. Dialogue in Witkacy's post-Strindbergian world is untrustworthy, memory faulty, speech and action disconnected. The mystery is gone, but the two friends reminisce about their supposed journey to the East and fantasize about an Eastern woman, drugs, and power. Even the Chinese Mummy's Chineseness is suspect, (all the more ironic because in Witkacy's time the actress playing the role would be white), and thus her otherness is bogus. She is a ghost haunting the characters' drug-induced dreams, but a ghost created by the dreamers themselves who are self-haunted.

Except for the domineering von Telek, the characters balk at accepting the identities that society has to offer them. Plasfodor—a fluid, malleable plasma—could never choose among his infinite possibilities and prefers to remain in chaos and nothingness without limits or contours.

In *Pragmatists* séance and orgy are activities by which the characters express their longings. Through the séance they hope to make contact with the mystery of existence—failing this, they themselves become ghosts at séances. Through the orgy they attempt to satisfy their insatiable desires. Instead of reaching a destination through a plot, they eternally relive repeated moments into which all essential experience has been emptied.

The action of *Pragmatists* takes place in a remote interior landscape—or existential limbo—beyond normal categories of time and space, in which the laws of cause and effect no longer apply. Instead, the unexpected reigns, based on a technique of omitting foreshadowing, preparation, and all the usual psychological and narrative interconnections.

Witkacy defied his critics to give a summary of the story of *Pragmatists*, promising a prize to anyone who could provide a synopsis. Several accepted the challenged, claiming the play was full of strident naturalism. In fact, there are many buried shards of plot taken from popular literature, but these fragments become components in a composition that is overwhelmingly pictorial, musical and kinetic rather than narrative.

Witkacy excels at portraying the collective consciousness of protagonists who share the same dilemmas, the same collapsing world, and the same despair. The group portrait of the dramatis personae is composed of interrelated and opposed traits held in ever-shifting patterns of tension and uneasy equilibrium. East and West, action and contemplation, business and art, life and death, male and female are the polarities on which *Pragmatists* turns. These sets of opposites are at war among the characters as well as within them, but the struggle produces only a stalemate. Plasfodor and his friends are "pragmatists" because instead of facing the ultimate mystery of existence, they attempt to find pain-killing evasions.

Witkacy characteristically brings the drama not to any resolution, but to an abrupt double ending with a "trick" *coup de théâtre*. By having Masculette's corpse rise Witkacy destroys the finality of death, rendering the violence and murder arbitrary and inconsequential. The dead will not stay dead, and the living are not truly alive. The Chinese Mummy leads off her band of walking dead through a dark door opening onto infinity; off-stage mute Mammalia screams on learning the mystery of eternal recurrence. Two gendarmes appear to arrest von Telek for identity theft. Nothing will ever change their situation, not even death. Witkacy has dramatized a state of consciousness in which the characters live the past over again and experience the future in advance.

THE PRAGMATISTS

A Play in Three Acts
(1919)

Dedicated to
Włodzimierz Mazurkiewicz

CHARACTERS

PLASFODOR MIMECKER—Thirty-two years old, thin, completely clean-shaven, jerky movements; dark eyes deeply sunken and outlined by very dark rings, dark hair parted on one side, quite long.

MAMMALIA—His dumb, but not deaf mistress. Medium height, dark eyes, a great deal of red hair. Twenty-six years old.

GRAF FRANZ VON TELEK—Rather fat, stands straight. Dark red hair combed smooth, large red beard. Sure of himself in both his movements and in his manner of speech; only the expression on his face is uneasy: his eyes rove. thirty-seven years old.

CHINESE MUMMY—Chinese mask instead of a face. A yellow garment wound around the body. Flowing, "bulging" movements. At rest completely rigid. She speaks with a woman's voice, but as though it had been filtered through a few cellars. Huge claw-like fingernails up to two inches long.

MASCULETTE—Sexless person, tending more however to the female side. A blonde with a high brush-cut. Slender and slight. Very thin ankles. Movements full of grace, seventeen years old.

TWO GENDARMES—In the style of Italian carabinieri, in tri-cornered hats.

NOTE: Everyone is to speak without exaggerated emotions and to say the speeches with particular attention to the significance of the words themselves.

ACT ONE

A room with one door upstage center, and another very far downstage right. To the left a window, through which somewhat orange afternoon sunlight falls. The walls are black with a yellow oriental motif. Stage center a small red three-legged table, on which there is equipment for making black coffee. To the right, a black sofa. Near the sofa a small cabinet made of black wood. On the floor a black rug with a red rectilinear design. Four dark red chairs.

PLASFODOR *sits at the table, his face hidden in his hands. He is dressed in white silk pajamas, patent leather shoes on his bare feet. MAMMALIA, dressed in a dark cherry-colored dressing gown, trimmed with white fur, sits on the small sofa to the right, not moving, gazing straight ahead. A long moment of silence.*

PLASFODOR (*without taking his hands away from his face*): That's enough! Oh, that's enough!—I can't stand it. (MAMMALIA *looks anxious.*) I don't know if I'll manage to live through this day. (MAMMALIA *gets up slowly and stands wavering; her whole figure expresses unbearable tension.*) And yet this ghastly torture is the essence of my life. Talking with a woman! My god! (*He uncovers his face and looks straight ahead with an expression of frightful insatiability.*) Was I created only to be something through which the stream of existence could flow, without ever stopping for even a second? (MAMMALIA *comes over behind him and listens to his words, visibly tormented; her lips move.*) There are two ways out: either to be what flows, or to be the screen on which the flowing creates a fleeting image. Which is more significant? (*Still standing behind him,* MAMMALIA *covers his eyes with her hands and seems to be trying to transfer her own thoughts directly into his head.*) Write, damn it, you filthy old hag! (MAMMALIA *runs over to the cabinet on the right, gets paper and pencil, takes the tray off the table and puts it on the floor, then kneels by the table.* PLASFODOR *takes her hand.* MAMMALIA *begins to write, looking hopelessly out into space.* PLASFODOR *reads slowly what she writes.*) "Barren torture guides the hand in the abyss of words, where senselessness meets sense and creates the soul of a nonexistent creature. Be that creature born of the word, who does not exist among the living." We've had all that before! Answer me clearly, or I'll kill you!! Oh! She doesn't know what torture this is! (*He squeezes her hand with all his might.* MAMMALIA *sways back and forth. Enter on tiptoe* MASCULETTE, *in a short rose-colored skirt and black stockings. The expression on her face is mischievous. The others don't see her.*) Answer me, damn it, or I'll torture you to death like the lowest . . . !! (MAMMALIA *begins to write again.* PLASFODOR *stops swearing and looks intently at the paper. He mumbles something incomprehensible, then begins to read.*) "Transform yourself and me into one inexpressible word, which no living creature can utter. He'll come to your aid—he's drawing near—I feel him . . ." (MASCULETTE *observes this scene with a laugh. Suddenly the upstage door opens [as a matter of fact, the door to the right remains closed until the end of the play] and, without knocking,* FRANZ VON TELEK *enters, dressed in a cutaway and striped pants with a white vest, a derby in his hand and a white cane with a gold knob.* MAMMALIA *springs up and runs over to him.* MASCULETTE *runs to him from the other side.*) That's all we needed! What do you want here, you personification of the most poisonous emptiness?

MASCULETTE (*hanging on* VON TELEK's *arm*): Don't you remember, Mr. von Telek? Don't you remember where we last met?

VON TELEK (*shoves her away brutally; turning to* MAMMALIA): I'm strong and healthy as a bull. I'm simply bursting with life.

PLASFODOR (*to* VON TELEK): You're just a poor puppet that anyone can dupe.

MAMMALIA *takes* FRANZ *by the arm and pulls him toward* PLASFODOR, *indicating a desire to reconcile the two of them;* VON TELEK *offers his hand to* PLASFODOR, *who puts his hands in his pockets.* MASCULETTE *laughs and goes to* MAMMALIA.

MASCULETTE: Everything will work out all right. Don't try to get the better of Plasfodor. I know what he's like.

VON TELEK: Quiet, women. I'm healthy as a bull, so I can afford the luxury of having that putrid carcass refuse to shake hands with me. I'm sure he'll talk differently in a few minutes. (*To* PLASFODOR.) You know, Plasfodor, I've invented a new kind of artistic creation. Perhaps you'd like to take it up? It's something between non-spatial sculpture and music which comes to a standstill in space. I even have an instrument . . .

PLASFODOR: You wretch: you want to rob me of my last disbelief. I know your devious ways. You're an ordinary businessman. Now that you've run out of ideas for new alkaloids, you're selling nonexistent drugs.

VON TELEK: Well now, there's an insolent beast lurking in this anemic milksop of ours! Remember the famous "apotransformine" that I extracted from the innocent bush of the Holparian tamarisk? Remember the wild visions you had then?

PLASFODOR: Shut up: don't remind me of those moments of decline and fall.

MAMMALIA *twists about between them, as if she were connecting some kind of threads. The men calm down.*

VON TELEK: Yes, I'm healthy as a bull. That's my essential strength. Now I'm director of the Department of Poisons at the Ministry of Trade. We want to monopolize all the poisons and form an independent union made up of the greatest good-time teetotalers.

He sits down on the sofa, PLASFODOR *next to him. They talk quietly.* MAMMALIA *goes over to them.*

PLASFODOR (*in a conciliatory tone, pointing to* MAMMALIA): Here's my last poison.

VON TELEK: Stop pretending, you quick-change artist! You're the one who's been poisoning her with your program of systematic sterility. To live means to create the unknown. After all, I learned that from you, didn't I?

MASCULETTE: What about me?

PLASFODOR (*to* MASCULETTE): You're forgetting you're only the maid.

MASCULETTE: Oh, is that so? Then can I tell the Count about the latest scene? Here are the papers! (*Grabs papers from the table and reads them out loud, avoiding* MAMMALIA, *who tries to snatch them out of her hand.*) "Transform yourself and me into one inexpressible word, which no living creature can . . ."

MAMMALIA *snatches the papers away from her and tears them into tiny pieces;* VON TELEK *laughs in a deep bass.*

PLASFODOR (*getting up*): I've grown younger in your company. Maybe all this is just an illusion. (*Pulls himself together.*) Oh, I love life too. Masculette! Come here. Can't a hundred and thirty pounds of live Masculette take the place of imaginary artistic creativity? But then why doesn't anything satisfy me? Von Telek is completely at home in his idiotic ministry, in his union of teetotaling good-timers. I alone have no place anywhere.

MASCULETTE (*going to him; naively*): There's a totally unknown poison in my heart. Whoever guts my heart out will get some really wild thrills from it.

VON TELEK: Now it's my turn. (*He embraces* MAMMALIA, *who, slipping away, leads him to the door.*) You're the one who's going to give me what I don't have and create a web of complex feelings in me. I conquer and discard. Just once I'd like to get in so deep that I won't be able to see the horizon at all.

He embraces MAMMALIA *and they go out through the door.* MASCULETTE *and* PLASFODOR *sit down on the sofa.*

PLASFODOR (*who has taken in this scene at a glance, speaks to* MASCULETTE): That was all just an illusion. Now, once again, I'm the same young boy I used to be years ago.

MASCULETTE (*ironically, but in a kindly way*): Poor baby.

PLASFODOR: Now I can understand my life over again from the very beginning—nothing ever happened to me. And yet I could have been whatever I wanted. But I didn't have that certain little spring.

MASCULETTE: You didn't have what creates a sense of reality so strong that you have to accept it just the way it is, and not some other way. I've known that torment of disbelief in one's own love. But absurdity I'll never comprehend.

PLASFODOR: You always understand everything in terms of love, even though you're a notoriously sexless person. There's a certain analogy, but in my case the object of doubt was all of life. The only way out was suicide. But I couldn't do it with a clear conscience; it wouldn't have been any solution at all. Oh, this conversation's wearing me out.

MASCULETTE: But you were young again just a moment ago.

PLASFODOR: Yes, yes. My friends at the Café Illusion think I'm a madman because I don't write poetry.

MASCULETTE: Don't let yourself get taken in by Francis's new swindle. I know what he's like.

PLASFODOR: I don't trust him either.

Off-stage VON TELEK *can be heard swearing frightfully. He comes rushing in, his clothes rumpled, traces of blood on his white vest.*

VON TELEK: The beasts! I treat you all like well-behaved ghosts, and they're more real than my whole ministry.

MASCULETTE (*getting up*): Did you kill her?

VON TELEK (*angrily*): What are you talking about? I got stabbed in the breastbone with a Japanese knife because I didn't want to be sufficiently real.

PLASFODOR (*getting up with satisfaction*): At last it's beginning . . .

MASCULETTE (*to* PLASFODOR): Stop making speeches. (*To* VON TELEK.) How did it happen?

VON TELEK: Quite simply, I refused her a certain little crime. She wanted me to kill her, today, right away, just like that, on the spot. It drove her into a perfect frenzy.

PLASFODOR: Then even she's incapable of doing it herself. Oh, that really impresses me.

MASCULETTE: Oh, so she couldn't either. (*Points at* PLASFODOR.) I tell you, Francis, he's stronger than you thought.

VON TELEK (*wiping himself off with a napkin*): There are certain moments when each of us is stronger than he really is.

PLASFODOR: I'm not concerned with any particular moment, but with their coming one after the other. (MAMMALIA *enters and draws near* PLASFODOR.) The infernal banality of existence. It's four o'clock in the afternoon. Then there'll be supper, then an orgy, then a séance, then the nightly bad dreams, then the usual dose of pills to give us strength to go on. Oh, it's unbearable!

VON TELEK: If you had to work the way I do, you wouldn't talk like that. There's only one life. It's so trite and obvious, yet few living creatures really understand it. The only thing that saves me is that I'm healthy as a bull.

MAMMALIA *embraces* PLASFODOR *with languorous movements;* VON TELEK *turns away in disgust and embraces* MASCULETTE.

MASCULETTE (*yielding*): Francis, is that true? You're not rejecting me, are you?

VON TELEK (*coldly*): I'm still not where they are yet. I'm still holding myself back. But whoever unleashes all the strength I've got in me—watch out. There'll be bloody mincemeat, bright red fluff coagulating on the blue sky of an ordinary everyday day.

MASCULETTE (*to* VON TELEK): Has she arrived?

VON TELEK: She's waiting for me at the hotel.

PLASFODOR (*shouting*): I've had enough of that! I've blocked off all the exits forever. Only death, hers and mine, will be my sole work. Masculette, coffee!

MASCULETTE *goes out.*

VON TELEK: Oh! Here's where I can help you. With your kind permission, I'll go now—just across the street, to the hotel. The memory of a certain event that hasn't happened yet is locked away in my room there.

MAMMALIA *approaches* VON TELEK *and clasps her hands together in supplication.*

PLASFODOR: Go ahead. I'm not afraid of anything now.

VON TELEK: All right then, I'm going . . .

MAMMALIA *tries to stop him;* VON TELEK *pushes her away brutally and goes out.*

PLASFODOR: Well, what now? The usual program. It's terrible how the strangeness of life has died out in us. (*By her movements* MAMMALIA *expresses her innermost torment.*) Stop twisting around like a marionette. Even talking with you has become a burden to me. Why can't I be lonely the way I used to be?

He sits down with the same gestures of despair as at the beginning of the act. MAMMALIA *stands behind him, her hands hanging limply. Pause. Enter* VON TELEK *leading the* CHINESE MUMMY *by the hand.* MAMMALIA *runs over to the* MUMMY, *who with bulging movements, advances slowly to stage center. The* MUMMY *kisses* MAMMALIA *on the forehead.* PLASFODOR *sits with his face in his hands.*

VON TELEK: Plasfodor! Plasi! Wake up and accept a new reality into your dried-up depths. (*Screams with all his might.*) Get up this instant!

PLASFODOR (*gets up and turns towards the* MUMMY. *To* VON TELEK, *indifferently*): Is that all?

VON TELEK (*to the* MUMMY): Speak!

MASCULETTE (*enters with coffee*): Something new, at last. I thought I was going to die of boredom.

MUMMY (*to* PLASFODOR, *in a voice which seems to come from the bottom of a bucket*): Remember that night in Saigon? When the opium entered our veins, swelling them with desire for the unknown . . .

MAMMALIA *stands between* PLASFODOR *and the* MUMMY, *with her face turned toward* PLASFODOR.

PLASFODOR (*in a hard tone*): I don't remember anything. You're Franz's new medium. But your Chineseness seems suspect to me.

MUMMY: And do you remember that night when you seduced me in the little bamboo hut in the shadow of the Ping-Fangs and drank the last drop of my blood through a straw made of dried Wu grass?

PLASFODOR: I seem to remember something like that. Yes, I think I really was somewhere near Saigon once.

Placing herself between PLASFODOR *and the* MUMMY, MAMMALIA *dances her desire to create an impenetrable wall between them.*

VON TELEK (*harshly, to the* MUMMY): Go on, Princess Tsui.

PLASFODOR: Tsui? That name is not unknown to me.

MUMMY: Remember when you sated your wild white lust, and your black-yellow lust was still unsated, do you remember what you did to me then? (*With her sharp claw pointed at* MAMMALIA.) That was when she went dumb, for the rest of her days.

VON TELEK (*in a hard tone*): Go on, keep going!

PLASFODOR: Yes, now I know I was in Saigon with you, five years ago, in May.

MASCULETTE *holds up* MAMMALIA, *who is about to faint, and leads her to the sofa.* MAMMALIA *weeps and moves despairingly.*

VON TELEK (*with the voice of authority*): Tsui! Tell him the final word. Transform both him and her into that word which no living creature will ever utter.

MAMMALIA *springs up and goes over to* PLASFODOR, *but stops a step away from him and moves as if unable to pass through a charmed circle.* MASCULETTE *observes the scene, laughing. The* MUMMY *puts her arms around* PLASFODOR's *neck and whispers something in his ear.*

PLASFODOR (*falling to the floor*): No! No! I don't want to . . . I don't want to . . . (*His voice trails off in a faint and he collapses on the floor.*)

VON TELEK (*to the* MUMMY, *with curiosity*): What did you tell him, Tsui, Princess of the Sky-blue Lotus? I'm healthy as a bull and I can take anything.

MAMMALIA *and* MASCULETTE *carry* PLASFODOR *to the sofa.*

MUMMY (*to* VON TELEK): I told him the word that could kill you too, you healthy bull. The word that she (*points to* MAMMALIA) couldn't tell him, because she went dumb at that very moment.

VON TELEK: Tell me what it is. Because I actually don't know what I'm creating here involuntarily, as a completely insignificant waste product of my being. I'll make a new poison out of it.

The MUMMY *takes a step toward him;* VON TELEK *moves back in terror.* MAMMALIA *goes over to him, takes his hand and escorts him to the door.*

VON TELEK (*going out the door*): This time I may have gone a bit too far.

The MUMMY *slowly draws near the sofa on which* PLASFODOR *lies unconscious.*

MASCULETTE (*holding* PLASFODOR's *head up*): It would seem that my master has had what the people at the Illusion call a significant experience. If only it hasn't been too significant for this anemic milksop.

MUMMY (*kneeling by* PLASFODOR): Shut up and hold his head straight.

ACT TWO

The same room as in Act One. Night. The little red table is placed near the sofa. On the table three candles are burning in a single candelabrum.

PLASFODOR *is lying on the sofa. The* MUMMY *sits to his right on the rug, her profile to the audience.* MAMMALIA *walks back and forth between* PLASFODOR *and the* MUMMY, *wringing her hands in despair, expressing terrible fear and anxiety by all her movements.*

MUMMY: Now you remember quite well who I am. Plas-fo-dor carried me off from the summer residence of my ancestors when I was still beautiful and young. The life I imagined for him was like an improbable dream, shadowy and bloody, white and innocent. He had everything: long, long ago he could have been a wise man and a warrior. I wanted to give him all that in the dream. You woke him up to your vile existence, where everything small and practical has enmeshed his great soul. Only his soul was beautiful; his body, eaten away by the terrible disease that consumes your common humanity, couldn't stand the fire of his spirit, which blazed like an inextinguishable torch in the immense black Nothingness of Absolute Existence. (MAMMALIA *falls on her knees before the* MUMMY *bowing until her forehead touches the ground; straightens up and prostrates herself again.*) And what good will that do you now, Countess von Telek? Even your brother's turned his back on you, your brother who loved you in your childhood with a love that wasn't at all brotherly. (MAMMALIA *keeps on bowing repeatedly.*) Get up and revive him now. How will he hear the mute cry that tears your insides out and burns you up with an unspeakable fire?

MAMMALIA *springs up and keeps turning about in the same spot in terrible torment. She gives the impression that a scream is trying to tear itself out of her and cannot.*

PLASFODOR (*without waking up from his dream*): I feel as though I'm falling with infinite speed into bottomless abysses, soft as down and black as the starless night. (MAMMALIA *listens intently.*) Everything's drifting over me in the shape of a hideous, bloated shirt front. For each point in reality there's a corresponding point in that cursed shirt front that keeps moving back and forth, drawing near me and then moving away. I could connect all the corresponding points with thread and join the dream to real life. But I keep sinking deeper and deeper and my torment will never end.

MAMMALIA *dashes over to him, then stops, and with sudden decision pulls a revolver out of the cabinet and, from where she's standing, shoots the* MUMMY. *The* MUMMY *does not move.* MAMMALIA *comes extremely close to the* MUMMY *and shoots her in the breast, almost pressing the revolver against her clothes. The* MUMMY *doesn't bat an eyelash.* MAMMALIA *once again prostrates herself before her.*

MUMMY (*calmly*): Don't get excited, Mammalia von Telek. That's not the way to overcome the essential strangeness of existence.

MASCULETTE (*enters in a rose-colored dressing gown and cap; terrified*): Why are you shooting, you naughty children? Will that help any? Oh! Francis told me such dreadful things before he left. All the time I kept on dreaming about monstrous teetotaling snouts slurping up horrible poisons: monopolized, systematized, mechanized. Oh, it wasn't a night of love in the normal sense.

MUMMY: The night of love won't come until tomorrow. Only death can resolve something as petty and insignificant as Francis von Telek's love.

MASCULETTE: Tell me, Princess Tsui, you dominate him completely?

MUMMY: Nothing dominates anything; everything comes into being by itself as part of the whole world, which is only the eye of Nothingness turned in on itself.

MAMMALIA *gets up and looks wildly at the* MUMMY.

MASCULETTE: And who is she, Mrs. Mimecker, my mistress, whom I despise so much?

MUMMY: She is punishment personified, which is self-embodied in life without anyone directing it, for the existence of the Supreme Being is based on His being His own sleep without dreams in the Infinity of all that is and ceases to be.

MASCULETTE: You're boring, mummy of an eminent person. I prefer your impresario, the bearded Franz. (*She goes out.*)

The MUMMY *grows abstracted and lost in contemplation.* MAMMALIA *prostrates herself before her. A pause. Enter* VON TELEK, *in black pajamas.*

VON TELEK: I thought there'd be at least a few corpses here. But it's only a short lecture course on metaphysics in the style of master Teng-Ts'en. (*To* MAMMALIA.) Get up, my poor poor little sister, then sit down and don't let the situation upset you. We've known a lot worse.

MAMMALIA *jumps up, her movements expressing the utmost indignation. She pushes away some nonexistent thing in the air, and tries to cry out but cannot. Finally she throws herself at* PLASFODOR *and tries to wake him. She tugs at him, embraces and kisses him—all in vain.* VON TELEK *laughs in a deep bass, the* MUMMY *joins in with subterranean chortles.* MAMMALIA *throws herself on her knees before* VON TELEK, *who, his right hand on the* MUMMY's *head, laughs ironically.*

VON TELEK: Humble yourself, you she-clown! I alone am the master of otherworldly powers despite my great sense of reality. You all wanted to cheat the most essential laws of existence and form a unity without content beyond life? I'll show you how!

The MUMMY *gets up slowly and stands beside* VON TELEK, *who puts his arms around her waist.*

MUMMY (*tersely*): Wake him up, Franz.

VON TELEK: Gladly. I don't specially care to have that idiot kick the bucket.

He goes over to PLASFODOR; MAMMALIA, *standing behind him, leans forward and watches each of* VON TELEK's *movements. He takes* PLASFODOR's *hand, turns it three times in a circle and tosses it on the sleeper's chest.* PLASFODOR *jumps to his feet.*

PLASFODOR (*rubbing his eyes and adjusting his clothes; to* VON TELEK): What, you here again? You wet nurse for incubi! You lesbian pimp.

VON TELEK (*slightly taken aback*): Plasi, express yourself more moderately: there are ladies present.

PLASFODOR *hits him in the face with all his might.* VON TELEK *covers his face with his hands.*

MUMMY: Hit him! Hit him as hard as you can! Don't show him any mercy! (*She chortles with satisfaction.*)

PLASFODOR (*in a rage*): Take that, you incestuous saltimbanque! Take that, you kept man of Astarte! (MAMMALIA *looks on in mute rapture;* VON TELEK *runs to the door and stops there.*) How dare you trick me in such a vile way? Who's master here?

VON TELEK (*rubbing his face*): How about talking calmly? You don't think I'm going to fight you, do you?

MUMMY: Now that score's been settled. Franz, I'm taking responsibility for your honor. And you, Plasfodor, tell us frankly once and for all if you love that woman even though she's mute and unbalanced, as far as everyday life is concerned.

PLASFODOR (*embracing* MAMMALIA): Oh! if I could only find out what love is, I'd gladly tell you, Princess Tsui. A long time ago, a very long time ago I knew what it was, alas. But in those days I used to write stupid little poems. Today it's all an extinct desert in which even all the weeping and earthly whimpering for mercy have fallen silent.

MAMMALIA *presses up against him.*

VON TELEK: Tsui! Are you against me too?

MUMMY: I only fulfill the role thrust on me by the Great Connection of Everything with Everything.

PLASFODOR (*to* MAMMALIA): It's just ordinary determinism. Or maybe it's simply that I do love you? To me you're what a mother is to her invalid son, who was once, perhaps in another existence, a titan.

MAMMALIA *winds herself around him submissively, with rather dog-like, yet at the same time cat-like movements.*

VON TELEK: Everything here looked so promising, but where is the strangeness of it all?

MUMMY: You only see strangeness in what excites your crude nerves: a strangeness of the second degree. But you don't have the slightest idea what a true transformation of the personality is.

VON TELEK: You forget you're only my baggage. You don't exist, you don't have any papers. But I've got a claim check for you, Princess. (*The* MUMMY *slowly goes to* VON TELEK; PLASFODOR *suddenly jumps up from the sofa where he has been sitting, and runs out of the room.*) Let's take advantage of the absence of that hysterical character and talk frankly for once. What have we really met here for? (*The* MUMMY *turns to him and slowly raises her arm;* VON TELEK *staggers and cries out in terror.*) Mercy! I don't ask for anything! I love you, Tsui, and I'm afraid of you. I'm healthy as the Farnese bull and, damn it all, I love life, just as it is.

He finishes on a lighter tone noticing that the MUMMY *is lowering her hand.*

MUMMY (*with contempt*): Coward! (*Points to* MAMMALIA.) If she weren't mute she could tell you such atrocious things that you'd die just from the torture of having to hear them.

MAMMALIA *looks at her in horror and makes a half-negative gesture. Enter* PLASFODOR, *followed by* MASCULETTE *in a night-gown.*

PLASFODOR (*holding a notebook*): Here's the kind of reading our maid does at night: *The Memoirs of Count Von Telek.*

He thumbs through the pages; VON TELEK *looks on indifferently.*

VON TELEK: I forgot about that, carried away by the madness of a purely sensual love for your soubrette, Plasi. But sooner or later we'd have had to put our cards on the table. You can stop looking through those papers. Now I'm going to tell you the principal mystery.

PLASFODOR (*reads*): " . . . Then we could tour the entire world with that pair of lunatics . . ." (*To* MAMMALIA.) That means us, and the noble Princess. He wanted to use us to open some kind of ghastly cabaret theatre!!

VON TELEK *grabs the notebook away from him;* PLASFODOR *laughs nervously.*

VON TELEK: The second mystery is much more important . . .

MUMMY (*interrupts him*): It's not time yet . . .

VON TELEK (*proudly*): Sometimes I too have a will of my own, Miss Tsui.

MUMMY (*ironically*): Knights appear on the stage in cabarets, but it's the titled riffraff who rule the peoples of the world . . .

VON TELEK (*interrupts her*): Right now this is life, not cabaret or metaphysics. With your kind permission I'm the one who directs events in life.

The MUMMY *squats, facing the audience.*

VON TELEK (*to* PLASFODOR): Mammalia has certainly told you about that mysterious man who seduced her when she was eight years old. I was that man. So I have more rights than you think.

MAMMALIA *stands petrified looking at the ground, then she moves as if attacked by a swarm of bees.* PLASFODOR *keeps silent.*

MUMMY: White people say so many useless things both in life and on stage. Slave of your own tongue, don't you know that what's going to happen tomorrow has to happen, even if you stir up all the demons in the world today?

VON TELEK (*ignoring her words*): Doesn't that fill you with hatred, Plasi? Have you really lost the possibility of feeling anything?

PLASFODOR (*in ecstasy*): I didn't know I owed my happiness to you. And my happiness is just that—that she is the way she is. At the thought of losing her, I simply cease to exist. Come here, my little Ma-Ma-Mammalia, give me your lips.

MAMMALIA *falls to her knees before* PLASFODOR, *who kisses her on the mouth, while raising her up from the floor.*

MASCULETTE: Oh, how I despise my mistress, Franz.

PLASFODOR: Your despising her is another indispensable chord in this symphony.

MUMMY (*indifferently like an automaton*): Take me back to the hotel, Franz.

VON TELEK (*angrily*): *I* can see I'm really not needed here. Thanks for last night, Masculette. I can't stand women who are rash or indiscreet.

MASCULETTE (*regretfully*): You're not really abandoning me, are you, Franz?

VON TELEK (*taking the* MUMMY *by the arm*): Definitively and forever.

MASCULETTE *laughs nervously.*

PLASFODOR (*with* MAMMALIA *in his arms*): Don't forget tomorrow morning, Franz. I'll be waiting for you at nine o'clock for a decisive talk. (VON TELEK *and the* MUMMY *go* out, followed by MASCULETTE. *Completely exhausted*, PLASFODOR *throws himself on the sofa.* MAMMALIA *paces nervously about the room.*) Don't let your forebodings get the best of you. I'm so tired—let me rest a moment. (MAMMALIA *stops pacing and gestures wildly as if she were going to jump out of her own skin.*) Isn't conversation the most significant way of experiencing life? Let's talk about anything at all . . . Actually, just the fact of talking itself . . . With words the wealth of possibilities is far greater than with events. If only it were possible to grasp what flows as the flowing itself, in its own terms, and not as something standing for something else. (MAMMALIA *seems to want to answer. "Oh, yes, that's just it."*) I can't decide on death. The fatigue felt by the individual, isolated being in his amorphous struggle against absurdity. Enclosed in a ball of glass, we roll among shattered worlds. And when I said that over there, at the Illusion, Hildesheim got up and asked me in all seriousness: "Well, all right, but have you read chapter three of Meyerspritz about triactical eudomnesia," or something like that. I haven't read it and I'm not going to. That pigeonholing of everything. Actually nothing can satiate me. I've lost the ability to feel any kind of pleasure, even if it's ten times removed from the immediate experience. Even the mystery seems to me to be something dead, ancient and fossilized in its unchanging sameness. Another idiot, Stanghuyzen, told me with a serious look on his face: "Dementia praecox." But for me it remains absolute. The criteria of those gentlemen don't interest me in the least. (*Stretches.*)

Only formulating something like this has value. It's something which doesn't get lost in the universe. Everything else passes and is scattered in nothingness. (*He yawns.* MAMMALIA *goes to him and takes his head in her hands. Suddenly she begins to listen intently, then stealthily goes to the window at the right. She stands there a moment and listens.*) I beg you, put aside these forebodings. For one moment at least I wanted to float in pure dialectics above life, even a life as unreal as ours. To keep in check the centrifugal expansiveness, the tension which goes into transforming reality. (MAMMALIA *draws the shade and opens the window.*) Oh, stop.

MAMMALIA *leans out the window and listens. In the distance the sounds of a mandolin can be heard. Nearer by, an oriental song without any melody, sung in a stifled, indifferent voice.*

MUMMY (*sings across the way in a window opening on the hotel courtyard*):

Ma a a a la ra ga a a a ta
Ka ma ra ta ka a a la.
Ma ga ra ta ma ga ha a
Me ge ere ka la wa ta pa a a.

MAMMALIA *listens.* PLASFODOR *gets up and goes to the window. They both listen for a moment.* MAMMALIA *shakes with fear, turns away from the window, wrings her hands and writhes in despair.* PLASFODOR *angrily slams the window and lowers the black shade. He takes* MAMMALIA *by the hand and pulls her toward the sofa.*

PLASFODOR (*sitting down*): That's enough, that's enough. That damned Mummy is the most real character of us all. It's because of her that reality's crept in among us. (MAMMALIA *stands in front of him and moves as if beseeching* PLASFODOR *to tell her something.*) You want to know what she whispered in my ear then? It seems totally unimportant to me now. She assured me that there is a future life, giving herself as supposed evidence. All that's a fraud. The life which *is* is the strangest. I don't need any other world. We'll never fathom eternity; and the other world, if it does exist, is only a certain variation on what exists here. That's not where the strangeness of existence lies. That's something to scare children with, third-rate mysteries, ghosts at séances. Oh! How that bores me!

MAMMALIA *implores him with gestures to stop talking as if his words were a sort of sacrilege for her. The* MUMMY's *song can be heard faintly through the closed window.*

ACT THREE

Scene One

The next morning.   The same room. MAMMALIA *and* PLASFODOR *are drinking chocolate at the small table.* MASCULETTE *waits on them. Enter* VON TELEK *drunk.*

VON TELEK (*throwing himself down on the sofa*): Now let's talk seriously. Does this life satisfy you? Is this really what we dreamed about as children, when I wanted to be a pirate, and you wanted to be an artist? No. There's no place in society for us. Not even for me, despite the fact that my position is all too clearly delineated. What was great in former times has become today—through the process of social pulverization— paltry, flat small-scale swinishness.

PLASFODOR (*ironic*): What's the use of making me realize those bitter truths? Even my sufferings are in another dimension. Desire, apathy, pleasure and pain, those concepts are foreign to me.

VON TELEK (*gets up quickly and pulls out his tie pin; sticking it into* PLASFODOR's *hand*): Does this leave you indifferent, too?

MAMMALIA *pulls him away.*

PLASFODOR (*cries out in pain*): Aaaah! You're a brutal beast. (*Sucks his hand.* VON TELEK *sits down on the sofa.*) I've got a body, damn it all to hell. What I'm talking about isn't any lousy teetotaling spirituality,

VON TELEK: And *I* don't like fraud.

PLASFODOR (*continues to drink his chocolate*): You understand everything in a different dimension. You're too real a bull, Francis, and you're far from understanding the way she and I live.

VON TELEK: Don't say anything more to me about that water hen, that whore-till-when. A dumb little animal. If she could talk, then you'd see her total nothingness. Besides, a woman should never talk. If I were absolute dictator, I'd have the tongues of all the women in my realm torn out, even if kissing lost some of its charm in the process.

MAMMALIA *writhes in indefinable suffering on the sofa.*

PLASFODOR (*with boredom*): We're using the same words, but we're talking about totally different things. That's where the poverty and wealth of language lie.

VON TELEK: That's enough palaver. What I'm interested in is creating a certain reality. Not necessarily a cabaret, but rather a sort of club, an association, various oddities, and you're the only one who could be the director of it.

PLASFODOR: I understand. Socializing and adapting certain towering creations of past ages to the leveling conditions of the present. You won't get me to fall for that.

VON TELEK: Why would that have to be a comedown? Isn't it worth the trouble to gather those fruits that heroism or true power once produced in this world, or in some other?

PLASFODOR: I wouldn't be able to go on being myself. I'd lose that don't-give-a-damn attitude to life that my total isolation has given me.

MAMMALIA *quietly sneaks up on* VON TELEK, *who doesn't notice what she's doing.*

VON TELEK: But that's just it—to rise above present-day life doesn't mean isolating oneself at all. In this very life you've got to produce the centers of infection that will destroy it. Points of inflammation throughout the whole society that no inventor of universal happiness will be able to control. (MAMMALIA *tips* VON TELEK*'s chair over onto the floor and sinks her hands into his throat;* VON TELEK *grabs her by the hair and they roll around on the floor.* PLASFODOR *calmly goes on drinking his chocolate and glances through a photograph album.* VON TELEK *roars hollowly.*) Let go of me! I'm choking . . . You slut.

MASCULETTE (*runs in and dashes over to save* VON TELEK): Francis! My poor Francis! Oh, how I despise my poor mistress.

MAMMALIA *lets go of* VON TELEK *and dances with joy stage left.* PLASFODOR *hasn't batted an eyelash.*

VON TELEK (*getting up; to* PLASFODOR): I kept telling you she was a stupid little animal.

MASCULETTE: Francis! I beg you, keep on loving me. Don't leave me in this horrible house.

VON TELEK (*impatiently*): Beat it, sour jelly-roll.

MASCULETTE (*falling on her knees before him*): Francis! I implore you, take me into your cabaret—there's no life for me apart from you!

Suddenly VON TELEK *pulls a large upholstery hammer out of the side pocket of his tailcoat and smashes in* MASCULETTE's *head with it as she kneels in front of him. She collapses on the rug without a groan.* VON TELEK *breathes hard.* PLASFODOR *calmly closes the album and takes another sip of chocolate.* MAMMALIA *continues to do her joyous dance.*

PLASFODOR (*suddenly rushing at* VON TELEK): Oh! I've had enough familiarities out of that "coq de la walk." (*He throws* VON TELEK *out and locks the door with the key; comes back, sips some more chocolate. After having reached the high point of satisfaction expressed by her dance,* MAMMALIA *calms down. He leads her over to the sofa.*) Even the death of asexual people doesn't affect me anymore. Masculette made the chocolate too sweet today. Well now, getting back to the subject before last, I've invented a new way of life. We're going to push our inner anxiety to a climax—by lying completely motionless . . .

They lie down side by side on the sofa. The curtain falls as he is speaking.

Scene Two

The same room, evening of the same day. Dusk is failing. Three candles are burning. The stage is empty except for MASCULETTE's *corpse, which sits on the sofa, its head heavily bandaged. There must be a pronounced cadaverous stiffness to the legs and arms. Enter* MAMMALIA *quietly, on tiptoe. She examines the whole room thoroughly, then listens attentively at the door and looks behind the window curtain. Suddenly she is overcome by fear. She is afraid of the corpse and the wide open door with the gaping blackness beyond. She goes stiff with fear, then seems to want to run away, then goes stiff again. Enter quietly the* MUMMY, *bulging.* MAMMALIA *throws up her hands and freezes in a state of monstrous fear. The* MUMMY *slowly draws near, embraces* MAMMALIA, *who is petrified with fear, and begins to kiss her passionately.* MAMMALIA *collapses. The* MUMMY *holds her up, then carries her over to the sofa and makes her sit down next to* MASCULETTE's *corpse.* MAMMALIA *is wide-eyed with fear.*

MUMMY (*screams, pointing at the sofa with her claw*): Get up! (MASCULETTE's *corpse and* MAMMALIA *get up simultaneously like two automatons.*) On the floor! Out of here!!

MASCULETTE's *corpse falls flat on its face and crawls on its elbows toward the door.* MAMMALIA *watches this for a moment, beside herself with fear, then falls in a faint on the sofa. The* MUMMY *still standing in the same place, leads* MASCULETTE's *crawling corpse toward the door by moving her finger with its giant claw. Voices can be heard outside the door. As they enter,* PLASFODOR *and* VON TELEK *pass the crawling corpse in the doorway. They step over the corpse without noticing it. The door remains open. The* MUMMY *sits down on the floor near the sofa.*

VON TELEK (*finishing a conversation already in progress*): And finally that way we'll get to the coast. I mean India, the Sunda Islands, and then Australia.

PLASFODOR (*distracted*): Yes, yes; but will I be able to create in all that a system isolated enough for my creativity in the realm of life?

MAMMALIA *awakens from her state of terror, rubs her eyes and goes unsteadily to* PLASFODOR.

VON TELEK (*noticing the* MUMMY): What independence!   There's my baggage taking a stroll without any claim check, going wherever it feels like.

MUMMY (*to* VON TELEK): You're careless, like a husband or too trusting a lover, whose sweetheart slips out of his hands imperceptibly without his knowing it.

VON TELEK (*waving his hand contemptuously*): I've got more important things on my mind than the problem of life beyond the grave. Sit down, Plasfodor, and send off that mute little animal of yours. (*With a gesture,* PLASFODOR *dismisses* MAMMALIA, *who paces up and down making odd gestures. The* MUMMY *emits uneasy murmurings, which, during the course of the two men's conversation, slowly change into an oriental song as in Act Two. As the* MUMMY *sings,* MAMMALIA's *movements become calmer, but* PLASFODOR *becomes more and more distracted and responds to* VON TELEK *like an automaton.* VON TELEK *sits stage right with his back to the* MUMMY, PLASFODOR *stage left;* VON TELEK *talks into space, not looking at* PLASFODOR. *Persuasively.*) You think that this is only some kind of mysterious business deal for me. Please, don't think that; from now on you don't have any right to think that. I can't live in what surrounds us either, and I'm looking for a way out. Only I don't have the strength, the way you do, to create it by isolating myself from the environment. I'd rather try and change the environment according to our metaphysical concept.   Produce metaphysical delirium on a mass scale, but not anything like the American sects—that's pure fraud, those are actually death throes . . .

PLASFODOR (*more and more distracted*): Yes, of course—I see that. That's truly great. But sometimes I have the feeling the game's not even worth the candle on the birthday cake.

VON TELEK (*interrupts him*): But can you be alone? Perhaps before, you could have become a hermit, but now that Mammalia is really yours, through the silence that surrounds her, you won't be able to be alone anymore.

PLASFODOR (*looking at the slowly-rising* MUMMY): I certainly won't. Death is the only thing that . . .

VON TELEK (*speaks, staring into space*): That's what irritates me, your constant flirtation with death. You won't kill yourself, that's for sure. You'd have done it a long time ago, if you were destined to. Now I'm dreaming of a wonderful life, in which humanity could blaze up one more time in a terrible flame of wild creation before plunging into the gray abyss that awaits it.

PLASFODOR (*unable to take his eyes off the* MUMMY, *answers totally without thinking about what he's saying*): Oh, yes, now I understand you. That's a fabulous idea.

MAMMALIA *goes over to the* MUMMY, *who bulges in various contortions and seizes* MAMMALIA's *hand*; MAMMALIA *begins to sway in time to the* MUMMY's *song, which grows fainter and fainter.*

VON TELEK (*not turning around*): Ah, at last that Chinese goat's finally stopping bleating. Now you can see, *mon cher Plasfodeur,* how you've underestimated me. For the sake of the great infection center of new creativity that we're going to ignite, I forgive you everything. But you've got to promise me one thing: that you'll get that poor little sister of mine ready in a suitable way. That's the only thing I'm not taking on myself, even though I'm actually healthy as a bull. Perhaps I did rub out your soubrette needlessly, but it's given me a new dimension for metaphysical crime without any motive whatsoever.

PLASFODOR (*gets up and stretches*): Why, of course—naturally—that's a mere detail . . .

VON TELEK (*looking at him for the first time*): Plasi! You look like a perfect idiot. What's the matter with you?

PLASFODOR *goes over to the* MUMMY, *who takes him by the hand and slowly, with terrible bulging movements, leads* MAMMALIA *by the right hand,* PLASFODOR *by the left, toward the dark gulf of the open door.* VON TELEK *turns around and, stepping backwards towards the audience, looks at the others, his arms outstretched. They pass by in silence without looking at him and disappear through the open door;* VON TELEK *stands there as though nailed to the spot. After a moment there can be heard, apparently from the stairs, the* MUMMY's *song and, with that in the background, a frightful scream from* MAMMALIA, *as if all her skin had suddenly been torn off at once, and then some unintelligible cries and gibbering from* PLASFODOR.

VON TELEK (*screams*): Mammalia!!!

Suddenly there is a dead silence beyond the door; VON TELEK *falls down heavily on the rug, his head toward the audience. A pause. Through the door at right—used for the first time—enter* TWO GENDARMES *in tricornered hats and black uniforms. Looking around timorously, they go over to* VON TELEK, *who is prone, and start prodding him with their feet.* VON TELEK *sits up on the floor and looks at them wide-eyed.*

GENDARME 1: Your papers, Sir?

VON TELEK (*mechanically pulls papers out of his pocket and hands them over*): I don't understand a thing.

GENDARME 2: You'll understand soon enough.

GENDARME 1 (*reads*): "Graf Franz von Telek. Department Head at the Ministry of Trade. Division of Poisons." You're just the person we're looking for, Count.

VON TELEK (*getting up*): That's not true; there's a different name there. My name is Lambdon Tyger.

GENDARME 2 *grabs and holds him.*

GENDARME 1 (*giving him back the card*): There it is.

VON TELEK (*reads*): "Graf Franz von Telek." Yes, really, everything's conspired against me.

GENDARME 2: Where are your things?

VON TELEK (*laughs sadly*): My things? All my baggage came to life a moment ago and went out that door. (*Points to the center door.*)

GENDARME 1 (*to* GENDARME 2): Stay here with this gentleman. I'll go have a look at that other exit. (*He goes to the door and leaves.*)

VON TELEK (*laughs in a deep bass*): This is only a dream, noble torturer. That card belongs to a friend of mine long since deceased.

GENDARME 2 *looks uneasily about;* GENDARME 1 *comes back.*

GENDARME 1 (*uneasily to* GENDARME 2): There's no way out through there. Or have I gone off my rocker?

GENDARME 2 (*terrified*): Let's get out of here. There aren't enough of us to handle this kind of business.

GENDARME 1 *looks at him wide-eyed with fear and they both rush to the right door in unison. Bumping into each other at the door, they fly off like madmen.* VON TELEK *stands there calmly.*

VON TELEK (*pulling himself together*): In our family no one has ever admitted defeat. (*Pulls out his watch.*) Starting tomorrow, I'm beginning a new life. (*Looks at his watch.*) Actually, starting today, which is much more difficult. (*He puts on his derby, takes his cane and with an assured step goes out through the center door. In the distance he can he heard whistling a kind of two-step.*)

22 August 1919

Stanisław Ignacy Witkiewicz
Fearing Oneself
circa 1910

TUMOR BRAINIOWICZ

A Drama in Three Acts with a Prologue
(1920)

Foreword

Written in late 1919 and published in July 1921, *Tumor Brainiowicz* was the first play by Witkiewicz to be staged. The premiere was given at the Słowacki Theatre in Cracow on June 30, 1921, followed by one subsequent performance. The director was forced to wait almost a year for permission from the Cracow censor, who found the play, and particularly the prologue, so unintelligible that it seemed subversive. Once approval was obtained and the rehearsals started, several actors withdrew in protest against what they considered to be total nonsense, and the director, fearing a scandal, announced in the press that the production would be of a private and experimental nature designed for those interested in new trends in the art of the drama. Special invitations were necessary, available only by writing to the theatre.

The performance itself went well. The author was called on stage after the second act and presented with an armful of lilies by the Cracow Mathematical Society. But the play was dismissed by the critics as the work of a madman. In March 1926, a second production of *Tumor,* planned at the Teatr Mały in Warsaw, was canceled when the actors went on strike after the first reading of the play. The first and only postwar Polish production took place in Olsztyn in 1974. Tadeusz Kantor's *The Dead Class* (1975) takes many of its characters and much of its dialog from *Tumor*, but these elements are totally transformed.

In the "Theoretical Introduction" to his first fifteen plays, the playwright calls *Tumor* "a fantasy on the theme of the revolution in mathematics and physics." At this time Polish mathematicians and logicians were starting to gain international recognition, and Witkacy, who knew many of them, was a pioneer in creating drama out of modern science. Instead of cultivating the drawing room comedy of ideas as a forum for discussion of science (as did several Polish physicist-playwrights in the 1920s and 30s), Witkacy puts the concepts of modern physics and mathematics—indeterminacy, complementarity, and relativity—into the warp and woof of the dramatic form itself. Georg Cantor's theory of sets, alephs, and transfinite functions become the source of the comedy. The revolution in science is not explained discursively, but directly embodied in character and action and rendered theatrical. In *Tumor* Witkacy makes the new mathematics both the subject of his drama and the cornerstone of its dramaturgy.

Witkacy imbues his drama with Freud as well as with Cantor. *Tumor* is a play about genius, portraying an exceptional individual at odds with the repressive institutions of family and society, which are constantly threatened by the subterranean, disruptive forces of the erotic and creative drives. Like a huge overgrown child, Tumor, an embodiment of the Id, has wild tantrums: he roars, stamps his feet, rolls his eyes, howls, wails, thrashes up and down, and smashes furniture.

Science quickly becomes a matter of global politics. Tumor—a wild plebeian Slav—must be tied up and kidnapped by the cool British secret agent Professor Alfred Green who comes to protect the empire and preserve the status quo. In Act II the tropics are introduced as the setting, when the love-sick Tumor pursues his step-daughter Iza to Timor, a remote island in the Malayan archipelago inhabited by a "primitive" people whose simplicity is coveted by the "civilized" Europeans. The drama shifts from a single focus to a confrontation between Southeast Asian and European cultures, pitting the natives' age-old animistic faith in the god of the volcano against Tumor's belief in the power of the aleph. National, racial, and class traits become central to the drama's conflicts. First Tumor and then the British imperialists seek to possess the island by colonizing it.

Naked bronze bodies, bright sarongs, and gigantic purple flowers contrast with the monotonous white of the Westerners' skins, tropical outfits, and pith helmets. Strong feelings are aroused by skin color and scent. The Rajah's son is in awe of Iza's white skin, Tumor boasts of his "white power," but whiteness is also the color of boredom, uniformity, and repression which lead to violence and aggression. After first killing the Rajah and assuming his role, Tumor sets himself up as a divinity to the natives, following in the footsteps of Conrad's Lord Jim and Mr. Kurtz. Witkacy, who visited Ceylon as part of a British scientific expedition, considers the hidden network of ties among knowledge, power, and imperialism. For the British science is a form of power—a gateway to imperialism based on knowledge—and colonial and scientific expansion go hand in hand. For a while Tumor plays at being Faustian man, aspiring to power through knowledge, but cannot long sustain the role because he lacks faith in his own authority.

The structure of the play—seemingly disjunctive, meandering, full of capricious playfulness and knockabout humor—actually makes new connections. Intellectual and artistic creation is both childlike and like giving birth to a child. Acts I and III take place in the children's nursery where the adults play absentmindedly with toys strewn on the floor.

The dramatic form of *Tumor* is appropriately childlike and primitive for a play that takes as its theme the kinship between the genius and the child, the creative and the primordial. Tumor is a victim of his own genius and fallible human nature. Creativity, like sexuality, is uncontrollable.

Driven by desire for his demonic step-daughter, Tumor starts to create a revolutionary system of mathematics based on new transfinite numbers he calls "tumors" that proliferate, just as his children have. As Tumor's name indicates, genius is a disease of the brain that spreads rapidly.

Through parody Witkacy builds his drama out of the works of others. In the "Preface" to *Tumor,* he mentions several sources. For the picture of colonialism, Witkacy draws upon *Almayer's Folly*, which he had begun to translate into Polish in late 1919. From Conrad's novel Witkacy takes the geography and local color dealing with the Malayan Archipelago. But it is also from Conrad that the playwright derives something more essential: use of the tropics as a critical perspective on Western civilization and a radical insight into human nature. The supposed savages, innately passionate and heroic in their single-minded devotion to their love and honor, are contrasted to the greed and deceit of the duplicitous Westerns.

The contrast between East and West, colored and white, savage and civilized, as developed by Conrad, becomes fundamental to Witkacy's world view. Half-naked, smelling of raw meat, and fearfully superstitious, the savages are nobler than the conquering Europeans who lack absolute values. The lowborn slob Tumor, who owes both his tremendous vitality and his creative and procreative energies to his plebeian heritage, is prince of numbers, but he envies the Rajah, son of the volcano, who is a true prince by birth.

Witkacy's white desperadoes, seeking to compensate for their lost sense of the mystery of existence, are haunted by colonial dreams of an exotic realm where they would have unlimited opportunity to act out their fantasies of power, greed, and lust. "Today's adventurers," Witkacy writes in *New Forms* (1919) "are a total rabble, chasing after profits along the least legal path; if they aren't locked up in jail in old Europe, such riffraff find a field for action in the colonies, where there still blooms a form of existence intensified by the risk of life and fortune."

Visited by the ghost of Patakulo, the Rajah he murdered, Tumor suddenly drops dead of a heart attack. At the very last moment, Lord Persville—a totally new character—appears out of nowhere and robs Tumor of his life work. Genius dies exhausted, and his great idea is stolen and exploited by others while the corpse still lies on the ground.

TUMOR BRAINIOWICZ

A Drama in Three Acts with a Prologue
(1920)

Dedicated to
Zofia and Tadeusz Żeleński

PREFACE to *TUMOR BRAINIOWICZ*

A few words by way of a preface won't do any harm, but it won't do much good either. *Tumor Brainiowicz* had its origins in a tumor of the brain, as is evident from the very title of the play. Any good book on diseases of the brain or a consultation with an honest doctor will tell you all you need to know about tumors. The names of the characters come from fantasy, life, and the works of other authors.   Fantasies on the theme of the contemporary revolution in physics and mathematics should not offend scholars; they are only the pretext for certain "dynamic tensions." As for the sources used in writing the play, I can with a clear conscience refer to the following works:

> Three orange-colored popular works by Henri Poincaré;
> *Allgemeine Theorie der unendlichen Mengen* by Arthur
>   Schoenfliess;
> *The Principle of Contradiction in the Light of Bertrand Russell's
>   Latest Research* by Leon Chwistek;
> *Julius Caesar* by Shakespeare ;
> *Almayer's Folly* by Joseph Conrad;
> *Nietota* and *In the Twilight of the Stars* by Tadeusz Miciński;
> My own posthumous works in the field of philosophy and my own
>   explorations (not works) in tropical and subtropical regions.

For a more complete explanation of the essence of the art of the theatre in general, see (attentively): *Introduction to the Theory of Pure Form in the Theatre* by the same author in *Skamander*.

S.I.W.
22 February 1920

CHARACTERS

TUMOR BRAINIOWICZ—Very famous mathematician of humble origin. Forty years old.

GAMBOLINE, DAUGHTER OF PRINCE BASILIUS—From the noble line of the Transcaspian Trunduhl-Bheds. *Primo voto*: Countess Roman Kretchborski; *secundo voto*: Mrs. TUMOR BRAINIOWICZ. Thirty-six years old.

He is a giant built like a wild ox. Low buffalo brow with a huge head of rumpled blond hair falling down over his face. Magnificently dressed. A red decoration in his buttonhole. Across his shirt front there can be seen the green ribbon of some Eastern order. A gray suit of the best cord and yellow shoes. Clear blue eyes. Close-clipped flaxen mustache. Otherwise clean-shaven.

She is a magnificently developed brunette with light down on her upper lip. Fiery black eyes. Somewhat Oriental. A wildly exciting thoroughbred.

BALANTINE FERMOR—Spinster. (The Right Honorable Miss Fermor.) Daughter of Henry Fermor, Fifth Earl of Ballantrae. Thirty-two years old. Beautiful, majestic blonde; healthy, very exciting thoroughbred.

PROFESSOR ALFRED GREEN—From the M.C.G.O. (The Mathematical Central and General Office). Blond hair, pince-nez. A thoroughly English type. Forty-two years old. Completely clean-shaven.

JOSEPH BRAINIOWICZ—Crafty peasant, seventy-five years old. Fit as a fiddle. Nothing like TUMOR. (TUMOR takes after his mother.) Peasant overcoat, glossy high boots. Brown hair going gray. Aquiline nose.

IBISA (IZA)—Countess Kretchborski. Daughter of GAMBOLINE and Roman Kretchborski. Eighteen years old. Red hair, blue eyes. An utterly wildly exciting, demonic young girl, a real thoroughbred. As like her father as two peas in a pod.

ALFRED BRAINIOWICZ—Sixteen years old. TUMOR's first born son from his third marriage with GAMBOLINE. The very image of his father. Dressed in a pinkish-gray sports outfit.

MAURICE BRAINIOWICZ—Fourteen years old. The next item in the collection of young Brainiowiczes. Very like his mother. Dressed in a gray-dun sports outfit. Turned-down collar. Raspberry *lavallière* tie.

IRENE BRAINIOWICZ—Twenty-three years old. TUMOR's daughter from his second marriage. Plain, very intelligent brunette of a slightly Semitic type.

LORD ARTHUR PERSVILLE—Fourth son of the Duke Osmond (future Duke of Osmond, Marquess of Broken Hill, Viscount of Durisdeer, Master of Takoomba Falls), the greatest demon at the Mathematical Central and General Office and the greatest of unpunished criminals; so-called "King of Hells" (*roi des enfers*) and gambling dens (amphibiology of the plural of Hell). Thirty-three years old. Sharpest geometrician on the planet earth. Student of Hilbert. Leader of fashion. Dressed in a tail coat and striped trousers and a top hat, with a cane in his hand. A youthful face of unusual beauty. Clean-shaven; black eyes. Brown hair, strong build, something between a true lord and a criminal type from the penal colonies. Refined gestures. His eyes never laugh but his beautifully drawn full lips, fixed in delicate, yet monstrously powerful jaws, have the smile of a three-year-old baby girl. Moreover, he is a person (if he can be called a person) who arouses the most diabolic jealousy and envy throughout the entire globe.

PRINCE TENGAH—Very beautiful Malay, son of the RAJAH PATAKULO of Timor. Twenty-three years old. Blue turban, red sarong. Kris at his side.

OLD RAJAH PATAKULO—Old Malay with a gray beard; sixty years old. Loin-cloth around his hips.

CAPTAIN FITZGERALD—Clean-shaven sea wolf. Commander of the cruiser *Prince Arthur*.

MALAYS OF THE GUARD—Dressed like TENGAH, with lances.

TWO OTHER MALAYS—In red turbans with lances.

A CROWD OF MALAYS

TWO WHITE MEN—In khaki outfits and pith helmets.

SIX CREW MEMBERS FROM THE CRUISER—Dressed in white sailor suits.

TWO OF GREEN's AGENTS—Impersonal beings.

FOUR PORTERS—In blue aprons.   Completely impersonal characters with beards.

ISIDORE BRAINIOWICZ—In diapers.

Prologue

Living salamanders' branded mugs
Cackle in the nameless planet's red expanse.
Serrated in the torment of surexistences,
Denticulated into baby puckers,
Enfolded into old senile dentures,
The funereal stilettos of living murderers,
Driven by their swollen hearts' desire,
Draw near the goal:
A hyperbolic comet's nodal point.
Into senile dentures' clavichords
I pack mashed words, by ardor exacerbated.
A monster's carrion, crushed at the crossroads,
Eats out its belly-button and drills holes into little birdies'
         rainbow wings.
I know that well.
And find it good that it is so.
The gesture of a ghost along the world's steep cliffs
Allays the torment of the cretinized masses.
Pubescent bards cajole one another
Amidst the fragrant shrubs and shady shrines.
Beyond the wall she (who?) cries out for "more"!!
On an irreversible slide to baneful lubricity,
Crushing body against bones, jaw backwards turned,
She bares her fiery teeth behind sharp corners
And poking with a pelican's beak,
In the cave that their shadows have seized,
Shadows of masses eviscerated by superbrutish torment
Extend the watery abyss with a faience cup.
I know that I am lying and that higher than laughter is only
         construction of truth,
Etching itself into darkness like a spiral Babylonian tower.
Babel, Jezebel, and English Mabel,
Who reads the Bible at insipid five o'clock tea,
While the thundering photosphere of our star
Snorts in an explosion of flaming gas.
Hydrogen burns and helium drifts aimlessly,
Illumining the expanses of intermediary dusk.
The old man without a beard measures out nightfall and daybreak

And at the edge of ultimate concepts
Sets the world's manometer on Nothingness.
To be him or remain oneself,
In metabrutish, rococo dress,
And keep on rutting in uproarious pastures.
Here's a crux worthy of great Caesar's lies.
Worn-out teeth still munch the food
Ruminated long ago in a double pouch
That proud Pasiphaë now glories in.
An electron in a magnetic field coddles
The blind glance of a ghost stopped in its tracks.
The relativity of space curves all the lines,
And the blind man licks objects robbed of their color.
Pure as a tear, a spirit ceaselessly vomits a nondescript fluid . . .
Mankind, that abhorred machine of former deities,
Piles on ancient Tiber's banks the pukings of desire,
Into tiger pleats and corn-cockle anthers.
(Somewhere a marabou is standing on one leg.)
It's all outworn, the pulp of words no longer flows
And fails to shroud the dread of bygone devils.
They abase themselves before a spit-out pip,
Tybalt fears the Cains and Abels.
In centipedes' embraces a panther bewitched,
Its mottles shining pink and proud.
Through high grass there crawls a splendid courtesan,
Her belly mashing far too lucid words.
Draw the curtain, behold—on stage enter
Tumor Brainiowicz himself, with a tumor in his brain.
To us what does it all really matter?
That flail-macerated flaneur with a lion's mane.

ACT ONE

The children's room on the second floor of GAMBOLINE's *house.* TUMOR BRAINIOWICZ *sits alone in an armchair. Many children's toys on the rug. A huge cylinder full of gas stands in the corner to the right. The furnishings of the room are the height of modern hygiene. Everything white as snow. The sun streams through large windows to the right and left. It is bright and warm. Upstage a blackboard for school work. To the left of it a door facing the audience. Another door to the left.*

BRAINIOWICZ: I'm banging away at top speed. Grips coming to grips, grips sinking into grips, and in the fiery splutter, stirring up a little dust in a storm beyond the grave. Cursed civilization! (*Bangs his fist on the back of the chair.*) Who's forcing me to pretend? Yesterday I read their whole new program. Simply makes you want to puke. Vomito negro.

Enter IZA. *Short black dress. Azure stockings. Shoes with red pom-poms.*

IZA: Mother wants to know if there's anything you need.

BRAINIOWICZ: I need a bull, a chariot, limitless horizons and your blue eyes, Iza. Tell your mother she is like Pasiphaë. She'll turn green with envy. She's so frightfully complicated, perhaps I'll burst in this whole whirlwind you're all creating.

IZA: Please calm down. I know a great deal—a great deal more than Mother or even than you.

Exit IZA. BRAINIOWICZ *gets up and winds his watch.*

BRAINIOWICZ: Cursed civilization. I don't have an ounce of the artist in me, not even that much! (*Indicates by holding his thumb and forefinger very close together.*) And yet the whole world is trying to make me believe I am an artist: "Oh, what great talent! Oh, what a genius!" If only she wouldn't think that! All my children look so much like me that I am simply terrified there hasn't been a single woman strong enough to be unfaithful to me.

Enter BRAINIOWICZ's *father in a peasant overcoat and high boots.*

JOSEPH BRAINIOWICZ (*an old but still spry peasant; broad-shouldered like his son; speaks with a peasant drawl*): You're invincible, sonny boy.

BRAINIOWICZ: Always full of bright ideas, aren't you, Father? So old and yet so foolish. (*Recites.*)

> In the depths of my soul
> Primordial vengefulness,
> My coat of arms
> A juicy maggot.
> Hordes of horses all aghast
> And officers with looks downcast
> Over the fate of harlots long, long ago departed.

(*Speaks.*) Besides being myself, I could be a waiter, an officer or a harlot. If I were a woman, I'd be a terrible slut.

JOSEPH BRAINIOWICZ: How fantastically beautiful you are, sonny boy. (*Picks up a doll from the floor and kisses it.*) That's what my little darling looked like, when she died. That's what your poor little sister Anselma looked like.

BRAINIOWICZ (*recites*):

> Worms are wriggling through my eyes
> In dark, dissolving images,
> Like a sharp-edged knife
> I'd like to use myself to slice
> Clean through speed-enamored space.
> Burdens I bear, the likes of which
> No Caesar of this world could weigh,
> And yet away it flies like wisps of hay.
> And everything seems light to me,
> Like the spider's insubstantial pelf,
> Like some unobtrusive little elf,
> Or his other, interplanetary self.
> My face I have powdered with greatness
> And I am a hideous marionette.
> Such disgust as I feel for myself
> None has known since worlds began.

JOSEPH BRAINIOWICZ (*staggering*): Oh, how lovely you are, sonny boy! Come on, let's go to the corner pub.

BRAINIOWICZ (*in despair*): Oh, go by yourself, Father. I still have to finish writing the rules and regulations for the new Academy of Sciences today. And besides they just sent me the proofs for my treatise on transfinite functions. But you don't even know the first thing about algebra, Father. Might as well talk to a stone wall. (*He hands his father a piece of paper which he pulls out of his pocket.*)

JOSEPH BRAINIOWICZ (*puts on round-rimmed glasses and reads*): "Über transfinite Funktionen im alef-dimensionalen[1] Raume," by Professor Tumor von Brainiowicz. Oh, how clever you are, sonny boy! And just for that they gave you a title of nobility. (*Sorrowfully.*) I had a dream. I saw you as a pagan idol in a kind of Oriental temple. You didn't recognize me and you were laughing at I don't know what. And I was thrown out by a guard—a puny little old man, trembling like a leaf. He had a face like our Fido, only human.

BRAINIOWICZ (*putting the proofs away in his pocket*): I never had time for anything, not even love. But what is love for me? My children are growing up. My son will soon graduate from high-school; my daughter already can integrate differential equations pretty well, but I can't even get a little rest. If at least I were religious. "Aber mir, keine Marter ist erspart, " as Franz Joseph used to say.

JOSEPH BRAINIOWICZ *nods and heads for the exit. At the door he meets* GAMBOLINE *dressed in a light* balachan, *a Russian peasant overcoat.*

GAMBOLINE: Joseph, I told you to take care of yourself. And here he's gadding about again!

JOSEPH BRAINIOWICZ: Oh, if die I must, may I breathe my last in distinguished company. And how is Your Ladyship feeling?

GAMBOLINE: Like a steam bull. (*She laughs. Exit* JOSEPH. GAMBOLINE *suddenly grows sad and goes over to* BRAINIOWICZ.) What's the matter with you? Tumor! Don't you love me?

BRAINIOWICZ (*picks up the doll and looks at it*): But you know the whole story. I'm a lowborn slob, an utter beast. I remember, I can't forget. I

---

[1] Aleph: Cantor's first transfinite number. [Author's note.]

smashed your cupboard into smithereens and you had to feel ashamed of me in front of all of them. But I couldn't help getting drunk.

GAMBOLINE: Don't give it a thought. It's all been made up for. I wish I could have a baby every month so there'd be more like you. I'd like to own one of those islands in the Pacific Ocean and have you there and our children, the whole lot big strong strapping boys like you, the whole lot math wizards, each one an exact copy of the others. The Academy would be right in the middle and you, my one and only, lord of all suns, king of numbers, prince of Infinity, shah of the world of absolute ideas, leaning back in the entire universe as though it were your armchair, you'd sit there mighty as . . .

BRAINIOWICZ: Stop—I'm choking on my power as on a pill too big even for the jaws of a whale.

GAMBOLINE: You don't love me. Do you want Isidore to come into the world with crooked legs and eyes on the side of his head?

BRAINIOWICZ (*hugging her impetuously*): No! No! Don't talk like that! I love you, I love you desperately. (*Suddenly goes limp.*) But I can't forget that you're a princess. There's something absolute about that. One has only to take a look at your legs. (GAMBOLINE *looks at her legs, then studies him carefully.*) If your father, Prince Basilius, could see you in the arms of a lowborn slob like me, he'd die a second death from shame. I tell you there's something absolute about that, about the whole question of birth. What good does all my knowledge do me? (*Flings the proofs against the wall.*) I can't be born again.

GAMBOLINE (*hugging him*): My one and only, my dearest darling Tumikins—you don't understand in the least. That's just what attracts me, and where the whole diabolical charm lies. That's why I left Kretchborski. I can't stand those demi-aristos. The cursed snobs. You are a monstrous slob and when I feel my blood, of a truly infernal blue, mingling with your crude, crimson peasant blood, and together we're creating a race of violet demi-gods, when I think about that, I have the urge to spurt into molten lava from some other world out of sheer happiness. (BRAINIOWICZ's *face lights up in wild triumph. Enter* ALFRED BRAINIOWICZ.) Look! There he is, my fetish. Fred—come here, let me give you a hug . . .

BRAINIOWICZ (*to* ALFRED): Did you solve the problems?

ALFRED (*kissing his mother, speaks in a quiet voice*): Yes, Papa. I made the solution more difficult for myself by using Whitehead's method. That atrocious old man knows how to make the simplest question impossibly difficult.

BRAINIOWICZ: Show some respect for that wise man. Remember, I was his student.

GAMBOLINE (*looking at them admiringly*): I'm not sure I'll survive this happiness. Oh, why, why can't I be a rabbit!

BRAINIOWICZ (*gloomily*): Remember the white rabbit who gave birth to brindled cats for the rest of her life. She was unfaithful to her husband only once. Alfred reminds me of Kretchborski a bit too much.

GAMBOLINE (*laughs, stroking* BRAINIOWICZ's *head*): Poor brainpan! Numbers have eaten up all your gray matter, Tumor!

BRAINIOWICZ (*roars*): Don't make fun of my name! It's quite well known throughout the whole world.

He stamps his feet and rolls his eyes in a mad fit. ALFRED *goes over to the blackboard and starts writing on it with a piece of chalk. Gigantic integrals and complicated symbols appear.* GAMBOLINE *gets down on her knees and starts building something with the blocks.* BRAINIOWICZ *remains where he is. He calms down and sinks into deep thought.* IZA *runs in with the youngest Brainiowicz,* MAURICE.

MAURICE (*pronouncing his words aristocratically and saying his "r's" very gutturally in the Parisian way*): But papa only writes poetry to keep his mental balance when the numbers have gone clean through all of his pores right into his soul. Iza is a true poet. Her poem has been published in our Futuristic children's magazine. Iza, recite it.

IZA (*recites*):
     Once there was a little fetus in the dusky by-and-by's,
     Someone gave a shove by chance, someone stole a secret glance,
     And out came pretty toes.
     First of all they had to christen, find a name and then baptize,

Then baptize it Moogle-wise.
Once there was a little kitten, once there was a soft green mitten
Ate its breakfast in the by-and-by's.
Someone gave a secret glance, someone stole a shove by chance.
They all cried out their eyes.
In the children's picture book, in the cozy girlish nook,
A new tableau arose.
In the dusky by-and-by's someone stole a secret glance,
The cat devoured Moogle-wise.
Whether it was only dreamed or really happened as it seemed,
In vain they would surmise.
Did the illustration by itself arise,
Did the dream out of the drawing spring alive,
Not a guess from even soft green mitten,
Not a guess from even Moogle-wise.

BRAINIOWICZ (*dolefully, tersely*): Makes too much sense.

ALFRED (*coming back from the blackboard*): All that's good for nothing. Father's a two-timer. Father's in love with Iza. That's why mama weeps all night long. I want no part of it.

BRAINIOWICZ (*screams*): Have you gone crazy?

MAURICE (*pointing at his father*): Yes, I know. He paces up and down all night and howls. He's a madman.

GAMBOLINE *jumps up*.

GAMBOLINE: Tumor!

IZA (*claps her hands with delight and jumps up and down*): The avalanche has started to come down!

BRAINIOWICZ (*beside himself*): I'll go stark raving mad! How dare they?

ALFRED: A perfectly ordinary story. There'll be a short news item in the papers tomorrow under the heading: "Impostor Unmasked!"

GAMBOLINE (*suddenly bursts out laughing*): The old brainpan is coming unscrewed, completely unscrewed!

BRAINIOWICZ (*sorrowfully*): It was so great and it's all gone completely to pieces. (*To* IZA.) Because of you, you aristocratic little demon! I always said, exterminate the Kretchborskis or else we won't get anywhere.

GAMBOLINE (*to the children*): Quiet! Calm down, all of you. There's still time to straighten all this out. (*Threateningly to* ALFRED, *hypnotizing him.*) That's not the way it is at all. Understand? (*Through the center door enter* JOSEPH *with an unknown gentleman wearing a pince-nez.*) Too late!

IZA: Good afternoon, Joseph. Who is that you've dragged in here with you?

JOSEPH: Well, you see, he was looking for Her Ladyship. He says to me, he says, he's first-class company.

STRANGER: Indeed, I am company and it seems I have come just in time.

ALFRED *comes over to the* STRANGER.

ALFRED (*to the* STRANGER): Don't you dare butt into our private business.

GAMBOLINE (*uneasily*): Quiet, children! It's my private business, and only mine. I'm so worried about Isidore. Leave, all of you. I must be alone with him.

BRAINIOWICZ (*dolefully*): With whom? With Isidore? (*To* IZA.) I told you, all this makes too much sense. (*Exit to the left.* MAURICE *and* ALFRED *try to hold him. He breaks away from them and gets away.*)

STRANGER: One moment more and it will be too late. I have found the last possible means of salvation.

MAURICE: I don't believe you. We've already been through all that. We keep going around in circles until our heads are literally spinning. We can't take any more.

ALFRED: That's right! It's all a masquerade for them, for the members of the Academy, but we're in very bad shape.

IZA (*falls on her knees in front of her mother*): Send that man away. Mother, send him away!

GAMBOLINE (*gently but firmly*): No, Iza. We must make a decision now. The tainted blood of the Kretchborskis is speaking through you.

STRANGER (*harshly, to* GAMBOLINE): You must choose between your daughter and him. The entire universe is watching you and you alone. He can't change the binding laws of mathematics just for the whims of that nymphet! He is capable of anything. I already know the proof he'll use to convince even the great Whitehead himself. It all started with the alephs; where actual infinity comes into play, his omnipotence is absolute. But for the whole of civilization, in the name of all the ideals which humanity has ever held until now, we have to stop this.

ALFRED (*begins to get the picture*): Moritz, guard the door. (MAURICE *stands in the center door.* GAMBOLINE *doesn't know what to do. In her face and movements she displays signs of a monstrous struggle with herself.*)

GAMBOLINE (*screams with sudden resolution*): Tumor! Help!!

STRANGER (*pulling a card out of his wallet*): That won't do any good. I am Professor Green from the M.C.G.O., the Mathematical Central and General Office. Green, Alfred Green.

In one jump IZA *is by the door.*

GAMBOLINE (*screaming*): Green!!

GAMBOLINE *faints.* MAURICE *grabs* IZA. ALFRED *whispers something in* GREEN's *ear.*

GREEN (*loudly*): My agents are out there. (IZA *breaks away from* MAURICE *and dashes to the door. The* TWO AGENTS *rush in and grab* IZA. *All the while* JOSEPH *splits his sides laughing and coughing senilely at the same time, spitting phlegm, and choking, until he simply squeals with delight. At this point* TUMOR BRAINIOWICZ *rushes in from the left and stops, absolutely petrified.* GREEN *yells to his* AGENTS.) Off to the automobile with her and away you go in fifth gear! (*With mad speed the* AGENTS *wrap a red scarf around* IZA's *head and run out through the center door holding her in their arms.* TUMOR *leaps over* GAMBOLINE's *prone body and dashes to the door.   GREEN blocks his way threateningly, but with respect.*) Professor! Not another step.

ALFRED *and* MAURICE *close in on their father from both sides, stalking him like cats.*

JOSEPH (*yells, setting them on*): Zoop!

The two boys hurl themselves at their father, trying to pin his arms behind his back. GREEN hurls himself at him from the front, seizes him by the throat and tries to hold him. A motionless and mute scene like Ursus with the bull in Sienkiewicz's Quo Vadis. *It lasts a very long time. The silence is broken by the loud panting of the combatants.* JOSEPH *makes his decision and like a predatory, wingless vulture creeps up to* BRAINIOWICZ, *grabs him by the legs around the knees and throws him to the ground. In silence they all tie* BRAINIOWICZ *up with scarfs and watch-chains.* GREEN *uses the rope which he had ready.*   BRAINIOWICZ *roars briefly, then gives in passively.* BRAINIOWICZ *lies bound. They all are sitting on the floor breathing heavily.*

GREEN (*calmly*): I've done my duty.

JOSEPH (*compassionately*): You see, sonny boy, what you've come to. I always said: don't pull the string or it will break.

ALFRED (*getting up*): That was no string, it was a rubber band.

MAURICE (*very aristocratically*): I have the impression that infinity is steaming out of papa's hair. (*He goes over to his mother.* GAMBOLINE *comes out of her faint.*)

GAMBOLINE: It's some sort of horrible dream.

GREEN *gets up and looks at his watch.*

BRAINIOWICZ (*lying without moving*): Who will ever beat my last idea? I'm invincible. You can put me in jail. I won't say a word, just leave me pencil and paper. My last poem has to be finished.

GAMBOLINE (*to* GREEN): Where is Iza? (*She gets up, brushing herself off.*)

GREEN: Sacred blue, as the French say. I wish I knew myself. It happened so quickly, I didn't have time to give them orders.

GAMBOLINE (*suddenly joyful, as if it had all become clear in her mind*): But perhaps that's the only possible solution! Perhaps that's exactly how it ought to be.

BRAINIOWICZ (*indifferently*): Perhaps it is. Who can say?

Enter BALANTINE FERMOR *dressed in a golfing costume.* GAMBOLINE *rushes over to meet her.*

GAMBOLINE: Thank goodness you've come. Do you see the disaster that has occurred? It's so wild and unlikely I can hardly keep from laughing.

BRAINIOWICZ (*recites. They all listen dumbfounded*):
    Above the planet's rim
    Across the starlit night,
    Into infinity crawl rows of alephs.
    And infinity infinitized
    Petrifies itself, self-cuckolded.
    Swirls of Titans, ghosts with horns
    Pour galaxies of stars
    Into threadbare abysses.
    Thought sunk its claws in its own innards
    And bites itself in its own abyss,
    But whose thought is this? It can't think itself, can it?
    As thunder thunders and lightning flashes all by itself.
    The point expanded into a space of nth-dimensions
    And space collapsed
    Like a pricked balloon.
    All the air rushed out. So nothingness inhales
    Its own emptiness
    And crushes every single thing in time that stopped.
    Hey! A glass of beer!

GREEN: Coming right up, Professor. I'm glad they didn't hear that poem at the M.C.G.O. I can just imagine the looks on their faces.

BRAINIOWICZ: Pure nonsense, my dear Alfred. Am I going to get that beer of mine one of these days? What a shame Iza didn't hear that poem. (*To* MAURICE.) Well, blockhead, still think I'm not a poet?

ALFRED (*to* MAURICE): Don't say anything to papa.

BALANTINE (*to* GREEN): Send for more of your people, Professor. We've got to take him off to jail immediately. (*Exit* GREEN.) And you, children, go for a walk. It's a glorious day. There's spring in the air. The buds are turning green on the trees. I even saw two butterflies, two brimstones, which awakened by the warmth, left their larvae and made broken circles in the air so drenched in aromas. The poor unfortunate creatures, they don't know there are no flowers yet and that what awaits them is death from starvation.

The boys' faces brighten. GAMBOLINE *kisses them on the forehead.*

GAMBOLINE: Yes, go for a walk. You're right, Balantine. You and I are like those butterflies you were talking about.

BRAINIOWICZ (*ironically*): And I am the flower that hasn't bloomed yet. But I'll still bloom. Never fear. (*Exit the boys.*)

JOSEPH: And if your Ladyship permits, I'll see them off.

GAMBOLINE: Yes, all right. Go now, Joseph, and then come back and have dinner with us. There'll be your favorite mush. (*Exit* JOSEPH, *bowing low. Enter* GREEN *with* FOUR PORTERS *in blue smocks who take* BRAINIOWICZ *and go out.* GREEN *goes out after them.* GAMBOLINE, *suddenly very anxious, rushes over to* BALANTINE FERMOR *and asks, imploringly:*) Tell me, what does it mean? I beg you, don't torture me anymore. By all you hold dear, tell me.

BALANTINE (*reassuringly*): Quite simply, you've all grown overly attached to certain ideas. Of all of you, Iza has the truest intuition about the future.

GAMBOLINE (*in despair*): Poor, poor Iza! (*She stares straight ahead of her with a pained look.*)

ACT TWO

The action takes place on the island of Timor (*the Sunda Archipelago*). *The seashore. In the distance the red cliff of the island of Amak Ganong. To the left, palm trees and bushes covered with gigantic purple flowers. To the right, a stockade with loopholes for rifles, and an entrance to the Malay Campong. Five-thirty in the morning. Pitch black. Canopus is in the ascendant. The crescent of the moon, like a canoe with its points turned upwards, barely gives off any light. At the gates of the stockade there are two* MALAYS *in red sarongs and blue turbans, carrying spears. They stand guard without moving. In the middle of the stage there are two Ceylonese deck chairs* (*Colombo style*), *the feet to the audience. Enter* TUMOR BRAINIOWICZ *from the Campong in a white tropical outfit, almost carrying in his arms the fainting* IZA KRETCHBORSKI, *also dressed in white. The* MALAYS *prostrate themselves in front of them, then get up.*

BRAINIOWICZ: So that brute Green fell in love with you. They've always been like that at the M.C.G.O. In the morning, abstract theory and pure multiplicity *per se*. After dinner, when they've downed their whisky and soda, they have time until the next morning to do the wildest things. How I loathe Europe. I'm a lowborn slob, a totally primitive brute, but I can't stand that mealy-mouthed democracy anymore.

IZA: I love you. Now you're a true prince out of a fairy tale.

BRAINIOWICZ *puts her in one of the Ceylonese deck chairs; he collapses in the other one which creaks under his weight. He sticks his feet over the arm rest of the chair.*

BRAINIOWICZ: This is all play acting. I don't have any feeling for reality, it's not in my blood. Pretend to be ruler of these brutes! That Anak Agong, Son of the Heavens, whom I defeated, was a true ruler! Oh! I'll make mincemeat out of him! Potted viande! That brute is better born than I am. His great great grandfather's father sits on that volcano, look, Iza, over there where Ganong Malapa rises up. (*He points to the audience. For a moment red lightning floods the stage from the direction of the audience and distant rumbling can be heard. Ganong Malapa is erupting.*)

IZA: You came out of that volcano yourself. The mystery is unfathomable.

Today I'd like to beat Malays with rattan rods. I'd like you to beat me like a true ruler. Yet at the same time I'd like to keep you in a cage, feed you raw meat and use you as only certain domestic beasts of burden are used. Leave you at moment of the highest, bestial, cruel sensual pleasure.

BRAINIOWICZ *thrashes up and down furiously on the deck chair, gnashes his teeth and bellows.*

BRAINIOWICZ: Shut up! The very demon of infinity is tearing apart my skull of steel. Don't force me to do something frightful. I can't satiate myself on you. You are flimsy as fluff and insubstantial as a spider's web, and yet you torture me atrociously. Remember, I now have greater power than all the Greens of this world.

IZA: I like it when the hippopotamus in you gets aroused. Who is better born: you or the first hippo who happens to come along?

BRAINIOWICZ (*rolls about on the deck chair and roars*): Oh! just let Green fall into my hands. I'll take care of him all right—in the Malay fashion, in cold blood.

IZA: You won't be able to. For that you have to be a thoroughbred. You won't even succeed in annoying him, Professor. In another moment you'll fly into your usual towering rage that I so love, that I so fear, that I so despise. And that gives me the invincible pleasure of enslaving myself, you and the whole world. I'd like to be even smaller; be a mosquito and drink your blood through a tiny little tube that was an extension of my body, and make you roar with fury.

BRAINIOWICZ (*gets up from the deck chair and, fists clenched, goes over to* IZA): Oh! If I could first calculate your differential, analyze each infinitesimal particle of your cursed, russet-colored blood, each element of your hot, parched whiteness, and then take it, mash it, integrate it and finally comprehend wherein lies the infernal strength of your unattainability that burns and consumes me down to the very last tissue of my lowborn, slobbish flesh.

IZA: Remember, if I hadn't seduced Green, you'd be rotting in jail now.

BRAINIOWICZ (*with a superhuman effort gets control of himself and sits up in the deck chair with his profile to the audience, his face turned towards* IZA. *He speaks calmly, in a wheezing tone of voice*): What took place between the two of you? How could you give him what was my property alone?

IZA: Property!! That from the great Brainiowicz, Tumor the First, Anak Agong, ruler of Timor and adopted son of the fire-breathing mountain. A vulgar display of jealousy! (BRAINIOWICZ *roars and beats his fists on his knees*.) You're old. A boring professor. I don't give a damn for those stupid alephs of yours. Your property? How dare you? If at least you were a poet, I'd forgive you half your wild strength. What Moritz is able to do with just a single word costs you entire mountains of ordinary brute energy. Someone's property is what that person takes and keeps, not refuse snatched by chance from the Mathematical Office. My infinity is no symbol. I am like the true Astarte. If I had come into the world earlier, I would have truly been a queen, not a cheap actress on some stupid island. You gave me to Green. That mathematical instrument was my first lover; since I cannot consider your six sons as lovers. You acted like a pimp! Too bad Isidore, about whom there's been so much talk now in your household, couldn't have been in my collection.

BRAINIOWICZ *gets up and yells for the* MALAYS. *Dawn suddenly breaks, red clouds drift across the sky. The palms sway in the morning breeze. In the distance the volcano erupts. Blood-red flashes of lightning illuminate the landscape, and muffled rumblings can be heard.* MALAYS *run up with raised spears.* IZA *lies motionless with her eyes closed.*

BRAINIOWICZ (*roars*): Get her! Run her through! Kaffirs, sons of dogs!

The MALAYS *prepare to strike, waiting for the final order. Unable to take his eyes off* IZA, BRAINIOWICZ *freezes in motionless ecstasy. Bright sunlight suddenly floods the stage and the shrieking of a thousand parrots can be heard.* BRAINIOWICZ *falls on his knees in front of* IZA *who stretches voluptuously in the deck chair, parting her lips slightly. She raises herself up slowly, looking with bright eyes into the sunny expanses of the sky.* The MALAYS *fall on their knees.*

IZA: If only you believed in yourself. If only your cursed brain, which is bursting apart that huge buffalo head of yours, didn't keep you from believing that you really are the son of the fiery mountain, if only you were just a little bit of a poet, I would be yours forever. Now I don't know. Who invited that atrocious expression: the metaphysical navel? Oh, yes, it was Alfred, your first-born half-breed, your blue and gray blooded son. That says it all. The two of you have killed the true beauty of life, without making death any less hideous. You can even kill me. I prefer the spears of those brutes to the knife of a famous surgeon. But I won't ever let you and your clever paws touch my body again. (*The parrots scream as though possessed. A Malay boat with a rectangular orange sail passes by.* BRAINIOWICZ *runs his hand through his hair.*) Bring the white rajah his pith helmet, you sons of dogs. You'll overheat your brainpan, Professor.

The MALAYS *come running into the Campong.*

BRAINIOWICZ: Now I'm really all riled up. I feel such monstrous insatiability that my brain is turning into hot mush. The kind I used to eat years ago in my little thatched hut. That's what's so frightful; the abyss that separates me, a civilized peasant, from these savages. The pettiness of this whole charade. I'm an ordinary fortune hunter and, when you come right down to it, a mealy-mouthed liberal—nothing more. All Tumor's problems, all the transfinite functions amount to absolutely nothing. (*The* MALAYS *bring his white tropical pith helmet and* IZA's *hat and, with signs of the deepest reverence, put the pith helmet on* BRAINIOWICZ's *head*.) But I'll play my role to the very end. (*To the* MALAYS.) Send for Anak Agong. (*The* MALAYS *run off to the left.*) Now I'll rise above mealy-mouthed democracy once and for all. First I'll be a cruel and menacing ruler, and then I'll institute total socialism. Let those brutes stew in their own juice.

Throngs of MALAYS *gather to the left among the bushes. Only the first rows are visible. In the distance, thunder can be heard and the sun takes on a reddish hue.* IZA *is lost in reverie. A pause.* TWO WHITE MEN *in pith-helmets and khaki uniforms lead in the old* RAJAH PATAKULO *from the left.* TWO MALAYS *in red sarongs and red turbans follow them. The gray-bearded* RAJAH *wears only a loincloth around his hips. The* MALAYS *set up a deck chair to the right.* BRAINIOWICZ *sits down in the deck chair. A* YOUNG MALAY *of unusual beauty approaches* IZA *and whispers something in her ear.*

BRAINIOWICZ (*to the* RAJAH): Patakulo: I, Tumor the First, ruler of Timor, son of the Heavens and of the Fiery Mountain (*the volcano flashes blood-red against the darkening, stormy sky*), I am the one who has the right to reduce you all to pulp, to dry up the sea and extinguish the mountain that gave birth to me. (*Ever thickening stormy darkness. More and more violent thunder and lightning. He points to the* RAJAH.) Measured against my white power, your former ruler is but the shadow of a shadow.

IZA (*interrupting her conversation with the* YOUNG MALAY): You're not reciting your lines well, Professor!

The MALAYS *whisper among themselves.* BRAINIOWICZ *becomes flustered.*

ONE OF TWO MALAYS FROM THE GUARD AT THE CAMPONG (*in a blue turban*): I saw it. He humbled himself before her. Our enchanted spears could not touch her body.

SECOND MALAY: She is the new divinity of the whites. The hand that held my spear turned to stone when I tried to strike her. The white Rajah worshiped her as a celestial being.

BRAINIOWICZ (*gets up; with one last effort he tries to gain control of himself. He pulls out a revolver and shoots the old* RAJAH, *who falls to the ground. Yells*): Boy! Lemon squash!! (*A pause; he continues speaking calmly.*) I, Tumor the First, ruler of Timor, am the sole master of this land. There are no other divinities. (*A* YOUNG MALAY, *who has run out of the Campong, serves him lemonade on a tray; to the whites in khaki uniforms.*) Bring her over here!

BRAINIOWICZ *points to* IZA. *She comes to him, and for a moment they look each other in the eye. A terrifying flash of lightning illuminates the landscape and thunder crashes from the clouds down onto the earth.*

IZA (*bursts into uncontrollable laughter*): Tumikins! You old ham. Did you really think I'd fall for a trick like that? You old minx in oxen hide!

BRAINIOWICZ (*resignedly, looking at her in complete submission*): I am helpless! Iza, Iza, what is all of mathematics and absolute knowledge compared to one square centimeter of your skin. Oh! If only I could be an artist!

The YOUNG MALAY *comes over to them with a snake-like smile.*

YOUNG MALAY: Oh, white Rajah! Give me your divinity. The volcano has fallen in love with her. Since she came to our island, Ganong Malapa has been trembling all over and breathing fire. He has not been so angry for centuries. I am son of Patakulo and rightful ruler, besides being great grandson of the underground fire. I shall marry her as a sister, and I shall honor her as I have always honored our gods in the Unity of Being beyond the grave.

BRAINIOWICZ (*furious*): They're two of a kind. The cursed aristocrats. The only art that matters is triumphing over the problem of one's birth. Iza, don't think I don't love your mother. But it was for you alone that I committed this hideous crime. (*To the* YOUNG MALAY.) You don't know her, Prince Tengah. She is no divinity. She's an ordinary bored white nanny goat. If you take her as your wife, a frightful punishment awaits you for defiling the fire of the mountains.

PRINCE TENGAH: You're the one who does not know her, white Rajah. You look at everything through your horrible cleverness which has concealed from you the true beauty of the soul, the sea and the mountains. You killed my father without even being his enemy. Could anything be more hideous!

BRAINIOWICZ: How does that colored pip-squeak know that?

IZA: You killed that old man to impress me. To impress me! Oh, how I despise you, paltry pedant of actual infinity. Go on begetting your degenerate brood on my poor mother whom you have been deceiving, but don't you dare enter my inner sanctum.

The storm passes by. The darkness slowly dissipates. Tired of the show, the MALAYS *slowly disperse, carrying off* PATAKULO*'s corpse.*

BRAINIOWICZ (*in despair*): Oh, how petty and drab everything seems! I don't know whether I'm an ultra-civilized human or only an ordinary brute pretending to be a featherless biped. Oh! Too bad Green isn't here. I can still impress them down at the M.C.G.O. There I can show them the class of numbers that I have designated by Persian numerals. But the quantity of alphabets is limited. Those numbers, my very own numbers, I call tumors. Tumor the First will not be the ruler of a miserable little island, but the first number in that monstrous series which will turn their brains inside out like an old glove.

IZA (*to* TUMOR BRAINIOWICZ): All the same in a certain sense there is something great in you. (*Embraces* PRINCE TENGAH.) But I love only him, true scion of the fiery mountain.

PRINCE TENGAH (*in wild rapture*): If the death of my father has allowed me to possess the love of a divinity, blessings upon you, oh, white Rajah!

He kisses her on the lips. BRAINIOWICZ *tosses aside his tropical pith helmet and wipes his sweaty hair.*

BRAINIOWICZ (*in greater and greater despair*): What should I do, what should I do now? There's no place in the world for me. I exist and I don't exist. Infinity has devoured my entrails. If I could at least write one little poem. Oh, what inhuman torture! (*To* IZA.) Do you think that savage loves you? He sees in you only the poetess. You've turned his head with your stupid poetry.

IZA (*recites*):
> In the dark and soulless fire,
> Sweaty flesh chokes out my light.
> Thus I feel a strange god's ire
> For the deeds of pigeons bright.
> Pigeons white, and young girls dreaming
> On wet grass the pigs are preening.
> You are one, and they are thousands.
> Would I had bodies as many as thoughts,
> And each body lovers as many
> As, say, numbers in the aleph-null.
> Little words: if only—oh, chasm fearful,
> Lumbering ox necks that bow and scrape.
> Would I had passions burned black as crepe
> Fastened in the months of sky-blue ore.
> Fastened forever the lock on the prison door,
> Built upon the world's wide wilderness
> By some triumphant god, titanic, bold:
> For devils sick and perverse angels
> The madman's ward, beyond whose threshold
> Goes no sage or prince of numbers.
> There forever to the black one sue,

Whom the fiery mountain brought to light,
And continue there to dwell—worm-white,
To the strange god ever true.
Writhe in some resplendent ape's embrace,
Hearing silence echo midst the stars,
Guzzle blackest blood, watch torture's hard grimace,
Icy laughter breathe on guts' raw scars,
Squeal with rapture, then kick rapture's face,
Till the final croak comes through the bars.
Be a girl pure, innocent and little,
Moisten my red tongue with sweetish spittle.

BRAINIOWICZ (*has gained complete control of himself*): You can put that in the children's Futuristic magazine Maurice edits. But, unfortunately, it doesn't impress me.

IZA (*pouts disdainfully, drawing away from* PRINCE TENGAH, *who keeps on trying to kiss her*): I'll show you something better yet. This black has a strange smell. Something in between mildewed linen and dried mushrooms. Oh, how hideous life is! Why is it that real people are nothing but wild beasts, why is it that their smell is repulsive to our corrupted nostrils?

BRAINIOWICZ (*laughs savagely, triumphantly*): See, you silly little European goose: civilization is winning out.

IZA: It's a triumph for you. That black idiot is downright repulsive. Something's come unscrewed in my head.

PRINCE TENGAH (*does not understand very clearly what is going on; to* IZA): What are you saying, daughter of the moon?

BRAINIOWICZ (*ironically*): She's opening wide the treasure chest of her civilization for you. Now you're going to find out everything, son of a father I bumped off, why, I don't know myself.

IZA (*sadly*): Unfortunately, you know quite well. Everything has come to an end. I don't know who to give the rest of my days to. That black prince was my last hope.

BRAINIOWICZ (*with anxiety*): What about me?

IZA: Oh, Professor, you will continue to be the prince of numbers, alephs, tumors of the nth-class and other such creations. I have lost what gave me strength in my dealings with you, Professor. Your daughter will effectively replace me at your side. Such an able young girl!

TENGAH *looks at them with growing astonishment, without understanding anything at all.*

BRAINIOWICZ: You know, something's come unscrewed in my head too. At least I have the feeling it has. It's lucky I haven't yet gone crazy. I wonder what Alfred would say if he could see my most recent ordeals. Not Alfred Green, of course, I mean my first-born reprobate of a son.

PRINCE TENGAH (*to* IZA): My one and only, my divinity. Why don't you notice me, why do you push me away? Doesn't your white body want to be sacrificed to the underground fire? I myself am like the fiery mountain. If you wish, I shall burn you up with one single breath of mine.

IZA: Prince, your breath doesn't smell of sulfur, only raw meat. No one ever burned up anyone yet with raw meat.

BRAINIOWICZ (*to* PRINCE TENGAH): I told you, black-yellow beast, she is an ordinary silly little white goose. Now you have the truth from those lips you kissed a moment ago with the highest love.

PRINCE TENGAH *staggers.*

PRINCE TENGAH (*in despair*): I have betrayed myself. Terrible are the lies of white people, frightful the venom in their souls poisoned by learning. Their words are more murderous than our swords, their weapons stronger than the holiness of our divinities. Oh, white Rajah! I shall not kill you, because I do not wish to defile my sword intended for enemies worthy of me. (*Pulls his kris out of its scabbard and runs himself through.*) May you be cursed, white worm for whom I betrayed everything that was sacred to me. (*He dies.*)

IZA: At last I finally got rid of that colored Casanova.

BRAINIOWICZ (*looks at her with cold admiration*): Iza! You are marvelous.

If it weren't for this insane heat and my new thought about an nth-class of tumors, I don't know if I wouldn't fall in love with you all over again. Really you're the only woman who . . .

Two MALAYS *in blue turbans rush in. They fall down on their faces in front of* IZA. BRAINIOWICZ *shows his displeasure.*

MALAY 1: Oh, Queen! A boat has come into the bay of Banggai. A white chief is coming here. They have brought a new divinity.

MALAY 2: She is bigger and fatter than you are. (*Notices the prone body of* PRINCE TENGAH.) But what is this? Our chief dead, run through with his own kris.

MALAY 1: He has put himself to death according to the precepts of his ancestors. (*They both prostrate themselves in front of the corpse—it becomes completely bright and sunlight floods the entire landscape.*)

MALAY 2: We have run out of rulers. Unless the new goddess has brought us someone from beyond the far seas. (*They get up and remain in an expectant attitude.* BRAINIOWICZ *pulls field glasses out of his pocket and looks between the bushes to the left.*)

BRAINIOWICZ (*looking through the field glasses*): I recognize her. The *Prince Arthur*, a cruiser first-class. They have just come ashore. Sacred blue! Green is getting off the launch. Balantine Fermor, Captain FitzGerald and . . . (*He lowers the field glasses.* IZA *grabs them and takes a look.*)

IZA (*stamping her feet in excitement*): Green is on his way! Green, Green has come! Balantine! She will be a consolation to you, Professor. She adores you so.

BRAINIOWICZ: But the fact is I am a criminal. I killed an innocent man.

IZA (*lowers the field glasses*): Really! To have scruples because of some Malay or other. Spit on that! Long live the alephs and the tumors! What is death in the face of actual infinity?

BRAINIOWICZ: Perhaps you are right. There's no such thing as crime. Just look at all the people nowadays who claim the rights of man just because they walk about on two legs. How can we tell a human from a brute—what is the criteriom? Once that was clearly known: nowadays, in times of mealy-mouthed demo . . . (*The roar of a cannon from the cruiser prevents him from saying more.*)

IZA: That's Green banging out a greeting on the twelve-incher aboard the cruiser. That's what we agreed on beforehand.

Enter from the bushes: GREEN. FITZGERALD, BALANTINE FERMOR *and* FIVE MEMBERS OF THE CREW, *armed from head to toe.*

GREEN: Hip! Hip! Hurrah! Brainiowicz is alive! Seize him, boys! Give the order, Captain. We're taking possession of this country. (*The* MEMBERS OF THE CREW *throw themselves at* BRAINIOWICZ *and bind him with ropes.* IZA *laughs, very embarrassed. To* IZA.) Iza! You are a marvelous woman. We mathematicians know how to savor the strangeness of life. What happened before is of no importance. Your past doesn't exist. The only thing that exists is science, for which everything can be sacrificed, even male honor. (*To* BALANTINE.) Miss Fermor, the right honorable Miss Fermor, please vouch for the truthfulness of my words. I love Miss Kretchborski; I renounce all the secret machinations at the M.C.G.O. Miss Fermor, please repeat these words to the sole woman who is worthy of bearing my name and perhaps even my title, provided that God in his mercy—mathematics and religion are two totally different aspects of the same thing—allows me to live longer than my cousins.

BALANTINE: Iza! I am here on behalf of your mother. (*To* BRAINIOWICZ, *who lies trussed up on the ground.*) A propos! Gamboline finally begat Isidore. Marvelous boy. His eyes are so close together you can scarcely see his nose, like all the Trundhul-Bheds. A born mathematician.

BRAINIOWICZ (*joyfully*): Oh, I'm grateful to all of you for having taken my will power away. I'm being poisoned by my own strength. I simply have too much will power and that's why I cannot make any decisions. Infinity actualized in total freedom of choice. Oh, the pleasure of being imprisoned. Iza! On behalf of your mother, and speaking as your stepfather, I give you a completely free hand. Green! You old scoundrel! You've got the prettiest girl in the world. She loves you . . .

BALANTINE (*interrupts him*): And besides, it will be no misalliance. Alfred is Green of Greenfield. He is the fifth son of the Fifth Marquess of Mask Tower. May his brothers enjoy a long, long life, but when they do die, he will be a peer and the richest man in England.

BRAINIOWICZ (*furiously*): Dogs' blood! I didn't know that. Sangua del carno! Why am I not something of that sort? From that vantage point you can look down your nose at everything.

GREEN: You are Brainiowicz. *Tout simplement*, Brainiowicz. *Maître*, I'd give you ten titles of nobility for that diabolical name, which I can't even pronounce.

BALANTINE: Isn't that the truth? There's something in that name that conjures up the smell of proto-slavonic forests, of hives of wild bees stirred to life by the heat of the sun in flowering glades, and of rivers and lakes full of golden fish and water sprites. Oh, how beautiful it is. Carry him off to the ship. Isidore is waiting for him. Isidore keeps waving his fat little fists and in his own mute language calls for the father he already adores. (*She notices the bodies of the Anak Agongs.*) Great heavens! Brainiowicz has made mincemeat of these Malays.

IZA (*in* GREEN's *arms*): It was an accident that happened quite by chance. That young black died out of love for me. The old one tried to kill the Professor. I shot him down like a dog. What else could I do? It was every man for himself.

GREEN (*losing control of himself*): How I love you, Iza! How is it possible . . . so short a time, so little opportunity . . . And then a separation like that. Oh, how I love you . . .

BALANTINE (*to the* SAILORS): Seize him, boys! And hold him tight. You see, he's the greatest brain in the civilized world. A bit twisted, since everything that's great has to be twisted, and perversity nowadays is simply synonymous with greatness.

The SAILORS *take* BRAINIOWICZ *and exit with* FITZGERALD *and* BALANTINE. GREEN *plants a pole with the British flag.*

IZA: And yet there's something I regret. But I don't even know what myself. Only the dream will remain. The memory of events that never took place. (*Making a sudden decision.*) Green—I've got to tell you everything—I was unfaithful to you with Tumor.

GREEN *curls up into a ball from pain and jealousy and at the very same moment stretches with wild desire.*

GREEN (*throwing himself helplessly at* IZA): I love you, I love you! Quiet! There are only these moments, and everything else is an illusion in the infinite infinities of being.

IZA (*submitting to him indifferently*): But it was so lovely, so strange. What a pity, what a pity . . .

GREEN *carries her off fainting to the left, into the flowering bushes.*

ACT THREE

The same room as in Act One. GAMBOLINE KRETCHBORSKI, secundo voto
BRAINIOWICZ, *dressed as in Act One, walks up and down with a young child
in her arms humming, to the tune of a Slavic lullaby.*

GAMBOLINE:
>Oh, ho, pussy cats two,
>Both of them black and both of them blue.
>Oh, ho, pussy cats three,
>Ate the gray brains of a flea.
>Oh, ho, pussy cats four,
>Papa went to see a whore.
>Oh, ho, pussy cats five,
>Mama's wild wish came alive.
>Oh, ho, pussy cats six,
>Tie infinity to sticks.
>Oh, ho, pussy cats seven,
>Papa said: With you, it's heaven.
>Oh, ho, panthers eight,
>Mama said . . .

Enter BRAINIOWICZ.

BRAINIOWICZ: How is Isidore doing?

GAMBOLINE: Isidore is doing quite nicely; but what about you, father
Brainiowicz, how do you feel in this ordinary everyday life of ours?

BRAINIOWICZ: I don't know how to stray from the path of virtue. More
important, what do you think of Iza's marrying Green?

GAMBOLINE: You know I am free from aristocratic prejudices about family.
Once his three brothers all die, it will be an excellent match for Iza.

BRAINIOWICZ: You have no idea what it means to me. (*Points to* ISIDORE.)
That's my last child with you. There's something about Isidore's face
that completely takes away any desire I might have to beget any more
Brainiowiczes with you. (*Making a sudden decision*.) I've applied for a

divorce today and I intend to ask for Miss Fermor's hand before the day is over.

GAMBOLINE (*indifferently*): There's nothing I want. Seven sons are enough. I am beyond all that. Slobbish, lowborn love and all forms of spiritual perversity. I have ennobled the race of Brainiowiczes. Alfred can ask for the hand of a lord's daughter. No one will refuse him.

BRAINIOWICZ: You forget that I too can ask for the hand of a lord's daughter, and even be accepted. I have lived alone, immersed in my calculations. I begat a new world. Cantor, Georg Cantor, is a mere infant compared to my definitions of infinity, and Frege and Russell are the paltry decanting of a Greek void into the void of our own times with their definition of number, compared to what I thought up this morning . . .

GAMBOLINE (*keeps on dandling the little sniveller*): A hideous compromise. Alfred told me about it . . .

BRAINIOWICZ: I'll murder that first-born cur of mine! He doesn't know anything. He's trying to denounce what he hasn't even been able to grasp. Don't you understand that certain brains are incapable of grasping certain things. My logic is irrefutable. Simply to formulate that series of arguments coherently, you've got to have a really first-rate head on your shoulders. The only one who has the strength for that is me, me. They sense that and that's why they're afraid.

Enter GREEN *with* IZA.

GREEN: Professor! Your theory is winning out. Today I got the latest bulletin from the M.C.G.O. Even Whitehead has been shaken.

BRAINIOWICZ: They can only accept what falls into categories that already exist. We, Brainiowicz, have given a new meaning to the very concept of logic. Those half-wits can't tolerate that.

GREEN: But what if you do win, Professor? What then? What's going to happen to the whole science of mechanics? What's going to take the place of the law of gravity? It's the first case in our times of pure deduction overturning a world view that has several hundred years behind it.

BRAINIOWICZ: Think I'm revealing the essential stuff? Can you really believe I would tell the truth in the presence of half-wits like you and your colleagues from the M.C.G.O.?

IZA: Oh, how happy I am that such a genius was in love with me for two whole months.

GREEN (*to* IZA): Stop it, you silly goose! (*To* BRAINIOWICZ.) Professor! Tell me and no one else but me. Tell me: how did you arrive at the formula for the nth-class of numbers. Tell me, what is tumor-one?

BRAINIOWICZ: You're a stupid nincompoop. I'll tell you and the next minute you'll forget. You've got to have the brains of a titan for something like that. Do you think that everything really is curved and that everything really is simultaneous?   Those are elementary questions in transcendental dynamics, of which my theory is simply a childish application.

GREEN: Just tell me the definition of that one little word, "really," Professor. That's all I ask. Tell me how you define "or" and "except"— just those two words.

He falls to his knees in front of BRAINIOWICZ.

BRAINIOWICZ (*dolefully*): The posthumous edition of my works will take up that problem too. In the meantime I can tell you only this: it's either you or me. The exponent of my ultimate thought is Iza, that miserable Iza, whose slave you are and who is unfaithful to you with all the ship's stewards during official expeditions, not to mention the members of the M.C.G.O. Get to know her well, future Fifth Marquess of Mask Tower. She embodies the mystery of the identity of those two little words: "or" and "except." I discovered that when I killed old Patakulo.

GREEN (*on his knees*): Go on! I think I'm beginning to understand.

BRAINIOWICZ: Do you think I understand it? My ultimate thoughts will be as difficult to decipher as Egyptian hieroglyphics. But where will they find a Champollion of logic, someone with sufficient brain power to decipher these thoughts and transform them into symbols intelligible to all?

GREEN: I'll do it.

BRAINIOWICZ: You, you simple-minded idiot? (*Laughs wildly.*) You have no desire for the truth, you dream only of universal mathematical blackmail!

GAMBOLINE *dandles* ISIDORE *with ever mounting passion.*

GAMBOLINE: They'll resolve it. Our children will. The entire future lies in their hands.

BRAINIOWICZ: You're wrong, my child. The next generation will have to give that up. We civilized slobs are the only ones who have that savage strength. In twenty years time there won't be any more of us lowborn slobs with brains the size of a buffalo's, but high-strung as a hysterical princess's nerves. That's where our whole western democracy is heading. And it's being opposed by the glorious movement of destruction the East is indulging in.

GREEN (*getting up*): Tumor Brainiowicz—an ordinary universal maniac for state socialism. What a fiasco!

BRAINIOWICZ: You're wrong there, you idiot! Turning the clock back on civilization. That's what ruling the island of Timor taught me. You know I murdered a man there, and another one killed himself because of me. Do you know what that meant for me?

IZA *falls on her knees in front of him.*

IZA: Tumor! You are the only great man I have ever known.

GAMBOLINE: Shame on you, Iza! In front of your mother.

BRAINIOWICZ (*to his wife*): Your dearest, darling Isidore is going to be a monstrosity, causing shame to all his ancestors: the brutish race of Brainiowiczes as well as the Mongolian Khans, headed by the Great Ghengis himself. Out of my sight, cursed bitch! I am master of the world!!

GAMBOLINE: Oh, so that's it, is it? So everything I've done is worth nothing? So I'm to be kicked too for lowering myself? You dare insult what is most sacred to me? I'll show you! You double-dealing comedian!

She dashes over to the window to the right and throws the diapered ISIDORE BRAINIOWICZ *through it; then she stands still, her face turned towards the audience, with a look of total madness. The frightful look of tension on her face, expressing animal pain, lasts for a moment. Then she falls to the ground and howls wildly like a she-wolf.*

GREEN: See here, Mrs. Brainiowicz! People don't do things like that. This is sheer barbarism.

IZA: Mother! I like monstrous things, but that's too much even for me. (*She dissolves in tears.*)

BRAINIOWICZ: It leaves me completely indifferent. The umbilical cord which tied me to my children has been cut. One more crime takes place because of me.

GREEN: I worship you, Professor. You are a titan. A glorious deed done involuntarily!! Could there be anything more delectable!

IZA (*to* GREEN): Oh, so you're that weak, Alfred? You can humble yourself in front of that old puppet? I have been a witness to his crimes. Merciful God! Involuntary crimes committed by a bungler unfit for life. The inner recesses of his soul exposed by the light of transfinite ethics. That lily-livered monster has a conscience. It makes him suffer. Can't you see that, Alfred? Is there anything more putrid than pangs of conscience?

GREEN: I must confess, that's something I've never been bothered with. After the most frightful orgies at the M. C. G. O., I felt quite wonderful. We used to kill little girls from the plebeian class in an indescribably cruel fashion . . .

GAMBOLINE (*covering his mouth with her hands*): You horrid rotter! You're the one who started this hideous conversation. It's your fault I killed poor Isidore . . .

Enter JOSEPH BRAINIOWICZ *holding a newspaper. He is followed by* TWO

PORTERS *in blue aprons who carry in the bloody diapers containing the pulverized remains of* ISIDORE BRAINIOWICZ.

JOSEPH BRAINIOWICZ: Begging your humble pardon. What I mean is they've written up my boy so nice here in the papers. A hero! A thinker! A genius at ideas and a genius at deeds. But where is that island? And is it true he claimed to be the son of a fiery mountain? Oh, my boy, that was wrong of you to disown your own legitimate father and you'll be punished.

BRAINIOWICZ (*very ashamed*): But Papa, but Father (*stammers*), but damn it all to hell, get rid of that filthy rag!

He grabs the newspaper away from him and flings it at the wall. Enter IRENE BRAINIOWICZ *in a black dress.*

IRENE: Father! *I'll* free you from these last bonds. I don't want any love. I know everything.

BRAINIOWICZ (*deeply moved*): I forgot I had another daughter. Dearest Rena! You're the only one who'll stay with me.

IRENE (*embraces him tightly and kisses him on the forehead with infinite tenderness*): Yes, Father! Give up that horrible work. You can have it published after your death. I know. Alfred doesn't understand a thing. The only thing he knows how to do is spy on you. He's very clever, but only up to a certain point. I know what he's like. I taught him the fundamentals of the theory of pure plurality. (*To* GREEN.) Green! How dare you burden that great intellect with all that nonsense? Have you all gone mad at that cursed M.C.G.O. of yours?

GREEN (*bows humbly*): I know quite a bit myself. You are very clever, Miss Irene, but what you don't know is that he has created a class of numbers designated by Persian symbols, and that he is now about to prove that the number of a certain plurality is higher than all the pluralities known to him and to Satan alone. He has even had the presumption to name it:—tumor-one.

IRENE *looks at her father in terror; then she takes the blood-soaked diapers away from the* PORTERS *and presses them to her breast.*

IRENE: Poor, poor Isidore!

JOSEPH BRAINIOWICZ: Even the poor child wasn't spared, son of a gun.

IRENE (*to* JOSEPH): Grandfather! Let's get out of here. It's simply impossible to breath here. I envy Leibniz so frightfully. He was a child just like this poor little corpse.

She takes JOSEPH *by the arm and goes out, clutching the diapers under her left arm; the* PORTERS *follow them out.* GAMBOLINE *regains her composure and smoothes out her dress. She gradually stops being a mother and a she-wolf, and once again becomes a woman in love.*

GAMBOLINE: Now you've been overpowered, Father Brainiowicz. I doubt you'll get back on your feet again. Even Rena has left you and your own papa-person has evaporated into thin air.

GREEN: I am still here. I'll stay with him.

BRAINIOWICZ: You wretched crab; you eavesdropper on unthinkable thoughts; you psychic kept man of a degenerate nymphet! I'd rather go into exile and fall prey to the Dyaks on the island of Timor than confide even one single thought to you.   He thinks he knows something because he can pronounce the words: tumor-one. It's not a secret spell for discovering treasure; to understand it you've got to have a head on your shoulders, not a bird-cage for multicolored fledglings. You blockheaded intellectual rag picker! You powder puff, you lackey of strumpeted infinity!

He suddenly goes weak in the knees and sits down on the ground. Enter BALANTINE FERMOR *in a pink dress and gigantic hat with a colossal black feather.* GAMBOLINE *rushes over to her.*

GAMBOLINE: Oh, dearest Balantine! I killed Isidore! Do you understand what has happened?   Poor little Isidore smashed to bits on the cobblestones, and it was all my doing. But he forced me to! That monster, that lowborn slob—Brainiowicz.

BALANTINE (*calmly*): In the first place, he didn't force you to, and in the second place, you didn't kill Isidore. A long time ago, almost from his very birth, I saw frightful tendencies in that boy. And most of all, a tendency to hideous diseases. Joseph told me about it. Decent old chap. He's so busy with the role he's playing.

IZA (*who has been diligently putting away toys all this time*): That person (*indicating* BALANTINE) has to spoil every last monstrosity, even the most unassuming. Everything is as clear and simple to her as integral equations. That's good for Irene. I tell you, she'll be back here in no time.

GREEN: Stop, oh, stop. I have the impression a whirlwind of spirits is flying through my head. Those drowning in the sea of death while still alive are not denied their final wishes. Iza! I feel you slipping away from me. Your tiny little soul is as slippery as a school of slithering sardines.

IZA: I must ask you not to attribute to me what is a pure play on words. I have created an entire little world from the scraps of the various words you have inadvertently let drop. Such a tiny little world, but for all that, mine, all mine.

BALANTINE (*ironically*): Oh, how touching. Don't go on that way; I feel the tears welling into my eyes.

Enter ALFRED *and* MAURICE BRAINIOWICZ. BRAINIOWICZ *gets up off the floor*.

ALFRED (*pulling a newspaper out of his pocket*): Listen! You too, Mother! Only I beg you, be brave, don't let this news upset you . . .

GAMBOLINE (*imploringly to* ALFRED): Spare me . . . I cannot stand it anymore.

IZA (*tries to calm her down*): There, Mother dear! Nothing more can possibly happen. It was a dream. Alfred and I will have you come live with us. Green! Isn't that right? You won't deny me that.

GREEN (*coldly*): On certain conditions.

ALFRED (*reads*): The heading is: "Monstrous compromise. Well-known pillar of present-day mathematical scholarship, Sir Tumor Brainiowicz, recently made hereditary baronet of Queensland, conqueror of the island of Timor and creator of a new constitution for the Malays in the third marine district, has fallen victim to his own weakness . . ."

BRAINIOWICZ (*dolefully*): Green wrote that. Remember what he said right here just a moment ago. He was lying flat on his face in front of me as though praying to a statue of Isis. Now isn't that just hideous swinishness?

MAURICE: Papa! Papa! Listen to the rest of it.

ALFRED (*reads*): ". . . his own weakness, which is revealed in his latest theory, published in the organ of the M.C.G.O., *Unity and Diversity*. This theory is concerned with the already known creation of a free class of numbers . . ."

GAMBOLINE: Green! How could you do something like that!

IRENE *runs in*.

IRENE: It's a lie, a monstrous lie! Green's trying to put father to the test. He gave Alfred the idea. I know everything. Joe just gave you away. He's running a fever and told me all about it. Green is a rat. He used Iza just to have influence over Alfred.

BRAINIOWICZ: But here it is in print. I know what will happen next. To make it impossible for me to carry on my work, I'm being presented as a person who's given up on the infinite series of numerical classes. I want to put a limit to these classes. I still don't have an overall proof. But the value called tumor-one is the highest value that can exist. No one, not even a transfinite mind, the mind of God himself, is going to create a series of tumors.

IRENE (*falls on her knees in front of her father*): Papa! I don't want to hear any of that. What have all of you done to Infinity?!

BRAINIOWICZ: So you're against me too. There are no more Brains left in the world. I thought my daughter, at least my poor little Rena, would accept me for what I am. No—apparently I've got to go through all possible torments right to the very end.

He sits down on the floor. For a moment he plays with the blocks, then he begins to cry horribly, despairingly. He almost howls, sobbing hysterically.

They are all petrified with terror and anguish.

IZA (*embraces* BRAINIOWICZ. GREEN *wrings his hands in despair*): Now I really love you. I wanted to see your weakness just once. The days are past when you could tame demonic women by force. I am a demon! (*Leaps up and, with a fiery glance, transfixes those present, and even those not present.*) I am a priestess of Isis. I have danced naked with a sunflower on my forehead. I have humbled Lord Persville, the greatest demon at the M.C.G.O. Green! You wretched wet noodle, cuckolded forty-five times over: Lord Persville—creator of a geometry which can be represented analytically only in intermittent, transfinite functions— writhed at my feet like a trampled worm. I did not sleep nights. I worked like forty steam oxen! Tumor! I feigned ignorance to be able one day to look at your weakness. I know everything! I know the theory of numbers that are variable in a continuous fashion! (GREEN *writhes in terrible sufferings.* IZA *embraces* BRAINIOWICZ *again.*) I alone truly love him. None of you knows what I've been through.

IRENE: The slut!

GREEN (*roars wildly*): Oh, the viper!!!

ALFRED: What about me! Father, the mathematics you taught me was false. That Futuristic nymphet knows more than I do.

MAURICE: Iza! So your poetry is all lies! Oh, I won't live through this.

BALANTINE *looks on with icy calm, holding the sobbing* GAMBOLINE *in her arms.* MAURICE *falls to the floor and cries uncontrollably.*

BRAINIOWICZ (*pushes* IZA *away with a sudden gesture; she collapses on the floor next to the weeping* MAURICE; *getting up, he speaks to* IZA): Out of my sight! I don't know you and I hate you. You thought you could degrade me that way—me, Brainiowicz, father of seven sons and an untold number of daughters? Out of here, you monkey!

GAMBOLINE (*stops crying and suddenly bursts into a savage laugh of triumph*): Serves her right. Let the cursed house of Kretchborski die out.

BRAINIOWICZ (*standing like a wounded wild ox whom pride alone keeps from falling*): I am completely alone. Where I get my strength from, none of you will ever find out, and I myself know little more about it than you.

GAMBOLINE: You won't be mine, then don't be anyone's. Father Brainiowicz: you are truly great.

ALFRED (*in despair*): And I spent all that time learning a pack of lies! My whole examination in transcendental dynamics is a cheap farce. But who are those criminals at the Academy? Who are they (*points at* GREEN), who are the scum from the M.C.G.O.? The earth has never borne such monsters. Oh, if only I could pluck out my brains from my skull, if only I could start to understand all over again from scratch!

MAURICE *calms* IZA *down. She gets up with a smile.*

MAURICE (*getting up with her*): We'll write poetry together. It's still not too late to work all that out.

IZA: Moritz, save me. Only you can. But won't it just be a repetition of everything that's already happened once before?

MAURICE: No, Iza. Remember our conversation on the green sofa yesterday? Do you remember what you told me?

IZA: That infinity is individuality turned upside down. That was your father's idea. I've got to create it in pure form.

MAURICE (*embracing her*): We'll create it together. It's a counterbalance to intellectual derangement. We'll create a lovely little gray bird who will fly off into the Void. Without any rainbows or colors. Understand? I know how to do it.

BRAINIOWICZ (*coldly*): By simplifying things artificially.

IZA: That's not true! You have no right to talk about art. I believe in Moritz's genius.

BRAINIOWICZ (*pulls out a notebook and writes something down*): I can stop talking altogether. Oh, when I remember that I once used to write poetry, I go cold all over from shame. Tomorrow, without further delay,

I shall marry Balantine Fermor and then off we go to Australia.

GREEN, *who has been observing* IZA *and* MAURICE *with daggers in his eyes, suddenly goes over to* GAMBOLINE.

GREEN: Madam! I have a strange premonition that the ship carrying my brothers off to war will sink tonight. If you wish to become the Fifth Marchioness of Mask Tower immediately, that's fine. If not, we can wait.

GAMBOLINE: See here, Alfred. People don't do things like that so fast.

GREEN: Very well, we can wait. But our business is done. (*To* BRAINIOWICZ.) Professor! Let's forget all this. I could have you put in jail straight away. But I believe that after all this you are going to be reasonable. Only the posthumous edition of your works will contain the ultimate proofs. Through prolonged exposure, ordinary mortals will eventually familiarize themselves with the problem. (*Sadly.*) And so will I, I hope.

BRAINIOWICZ: Stop this nonsense, Alfred. You're an intelligent fellow. So why not tell me when the *Euripides* of the Green Star Line sails and reserve a cabin for two. I promised the Maharajah of Penjar a game of poker once we're aboard.

GREEN: I see that time really has stood still for you, Professor. The *Euripides* sailed two weeks ago. The *Eurigone* sails today, but Penjar leaves on the *Euripontes* in two weeks' time. That's the fact of the matter. I am glad that Europe will have a chance to catch its breath. Reserve a cabin then, shall I?

BRAINIOWICZ (*to* BALANTINE): Two weeks all right with you?

BALANTINE (*she stretches in anticipation of unknown sensual delights*): Of course. With you, Tumor, even these two weeks in Europe will be superhuman bliss. But permit me to give myself to you definitively only after we're aboard the ship. I want to bring back the former atmosphere. After all, FitzGerald wooed me assiduously. It was in his company that I saw for the first time the Southern Cross and the hyper-sun of dreadful Canopus. Once Canopus is in the ascendant again, I shall be yours. How long I've been tormented by my virginity! Only sport saved me from Persville! Do you realize that demon begged me for mercy like a tiny little child?

GREEN *and* GAMBOLINE *whisper together.*

BRAINIOWICZ (*to* BALANTINE): That no longer concerns me. Fortunately, you don't know the first thing about mathematics. You will be the last cold compress on my head, on this poor old brainpan. But I shall love you like a young man, like a raving boy.

BALANTINE *leans against him with a smile; they both stand like statues.*

GREEN: We'll bring up your sons for you to be healthy mathematicians with real heads on their shoulders. Only Moritz didn't work out too well. But that's a kind of expiation.

IZA: I'm taking full responsibility for Moritz. The likes of that decadent have yet to be seen on this or any other planet. Given the contingency of art, he'll reduce all absolute values to sameness in a tiny circle closed in upon itself.

ALFRED: Father, I forgive you everything. And I wish you well. I'll find some decent young lady and start a new life.

BRAINIOWICZ *suddenly clutches at his heart.*

BRAINIOWICZ (*uneasily*): I have such a strange empty feeling in my heart. (*Cries out.*) Patakulo! Don't look at me like that! (*He falls as though struck by lightning. BALANTINE lets out a wild cry of panic. They all dash over to him. GREEN feels his pulse. He gets up. They all wait in a state of frightful anticipation.*)

GREEN: He's dead. So the ultimate proof will never be known to anyone.

BALANTINE (*throws herself on BRAINIOWICZ's corpse with a wild laugh. The others remain where they are, rooted to the spot*): See how my virgin dream has been fulfilled. Go for a walk, children. The spring is the same as it was then. The buds are growing green upon the young branches and warmth pervades the faded azure and the spidery clouds in the sky. Go, leave me alone with him. (*She laughs gently and quietly. GREEN offers his arm to GAMBOLINE; MAURICE, to IZA. ALFRED puts his arms around* IRENE, *who is petrified by pain, and one after the other they file out in silence through the center door.* BALANTINE *suddenly gets up and stretches voluptuously.*) No one knows that I, too, devoted my life exclusively to mathematics and am intimately acquainted with all Tumor's theorems. (*The door to the left opens and* PERSVILLE *enters. He goes over to* BALANTINE.) Arthur! Arthur! My happiness, my life, my everything!   (BALANTINE *throws her arms around him with wild passion.*)

PERSVILLE (*coldly*): Now you are mine. We're going to Australia. I was on the telephone just a moment ago. I've been appointed visiting professor at Port Peery. Now we'll apply Tumor's theory to my geometry and create true transcendental dynamics. Not what they're studying at the Academy, which Alfred failed twice.   True transcendental dynamics, my love, true transcendental dynamics.

BALANTINE *laughs voluptuously, almost completely unconscious.*

Stanisław Ignacy Witkiewicz
Self-portrait
circa 1910

GYUBAL WAHAZAR

or

ALONG THE CLIFFS OF THE ABSURD

A Non-Euclidean Drama in Four Acts
(1921)

Foreword

Once embarked on his career as a playwright with *Pragmatists* and *Tumor*, Witkacy wrote as one possessed, in a frenzy of composition. After completing *Gyubal Wahazar, or Along the Cliffs of the Absurd*—a large-scale political work of dystopian science fiction—in just two and a half months on June 14, 1921, Witkacy wrote to a friend that he had now written fifteen plays in two and a half years of intense effort. "That's too much," he declared. "Now I'm quitting. I'll paint."

Rather than abandoning playwriting as he had threatened, Witkacy continued to cultivate the political genre, making it the highest reach of his artistic vision. *Gyubal*, subtitled "A Non-Euclidean Drama in Four Acts," presents a frightening picture of the automated political realm of the future, which Witkacy calls "a six-dimensional continuum." It is Witkacy's most searching portrait of the modern dictator and the totalitarian state, revealing its roots in modern science and pseudo-science and its connections to the occult and alternative religious sects.

In 1921 Witkacy's insightful predictions about dictatorship would have seemed farfetched. Soon, however, his apocalyptic premonitions began to be realized throughout Europe, including Poland. When in 1926 *Gyubal* was being considered for performance at Warsaw's Mały Teatr, Pilsudski's May *coup d'état* intervened and made it unwise to put on a drama about dictatorship.

In communist Poland the play became even more dangerous. Although the 1966 premiere of *Gyubal Wahazar* was uneventful in a Poznań production that avoided controversy by stressing the comic, the next two productions—at the Student Theatre Kalambur in Wrocław in 1967 and at the Teatr Narodowy in Warsaw in 1968—were forbidden by the censor after the dress rehearsal. Since 1972 when the ban on the play was lifted, *Gyubal* has been one of the author's most widely performed and acclaimed dramas.

Witkacy's works are interrelated. Not only are issues carried over from play to play, but characters from earlier dramas are discussed or even reappear in later ones. A point of origin for *Gyubal* is his first play, *Maciej Korbowa and Bellatrix* (1918), which introduces Wahazar sixteen years earlier, when as a young man—known as Maciej Korbowa—he heads a decadent secret society and subsequently betrays his former friends to gain power in a world of revolutionary violence. The immediate impetus for *Gyubal* came from Witkacy's reading of Georges Ribemont-Dessaignes's Dadaist drama, *L'Empereur de Chine* (written 1916, published 1921), which depicts an arbitrary political realm of the future where almost abstract violence occurs according to mathematical principles.

Witkacy's exposure to the early twentieth-century revolution in science had an incalculable impact on his work. All of his plays are informed by recognition of a plurality of worlds and consciousness of man's new position in the universe as an individual living on just one planet in infinite space. Rather than using classical mythology, in which he shows little interest, Witkacy draws upon the new mythology of science fiction, which he often combines with near-Eastern myths of death and rebirth fundamental to cultural anthropology that he knew from Frazer's *Golden Bough* and from his conversations with Malinowski.

Dramas depicting utopias or dystopias usually make use of old-fashioned plotting for their narrative framework and traditional psychology as the basis for their characters, who talk and behave like ordinary human beings of the past. In *Gyubal*, Witkacy found a new and original dramatic shape to convey his vision of the future. Abandoning the principles of causal and discursive dramaturgy, he creates a fluid dramatic form by imagining future totalitarianism as indeterminacy and endless trans-formation, based on the postulates of modern science. Human nature has become something infinitely malleable, subject to control and transmutation. The mutability at the heart of *Gyubal* is not only social and political, but biological and physical as well, affecting the very nature of matter. The fission of psychic atoms, the cloning of Wahazars, and the mechanical reproduction of interchangeable people reveal that nothing solid is left, once the immovable centers of nature have been perverted. Humanity can be endlessly transformed to suit the needs of social technology. Any one can be turned into a Wahazar; there are Gyubal imitators in Albania, a Wahazar doll for children to play with, and gland injections to produce future Wahazars.

The play unfolds like a wall scroll, panorama, or fresco. Rapidly shifting images float by and dissolve, but each of the fragments in the kaleidoscope is bright and hard. Sharp focus and firm contours impart to the most inscrutable details the superclarity of a nightmare. From the very first moment of their appearance, characters are externally established and imprinted on the imagination by precise definition of costumes, colors, shapes, features, and manners of speaking.

Authors of dystopian fantasies typically focus on the sympathetic victims of a cruel totalitarian regime, with whom the audience can identify. Striking out into unexplored territory, Witkacy abandons the humanist hero and his romantic love affair forbidden by the state and centers *Gyubal* on the dynamic interplay between the dictator himself and the masses. We watch the crowd's rhythmic movements in response to the paroxyms of the hero—his foaming at the mouth, swearing, kicking, falling into abject states of stupor, then waking up with new bursts of frenzied energy. The actors' bodies are the principal medium of the drama.

Instead of making the new regime a revolting aberration seen from the point of view of traditional human values, the playwright enters imaginatively into the workings of the mechanism of dictatorship and dramatizes the deep bonds between oppressor and oppressed that have their sources in the changing demands of an evolving human nature. Future mankind no longer wants or needs freedom of the spirit, but rather must be transformed into purposefully functioning insects in order to regain the mindless happiness known only to members of the most primitive clans in prehistory. By the new standards, the terrifying tyrant is a charismatic leader and father to his people, as well as a saintly martyr ready to immolate himself for their welfare.   The oppressor actually becomes the oppressed and the essential action of the play is the slow martyrdom of Gyubal Wahazar, culminating in his ritual murder so that the new ruler can become Wahazar II.

Wahazar's death is a modern re-enactment of the central myth in *The Golden Bough*, the ritual killing of the divine king and even includes the tearing apart and eating of the sacrificial body; to become the new Wahazar, Unguenty must be fed Gyubal's glands while they are still warm. The survivors genuinely lament the death of the monstrous dictator, who was the last individual of towering proportions in a world of growing pettiness and conformity.

The combination of non-Euclidean coordinates and primordial, mythic patterns produces in *Gyubal* a drama of terror, mystery, and complex emotional and intellectual resonances.

GYUBAL WAHAZAR

or

Along the Cliffs of the Absurd

A Non-Euclidean Drama in Four Acts
(1921)

Motto:
Es ist doch teuer zu Macht zu kommen—die Macht verdummt.
Friedrich Nietzsche

Dedicated to
Tadeusz Langier

CHARACTERS

GYUBAL WAHAZAR—Looks about forty years old. Long, black walrus mustache, disheveled black hair, black eyes. He froths at the mouth at the slightest opportunity. (It's very easy to do by first stuffing one's mouth full of soda tablets or Piperazina flakes from Klawy's drugstore.) Very wide light green pants and long violet shoes visible beneath them. Crimson jacket. Black soft hat. A titan. Hoarse voice.

PIGGYKINS MACABRESCU—Ten-year old girl, blonde, dressed in white with pink ribbons. Beautiful as a little angel. Huge black eyes.

DONNA SCABROSA MACABRESCU—Her mother, twenty-six years old, blonde, very beautiful. Like her daughter, angelic-looking. Light eyes.

DONNA LUBRICA TERRAMON—Twenty-three years old. Red hair with black eyes, a friend of DONNA SCABROSA's.

SWEETHEART—DONNA LUBRICA's eight-year-old son. Fair-haired, generally quiet.

NICHOLAS CLODGRAIN—Miller. Fifty years old. Fat. Completely clean-shaven. Fair-haired with a fat red face.

JOSEPH RYPMANN—Doctor. Tall, thin. Short mustache. Fair-haired.

LYDIA BOCARINA—Dressmaker. Brunette. Thirty years old. Rather pretty, but vulgar.

APPLOSIA MUSTOLET—Maid. Twenty-three years old. Pretty. Dark hair. Light eyes.

FLAYTRIX DIMMONT—Literary man. Thin, small, thirty-eight years old. Long, fair hair. Completely clean-shaven.

FATHER UNGUENTY—Ninety-two years old. High Priest of the perfidious sect of Perpendicularists. Gray-black hair. Completely clean-shaven. Theorist. Long, black, close-fitting garment with white buttons in a row. Tall, black, conical hat with black flaps.

FATHER PUNGENTY—Monk. Fifty-four years old. Grand Fakriarch of the perfidious order of Barefoot Pneumatics. In sandals. FATHER UNGUENTY's brother, and looks exactly like him, but is distinguished from him by a black beard which reaches to his knees and a gigantic mass of black hair hanging down to his waist. Brown habit with yellow circles, fastened with a yellow cord.

FOUR PERPENDICULARISTS—Completely clean-shaven elderly gentlemen, dressed exactly like FATHER UNGUENTY but without flaps on their hats, which have the points cut off.

TWO BAREFOOT PNEUMATICS—In sandals. Dressed like FATHER PUNGENTY, but without the yellow circles.

FOUR HANGMEN—In red tights and red tricorn hats *en bataille* with black feathers. Short black tunics reaching midway between their hips and their knees.

FIRST HANGMAN—Gray-haired with a close-trimmed gray mustache, short hair.

SECOND AND THIRD HANGMEN—Black-bearded.

FOURTH HANGMAN, (MORBIDETTO)—Young man with a cruel, womanish face. Slanting green eyes. Masses of curly red hair.

WAHAZAR'S SIX BODYGUARDS—Dressed in khaki uniforms of English cut with white facings. Black fitted hats with sky-blue feathers, placed the usual way. Clean-shaven.

BARON OSKAR VON DEN BINDEN-GNUMBEN—Commander of WAHAZAR's guards. Beautiful, clean-shaven gentleman, thirty years old. Dressed like the soldiers, but he has golden epaulettes with red stripes.

CROWD OF PEOPLE WITH PETITIONS—WORKERS, GENTLEMEN IN TOP HATS, OLD WOMEN, ELEGANT LADIES, DANDIES AND DANDYETTES.

AUTHOR'S NOTE: Primary colors in the costumes and settings are to be the following shades: yellow—cadmium lemon; red—French vermillion; black—elephant black.

Act I—Waiting room outside the audience chamber in WAHAZAR's palace.
Act II—Another room in WAHAZAR's palace.
Act III—Basement in the prison on Ragamuffin Genius Street
Act IV—The same room as in Act I.

ACT ONE

Waiting room outside the audience chamber in WAHAZAR's *palace. A door at the back and one stage left. Black walls. No windows. A red design: a single line of irregular zigzags, ending in points of yellow flame. Two yellow columns with red spiral stripes. In the corner by the door at the left a table with a gigantic blue siphon full of soda water and a glass. Nearby on a small hook on the rear wall hangs a crimson army coat with gold braid and gold trimming. No chairs at all. The right wall is taken up by a gigantic cabinet bookcase with glass doors. To the right of the upstage door hangs a gigantic portrait of* WAHAZAR, *cubist in style but despite that a very good likeness. On the floor a black rug with a red center with a radiating yellow star. One lamp above. On two columns two others are burning, facing each other by means of reflectors. The stage left door is padded with brilliant red featherbedding. Above the door, a gigantic purple stuffed bird with a blue chain in its beak.*

     A CROWD OF PEOPLE WITH PETITIONS, *jammed together near the upstage door. Sometimes separate individuals walk about here and there in a state of nervous agitation. They all hold huge sheets of paper, written on one side only, which from the other side look exactly like the rug, black with a red center and a yellow star. In the crowd are:* DONNA SCABROSA *with* PIGGYKINS, DONNA LUBRICA *with* SWEETHEART, FLAYTRIX DIMMONT, LYDIA, APPLOSIA, FATHER PUNGENTY *with* TWO BAREFOOT PNEUMATICS, WORKERS, GENTLEMEN *in top hats,* OLD WOMEN *and* ELEGANT LADIES, DANDIES *and* DANDYETTES. SCABROSA *in a light blue dress,* LUBRICA *in a green dress.* FLAYTRIX, *a beret on his head, light gray-green raincoat, white gloves.* APPLOSIA *in a worn-out violet dress and aquamarine kerchief.* SWEETHEART *dressed in dark blue.* LYDIA *in deep mourning. They all whisper, then speak more and more loudly; finally distinct shouts begin to be heard.*

FIRST GENTLEMAN (*looking at his watch*): It's three in the morning. I propose we just leave.

DANDYETTE (*in an orange dress*): It's not possible. I've been standing here waiting for six hours.

FIRST OLD WOMAN (*gray kerchief, rags*): What we've got here is a complete deassessment of the whole valuation of facts. I'm going to stick it out.

SECOND GENTLEMAN: Don't bother me about the valuation of facts.

FIRST LADY (*dressed in black*): We don't have any criteria for that.

SECOND OLD WOMAN (*red kerchief, rags*): No. In a state with a six-dimensional continuum all criteria are really too trite.

DANDY (*rubbing his knees*): Oh! They're really killing me!

PIGGYKINS: Rub them with camphor oil.

SCABROSA: Quiet down, honey! This child is driving me to despair with that endurance of hers.

SECOND LADY (*dressed in red, falls on her knees with her face turned toward the left door*): He's in there! Our ruler! The only master of all the elements and boundless fields of universal gravitation!

SECOND OLD WOMAN: What a lunatic! She doesn't think any of us knows Einstein's theories. They're teaching absolute differential calculus in high school now.

FIRST OLD WOMAN: Long live Gauss! Long live general co-ordinates! Now we all know what tensors are!

SECOND LADY (*prostrating herself before the door*): I'd like to go on waiting till I drop dead. I think I'm flying at infinite speed into the abyss of absolute certainty. Every second is infinity.

FIRST GENTLEMAN: But I've had enough! Let's all go right into his office and tell him we won't put up with it anymore.

DANDYETTE (*clucking*): Yes, yes, yes. Let's go. (*She goes toward the door.*)

SECOND LADY (*grabs* DANDYETTE *by the leg, laughing hysterically*): Don't go in there! Can't you hear? Our ruler, our cruel god is angry.

They all listen. From behind the door at the right can be heard WAHAZAR's *thunderous gibbering and another man's groans.*

FIRST GENTLEMAN: Oh, It's just rotten! I can't stand it anymore.

FLAYTRIX (*coming up to him*): How long have you been waiting, Monsieur le Duc?

FIRST GENTLEMAN: Five hours! It's unbearable! (*He crumples up his paper and flings it on the ground.*)

FLAYTRIX (*bursts out laughing*): Ha, ha, he thinks he's been waiting! Do you know how long I've been waiting, Monsieur le Duc? Three months! Three whole months—for six hours a day. It's about putting my plays on.

VOICES: Yes! We have too! I've been waiting forty-five days! I've been waiting two weeks!

SECOND LADY (*all the while on her knees, out-yelling all the others*): I'm going to wait myself out! I'm at my guts' end from waiting! Everything inside me is bulging out all over from waiting, endlessly waiting. There aren't any tortures in Hell. There's only waiting. Hell is one gigantic waiting room.

VOICES: We're going! I can't stand it anymore. Break the door down! Let's go!

The CROWD *seethes tumultuously on the spot. Pushing the* CROWD *aside,* GNUMBEN *enters through the center door. Those who've seen him fall silent. There is total silence.* GNUMBEN *makes his way through the hall, looking at everyone venomously and searchingly.*

FIRST GENTLEMAN (*to* GNUMBEN): Captain, there's a woman here who's gone mad from waiting. (*Points to* SECOND LADY, *who hasn't stopped prostrating herself.*) Things just aren't done that way. It's . . .

GNUMBEN (*coldly*): Shut up!

FIRST GENTLEMAN *is quiet. They all step aside in silence before* GNUMBEN *as he leaves. Exit* GNUMBEN. FIRST GENTLEMAN *picks up his crumpled paper and carefully smoothes it out on his lap, swearing quietly.*

SECOND LADY (*pointing to the military coat hanging next to the table*): Look!

There's the symbol of his authority. The Pure Form of his power, waiting to expand in the sensuous movements of his frightful body!

FIRST GENTLEMAN (*under his breath*): Oh, the scum! Oh, damn it all! Oh, hell! Oh, damn it to hell!

FLAYTRIX (*to* FIRST GENTLEMAN): Calm down, Monsieur le Duc. It's one big joke. I'm enduring it all because I see everything as a piece of fantastic fiction.

FIRST OLD WOMAN: Yes, when you live the way we do, there's absolutely no need to read melodramatic novels. Life itself is . . .

The door at the left is flung open and, kicked with full force, NICHOLAS CLODGRAIN *flies out through it, in clothing smudged with flour, a huge sack in his hands. He tumbles down beside the* SECOND LADY *on his sack, which bursts, spilling flour about. The door remains open for a moment. Petrified with terror, they all look to the left. The* GENTLEMEN *have taken off their top hats,* FLAYTRIX *his beret.*

SECOND LADY: It's him, our one and only—tin god of perpetual waiting. Come! Let a sacrifice of suffering be performed!

WAHAZAR (*bursts out through the left door, frothing at the mouth and spraying white foam all over his crimson jacket. He bellows*): Haaaaaaaaaaaaa!!! (*Comes to a stop and puts his hands in his pants pockets. The next moment he pulls his right hand out and points to* SECOND LADY.) Throw that old carcass out! (SECOND GENTLEMAN *and one of the* WORKERS *grab the* SECOND LADY *and drag her off quickly through the center door.*) Good! (*To* FIRST GENTLEMAN.) Get going. You first!! (*Points to the left door.*)

FIRST GENTLEMAN (*hesitates, then humbly*): Perhaps after Your Onlyness. *Après vous* . . . If you please.

WAHAZAR *grabs him by the scruff of the neck, hustles him off into his office and slams the padded red door shut after them. A moment of silence. The* SECOND GENTLEMAN *and the* WORKER, *who dragged the* SECOND LADY *out, come back.*

WORKER: They've taken her to the yellow house.

SECOND GENTLEMAN (*mopping his brow*): Oh! How atrocious! She over-waited. What could be more ghastly!

SECOND OLD WOMAN: Sooner or later that's what awaits all of us: we'll all over-wait till doomsday.

From behind the left door, WAHAZAR*'s infernal swearing can be heard. all listen intently.*

FLAYTRIX (*breaking the silence*): But sometimes if you hit on the right moment, you can do anything you want with him. You just have to really go to it, rough and ready. The way that scoundrel's mind works is weird.

CLODGRAIN (*getting up*): Oh, that I've got to try.

FIRST OLD WOMAN: But watch out, Nicholas. If it doesn't work the very first time—it's death.

RYPMANN *comes out through the left door. While the door is being opened* WAHAZAR*'s monstrous roaring can be heard.*

RYPMANN: Do you all have your papers in order?

VOICES: Yes, Doctor. We all do! Everything's in order.

RYPMANN: Not so loud. I'm very worried about the condition of His Onlyness's heart. His pulse is 146 per minute. Don't excite him, or I'll have to break off this session.

DANDYETTE: For God's sake, Doctor! I've already been waiting seven hours. I can't even feel my feet at all. (*She sits on the ground.*)

RYPMANN: Are you joking or what the hell? There are people here who've been waiting for months, ten hours a day, and she shoots off her mouth about seven hours! A great lady!

FIRST OLD WOMAN: I'm literally terrified by His Onlyness's fantastic asexuality.

RYPMANN: That man's got superhuman strength. I'm a doctor and I don't understand the first thing about it. Those are unknown sources of psychic energy. I've racked my brains, and everything else too, to see what it could mean.

FLAYTRIX: Drugs?

RYPMANN: What are you talking about? Of all the teetotalers I know, His Onlyness is the most total. He sleeps an hour, some times an hour and a half. Then he works like sixty steam hippopotami. I still haven't been able to bring the Illyrian Ambassador back to his senses after the session he attended today. They've drawn up a new plan for educating young girls. A masterpiece. Makes your mouth water.

DONNA SCABROSA: That's something for me. I'm here for the first time. Explain it to me please, Doctor.

PIGGYKINS: To me too. I want to be a lady in waiting to His Onlyness. I want to have it written on a red card, like the little Princess of Valpurgia.

RYPMANN (*to* SCABROSA): Why, certainly. That's the easiest thing in the world. I admire you. (CLODGRAIN *leaves through the center door. They all listen to the conversation between* SCABROSA *and* RYPMANN.) There aren't many mothers who consent to it, and yet the results are simply wonderful. But a total separation is requi . . .

The left door opens and the FIRST GENTLEMAN *falls in, kicked hard in the rear.* WAHAZAR *follows him—his entire jacket covered with foam. The* DANDYETTE *gets up off the floor.*

WAHAZAR (*roars*): Haaaaaaaa!!! You filthy pig, you kickasker! You pimple-faced louse egg! (FIRST GENTLEMAN *falls on the floor.*) You dare come here with a crumpled-up piece of paper and you even dare sign it "Duc"—eh? You sawed-off runt! You multi-slotted sisygambis! (*Looks over the* CROWD.) Listen! I've told you that in my presence you're all equal. You old toad and you degenerate slob about town, and you slut, and you great big weakling. (*Points in turn to the* FIRST OLD WOMAN, *to the* WORKER, *to the* DANDYETTE *and to the* FIRST GENTLEMAN, *who gets up and stands "at attention."*) You're nothing, absolutely nothing. It's for you that I'm devoting myself to that most difficult task of all, complete solitude. I have no equals. I'm not like emperors and kings— I'm in another spiritual dimension. I'm such a great genius at living that

Napoleon, Caesar, Alexander and other caper-cutters like them are nothing compared to me: specks of dust, just like you! Understand, you shrivelled up, sluttish old bags? I've got a brain like a barrel. I could be anything I wanted to be, whatever I took a fancy to. Understand? Huh??

FLAYTRIX (*in a quaking voice*): I think to a certain extent I'm beginning to grasp it a little.

WAHAZAR: I'll give you "to a certain extent!" How'd you like to die to a certain extent, you lousy scorpion? Huh??

FLAYTRIX (*looking wildly*): I . . . nothing . . . I . . . Your Onlyness . . .

WAHAZAR (*more mildly*): Then shut up and listen. I see you're reasonably intelligent. (*To everyone.*) I'm sacrificing myself for all of you. None of you can appreciate that and I don't expect you to. I know you say monstrous things about me. I don't want to know anything about that. I don't have secret informers and I'm not going to, just as I don't have any ministers. I am alone, like God. I alone rule everything, and I'm responsible for everything, and answer only to myself alone. I can condemn myself to death, if I feel like it—if I become absolutely convinced that I'm wrong. I don't have any ministers—therein lies my greatness. I am a lone solitary spirit—like the steam in the engine, like the electrical energy in the battery. But then I really do have a machine under me, and not some living pulpy mush. My officials are automats, like the ones you see in train stations. I put a penny in and out comes a chocolate, and not a peppermint: a cho-co-late. (*To* FLAYTRIX.) Understand that? Huh??

FLAYTRIX: Yes, now I understand completely. For the first time . . .

WAHAZAR (*interrupts him*): Well, thank God. Be glad you've understood and shut your trap. (*In a lofty tone.*) I'm transporting you to a happiness such as you couldn't even imagine now. I alone know. Everyone will be set in his own little box filled with cotton, like a priceless gem—solitary, single, unique in the superhuman dignity of his deepest being: exactly the way I am now. But the difference is, I suffer like the very devil, because I'm sacrificing myself for you and I even have to put up with your considering me a wild slob, just like all of you—(*to* FIRST GENTLEMAN)—including you, Monsieur le Duc. I am pure as a solitary virgin thinking of the white flowers of metaphysical love for the Sole

Deity. I am alone like a strange metaphysical flower, growing out of the dark center of the universe, I am solitary like a pearl in an oyster forgotten in the depths . . . (FLAYTRIX *bursts into hysterical laughter and falls on the ground in convulsions*.) Laugh, you idiot. I know I can't talk your lousy literary language. Laugh. I don't hold it against you. Each one of you can tell me everything right to my face, but not one of you dares, because, my good people, for that there's death. What do you expect? But I don't have informers. There lies part of my greatness. I'm telling you: you can create new people only by destroying, and not by putting beautiful thoughts into everybody's head, the way that Mr. Flaytrix does. Let him have his fun, but I'm going to destroy for the sake of the most beautiful treasures, for the sake of those wonderful flowers that will bloom in your children's souls when they awake in the desert of the spirit and howl for one drop of that something immutable, great, and yet so small that you can find it in every earthworm, in every blade of grass, in every crystal hidden in the rock . . .

FLAYTRIX (*getting up, interrupts him*): And even in the bedbug that bites you during the night, Your Psychic Non-Euclideanness?

WAHAZAR (*coldly, in a trembling voice*): What?

FLAYTRIX (*bluntly*): I'm asking you, can you find it in a bedbug too? You old ham!

WAHAZAR *whistles through his fingers; the* CROWD *makes way; with mad speed the* SIX GUARDS *with* GNUMBEN *at their head rush in.*

WAHAZAR (*points to* FLAYTRIX): Shoot that clown immediately!

GNUMBEN: At your orders, sir. (*Points out* FLAYTRIX *to his men.*)

With mad speed the GUARDS *drag out* FLAYTRIX*, who goes limp as a wet noodle.*

WAHAZAR (*finishing his speech*): Well, that's just a little sample of what I'd like to give you. And I'll give it to you, even though you have to go through such tortures you'll think what's going on now is superhuman bliss in comparison.

They all listen, paralyzed with fear.

FIRST OLD WOMAN: That's all very well, Your Onlyness, but what's going on now is what we're really concerned about. I keep hearing about it, but I don't understand it very well, although I do know Einstein's theory pretty well.

WAHAZAR (*wiping the excess foam off his jacket*): You see, old girl, I don't understand it myself. Here even Einstein won't help either you or me. I could know it, but I don't want to. I'd lose my power to act. (*To everybody.*) You all understand? Eh? (*Silence.*) If I really knew what I was after, if I understood it as well as that old girl, and I too, as far as that goes, understand Einstein, I wouldn't be able to do a single thing for you. (*A burst of rifle fire is heard off-stage.*) Oh—now there's one less literary man. Right away the air's clearing. I don't like writing myself, and I can't stand scribblers. A dog's breed, damn it! Well?

OLD WORKER: That's all very well, Your Onlyness, but you yourself say that for now there's nothing but torture. I can believe that maybe our grandchildren will be happier, but what about us; what good'll it do us?

WAHAZAR: Probably none, but it's not at all so tragic as it seems. We've got to go beyond the individual—otherwise we won't create anything. I want to restore to all of humanity what it has lost; and despite the price it has paid to get where it is, mankind is trying to become, if it hasn't already become, something exactly like a beehive, an ant hill, a swarm of locusts, a nest of wasps, or something similar.

FIRST OLD WOMAN: All right, but we old people, we'd like to get some rest too. Your Onlyness, you've already lived, you've enjoyed life. But we haven't. It's the same old thing all the time, only worse and worse.

SCABROSA: Yes. He's enjoyed everything to the hilt. I know him.

WAHAZAR (*to* SCABROSA): You there, don't interrupt! (*To the* OLD WOMAN.) Do you think that all this has to do with you, with what you are? Far from it. Who told you that? It doesn't even have to do with me, with me. Of all of you, I suffer the most. Be glad you're suffering in the company of a man like me. Don't force me to make hollow speeches, and especially not to think. Besides, if I wanted to, I could think it all over during the night; tomorrow I'd get up a completely different person and I wouldn't be able to do anything anymore, literally not anything. You complain that sometimes you have to wait two months or so with a petition. The Jews have also been waiting, for the Messiah, and that's why now they've come up with Georg Cantor, Husserl, Bergson—oh, how I hate that faker—Marx and Einstein. Don't think I'm a Semitophile, but it's a fact.

FIRST OLD WOMAN: So, the Jews were waiting, and they waited and waited till they over-waited, and when the Messiah finally came, they killed him.

WAHAZAR: Don't make me lose my patience, old lady. If you won't be happy, at least your granddaughter will.

OLD WORKER: But what about me? Me? What good'll it do me?

WAHAZAR (*mimicking him*): Me! Me! Me! If I'd thought like that, you'd be a flock of sheep now. As it is, at least you're waiting for something. (*Laughs.*) You probably think I'm shooting my mouth off too much, and that in this time I could have taken care of everything. Fine! All right then! Give me your paper—any one at all. (*He snatches the* OLD WORKMAN's *paper out of his hands.*)

RYPMANN (*while this is going on, grabs his hand and feels his pulse*): Your Onlyness—175. Not a minute more. Time's up.

CLODGRAIN (*dashes in with a bottle of wine in his hand, pushing his way through the crowd*): Hey there—Gyubal! Get on over here. I got some business. (*Hits* WAHAZAR *on the neck with his fist.*) Read it, dammit all, or I'll smash every bone in your body.

WAHAZAR *keeps on reading the* OLD WORKER's *petition in silence.* RYPMANN *takes his temperature under his jacket.*

FIRST OLD WOMAN (*in astonishment*): And to think no one dares kill him!

WAHAZAR (*yanks the thermometer out from under his arm and flings it on the ground*): You see, old lady. That's the kind of psychic fluid I've got. (*He tears the* OLD WORKER's *petition into pieces.*)

CLODGRAIN (*a bit crestfallen, tries a second time; hits* WAHAZAR *on the head with his fist*): You're going to answer me, muddlehead. The mill's got to run. I don't have time for your whims!

WAHAZAR (*waking up as though he'd been dreaming*): What?

CLODGRAIN (*in despair*): The mill's got to run today! Sign, dammit all, and we'll drink to it.

Tension mounts in the CROWD.

WAHAZAR (*in a fog*): Hm . . . that's very interesting . . .

CLODGRAIN (*completely beside himself*): Sign it, hang it all, and have a drink!

WAHAZAR: Well, what'll you get out of it?

CLODGRAIN (*flabbergasted*): N-nothing. The mill will run if you sign. (*Suddenly furious.*) Quit joking, twitchtripe, or you won't draw another breath once I get through with you!

WAHAZAR (*taking* CLODGRAIN'*s paper*): I'm of just the opposite opinion, but I can sign it. (*Signs with a fountain pen and gives the paper back to him.*) But I'm not going to drink any wine with you, Nicholas. Now hurry back to your mill. (*He shakes his hand,* CLODGRAIN *goes out clutching his head.*)

RYPMANN (*speaking above the whispers, which burst out after the previous tension*): Your Onlyness, not one petition more, or it means death. This woman is the only one I'm still going to let Your Onlyness receive. Her daughter wants to be a lady in waiting of the new type. (*To* SCABROSA.) Come closer. The rest of you can leave the room.

The CROWD *slowly leaves muttering, pressing at the door. Only* SCABROSA *with* PIGGYKINS, LUBRICA *with* SWEETHEART *and* LYDIA *remain.*

SCABROSA (*approaching*): Don't you recognize me, Uncle Dick?

WAHAZAR (*uncertainly*): No.

SCABROSA: Don't you remember when you were president of the union? I'm Gina, daughter of Baron Vessanyi, the one who saved your life and died. That's why I was your ward for two years. Because you really are Dick de Korbowa.

WAHAZAR: Maybe I was Dick de Korbowa and maybe that's all true, but it doesn't have anything to do with this. I've completely wiped out my past. Go on.

RYPMANN: Yes, Madam, in his present state of health His Onlyness can't stand remembering anything.

SCABROSA: All right then. The point is that my daughter absolutely insisted on being a lady in waiting in Your Onlyness's court. Come here, Piggykins. Say hello to Grandpa.

WAHAZAR (*to* PIGGYKINS): Come here, my child. I'm very pleased you're so sensible.

PIGGYKINS: Oh, grandpa, but I don't want to have to wait like all those people, even Mama. I want to have everything right away.

WAHAZAR: And you'll have it right away, my child. (*To* SCABROSA.) The adorable little angel. I'll do what I can for her. I'm bringing up ladies in waiting so they'll be ideal specimens of mechanical mothers. (*To* PIGGYKINS, g*iving her some candies he pulls out of his pants pocket.*) Here, have some candy, my precious. (*Lifts her chin up.*) What intelligent eyes you have, my little birdie.

RYPMANN (*restlessly*): Your Onlyness, perhaps Your Onlyness isn't feeling well? Perhaps a little soda water?

WAHAZAR: You think I've gone off my rocker from overwork, Dr. Rypmann? Quite the contrary, I feel wonderful. But give me the soda water anyway, if you want to. (RYPMANN *goes to the table where the siphon is and pours the soda water. To* SCABROSA.) And you, Madam—do you agree to a total separation? Today we've just drawn up the final plan for the education of young girls. Something wonderful. But all mothers clear the hell out of here.

RYPMANN *brings the soda water.* WAHAZAR *drinks.*

SCABROSA: But Your Onlyness, maybe I could too . . . Perhaps some place could be found . . . Maybe one single exception, Your Onlyness?

WAHAZAR (*giving the glass back to* RYPMANN): No, Madam; I can't stand ordinary women in my immediate circle, and anyhow my aim is to mechanize them completely. I divide women into quote "real women"— I mechanize them without mercy—and masculettes, that I turn into men by means of the appropriate transplant of certain glands. Dr. Rypmann! Isn't that right?

RYPMANN: That's right, Your Onlyness. (*To* SCABROSA.) We've obtained fantastic results.

SCABROSA: But, Your Onlyness, I'd like to be myself . . . Just myself, if only life could be a little better for me.

WAHAZAR: Not another word. You've got something of the masculette in you. Your eyes are too intelligent! (*He laughs.*)

LUBRICA (*coming over to them*): I beg Your Onlyness—she's my friend.

WAHAZAR: What? You here too? Someone who's been pestering me to death for a year with her unrequited love for me? (LUBRICA *covers her face with her hands.*) Oh yes, you ought to be ashamed of yourself— you're not fit to be mechanized. It's a good thing I remembered about that. (*To* RYPMANN.) Here's a clever old bag—she'd make us a wonderful functionary for the High Commission on Derivative Sects. Eh? Dr. Rypmann?

RYPMANN: That's right, Your Onlyness. She's no model for a mechanical mother.

WAHAZAR: All right then, Dr. Rypmann, send these two women to the Review Commission. *A propos*: All the old women in the Fourth Workers' District are to be shot by nine tomorrow morning. *Bon!*

LUBRICA: Gyubal Wahazar, beware of the curse of the species. It exacts its own vengeance. You're going to create a society in which the females will devour their men the way certain insects do. You'll be drones that we'll tear to pieces when they become useless.

WAHAZAR: Ha! Ha! Ha! (*To* RYPMANN.) Dr. Rypmann, how wonderfully she talks. What intelligence. We'll make a marvelous functionary out of her.

LUBRICA (*falls on her knees*): Gyubal Wahazar, I beg you! Have pity on us at least.

SCABROSA: But my Piggykins! What about her? What will she become? What do you want to make her into?

WAHAZAR: That's what the Commission on Supernatural Selection will decide after two weeks of preliminary training. My system is *inébranlable*. It transposes my own torments into universal values. I am the first martyr of my six-dimensional continuum. No one has the right to suffer less than I do. What's more, I'm completely alone.

PIGGYKINS: Grandpa, don't lie. You're not alone. Someone's walking behind you and whispering incomprehensible things in your ear.

WAHAZAR (*embarrassed*): Those are just stories. You've been listening to the local gossip, my child.

SCABROSA (*falling on her knees before him*): Your Onlyness! Please believe her. She's clairvoyant. A whirlwind of the astral bodies of unknown beings is ceaselessly spinning around her.

WAHAZAR: Nonsense. Quit pestering me.

PIGGYKINS (*mysteriously*): Grandpa, it's not nonsense. I feel that that someone is very near.

WAHAZAR (*glancing at his watch*): It's almost four already. I've got to go.

PIGGYKINS: You won't get away. Stay where you are and look me in the eye. I can see to the bottom. And at the bottom horrible red earthworms with black heads are crawling. I see what's there behind you. Why are you torturing yourself, Grandpa? Stop torturing yourself.

WAHAZAR: My psychic juices aren't working. Dr. Rypmann, I feel weak . . .

RYPMANN *holds him up*.

SCABROSA: Your Onlyness! This moment is unique. There's still time to turn back. Listen to us, listen to my Piggykins!

RYPMANN (*feeling* WAHAZAR's *pulse*): Your Onlyness—go to sleep, go to sleep immediately. No pulse at all. (*To the women.*) This is what's called internal anaesthesia. He's being poisoned by the secretions of some mysterious gland. I've always said that the future of medicine lies in the glands.

PIGGYKINS: Grandpa, now you're where I am. You're seeing the same thing. Think a minute more, and you'll understand everything.

WAHAZAR: Piggykins, don't talk like that. A frightful world of gentle quiet beauty is opening up before me. (*In a faltering voice.*) Dr. Rypmann, water . . . (RYPMANN *rushes for the water,* WAHAZAR *sways.*) It's nothing. Glands. (*He undoes the collar of his jacket.*)

PIGGYKINS: It's not the glands. He's walking around you and he's tempting you. It's not the devil. It's yourself. You're coiling around yourself like a snake. Now you see a green meadow and a little shed. And a small dog with a little red ribbon is sitting in the shed. I see the same thing every night as I fall asleep.

WAHAZAR *looks at her as if hypnotized. The* DONNAS *kneel on each side.*

LUBRICA: Gyubal Wahazar, listen to the promptings of your true "I."

SCABROSA: For the sake of that highest idea you love so—don't turn us into automatons.

WAHAZAR *drinks the water* RYPMANN *gives him.*

WAHAZAR: Wait, wait, this is a unique moment.

RYPMANN: Your Onlyness! Sleep!

Through the center door enter the FOUR HANGMEN. *They approach quietly, take off their hats, make a low bow with them and put them under their arms.*

SWEETHEART (*who until now has been standing motionless in front of the left column*): Good morning, Hangmen. I belong to the masculine bloc.

The WOMEN *turn around and shriek with terror, then, without getting up, they cover their eyes with their hands and remain that way. With a venomous smile,* MORBIDETTO *silently goes over to* WAHAZAR *who can't take his eyes off* PIGGYKINS. WAHAZAR *gives a start. He drops the glass which falls on the floor and breaks.* MORBIDETTO *looks him in the face, standing to his right.* WAHAZAR *suddenly starts to bestir himself and wakes up from his stupor.*

WAHAZAR (*roars*): Haaaaaaaa!!! (*Foam gushes from his ugly mug.*) Those two sluts go tomorrow to the Commission on Supernatural Selection! Shoot all the old bags in the Fourth district! Cancel all authorizations for exceptional marriages! Summon all third class educators for a special meeting today! Haaaaaaaa!!! (*He froths at the mouth.*)

All this time LYDIA *stands motionless leaning on the right column.*

RYPMANN: But now sleep, Your Onlyness!

MORBIDETTO *takes* WAHAZAR *by the arm and leads him slowly to the left.* WAHAZAR *wipes off the foam which drips from his ugly mug.*

WAHAZAR (*walking slowly*): Thanks, my Morbidetto. I had a moment of weakness.

They go out. The rest of the HANGMEN *slowly follow them.*

RYPMANN (*taking* PIGGYKINS *by the arm*): And, my child, you're going to come with me to our boarding school in the palace.

SCABROSA *uncovers her face and, still on her knees, holds out her arms to* PIGGYKINS *in silence.*

PIGGYKINS: Don't be afraid, Mama. I'm not scared of that roaring. Nothing's going to happen to me.

RYPMANN *gently leads her out stage left.*

SWEETHEART: What a ridiculous situation! I belong to the masculine bloc and none of this has anything to do with me.

SCABROSA *bursts out crying,* LUBRICA *gets up and presses* SWEETHEART *to her motherly bosom. Enter* GNUMBEN *through the center door.*

GNUMBEN (*coldly*): This way, ladies. (*With his left hand he points to the center door.*)

LUBRICA (*To* SCABROSA): Come, Gina. Someday my Sweetheart will even things up.

SCABROSA *gets up with difficulty and, wiping her eyes, goes toward the center door. She is followed by* LUBRICA *with* SWEETHEART *cuddled in her arms,* LYDIA *comes after them.* GNUMBEN *stays where he is to the left, his right profile turned toward the audience.*

ACT TWO

The red chamber in WAHAZAR's *palace. The walls are hung in red; on the floor a red rug with a yellow star in the middle of a black center. Fantastically shaped lemon-gold furniture, as wild as you like, with wings along the arms, etched in black designs. In the back a window through which can be seen hilly countryside, full of fresh greenery. In the distance a city with towers and smoking chimneys.*

The women are sitting in a circle, grouped as follows: LYDIA, SCABROSA, *and, in an armchair with* SWEETHEART, LUBRICA.

LUBRICA (*holds a gigantic black envelope with five yellow seals*): My God, my God—what'll happen to us now! What didn't they do to us in that Commission!! Words can't describe it.

SCABROSA (*depressed to the point of utter apathy, holding the same kind of envelope*): And now we're going to go on waiting until we go mad. We don't know anything about what's in these cursed envelopes. They sentence you for the rest of your life. If only they'd told us right away, the beasts!

LYDIA: Don't get upset, ladies. I've been through it all and I feel just fine.

SCABROSA: Yes, but they didn't turn you into a masculette or anything like that. What'll happen to us the devil alone knows. Just thinking about it gives me chills all over.

LYDIA: You should be proud. I was too stupid for that. Now I'm just an ordinary mechanical mother and nothing more.

LUBRICA: When I was little I always dreamed of being a boy, but now just the thought of it makes me feel sick. Oh! What a terrible age we're condemned to live our lives in!

SCABROSA: At least you've got your Sweetheart! They don't have a scheme for educating boys worked out yet. But what about me? I'm absolutely alone and they've even torn my poor Piggykins away from me. Oh, my God, my God! (*Weeps.*) I don't care for myself; I'd even be willing to become a masculette, if only my poor little girl would be happy!

LYDIA (*gets up and comforts her*): There, there, dear Madam, they just sent for me to take the measurements for Piggykin's new dresses. She'll look lovely in these clothes. (*She strokes the sobbing* SCABROSA's *hair.*) Calm down; you don't want to upset your little girl. She'll be here any minute.

LUBRICA (*feverishly crumpling her envelope, so that the sealing wax breaks*): If only they'd hurry, if only they'd hurry up. I can't wait any longer. The application I made yesterday to go to Illyria isn't worth the paper it's written on now. (*She gets up and paces about.*)

Pause. From the right side enter APPLOSIA *leading in* PIGGYKINS *by the hand.* PIGGYKINS *is carrying a gigantic doll, a caricature of* WAHAZAR, *dressed as he was in Act One.*

PIGGYKINS: Mama! Mama! Look how nice Grandpa Wahazar is. When I pull his mustache I know everything he's thinking. (*She runs over to her mother and puts the doll on her lap;* SCABROSA *hugs* PIGGYKINS *and holds her silently for a long time.*) What are you crying for, Mama? I'm not afraid of anything.

SCABROSA (*sobbing*): But I won't see you anymore, maybe not until after you're all grown up.

PIGGYKINS: Mama, shame on you for crying like that. I slept wonderfully. They gave me cocoa and cookies. And what a lovely bathtub I've got! All done in little pink cats with black eyes. When I grow up, I'll give you one just like it.

SCABROSA: Poor, poor child. If only I were sure you'd be happy. (*Gets up, knocking the* WAHAZAR *doll onto the ground; laughs through her tears.*) Ha, ha, a bath with pink cats. Maybe he has the same kind himself, that scoundrel, that mad comedian, who's getting revenge for his own emptiness! Oh! (*She clutches her heart and bursts into wild laughter.*)

PIGGYKINS (*laughing, picks up the doll and dances around the room with it*): See how Grandpa's playing with me! He doesn't have the time himself, so he gave me this puppet.

LYDIA: All right now, Piggykins, come here! I've got to take the measurements for your new dresses. (PIGGYKINS *sits the doll up on the chair in* LYDIA'S *place and stands before her radiantly.*) They'll all be in blacks, yellows and reds. You'll look just lovely in them. (*She measures her and jots down the measurements in a notebook. Enter* RYPMANN *from the right, in a white smock.*)

RYPMANN: Good morning.   Good morning. Were you ladies at the Commission?

DONNAS LUBRICA and SCABROSA (*rushing to him*): Yes, yes. Tell us, Doctor! What's going to happen? What are the results? Maybe you could open these envelopes?

RYPMANN: I don't know anything about it. I'm not authorized to open these envelopes. The only person who can do that is His Onlyness, Gyubal the First.

Disappointed, the women move back.

LUBRICA: Oh, let's hope he's the last.

RYPMANN (*severely*): You're wrong! With your narrow little mind you can't grasp the full scope of such a genius's thought. These aren't artistic pipe dreams or high-principled do-gooding, this is Reality with a capital R.

LUBRICA: It's cheap Claptrap with a capital C. I'm surprised a man as intelligent as you lets himself get so hopelessly taken in.

RYPMANN: Madam, believe me. I still don't understand everything, but I do know quite a bit. His Onlyness is the Ramses II of the contemporary age. He wants to demechanize humanity, but leave it all the advances of social evolution. He's already done this in part, only we can't realize it yet. We're looking through a magnifying glass at what requires a distance of thousands of light years and gigantic reflecting telescopes in order to be viewed. You shouldn't listen to his words, but look at his actions from that distance. He's a great martyr, and only the fact that he's being poisoned by the secretions of certain unknown glands can explain in biological terms this superhuman energy of his. By analogy with chemistry I'd call it the fission of psychic atoms. Just as radium changes into other bodies by giving off fantastic amounts of energy, he must change into somebody else. If he doesn't, I'll have to declare that medicine is bunk.

LUBRICA: But that's insane. You live here comfortably and have a psychiatric laboratory right on the spot with the most interesting specimen of a madman in the entire world. But the way we live—even your patient himself doesn't have any idea. Oh! If only someone could kill him!

RYPMANN: That's just where the whole art lies. The fact that they don't is no miracle at all, as the foreign ambassadors claim it is. It's instinctive on the part of the masses, who know that this man is suffering for them, at the same time that he inflicts the most monstrous tortures on them. The masses know he's leading them where no one else could. The man who could kill him would have to be some super-madman. And anyhow, this same radical change is beginning in other countries too.

LUBRICA: And it's all going to end in a total fiasco such as the world has never seen, or even . . .

The left door opens with a crash. Enter WAHAZAR*, wearing the same green pants as in Act One, a shirt of the same color, and the same unbuttoned brown army coat with gold trim that was hanging over the little table with the siphon in Act One. A black hat on his head.*

WAHAZAR: Ha! Ha! All right! I don't want to force mothers. I like to have them agree to it of their own free will. (*In another tone.*) Believe me, ladies, I'm not in the least violent by nature. I'm forced to be—forced. But when someone dares try to force me, he's got to face the consequences. Papers ready?

SCABROSA *and* LUBRICA *run to him with their envelopes.*

LYDIA: Thank His Onlyness for not making you wait. Sometimes it takes months.

WAHAZAR (*ripping open the envelopes*): That's right. It's not my fault if I don't have time. You're all forcing me to do it. Mothers are the only ones I don't force, because I want the new generation to be as strong as I am. Understand?

SCABROSA and LUBRICA: Yes, Your Onlyness! What's in the letters? Take pity on us, sir!

WAHAZAR (*stuffs the letters in his coat pocket*): Dr. Rypmann, have all the old ladies been shot, as I ordered?

RYPMANN: Yes, Sir, Your Onlyness. All the officers of the Infantry Regiment staged a revolt. They're all in prison.

WAHAZAR: *Bon!* Hang them all but leave me one small one, that little lieutenant from the Seventh Company. I'll use him to restock the pond. Bring him to the torture chamber at ten tonight.

RYPMANN: At your orders, Your Onlyness.

WAHAZAR: Dr. Rypmann, today there's to be chocolate pudding for dinner. Piggykins loves chocolate. Lydia, Piggykins's party dress is to be ready by seven.

LYDIA: Yes, Your Onlyness.

WAHAZAR: Dr. Rypmann, get the gelatin ready for the pudding. Tomorrow morning at ten I have to make a banner for the anniversary of the United Army Tailors' Association.

RYPMANN: At your orders, Your Onlyness.

SCABROSA: Your Onlyness . . . Just one little minute . . . What's in those papers?

WAHAZAR (*roars*): Haaaaaaa!!! I don't force mothers! But if one of them so much as lets out a peep, that's the end, it's curtains. (*More calmly, wiping the foam off his army coat.*) Now that wasn't very nice of you, my little lady. You ought to be ashamed for pestering people like that. (*To* RYPMANN.) Dr. Rypmann, don't let anyone in to see me today until two P.M. I have a meeting with the Albanian ambassador. Some nobody down there has started pretending to be me, and they're having trouble with him. Pretending to be me! Me! Did you ever hear of such a thing, Dr. Rypmann! Eh? And they're asking me for advice. Ha! Ha! I'll teach them a little Albania. We'll send the Prince of Valpurgia there as ambassador. He'll shake them up a bit. Appoint traitors as ambassadors. A superb technique. The sixth dimension! The non-

Euclidean state!! Ha! Ha! Ha! Ha! Ha! Ha! (*He chokes in an attack of infernal laughter, frothing at the mouth.*)

PIGGYKINS (*whom* LYDIA *has just stopped hugging, jumps up and down and laughs too*): Grandpa, come dance with me!

She grabs WAHAZAR *by the hand and for a moment both dance like little children.* LYDIA *looks on good-naturedly,* RYPMANN *with a fatherly smile.*

RYPMANN: That's enough, Your Onlyness! Your pulse.

WAHAZAR: That's right, my pulse. (*Feeling his own wrist with his other hand.*) But it's nothing serious, 150 at the most.

PIGGYKINS: Grandpa, let me pull your mustache.

WAHAZAR (*bending over toward her*): Go ahead. Pull. Yank it all you want. You can play with me the way you would with that doll.

He points to the puppet on the chair. PIGGYKINS *grabs him by the mustache and pulls his face down to hers.*

PIGGYKINS: Look me in the eyes, Grandpa. What are you pulling away for?

WAHAZAR *closes his eyes.*

SCABROSA: Still, deep down, he's basically good. (*Suddenly remembering.*) But that paper. You know, Lubi, I can't take anymore.

RYPMANN: Easy does it, ladies! His Onlyness is resting. This happens to him once every two years.

The women keep quiet.

PIGGYKINS: Grandpa, look me in the left eye. (WAHAZAR *leans over and looks in her eyes.*) I see your soul, your tired little soul. It's blue and it walks amongst the mosses and fondles little junebugs that are making love.

WAHAZAR (*apparently hypnotized, sits down in front of her on the ground*): You're taking away my loneliness, Piggykins. (*Closes his eyes.*) With you I'm not alone. Somewhere very far away I see a completely different world, a kind of meadow in the middle of a forest. I see you, as a young lady, with a big dog and a young man . . . Oh, God! It's me. (PIGGYKINS *strokes his hair.* WAHAZAR *covers his closed eyes with his hand.*)

PIGGYKINS (*softly*): Go on further and keep looking. Don't turn your eyes away from what you see.

WAHAZAR: My God! It's me. How long it's been since I've seen meadows and trees. I see butterflies; they're chasing one another . . . Lead me wherever you want, Piggykins. I'll do anything you say.

LUBRICA (*softly, to* PIGGYKINS): Ask him to show us what's in those envelopes.

WAHAZAR *gives a start. He wakes up with considerable effort.*

PIGGYKINS (*wringing her hands*): Oh, Auntie, now you've spoiled everything! Like a naughty little girl who smashes her toys.

WAHAZAR (*jumping up with a terrifying roar*): Haaaaaa!!! I've had my rest! I've been resting for ages. Now I've got to get to work. I can feel the strength of sixty electric bulls. I want to twist everything up, crumple it into a pulp. Dr. Rypmann! To work, to work!

SCABROSA: Sir! Take pity on us. Read through these papers first!

WAHAZAR: Haaaaaa!!! You'll find out in good time, turtledoves. You can just wait. Bring me that Albanian in here! They dare pretend to be me down there! Me!! (*Beats his breast, frothing at the mouth.*) Haaaaaa!!!

The right door opens. FOUR PERPENDICULARISTS *carry in* FATHER UNGUENTY *on a stretcher covered with black oilcloth, a peaked hat on his head, its end sticking out over the end of the stretcher. The* PERPENDICULARISTS *keep their hats on.*

FATHER UNGUENTY (*in a soft voice, but penetrating to the very psychic marrow*): You don't frighten me with that bellowing of yours, Dick Gyubal Wahazar with your two first names! You used to be a student of mine. Remember all the times I gave you "F" in differential equations! All the times I kept you in after school!

WAHAZAR (*speechless for a moment*): It's you, Professor!

FATHER UNGUENTY: I'm not a professor anymore, I'm the priest of a new religion. Today we've come out into the world. I have over twenty thousand followers supporting me. I've brought forth, in subterranean quiet, a new world, but a terrible one for liars.

WAHAZAR (*interrupts*): I don't lie. I'm the sole truth of contemporary life. They're forcing me to rage like a wild beast. And whoever forces me will have to face the consequences. I don't lie.

FATHER UNGUENTY: And nobody's saying you do. At least I believe in your truth. But without any faith you won't create anything, you scamp. You're as much in the dark as any living creature—from the most miserable worm up to me, and I know as much as any finite, limited being can know.

WAHAZAR: Then you know—you don't believe.

FATHER UNGUENTY: The highest knowledge touches the highest faith, because it serves only to reveal the unattainable profundity of the Mystery. (*Raising his voice.*) Look at me, I've got arthritic inflammation in all my joints and I suffer as none of your guests in the torture chamber has ever suffered. Anchylosis has petrified me into one single slab of inhuman anguish.

WAHAZAR (*ironically*): I know—we used to down a few drinks in the old days.

FATHER UNGUENTY: And I'm still drinking now and I don't care about my pain which keeps growing and can have no limits. (*Raises his hand and immediately howls in pain.*) Owwwww! Oo! Set me on the ground, surrogates. (*The* PERPENDICULARISTS *place the stretcher on the ground.*) I'm a heap of aching bones, but I've created something without which your work is the raving of a lunatic, the gnawing out of your own and others' very navel of essential individuality. You have got to join with me. (*He utters the last words with frightful force.*)

WAHAZAR (*coldly*): Whoever forces me will have to face the consequences himself.

FATHER UNGUENTY: Oh, don't worry, I will. You have got to be with me, because without faith founded on ultimate wisdom you will never be anything but a caricature, like Alexander the Great, Peter the Great, and all those other "greats." "Wahazar the Great," but at bottom a poor little madman—a tiny fish strayed into the net of metaphysical contradiction, a bogeyman to frighten naughty children.

PIGGYKINS: I told you practically the same thing, Grandpa—you didn't want to believe me.

FATHER UNGUENTY *turns to her.*

WAHAZAR (*impatiently, but gently*): Wait, Piggykins. (*To* FATHER UNGUENTY.) I know all that nonsense. A philosopher on the throne. The Persian Sapor, Marcus Aurelius and so on, and so forth. Ho, ho, Professor, philosophy and life are two mistresses of one and the same guy, yes—that's right, guy—you can't make them get along, wise-aches.

FATHER UNGUENTY (*shudders with revulsion*): Not philosophy, but true knowledge which inspires faith. Faith and philosophy are what you say: mistresses of the same man. There's only one life, and what I want is the summit of life. To achieve faith through knowledge, not through theosophical hogwash created for nonentities and flops. Humble yourself before me, you miserable caricature of the Caesars and other megalomaniacs. Today I read a lampoon that they've got stuck up everywhere in the Fourth District. Here's how it ends:
"Satan calls me a tumor of the umbilicus,
Louse of Infinity is what ancient deities call me."

WAHAZAR: What?

FATHER UNGUENTY (*angrily*): Humble yourself, that's what.

WAHAZAR: How do you mean?

FATHER UNGUENTY: Here's what I mean: Pay me the homage due me—fall on your knees.

WAHAZAR (*indifferently*): I don't see anything special in that.

FATHER UNGUENTY: Have you gone completely stupid? He's a sheep, not a man. Humble yourself, it'll do your brains good.

WAHAZAR: I'm an obliging person and if need be, I can humble myself. (*Kneels and bows down three times before* FATHER UNGUENTY.)

Enter FATHER PUNGENTY *with* TWO BAREFOOT PNEUMATICS.

FATHER PUNGENTY: Oh, pardon me. I didn't mean to disturb you. I am the Grand Fakriarch of the Barefoot Pneumatics. I've heard my brother has achieved his goals. We've come to humble ourselves. Excuse me, may I?

WAHAZAR (*angrily, getting up*): Why, of course, go right ahead, Father. This was only a little rehearsal of a play called *Henry IV and Gregory VII*. We'd finished.

FATHER PUNGENTY: Yes. We're all perfidious and heretical beings. Religion has fallen apart. There's no help for it. Still, I will humble myself before my beloved brother. (*To the* PNEUMATICS.) And you too, brothers, humble yourselves. Religion has fallen apart because of heretical sects.

He falls on his knees before FATHER UNGUENTY. *The* PNEUMATICS *do the same. The* PERPENDICULARISTS *remain like mummies.*

FATHER UNGUENTY: It is good, my brother, that you have humbled yourself. You've come to the right person. But you're wrong; the creation of different sects is a proof of the vitality of a given church, and not of its collapse. That's why I allow all possible forms of heresy, on this condition: you first must understand in the depths of your being, and then, by holding to certain irrefutable axioms, create a sect. Everybody can create a sect of which he'll be the only member, but first he must understand the one and only Truth.

FATHER PUNGENTY: Oh, how happy I am, dear brother. I'll found a new religious order this very day. (*He falls flat on his stomach before* FATHER UNGUENTY.)

PIGGYKINS (*runs to* FATHER UNGUENTY): Me too—I'm going to start a new little church. I've been dreaming about something like that for a long time now. Only I didn't know how to do it.

FATHER UNGUENTY: I bless you, my little child! You have great things ahead
of you.

PIGGYKINS *kneels before him.* WAHAZAR *suddenly roars in an inhuman
voice and throws himself at* FATHER UNGUENTY, *knocking down the*
BAREFOOT PNEUMATICS.

WAHAZAR: Haaaaa!!!!!!!! I'll let you have it, you mournful dry-rot!!
I'll show you what it means to have an ache in the bones!!!! (*Using all
his force,* WAHAZAR *crumples* FATHER UNGUENTY *up like a piece of
paper;* UNGUENTY *literally howls with pain.*) All right? Now do you know
what absolute knowledge is? Now do you know how to create faith out
of knowledge?

The PERPENDICULARISTS *pull* WAHAZAR *away from* FATHER UNGUENTY, *who
has fainted from pain and lies stretched out as if dead. The three women
dash over to revive him. Silently, without moving,* PIGGYKINS *looks over
everyone in the room, scanning them with extraordinary intensity. The*
PNEUMATICS *and* FATHER PUNGENTY *jump up and regroup fearfully at the
right. At the left the* PERPENDICULARISTS *hold* WAHAZAR, *who bellows
quietly, frothing at the mouth, then stops struggling and stands motionless,
dripping with foam, his eyes lowered.* RYPMANN *watches all this with
professional curiosity.*

WAHAZAR: Dr. Rypmann, I've made a fool of myself. It's the first real
mistake in my life.

The women busy themselves with FATHER UNGUENTY *in silence.* PIGGYKINS
goes to the left, takes the WAHAZAR *doll, sits in the armchair and rocks the
doll like a baby,* SWEETHEART *hasn't batted an eyelash, seated all this time
in his armchair up stage.*

RYPMANN: Nothing surprising about that, Your Onlyness: ptomaine
poisoning due to overwork.

WAHAZAR: Dr. Rypmann, tell them to let go of me. I'm weak as a child.

RYPMANN (*to the* PERPENDICULARISTS): Let go of His Onlyness. I take
responsibility for everything.

The PERPENDICULARISTS *let go of* WAHAZAR *and stand, silent, not moving.*

WAHAZAR: How terribly unhappy I am! Won't anybody ever understand me? All I need is a little warmth, a tiny bit of warm-heartedness, just a few crumbs of feeling. Once a year, once every two years. I mean, I do work like a galley slave, like a Negro on a coffee plantation. Yes, I am alone, and my greatness lies in the fact that I have no equals. But does that mean I don't have the right to ask for what's given the lowest ragpicker and pimp?

LUBRICA (*jumps up and, abandoning* FATHER UNGUENTY, *who lies as if dead, runs to* WAHAZAR): Gyubal! I've always . . . I'm with you!

SWEETHEART (*without getting up*): Mama! Mama! Leave him alone! I belong to the masculine bloc, but I won't he able to stand this.

WAHAZAR: That's not what I mean. What I'd like to have is a mother, damn it, a sister, damn it all! It's just unbearable.

LUBRICA: That's what I wanted to be! That was your most fatal error—imagining that I was in love with you. Not one bit. Believe me.

WAHAZAR: Bla, bla, bla. I know a little something about that. We'll see what the indexes from the Commission on Supernatural Selection tell me.

SCABROSA (*also abandons* FATHER UNGUENTY *and goes to* WAHAZAR): Your Onlyness, Dick, I beg you, burn those papers and don't make us into anything. Let us live in peace.

WAHAZAR: Oh, how misunderstood I've always been! How cruelly everybody persecutes me!

LUBRICA: Who? Us? We only want you to take a little rest.

SCABROSA: We don't want anything. Just to have you drop in on us from time to time to drink a cup of tea, have a little chat, relax.

WAHAZAR (*covering his eyes with his hand*): Oh, God, God! How all this wears me out!

PIGGYKINS (*throws her doll down and runs in between* WAHAZAR *and the two women*): Mama! Auntie! Leave him alone now. He's so unhappy.

SCABROSA (*to* PIGGYKINS): You don't understand anything. You're a stupid child. I'm beginning to think you're crazy. Leave us, please!

WAHAZAR *is pensive.* SCABROSA *tries to take* PIGGYKINS *away, but she resists. From the left enter the* FOUR HANGMEN, MORBIDETTO *at their head. No one pays any attention. They stop at the door, take off their hats, bow, then stand up with their hats under their arms and quietly watch.*

PIGGYKINS: Mama! Mama! This is a unique moment. You want to spoil everything. Everything can still go the other way. Please, I beg you, go away! Mama!

WAHAZAR (*angry, hitting* PIGGYKINS *on the shoulders*): Leave your mother alone! You can see she doesn't understand anything. (*To the women, in a very official tone.*) Now I'll take care of this business of yours. (*Pulls some papers out of his pocket and reads.*)
"Donna Scabrosa Macabrescu:
    30%—woman
    65%—masculette
    5%—insignificant psychic trash."

(*Speaks.*) Bon! (*Continues reading.*)
"Donna Lubrica Terramon:
    43%—woman
    55%—masculette
    2%—insignificant . . . "

(*Speaks.*)   Fine. Dr. Rypmann, you'll take care of these ladies. (RYPMANN *bows.*) The womanliness index came out the way it should. (*The* DONNAS *cover their faces in despair.*) And to think that there are so few genuine mechanical mothers today! But just wait, in two years there won't be any more demonic women at all!

FATHER UNGUENTY *recovers consciousness and groans quietly, propped up by* LYDIA.

SCABROSA (*furious*): Yes, there won't be any demonic women, there'll only be hermaphroditic horrors like that scum!

She points to MORBIDETTO, *who smiles indulgently and ironically.* WAHAZAR *turns around.*

LUBRICA (*to* SCABROSA): What do you keep talking for? Don't you see that all is lost! (*She sinks into the armchair.*)

WAHAZAR (*to* MORBIDETTO): Oh, it's you, my only friend! Save me. I had a moment of frightful weakness. I need someone, someone totally average, who'd stroke my head and then go away for a couple of years at least.

MORBIDETTO (*slithers suddenly like a snake, thrusting himself between* WAHAZAR *and the women and* PIGGYKINS, *always looking at* WAHAZAR): What! You dared have such thoughts, did you? You—I'll kill you! (*He utters the last words in a squealing, stifled voice, slowly bringing his face closer to* WAHAZAR's, *making him move back.*)

SCABROSA (*indicating* MORBIDETTO): He's the only one courageous enough to stand up to that monster. Wahazar loves the scoundrel.

WAHAZAR *and* MORBIDETTO *move to the left.* PIGGYKINS *keeps between them and* SCABROSA.

PIGGYKINS: Mama! Stop. It's too late now. The two of you have spoiled everything.

MORBIDETTO (*turning to the women*): Yes—it's too late. You can both go to the clinic. Dr. Rypmann, take these old girls off.

RYPMANN (*coldly*): I'm accustomed to taking orders only from His Onlyness.

MORBIDETTO (*instinctively starts to hurl himself at* RYPMANN, *but restraining himself, turns to* WAHAZAR, *who remains motionless, but tenses up terribly*): Wahazar! For the last time I implore you in the name of our friendship! You know that I'm the only one who can kill you. And that's what'll happen once you betray yourself.

WAHAZAR (*suddenly roars, frothing at the mouth*): Haaaaaaaaa!!!!!!! You think you're the one?! They're the ones who are forcing me and they'll have to answer for it. Haaa!! You're a miserable little abortion like all the others. The usual scum come sniffing around me and dishonor my deeds! As for my ideas, no one can sully them, because I don't express them! My superiority over every one else is that I create reality and not wretched delusions. You're a ghost, Morbidetto, like all the others I have to live with. I'd like to forge some infernal castle of porphyry, but as raw material I've only got a pulpy mass of wet noodles. How revolting!

MORBIDETTO: That's what you wanted. You're the one who reduced them to coming here. You covet your own weakness. It's your last drug now that you've exhausted all forms of abstinence—which is likewise a drug for you. You lacked material in yourself to torture yourself with, so out of an excess of strength you artificially created your own weakness. Gyubal Wahazar's incipient old-biddiness, on a foundation of fatherly pseudo-sentiments! What a monstrous degeneration. And this pseudo-wise man with his absolute knowledge! After all, everyone knows that nothing can be expressed without contradictory and limit-point concepts. And once you admit contradiction, what's the criterion for telling truth from falsehood?

WAHAZAR: I think you're right. Only the trouble is that I'm not sure whether you are. What am I to do?

PIGGYKINS (*rushing to* WAHAZAR): Grandpa! I'm the only one you can believe. I'll lead you out of this labyrinth. You can't understand that yet.

MORBIDETTO: I'm a match even for the mouths of babes when it comes to straight talk. I don't tell lies and that's why I can talk even with children. I'm a super-scum—a downright, unmitigated, premeditated super-scum. I stand here before you now because I know what the essence of Existence is: metaphysical swinishness.

FATHER UNGUENTY (*moaning*): Yes, that is the truth. But I know how to elude it in reality, and not only in abstract thought.

PIGGYKINS (*to* MORBIDETTO): I know how too. I not only know how, but I'll do it.

MORBIDETTO (*stroking her hair*): You don't understand a thing, little girl. Calm down and play with your doll. It'll teach you more than you can teach us or we you.

PIGGYKINS (*drawing back in disgust*): I know now, you're smart because you're trying to be smart, like him (*points to* FATHER UNGUENTY) or like Grandpa if he wanted to be. But he doesn't want to and he's right. You're all too smart, and yet so stupid! (*Taking the doll from the armchair.*) You're all stupider than this doll, even stupider than I am. I won't play with you today. Mama, come here, we're going to whisper something to each other very softly and then say goodbye for a long, long time.

SCABROSA: But don't you understand this, Piggykins: you're so smart, and you still don't know that he wants to make me into a masculette.

PIGGYKINS (*clapping her hands*): A masculette! A masculette! Father Unguenty, you're the only one who can understand what that means.

WAHAZAR (*roars*): Haaaaaaaaaa!!!!! That's enough—I am alone!! (*To* FIRST HANGMAN.) Let there be night! (FIRST HANGMAN *lowers a black curtain over the window. A moment of complete darkness.* THIRD HANGMAN *turns on the electric light.* To FOURTH HANGMAN.) Morbidetto, you'll never kill me. You're the same kind of lying guttersnipe as all the rest. Splattered up to my ears in the molten lava of mysteries, I'll go on to my very limits, to those final precipices. I'm like a black star against the white-hot night! Haaa!!! Dr. Rypmann, the Albanian ambassador goes to the yellow chamber. Get a room ready for special tortures! Come, Morbidetto! You've saved me from the last remaining act of weakness toward myself. I'll never forget what you've done. Dr. Rypmann, arrest everyone. Everyone, is that understood, everyone who's here and take them to cell No. 17 in the prison on Ragamuffin Genius Street! Is that understood? I'm going to get to work. To work! To work! Haaa!!! Do you understand, Dr. Rypmann??!!!

RYPMANN (*coldly*): At your orders—Your Onlyness.

WAHAZAR (*leaning on* MORBIDETTO): I'm leaving, and from this moment on my soul will not know the luxury of weakness. Oh, not face to face with anyone else, nor when confronting the particular case of this or that man or woman—not even weakness confronting myself, face to face with the unfathomable Mystery of why I am just who I am and not someone else. I have my destiny in this accursed limited world and I'm going to fulfill that destiny if everyone here has to die for it by the most frightful tortures. (*Starts to go out left. At the door.*) Dr. Rypman cancel hanging the officers of the 145th Regiment. Send them all to be tortured at eleven tonight.

RYPMANN *bows.* WAHAZAR *and the* HANGMEN *disappear off left. Pause.*

PIGGYKINS: I'll straighten it all out yet. I've got time. I'm still little. But don't ever try to come between Grandpa and me again, Mama. All right?

SCABROSA (*falling into the armchair*): All right, all right. It doesn't matter to me. I'm finished, wiped out. There's only one life, and they've torn mine to pieces, trampled on it, and rubbed it in the dirt . . . It's all over and I don't care about any of it. (*Weeps.*)

SWEETHEART: I belong to the masculine bloc. We're on the Committee—I mean Tommy, Bobby, and I are, and we'll hold our own.

LUBRICA *cuddles him in her arms.*

PIGGYKINS: Don't anybody bother me, and I'll be able to win out too. I feel I love him like a father.

SCABROSA (*putting her hand over* PIGGYKINS'*s mouth*): Don't talk like that. Don't talk like that!

FATHER UNGUENTY: Come to me, my child. You're the only one who knows the truth, although you haven't recognized it. (PIGGYKINS *tears herself away from* SCABROSA *and runs to* FATHER UNGUENTY.) You're a little lunatic, a poor little demented soul, who has to sacrifice herself for others in life. You'll die, but you'll accomplish what I'm dreaming about . . .

RYPMANN: Father Unguenty—don't give her ideas. The answer to this problem is a simple question of glands. For the time being I'm experimenting on mice, but if only His Onlyness would agree to experiments on people, I'd know everything. The concepts "genius" and "moron" will become in relation to the concept "man" what ice and water are to the concept H_2O. Father Unguenty, you'll see that science isn't in such bad shape as you think.

FATHER UNGUENTY: Who told you that I thought science was in bad shape?

Even Einstein's theory is incorporated in my system, as a small detail. For physicists, the world is finite and non-Euclidean, for me it's infinite and amorphous. Real space has no structure—that is the Absolute Truth, which includes Physical Truth as a mathematical convenience, good for a certain method of grasping phenomena. Understand?

RYPMANN: Well, now, that's enough discussion. Once I transplant a little of the despair gland into you, you'll despair even of your own truth. (*To the women.*) But now, good ladies, follow me to the laboratory for Supernat . . .

From the left enter GNUMBEN. *At each of the two doors,* THREE SOLDIERS.

GNUMBEN: Everyone in the red chamber is under arrest. By order of His Onlyness.

RYPMANN (*laughing*): Except me, of course?

GNUMBEN: Everyone—do you understand, Dr. Rypmann? You undoubtedly know that I do not make mistakes?

RYPMANN: It's a mistake!

GNUMBEN (*emphatically*): I never make mistakes, Dr. Rypmann. Get up and come with me. (*He goes out left.*)

PIGGYKINS: All this is just a joke. Grandpa wants to play a totally new trick. I'm leaving.

She goes off left. The PERPENDICULARISTS *lift up* FATHER UNGUENTY; *the terrified* PNEUMATICS *follow them out. They are followed by the women and* RYPMANN, *who is shoved by the* SOLDIERS *stage right with their rifle butts. The women moan.*

RYPMANN (*exiting*): Oh, God!! God!! The glands can always give you a surprise or two!

ACT THREE

Cell No. 17 in the prison on Ragamuffin Genius Street. Dark brown walls and yellow columns. Full of smoke. Straw to the left and to the right. Upstage center, a flight of wooden stairs, ending in an iron door on which every five minutes someone pounds as hard as he can with a hammer. The room is lighted by small orange lamps placed in two rows high on the walls; their light is reddish and dim because of the thick coils of heavy hanging smoke.

The whole company, y compris *the* FOUR HANGMEN, *except for* WAHAZAR, CLODGRAIN, *and* GNUMBEN. PIGGYKINS *is wearing a black dress with red and yellow patterns.* LYDIA *is just finishing fastening something for her in the back. At the left, the* HANGMEN, LUBRICA *and* SWEETHEART. *At the left,* FATHER UNGUENTY *and the* TWO PNEUMATICS, SCABROSA *and* RYPMANN, *without his lab coat. They are all lying apathetically on the straw.* LUBRICA *and* SCABROSA *are dressed like men in gray suits.*

LUBRICA (*to* MORBIDETTO): What now, Mr. Hangman? Maybe you're going to entertain us with your conversation? Maybe you're going to think up some unknown tortures for us?

MORBIDETTO (*yawning, significantly*): That'll come in due time. But I don't think we're going to stay here long. It's not worth starting. Our master-of-life is quite quick in his actions.

LUBRICA: And considerably more ponderous in his thoughts.

MORBIDETTO: Particularly in those he doesn't even express.

LUBRICA: But what they say in town, and even here among ourselves, is that you, Most Revered Hangman, know everything.

MORBIDETTO: I know him in his moments of anger and fury. But I don't understand some of his reactions when he's calm and mild.

LUBRICA: Aren't those moments of relaxation?

MORBIDETTO: No, definitely not. At those moments he deliberately flies low, lies in ambush, and gives in to his worst impulses in some inhuman, calculated way. But it's not weakness.

LUBRICA: On what evidence do you base that supposition?

MORBIDETTO: On the fact that I'm locked up here with you. If HE succeeded in imprisoning me, ME, it means that his spirit knows no weakness. Do you realize that from that moment on I've begun believing in his absolute, superhuman strength?

LUBRICA: And up till then what had you believed in?

MORBIDETTO: In myself, in my absolute, metaphysical swinishness. Now I don't believe in anything. (*He buries his head in his hands.*)

SCABROSA: If that scoundrel has already despaired about everything, it means we're lost without any hope of being saved.

RYPMANN: You all seem to forget that I'm imprisoned, I am, Rypmann, the famous Dr. Rypmann! Either the theory of glands has collapsed, or else a miracle will have to happen which can confirm my conception of the fission of psychic atoms. (*With sudden despair.*) Oooh! All this ridiculous talk. Death awaits us—if only we won't be tortured. We can be happy, as long as we won't be tortured. I know what he's like.

MORBIDETTO: Now, now, now, Doc! There's no telling which of us has been most important in all this business. Remember, for informing—true or false—it's death by torture, just as it is for treason.

RYPMANN: But I never betrayed anyone, and I never informed on anyone even by innuendo. I've always been a humble scientist—nothing else.

MORBIDETTO: Just like me. I was only a humble hangman. I always tortured when I was told to. And if our ruler liked to have me do it, that was none of my business. I don't want to pry into matters that are so very personal.

SCABROSA: How monstrous! Then you mean he . . .

MORBIDETTO: She's finally figured it out, the silly goose.

RYPMANN: What's she figured out?

LUBRICA: Yes. Yes. What's she figured out? Gina, tell me.

SCABROSA: I haven't figured out anything . . . He's the one . . . (*Points to* MORBIDETTO.)

MORBIDETTO: I haven't either. I haven't thought anything or figured out anything.

RYPMANN: He's a sharp one. He knows what he's doing. (*Nods his head knowingly.*)

MORDIBETTO (*flippantly*): And maybe I'm not imprisoned at all? Maybe our ruler had me locked up here so that I could get to know what you're thinking better? Hm? What do you say to that?

RYPMANN (*uneasily, trying to convince himself*): He could have found better subjects for observation than us.

MORBIDETTO (*looking at him out of the corner of his eye*): Now, now, now, Doc. Isn't that excessive humility?

RYPMANN (*getting up*): I assure you, it's not. I've always been a humble scientist. My goals have been purely theoretic. I lived only to accomplish certain work, nothing more.

MORBIDETTO: Yeaaah, the glands. We know a little something about that. The Commission on Supernatural Selection and certain little nocturnal trips to the Fourth District.

RYPMANN (*with forced jollity*): Good heavens, Morbidetto, you must be joking. Instead, tell me whether you have any cigarettes or not. I haven't had a cigarette for four days. It's enough to make a person go stark raving mad.

MORBIDETTO (*taking a pack of cigarettes out of his jacket*): Have one, Doc. I don't smoke, but I always carry some with me in case of emergency.

RYPMANN (*greedily flinging himself on the pack*): A Laurens "Figaro." (*Smokes.*) Oh! What bliss! But this is really suspicious.

MORBIDETTO (*getting up*): You're dumb as a doorknob, Doc. You want to pass yourself off as some kind of Sherlock Holmes. I give you my word as the greatest scum that I've been arrested absolutely *en règle*. And to be arrested by His Onlyness is worse than death; there may be (*high-pitched*) tor- (*bass voice*) tures.

RYPMANN: Damn! I'm starting to shiver. Anything—but not that. Oh God, God!!

MORBIDETTO: A person could end it all by committing suicide. There's an idea.

RYPMANN (*whimpering*): God preserve us. Isn't there any more hope at all?

Silence.

FIRST HANGMAN: Pray, each one of you, to that divinity you've forgotten about in good fortune and pleasure.

RYPMANN: I have no such divinity. I've believed in only one thing: the reduction of life to chemical processes, to what I've called the fission of psychic atoms. We've got to assume a new type of hypothetical molecules—or else we won't get out of this.

MORBIDETTO (*ironically*): Molecules won't help you much now, Doc, no matter what kind you assume.

RYPMANN: I feel a hideous emptiness—hideous, I tell you.

FATHER UNGUENTY: I believe you, my son. I wouldn't want to be you, not even for a second. As I hear you talking, I think to myself: Is it worth it for sages, prophets, and artists to take so much trouble for such a crew, for such a hideous pulpy mass of rotten worms? (*To* RYPMANN.) You've seen the prison toilet? Soup with live vermicelli! I have the same impression when I look at you, gentlemen. And these are the heights of mankind! Merciful God!

RYPMANN: I'm ashamed, but I'm scared. At least I'm sincere.

MORBIDETTO: When there's nothing more to lose, everyone's sincere. And that's when a man shows his true colors: a hideous flatworm. There's no courage—only pretending. But to pretend well is the highest art. We're not really artists—but at least let's pretend the best we can. Be a little less sincere, Dr. Rypmann. Don't pollute the air here; it's foul enough as it is.

RYPMANN (*in a trembling voice*): I'll try. I'll do anything.

FATHER UNGUENTY: There are women present, doesn't that mean anything to you? At least try to be a gentleman, Dr. Rypmann. Oh, how far my Truth is from Reality! Oh, Reality—what are you really?!

PIGGYKINS: Stop talking, all of you. Let there be silence.

MORBIDETTO: And why have silence? So we can hear the stinking psychic gasses, the stinkingest in the world, leak out of our souls?

RYPMANN: Listen, Morbidetto, you were free four days longer than I was. Tell me again exactly what happened.

MORBIDETTO: Nothing. Albania—ambassador got sick from exhaustion. Then we tortured the officers from the 145th Regiment for sixteen hours. After that they put me in a car and here I am.

RYPMANN: That's terrible . . .

PIGGYKINS: There's nothing terrible about it. It just means that something very strange will descend upon us. We've only got to stand firm.

FATHER UNGUENTY: Listen to that innocent child. Through her speaks that same spirit which in me is transformed into concepts.

MORBIDETTO: Nonsense. Nothing's going to happen. Let's simply accept the fact that the worst has happened. It's what we've all been expecting all our lives, when everything was going too well for us.

PIGGYKINS: Let there be silence. I know something holy. I'm going to tell you everything and then you'll all be just like me. We'll meet once more in Infinity. And once more, and once more, and so on and on forever infinitely.

FATHER UNGUENTY (*enraptured*): Go on, little girl. Cantor's theory of sets caricatured in the mind of a child! We're transforming everything into Infinity—here, here on earth. Oh, great faith, which flows from the Infinity of Existence! Oh, what a miserable creature Einstein is! So great as a physicist, but as a philosopher such a nothing, such a speck of dust driven hither and thither, such a poor little worm!

PIGGYKINS: You don't understand it either, Father Unguenty. It's beyond me, beyond Infinity. It is this moment, and not any other, and yet mine, mine . . .

She hugs the air to her breast. The door opens. Daylight pours in. A racket is heard, and then shoved by someone from above, WAHAZAR *comes rolling down the stairs; he is wearing the same army coat as in Act One.*

WAHAZAR (*crashing down at the foot of the stairs*): Haaaaaaaaaa!!!!! (*Immediately gets up.*) Wretches!! Pseudo-democracy and leveling triumph, and autocracy personified in the non-existence of other worldly powers! Everything triumphs over everything, nothing triumphs over everything, everything triumphs over nothing, Nothing, with a captal N!!! Do you hear that, you metaphysical courtesans! Do you hear, sages and you, you earthbound theoterranean bambino, you lambkin, you lambskin for frostbitten brains, you sheep, you, you, you!!! Piggykins!!! (*He crashes down on the floor again, frothing at the mouth.*)

RYPMANN: What's this? Your Onlyness . . . ??

MORDIBETTO: Everything's done for! So our regime is a total loss?

WAHAZAR (*getting up*): A total loss! A total loss! A total loss! It was all a comedy! I'm ruined, I've been imprisoned. Tomorrow death by torture awaits me. Me and all my followers. You're my followers. You're dying with me. He has conquered me, he has, he has!!! (*He crashes down, foaming at the mouth.*)

SCABROSA and LUBRICA: Who?? Whoooooo!?

PIGGYKINS: Whoooooooooo???!!!

WAHAZAR (*getting up*): He has! He has conquered me! He has—that cursed he I've always been afraid of. And I believed that they (*points to* RYPMANN *and* MORBIDETTO) would free me from him. And those two let me down. I am alone in my fall as I was alone in my power. I am the one and only. That is enough for me. (*He crashes down on the floor, frothing at the mouth*.)

MORBIDETTO: I knew there was somebody stronger than he was. I had an inkling about it while I was torturing that lieutenant. A new world appeared to me at that moment. I know who he is. He's the one I don't know. The one I had an inkling about. Wahazar, tell me!

WAHAZAR (*still lying down, his hands over his eyes*): Yes. It's him. HIM. We're all done for.

RYPMANN: I knew it too. I saw him in my dreams and in my waking moments. I know his face. But I can't remember what he looks like. That's the one it was, that one, that one! Oh! what torture it is not to be able to remember!!

WAHAZAR (*uncovering his face*): Yes—you're both thinking about him. It was him. Only him. I was nothing. He has conquered me for ever. A total loss—all a total loss. I'd just decided to try to get along with him (*points*), with Father Unguenty. I'd decided to embrace his faith, a faith based on Absolute Knowledge! All a total loss. He has conquered me, because the crowd can tell who is really on its side! Oh, what torture! How could I have known that I'd be here with you? With you whom I despised and adored! With you, for whom I have fought against your enemies and mine and against you yourselves! Oh! Oh! It's unbearable! I'm going to die! Kill me! Let it be finished once and for all! (*He falls on the straw to the left and howls dully*.)

MORBIDETTO: Ha! Ha! Ha!! That's the solution. To betray him or not by killing him?! Perhaps in return for this betrayal life awaits us, a new life, starting all over again from the beginning—a life without Wahazar! Who can even imagine the beauty of such a life? No one.

FATHER UNGUENTY: But who will take up this hellish burden after he's gone? No one. He alone had the strength. The one who will come after him must surely be weaker in mental powers than he. This is the limit point of intensity for strength of mind in our species of Individual Beings.

RYPMANN (*voluptuously inhaling his cigarette*): Nothing but poisoning by the venom of unknown glands. I've always said that all this Wahazar business was a hoax. If I could find those glands, I'd turn every human being into a new Wahazar. What am I saying—human being?! A hyena, a jackal or even a bedbug—it doesn't matter—it's just a question of time. Wahazar—a misshapen psychic abortion! If he, the one who has succeeded him, lets me, you'll see frightful things: the domination of the glands over the species. The fission of psychic atoms has already begun. There is no Wahazar. The nightmare is over. I'm willing to die for anything at all, but not for him.

MORBIDETTO: Let's not worry about the future. If we get out of this trap, we'll have time enough to talk about who we are really supposed to be. Actually, all this Wahazar business is only a ridiculous case of the power of suggestion. I spit on Wahazar. Do you hear that, all of you? He has always been a puppet in my hands. I have an instinct for cruelty—I admit it—but who has dared to use me, to use me by means of a shabby trick . . . ? Oh! It's too hideous for me to talk about. (*Points to* WAHAZAR.) There he is. That pitiful puppet eternally frothing at the mouth. I spit on myself; from this moment on I'm starting a New Life. I'll really be a scum.

PIGGYKINS: You're lying! You're lying! You're nothing. He pulled you out of nothingness. You're killing yourself with those words.

FATHER UNGUENTY: Verily, "Boo hoo I tell you"—as Tytus Czyżewski once said. She's telling the truth. We don't know what awaits us. I take refuge in my wisdom, like a snail in his shell, and I'm waiting, waiting. I've been waiting whole years, I can go on waiting. But it's not with you, abortive titans, that I'll create a New Life. Wahazar alone was worthy of an alliance with me, but look what we've got instead: a putrefied little heap of inert matter. I forgive you all. (*He wraps himself up in his coat, head and all, and appears to go to sleep.*)

PIGGYKINS: They're all lying. How strangely everything is turning out! I'm the oldest one of you all and I believe that Grandpa will triumph.

RYPMANN: Madam Scabrosa, restrain that imp. I've had enough of that. I'm beginning to have some hope and I can't stand the cawing of adolescent crows.

SCABROSA: I don't want to know anything. Piggykins is a lady in waiting—I hope she enjoys it. My life is finished. I can become the mistress of the one who's taken over. If only I don't have to sleep on straw. Oh, mattresses with inner springs! Oh, beefsteak and eggs! Oh, mayonnaise! All I want is a hot plate and a tiny little room of my own. Piggykins, I renounce you forever. Let HIM come. (*She hides under a quilt.*)

MORBIDETTO: It can't go on like this. Let's revolt. Let's light up a new star, here in this black hole. Let's create a vision of a New Life which will eclipse all the plans of that poor daydreamer. I'm objective. My point of view is clearly defined. Father Unguenty, you and I will create the monstrous duumvirate of the future. I'm ready to believe in anything.

FATHER UNGUENTY (*wrapped up in his coat*): For the time being—no. I'd first have to believe in your creative strength, Morbidetto. I don't know you and I must admit, at the moment I despise you. (*He wraps himself up still more tightly, moaning with pain.*)

LUBRICA: No—I can't stand this vileness. I love Gyubal like a brother. I stand by him in his misfortune. There's my superiority to the rest of you. (*She goes over to* WAHAZAR, *who lies there as if dead, sits next to him and strokes his head.*)

MORBIDETTO: I tell you, let's start an open rebellion among the prisoners. Let's go out shouting, "Long live HIM." It doesn't matter if we don't know who he is. Maybe there are a lot of them, maybe what's happened is that the secret government I once tried to form has come to power. Maybe they've only forgotten about us. Let's remind the world that we exist. Who's with me?

SWEETHEART: I am. I belong to the masculine bloc. What do I care?

MORBIDETTO *goes to the door.* SWEETHEART *follows him.* SCABROSA, LYDIA, RYPMANN, *the* THREE HANGMEN, FATHER PUNGENTY, *the* BAREFOOT PNEUMATICS *and the* FOUR PERPENDICULARISTS *follow them.*

FATHER UNGUENTY: Stop. This is ridiculous. I have the feeling I know exactly what will happen.

PIGGYKINS (*rushes over to* FATHER UNGUENTY): Yes, Father. We'll stay here. You and me. No matter what happens. I believe that Grandpa will triumph. He's good, but he's just gone a little mad. I don't want to talk with him now; he wouldn't understand me.

FATHER UNGUENTY *presses her to his breast, moaning with pain. Standing on the stairs,* MORBIDETTO *beats on the door. The others are gathered around him.*

MORBIDETTO: Hey!! Guard!! Open up!!!

He beats on the door with his fists. The door opens and daylight pours into the dark cell. CLODGRAIN*'s silhouette can be seen in the entrance.*

CLODGRAIN: What's going on there?

MORBIDETTO: We want to get out. In the name of the one who's taken over. If there's a large number of them—we'll honor them too. We don't care.

CLODGRAIN: So-ooo-o? You want to get out? That's no surprise. Who wouldn't want to get out of a dungeon? Sure. But it's not as easy as you think.

MORBIDETTO: Stop joking, Nicholas. Let us out. We'll take Wahazar with us and hand him over to the one who's now in power. Just let us out of here.

RYPMANN: Come on, Mr. Clodgrain. Tell us what happened, will you?

CLODGRAIN: Nothing much. Everything's all right.

PIGGYKINS (*shrieks*): People! Turn back while there's still time . . .

SCABROSA: Mr. Nicholas, it's not nice to keep us in a dungeon like this. Let us out. Please. We're all begging you. We all hate Wahazar. We really do. I'm not joking.

MORBIDETTO: Oh! What's the point of asking? What's if that idiot won't let us go, let's make a break for it!

He punches CLODGRAIN *in the stomach and gets out at the top of the stairs. At this moment* WAHAZAR *gives a terrible roar. Everyone stops, and at the same time* MORBIDETTO, *pushed backward, crashes down the stairs. The* GUARDS *with* GNUMBEN *at their head throng at the door. Everyone looks at* WAHAZAR.

WAHAZAR (*getting up, roars and froths at the mouth*): Haaaaaaaaaaaa!!!!!!
(LUBRICA, *terrified, collapses on the floor. The* GUARDS *squeeze in through the door, shoving the prisoners aside. The door closes.*)
Haaaa!!! Now I know everything!! And did you really think someone could imprison me? You miserable asthmabilicals? Haaa!!! A lousy breed of spiritual starvelings. Me and prison! Ha! Ha! Now I know everything and I'll act appropriately. You yourselves are forcing me. And whoever forces me will have to face the consequences.

All those near the door fall on their knees and crawl toward WAHAZAR. *The* GUARDS, *convulsed with laughter, beat the grovelers with their rifle butts.*

CRAWLERS: Your Onlyness!! Mercy. We didn't mean anything! It was prison psychosis! Persecution complex!

RYPMANN: Nicotine withdrawal! Mercy!!

WAHAZAR (*laughing savagely*): Ha, ha, ha, ha, ha, ha!! Crawl, currish crumbs! Crawl, lousy ganglions! Here, here, closer! Lick the straw, pestilential carrion. Wallow to your heart's content, parrot appendixes!! Ha, ha, ha, ha, ha, ha, ha!!!

GNUMBEN (*goes to* WAHAZAR *and salutes*): Mission accomplished, Your Onlyness.

WAHAZAR (*pulling a revolver out of his back pocket*): As a reward you get to die with your boots on, Captain. (*He shoots* GNUMBEN, *who slumps to the floor without a groan. The* GUARDS *stand at attention. To the crawlers.*) Get up!!!!!! (*They get up.*) Morons! Fatheads! Psychic frumps! I forgive you for everything. You're free. Lubrica, get up, damn it all! Gina! Hey! I'm not turning you into masculettes. You can do whatever you want. (LUBRICA *rises and kisses* WAHAZAR's *hand. He ignores this.*) Dr. Rypmann, you keep on with your work in the laboratory. But watch out for those glands. Your theory is inspired, but in actual practice: ho, ho, ho, be a little more careful, Dr. Rypmann. (*To the noncommissioned* OFFICER *of the guards.*) Hey, Sergeant, you become the captain and commander of the guard. Understand?

COMMANDING OFFICER (*saluting*): At your orders, Your Onlyness.

WAHAZAR (*to* PIGGYKINS): You, my child, you remain a lady in waiting. (*To* FATHER UNGUENTY.) I'm half converted to your faith, Father Unguenty. I won't be able to do it all by myself. I'm taking you into partnership, "Wahazar, Unguenty & Co." How about it?

FATHER UNGUENTY *remains silent.*

PIGGYKINS (*dashing over to* SCABROSA): You see? Didn't I say so? Mama, thank me. Grandpa's been converted to the New Faith because of me. (SCABROSA *hugs* PIGGYKINS.)

LUBRICA: And what about me?

WAHAZAR: Be whatever you want, but stay out of my way, darling. That's all I ask of you. (*To* FATHER PUNGENTY.) And you, Father Pungenty, you're a big zero in this whole affair. You and your Pneumatics, go on being a zero.

FATHER PUNGENTY: I thank Your Onlyness for imprisoning me. In silent communion with myself, I've thought up a new sect. What it is is . . .

Enter CLODGRAIN, *dressed as he was in Act One.*

WAHAZAR: We'll talk about it later. (*To* FATHER UNGUENTY.) All right, Father Unguenty, I propose that we settle everything once and for all. Do you agree or don't you? Professor, it's a former student asking you, and not just any old student—Gyubal Wahazar himself is asking you. Huh? Now isn't that the height of honor! (*Pause.*) All right, Father Unguenty, agreed?

FATHER UNGUENTY (*lying on the straw*): Hm. My God. Yes, certainly. I always dreamed of an alliance with you, Dick. It's just that it's all taken on a somewhat strange shape. But in the last resort I agree. What else can I do—I won't find anything better than you. Death is near, and the way is far.

WAHAZAR: *Bon!* And now I invite you to come with me to a banquet. Piggykins, give me your hand.

PIGGYKINS (*runs over to him*): My Grandpa! My dear Grandpa! I knew you'd be converted.

WAHAZAR (*loudly*): I'll tell you a secret, my child. I knew it too. But what have I actually been converted to? I've completely forgotten who I used to be, and I don't know too well who I am.

PIGGYKINS: You'll find out later, Grandpa. I'll tell you everything. Now let's go.

WAHAZAR: All right! Perpendiculars! Take the Fakriarch and bear him to the palace. Guard, attention! Forward! March!!!

The GUARD *leads the way. The* PERPENDICULARISTS *pick up* FATHER UNGUENTY, *who moans, lay him down on the stretcher and follow the* GUARD. *After them comes* WAHAZAR, *arm-in-arm with* PIGGYKINS. *The* HANGMEN *and the rest follow.*

MORBIDETTO (*runs to* WAHAZAR): Your Onlyness . . . Will I . . . Will I be free to . . . ?

WAHAZAR (*stops*): The more dangerous a creature you are, my dear Morbidetto, the better I like you. (MORBIDETTO *kisses* WAHAZAR's *hand.*) But we'll give up torture absolutely. From now on you won't torture any one but me. Agreed?

MORBIDETTO (*still bending over*): I can't stand it any longer! I'm going to burst!! (*Suddenly jumps for joy.*) What a mad comedy all this is!

WAHAZAR: Now, now. Don't get carried away. Let's go.

He goes to the door with PIGGYKINS. *All the others follow them.*

ACT FOUR

The same room as in Act One. Between the columns a huge yellow banner with the inscription, in red: "THE CONVERSION OF GYUBAL WAHAZAR." *Down lower a smaller banner with the inscription:* "LONG LIVE WAHAZAR AND FATHER UNGUENTY." *At the right there has been set up a black throne with yellow stars, facing to the left.*

FATHER UNGUENTY *is standing on the steps of the throne, dressed as in the previous acts, but with a yellow sash across his chest. On the left side of this sash hangs a gigantic, red, star-shaped decoration. Upstage, the same crowd as in Act One. The mingled buzz of talking and whispering can be heard. All the characters are in the crowd except for* WAHAZAR, CLODGRAIN *and* PIGGYKINS, FATHER PUNGENTY *and the* TWO PNEUMATICS. *The women are dressed as in Acts One and Two.*

FATHER UNGUENTY (*beats with a yellow staff on the steps of the throne; the whispers die down*): Poor souls, beggars of the Spirit, cursed undertakers who carted faith off to the graveyard of crumbled passions: First of all, down with pragmatism and equal rights for the sake of the utility of all kinds of rubbish. There is only one Truth and only one Faith springing from this Truth. Down with intuition, the conscious instinct and other similar hoaxes of intellectual pimps. I greet you in the name of what is about to happen. I am alone, and my knowledge is frightful. I need a driving force. Gyubal Wahazar, my partner in building a new world, will be this driving force.

A WOMAN'S VOICE (*from the* CROWD): That's too banal!!

FATHER UNGUENTY (*beats with his staff*): Quiet! I'm in good health thanks to the medicaments of the brilliant Rypmann, who, by the way, has come over to our faith without losing any of his experimental perspiration or skill at all. (*Bows to* RYPMANN, *who waves back;* RYPMANN *is wearing a red apron, on which is embroidered a yellow nervous system and black glands.*) The facts lead us to believe that the personality cannot be infinite and that is why the most important species, or classes, occupying the highest positions in the hierarchy of Individual Beings, have to huddle together in a pack—forgive me, I'm talking in the most popular terms—creating repulsive ant hills without any faith in the Mystery of Existence. Wahazar tried to fight against this, but through a terrible opprestification by his intellect he argued that civilization had to regress. Once I had acquired the ultimate knowledge which is contained in symbols comprehensible to everyone and can be presented as freely as you want in popular terms, the way Einstein's theory can, I came to accept the idea of the Mystery, the quintessence of which is, generally speaking, limitedness in Infinity. The Mystery kindles faith, not just any kind, the way the pragmatists want, but faith based on Absolute Knowledge. Long live the one and only faith, where contradictory and limit-point concepts touch the Mystery of Existence! (*Silence. Pause.*) I see that you do not understand me. I don't see any enthusiasm on your masks of scared bestialitude. What does that mean?

MORDIBETTO (*steps forward, raising his hand like a pupil in class*): Allow me to ask you, Father Unguenty, what is Existence in its totality?

FATHER UNGUENTY: Either it's an Individual Being within its own limit or an organization of such Beings, as for example, all plants. It can't be solely an agglomeration, because then we wouldn't be able to admit the movement of dead systems which are composed of Individual Beings, of living creatures. The physical view of the world, which we have to accept, wouldn't be valid.

A WOMAN'S VOICE (*from the* CROWD): That's boring. That's not faith. That's just common, ordinary hammering away on the ganglions with ideas long since dead and stinking.

FATHER UNGUENTY: Quiet!!

MORBIDETTO: I can't understand this "Either/Or." Either there is a Supreme Being or there isn't. No one can believe in "Either/Or"—there has to be a single object of faith.

VOICE (*from the* CROWD): That's not true! There's only one way out.

FATHER UNGUENTY (*spreading his arms out wide*): Create sects. No one's stopping you. Wahazar has understood this and he is with me.

MAN'S VOICE (*from the* CROWD): And what sect does Wahazar belong to? To the sect of the Unity or of the Plurality of Organizations?

FATHER UNGUENTY: Wahazar is with me. We are above sectarianism. Only the highest minds can take a dualistic position. But the choice of any one point of view does not contradict Absolute Truth. That's the superiority of faith founded on absolute knowledge. The phenomenologists could reach that point, but they don't have the courage. We're recklessly courageous in our thinking. We take the Mystery by the horns like a bull. (*Loud talking in the* CROWD.) Never mind, go ahead and argue. Create a sect, each of you! We're opening free colleges of supreme knowledge. Everything will be made clear and there's not an idiot living who won't he able to understand it. We'll create a life whose everydayness will he steeped in the Supreme Mystery. Even the shoemaker making shoes will experience what was up to now the lot of only the greatest minds. He'll experience it, but in a popular form, exactly the way workers today have ideas about Einstein, just as the great names in physics and mathematics do.

MALE VOICE (*from the* CROWD): Enough of that! This is no college here. We've come for a ceremony! We want a new life, not boring lectures.

FATHER UNGUENTY: I understand how insignificant desires keep flashing before your eyes and I promise they will be gratified. Every physical theory, duly checked in its metaphysical greediness, will find a place in our system. Dr. Rypmann is transforming the personality. I'll tell you in confidence that by transplanting certain glands from my partner to me he's slowly changing me into Wahazar. I feel boundless possibilities. I incorporate the fission of psychic atoms into my system as a brilliant concept.

RYPMANN (*coming forward to foot of the throne*): Ladies and gentlemen, up until now, we have been transforming by force. Now we'll create such conditions that the unfit species will die out by themselves. I thought I was a magician. I wanted to be a Wahazar too, but here my knowledge suddenly evaporated. Not all glands "take" on everybody. That is the terrible truth of my metabiochemistry. The individualizing of gland-ularization—I owe this to the theoretical works of Father Unguenty who in his brilliant introspective deducto-induction—please don't confuse this concept with Dadaism—has anticipated even this eventuality. I'm simply beside myself with joy! We have wonderful things to look forward to! Whoever wants to, whoever really wants to, can be anything within the limits of the transformability of the cerebro-spinal system. And with time we'll even succeed in influencing the self-generation of new ganglions, once we've gained experience of the creative will of this new type of Individual Beings. I am happy and so are you! Tomorrow will see no differences between us! We'll be flooded from inside by the infernal revelation of the transformations according to my formulas, the famous Tables of Rypmann! People! Do you understand? Each will be this, that, women, men—one big mish-mash of transformational possibilities, adjustments, and adaptations. This isn't nonsense! This is the marvelous Truth!

A murmur of adoration in the CROWD.

VOICES: Long live Rypmann! A new life! Down with mystical drivel! Biological Truth! The glands!!! Hurrah!!

RYPMANN (*pointing to* FATHER UNGUENTY): You owe it to him! With his great idea he has enlightened my experimental faculties. Without him I would be nothing. Fall flat on your faces.

He prostrates himself before FATHER UNGUENTY. *The entire* CROWD, *except for* MORBIDETTO, *does the same thing.*

MUFFLED VOICES OF THOSE LYING FLAT ON THEIR FACES: Long live Unguenty! Long live transformation! Long live the fission of psychic atoms!

CLODGRAIN (*enters through door at left, dressed in a red costume with a yellow star on his stomach and a gigantic yellow bearskin cap on his head, announces*): Their Onlynesses: Gyubal Wahazar and his spiritual daughter, Piggykins Macabrescu!!!

Enter WAHAZAR, *dressed as a* PERPENDICULARIST, *with the same yellow sash as* FATHER UNGUENTY, *leading* PIGGYKINS *by the arm, dressed as in Act Three with a lemon-yellow veil on her head. She holds a bouquet of pink roses in her hand. Off-stage the orchestra plays a cavalry march.*

WAHAZAR (*very loudly*): There's no way out. Got to wade through every humiliation. Let's keep going.

PIGGYKINS (*loudly, shrilly*): Don't worry, Grandpa. I'm here with you.

The orchestra breaks off in mid-beat.

WAHAZAR: Fine. I'm glad. Thank you, my child. It's just that I'm so frightfully bored. This whole business doesn't amuse me the least little bit.

He approaches the throne. MORBIDETTO *pulls out a blue lasso from under his tunic and goes and stands by the open door at left.*

PIGGYKINS: Tell them to get up, Grandpa.

WAHAZAR (*roars, frothing at the mouth*): Haaaaaaaaaaaaaa!!!!!!! Get up!!!!!! (*Everyone gets up. They rub their eyes and look around uncomprehendingly, like people aroused from sleep. Muttering in the* CROWD.) Shut up!!!!!!!! (*Silence. Calmly.*) I exist—that's the whole truth that can be extracted from this hideous situation. Let's finish this comedy quickly. I continue living after my own life has ended. I'm going to tell you a secret. Rypmann took out a certain gland of mine while I was asleep and transplanted it into Father Unguenty while he was asleep too. (*Points to* FATHER UNGUENTY.) I'm a mannequin and I'll carry it all through to the very end.

PIGGYKINS: Grandpa, calm down. That's not true.

FATHER UNGUENTY *looks on speechless, spreading his arms out wide in terror.*

WAHAZAR: I can afford to lie. (*To* FATHER UNGUENTY.) You begin, Professor.

FATHER UNGUENTY (*with a smile*): I'm beginning. Hear me, faithful followers. (*Sings in a quavering voice without any well-defined melody.*)

> Now I—now he: behold,
> In the soul a bell begins to toll.
> In my soul small bells are ringing.
> Come here, sisters and small sons clinging.
> I am one.
> We are two.
> Eden now.
> Down soft as dew.
> Edens too and eiderdowns,
> Poppies, pansies, and golden crowns
> Change their flowers into flue
> And motion's died in depths below

Butt him in the gut—do!
Butt him in the gut—do!
Truth awaits,
Glitters lonely,
Equivocally, not once only,
Have I kittened chasm's breath!
Moss grown over heart of Truth!
Not once only, ever lonely,
In empty echoes' blackened depth,
I filled the goblet to the brim.
Arise, all seers and phantoms dim.
Here's a corpse—here's a corpse—a cadaver . . .
Take it, as from a bird pluck the feather,
Since nothing now is left of the soul,
Of the great soul,
Immersed in the cold
In the fog of fate besplattered,
Crudified, bespoiled and tattered.
The soul itself no more suffices
From the iron shield of death
To rouse to life the meat-red masses.
Buy a body at dirt-cheap prices!
Though the eternal watchman bares his tooth,
Pry into the mysteries' private places
Though fear will barter off the Truth,
For all—still try, try all devices.

(*Stops reciting.*) Excuse me, ladies and gentlemen. I'm strictly a philosopher, not a poet. I improvised that little poem as well as I could. (*To* WAHAZAR.) Kneel down, Wahazar, and symbolize your oneness with everlasting Truth. And you kneel down too, Piggykins, unwitting child of perverse desire.

WAHAZAR *and* PIGGYKINS *kneel at the foot of the throne.*

VOICES (*from the* CROWD): What a disgusting comedy.

The tolling of a great bell is heard off-stage.

FATHER UNGUENTY: The more disgusting it is, the greater its effects can be. Truth must be shrouded in a cloak of falsehood in order to he more alluring. Anyhow, truths of any kind bore you. You wanted a ceremony—well, now you've got one. (*Unctuously.*)

> Now she—now he: behold,
> A strange bell strangely starts to toll
> And its reverberations roll
> Under this throne
> (*In a different tone.*)
> Under my throne.
> I hear them groan,
> I hear them moan,
> The mob tilling the crusted earth
> Scattering the seed of Truth
> For every separate brain the spoil.
> You there, raise it from the soil.
> And you, my little sister soul,
> You, pale dessicated pole,
> Give your solitude as spoil
> To the sovereign without precedent
> Most, most omnipotent.

(*Stops reciting.*) Excuse me, ladies and gentlemen, I'm improvising, and I never was a poet. That's the curse of my whole life. (*Kisses* WAHAZAR *and* PIGGYKINS *on their foreheads.*) But now that's enough ceremony. I never was a specialist in those relics of disguised Truth. Now listen to me, Gyubal Wahazar. You're the lowest type of comedian I know, the most perverse type who through perversion has arrived at complete mastery over the body, the type of degenerate ruler before whom the most immoral of the Caesars and Persian satraps could bow down . . .

WAHAZAR (*interrupts him*): Ah! If it were only like that! But it's not even . . .

FATHER UNGUENTY: So you want to degrade me and render me harmless by your own pseudo-sincerity, do you? All right. You are a complete zero. Both you and those who came before you, those damned do-gooders who sacrificed themselves for the common welfare. They're all just leftover scraps of something that's lost forever. Unless what I desire wins out. Understand? You don't exist at all.

WAHAZAR (*kneeling, coldly*): I can't refuse to agree to all of that. The fact is that this is the strangest moment in my life. I don't know who I am. Do you understand, you deceitful old man? You don't know what it means not to know who one is. Haaa!! (*He roars briefly, on his knees, then becomes quiet.*)

FATHER UNGUENTY (*triumphantly, to the* CROWD): I've conquered him, I've completely conquered. He can't even be my driving force. Wahazar, you don't exist for me, and that means you don't exist at all. There isn't any you. Tell me there isn't any you. Make an old man and a martyr happy with your last confession.

WAHAZAR (*getting up*): There isn't any me—that's not saying enough. I live in indeterminacy. I feel I'm everything. I'm gorging myself on all Being. Everything is intensifying into Infinity. Kill me, or I'll burst with ecstasy at my own self. Oh! What happiness! What bliss! Not to know who one is—to be everything!! (*He holds out his arms in front of him in wild ecstasy.*)

PIGGYKINS (*getting up*): Grandpa! Grandpa! Don't be so beautiful! Don't talk like that . . . (*She freezes in ecstasy from looking at* WAHAZAR.)

FATHER UNGUENTY (*making a sign to* MORBIDETTO): Morbidetto, It's time, high time!

MORBIDETTO *rushes over from the door and throws the lasso around* WAHAZAR's *neck.* WAHAZAR *falls over backward, his arms stretched out in front of him.* MORBIDETTO *pulls the noose tight, standing with one foot on* WAHAZAR's *chest.* WAHAZAR's *legs twitch a few times and he dies. Silence.*

PIGGYKINS (*falls on* WAHAZAR's *corpse*): I loved him, only him!!! (*She throws her arms around him and remains frozen in that pose.*)

FATHER UNGUENTY: It's happened! We're free! Dr. Rypmann, take out those glands of his immediately—you know—those Carioxitates Rypmanni, and prepare an injection for me while they're still warm. I'm old, but I have the strength of ten men. All right, Dr. Rypmann, get a move on. (*The* CROWD *mutters.* FATHER UNGUENTY *whistles through his fingers. Through the door at the left the* GUARD *runs in, led by a platoon* COMMANDER *dressed the same way* GNUMBEN *was. Through the center door* FATHER PUNGENTY *with his* TWO PNEUMATICS *elbow their way through the* CROWD.) Drive them all out into the courtyard. There the new edict will be read to them. I am now Unguenty-Wahazar in a single person. That's what I have always been. Charge bayonets!

The GUARD *advances with lowered bayonets on the* CROWD *pushing at the door.* MORBIDETTO *takes his foot off* WAHAZAR's *corpse, pulling it out from under* PIGGYKINS's *prone body, lets go of the lasso and goes and stands at the left, arms folded, watching what happens with a smile. There are left in the room:* MORBIDETTO, RYPMANN, CLODGRAIN, FATHER PUNGENTY *and his* TWO PNEUMATICS, LUBRICA *and* SWEETHEART, *and* SCABROSA; *the* THREE HANGMEN *and the* FOUR PERPENDICULARISTS *remain upstage left.* SCABROSA *comes over and gently embraces* PIGGYKINS, *who lies stretched out on* WAHAZAR's *corpse. The* GUARDS *stand by the center door.*

SCABROSA: Poor, poor child . . .

FATHER UNGUENTY (*coming down from the throne*): Morbidetto, now you are mine. You will be my driving force, my relaxation, my court absurdity of life. The only possible way to relax is in total absurdity.

RYPMANN *stands gazing lugubriously at the group:* WAHAZAR—PIGGYKINS—SCABROSA.

MORBIDETTO: Yes, Your Onlyness. I am yours. Everything else was just a prelude to truly significant things.

FATHER UNGUENTY: Oh, how happy I am, how infernally happy I am! Youthfulness of spirit expands within me, creating non-Euclidean tensions of multi-dimensional, amorphous space. Come, Morbidetto, now we're going to devise a new program which will be the synthesis of Wahazar's insanity and the supreme import of my Absolute Truth. (MORBIDETTO *smiles lasciviously.* FATHER UNGUENTY *leans on him as they go out through the center door. At the door* UNGUENTY *stops and turns to* RYPMANN.) Dr. Rypmann, let's not get too sentimental. Don't worry about this touching scene, get to work on your own specialty, the glands. Ha, ha! (*They go out.*)

RYPMANN (*to* SCABROSA *and* PIGGYKINS): You ladies will excuse me, but I've got to carry out my duties while the tissues are still alive. In a quarter of an hour it may be too late. And taking them out of someone still alive meant risking instant death.

SCABROSA (*rising up*): Rypmann, don't be cruel. After all, he is her father.

She feels it and that's why she's so heartbroken.

PIGGYKINS (*suddenly getting up; indifferently*): R-r-really? I didn't know anything about that. I thought it was pure chance that I loved him so much. But even if he is my father, it doesn't matter to me. Take him away, Rypmann.

SCABROSA *looks at her in amazement.*

RYPMANN: Strange, these perversities of the subconscious states. No glands will do any good here. (*To the* GUARDS.) Take His Former Onlyness's body off to the biochemical lab.

The guards take WAHAZAR's *body and carry it off left. Through the center door enter* FATHER UNGUENTY, *followed by* MORBIDETTO. LUBRICA *suddenly dashes after the* GUARDS *carrying the body.*

LUBRICA: I'm the only one who could have saved him. Oh! What monstrous swinishness! (*She runs out left.*)

FATHER UNGUENTY: Dr. Rypmann, the depths of that scum's perverse soul are frightening. (*Points to* MORBIDETTO.) I'll never free myself from him ever again.

RYPMANN: That's always been the curse of the great: they have to have some hideous little louse who ends up sucking their blood. I'm leaving—I don't have time for practical everyday matters. (*He goes out left.*)

FATHER UNGUENTY (*calls after him*): And don't forget about the injections, Doctor. (*Sits on the steps of the throne.*) I'm tired. I must be with some absolutely simple-minded nonentity. I must rest. Clodgrain! Come here and talk with me a little. (CLODGRAIN *comes and stands beside him.*) Give me your hand. I am weak. (*To* FATHER PUNGENTY.) Well now, brother and Fakriarch, what does your intuition tell you to do at this particular moment? I wonder if you know what I'm thinking of?

FATHER PUNGENTY (*pointing to* PIGGYKINS): Of killing that little one? She knows too much.

FATHER UNGUENTY: Yes. Your intuition about life is incredible. You will be the person I was supposed to be for Wahazar. I am Wahazar II. I'm a bit old, but that can't be helped. You will be my successor in this infernal six-dimensional continuum of Absolute Nonsense.

FATHER PUNGENTY *throws himself at* PIGGYKINS *and begins to strangle her.* PIGGYKINS *lets him without any resistance.* SCABROSA *looks on, unable to move.*

MORBIDETTO: Ha! Ha! Ha! Now I see the whole superiority of the new system. A miraculous way to overcome all scruples. That's just what we lacked, Wahazar and I.

LUBRICA (*runs in from the left*): Go to it, Sweetheart!! Show what you're worth for once in your life, sonny!!

She gives him a stiletto. SWEETHEART *rushes over and stabs* PUNGENTY, *who crashes down on top of* PIGGYKINS. *She jumps up from underneath him. The* PNEUMATICS *pin* SWEETHEART's *arms behind his back.*

PIGGYKINS (*gasping*): Thank you, Sweetheart. I'll take you under my wing and bring you up, and I promise I'll make somebody out of you. (*To the* PNEUMATICS.) Let go of him this instant!!

The PNEUMATICS *let go of* SWEETHEART, *who falls flat on his face before* PIGGYKINS.

SWEETHEART (*on the floor*): I renounce the masculine bloc. I'm yours.

PIGGYKINS *kisses him on the forehead.*

FATHER UNGUENTY (*in a fog*): Well, all right, but what does all this mean?

MORBIDETTO: There, there, there, Father Unguenty, don't be scared. It's one of those problems which will only serve to accentuate the greatness of our conceptions. We have to have a backdrop, a contrast, a kind of *repoussoir*. Otherwise nobody will see us, nobody will be able to tell us apart from all the rest. Leave them all as they are. Everyone has to have his own dangers; we do too.

FATHER UNGUENTY: Perhaps you're right, Morbidetto. As a theorist of life you are unequalled.

PIGGYKINS *presses the sobbing* SWEETHEART *to her breast.* RYPMANN's *head appears from behind the red door.*

RYPMANN: The injection for Your Onlyness is ready. I have all Wahazar's glands in hand. Hurry, or they'll get cold.

FATHER UNGUENTY: But isn't it too late? This final transformation frightens me.

MORBIDETTO: Get a move on, Your Onlyness. It's never too late for anything, if you've nothing ahead of you anymore. Get going, you old geezer. (*With a laugh he pushes* UNGUENTY *out through the door at left.*)

PIGGYKINS: Don't cry, Sweetheart. Someday we'll show them what the Truth is. But until that day comes, study like mad. Grit your teeth and study. Do you promise me?

SWEETHEART (*sobbing*): Yes, yes. I promise. I'm going to be strong like Grandpa Wahazar, even like Father Unguenty himself, like Morbidetto. I don't understand it all yet, but I know a lot. I really do. Don't you believe me, Piggykins?

PIGGYKINS (*hugging him*): I believe you. I believe you completely. But now come relax and play dolls with me. (*She pulls him off to the left. They exit.*)

SCABROSA (*watching them leave*): Poor, poor children, if they knew what was in store for them!

CLODGRAIN: But it's nothing like that at all, my dear lady! They'll change, adapt, adjust, then there'll be some new injections for them. Don't worry, Dr. Rypmann's sure to think up a few new tricks.

He puts his arms around her and kisses her on the mouth. Upstage the THREE HANGMEN, *the* TWO PNEUMATICS *and the* FOUR PERPEN-DICULARISTS *burst out in savage laughter.*

SCABROSA (*yielding to* CLODGRAIN): Ah! Ah! Ah! And yet life lost its last remaining charm when Wahazar died . . .

Stanisław Ignacy Witkiewicz
circa 1930

THE ANONYMOUS WORK

Four Acts of a Rather Nasty Nightmare
(1921)

Foreword

Witkacy wrote his plays at high speed, with scarcely a backward glance, and yet we know that the seeds of these works were often planted many years earlier. The next play in the collection is a case in point. Witkacy began writing *The Anonymous Work,* "Four Acts of a Rather Nasty Nightmare," in mid-September 1921 and completed it on November 27. It remained unpublished until 1962, and was first performed in 1967.

The play takes Shakespeare as its starting point. The title of *The Anonymous Work* comes from *Macbeth*, Act IV, Scene i. In response to Macbeth's question, "How now, you secret, black, and midnight hags,/ What is 't you do?" the Three Witches respond, "A deed without a name," which, in the nineteenth-century Polish translation, is rendered, "Bezimienne dzieło," or "Anonymous Work."

As a child Witkacy knew this scene and the lines quoted above from the captioned illustration by the British artist Henry Selous in his father's three-volume Polish edition of Shakespeare. Selous's woodcut showing Macbeth's visit to the Witches' cave is teeming with winged beasts, strange monsters, and hideous little creatures; it left its mark on Witkacy's creative imagination and served as a model for the grotesque figures that people his paintings and drawings.

In Witkacy's play, revolution is the anonymous work, created spontaneously from below, without any discernible author. For creativity both in art and in revolution, the true sources of power are subterranean.

The scene with the gravediggers in Act One, which takes its cue from *Hamlet*, appears as a motif in two of Witkacy's paintings. *The Gravedigger's Monologue,* of September 1916 done in charcoal and pastels, depicts Hamlet as Witkacy's friend Tadeusz Langier standing in a gave with three skulls and several bones. On his left we see a Gravedigger clutching a shovel; to his right there is a demented Ophelia and a bent-over figure. Four years later, *Composition with Gravedigger,* unrelated to *Hamlet,* anticipates the first scene of *The Anonymous Work.*

In Witkacy's treatment of motifs from *Hamlet* in *The Anonymous Work*, the gravediggers climb up out of the dirt, which has been their element, and replace the Prince as heirs to the kingdom. They then continue their work of interment; Lopak, the First Gravedigger, is the artist as undertaker, gleefully burying the old regime with a sneer.

The play's motto, "The Grizzloviks yelp at the sight of Black Beatus the Trundler," comes from a dream of 1912, when Witkacy was undergoing psychoanalysis. Reappearing in his novel *Insatiability* (1929), this unfathomable phrase has a mysterious significance for the author, as did certain words and combinations of sounds throughout his life.

In September 1921, just before the writing of *The Anonymous Work*, Witkacy and two friends, Langier and Niesiolowski, published anonymously *Litmus Paper*, a four page brochure parodying Dadaist and Futurist works. Witkacy's short one-act autoparody, *The Redemptors*, has four characters whose names reappear as major figures in *The Anonymous Work*; at this point they are only names in search of characters. These are the underground sources—his reading, his dreams, and his own earlier works, both literary and visual—which Witkacy tapped when he began composing *The Anonymous Work*.

According to Witkacy's theory of Pure Form, the sequential happening on stage of one thing after another is the essence of drama. For this reason his purposes are well served by appropriation of forms of popular literature featuring rapidly unfolding narrative and surprising transformations. Key to the craft of *The Anonymous Work* (and all of Witkacy's plays) is metamorphosis; the characters and situations constantly keep changing.

In *The Anonymous Work* Witkacy parodistically utilizes, as elements of formal composition, the intricate plotting and suspense of the spy romance. In keeping with the genre, the play takes place within ordinary categories of time and space, with no suspension of the normal laws of human behavior or traditional dramaturgical practice.

On a thematic level, *The Anonymous Work* is a play about the relation of art to politics and the state. In tandem with his next drama, *The Cuttlefish*, which deals with the same issues, it offers Witkacy's fullest portrait of the artist in a totalitarian regime. These farsighted works not only accurately predict the imminent rise of repressive dictatorships in Europe, but they also reveal the dilemmas that innovative artists face when they discover the unbridgeable divide between the artistic and the political avant-gardes.

In the 1920s and 30s—an age of collective movements seeking radical social change by violent means—avant-garde artists were forced to make political choices and join parties, or risk being shunted aside as weak-kneed and indecisive. The sickly consumptive painter Plasmonick Blödestaug—hero of *The Anonymous Work*—has with his art sought to subvert accepted modes and norms, but confronted with demands to be politically engaged and help change the world, he grows restive and unwilling to commit himself. When politics swallows art, when ethics replaces metaphysics, and the mass absorbs the individual, for alienated artists like Plasmonick authentic existence becomes impossible. He soon experiences difficulty in retaining his identity in a rapidly shifting political landscape.

Son of a bourgeois aesthetician, entangled in familial, financial, and erotic bonds to his society, Plasmonick is unable to escape the compromises that have made him captive to the outworn ideology of the crumbling dominant order. When the first revolution break outs, toppling the old regime, Plasmonick, who cannot opportunistically switch allegiances, goes to prison where he is forced to use his art for propaganda purposes by painting a modernist-tinged socialist-realist portrait of the great ideologue, Grizzelov, who is the fountainhead of the new Grizzlovik creed.

The Anonymous Work reveals the theocratic nature of future totalitarian regimes based on pseudo-ideologies. The masked power structure of society, in which nothing is what it seems, conceals the true operations of the political mechanism. Initiates in the cult of the Grizzloviks actually believe in nothing; the seemingly revolutionary doctrine is hocus-pocus hiding the emptiness and bankruptcy of ideology.

But *The Anonymous Work* is a play about a double revolution, the second occurring within the first, when the faceless rabble rises up and seizes power from their leaders, who have deceptively manipulated them.

Borders are eroded between the decaying aristocratic world and the underground movements and secret societies claiming to act for the masses. Colonel Manfred, Count Giers joins the bizarre sect of Grizzloviks, but Prince Padoval—more ruthless and pragmatic—puts on the black pointed cap of the extreme levelers. In a world of total appearance, class identities are fraudulent, systems of belief fictive, and revolution itself is a mystification serving to help the ruthless seize and hold onto power.

After the second leveling revolution, Plasmonick sees that the unity of his personality will be lost in endless role-playing and that he can no longer be creative under the aegis of the gray anonymous mass. Committing a deliberate murder so that he will be incarcerated for life, the artist declares, "In our times there are only two places for metaphysical individuals: prison or the insane asylum."

The Anonymous Work is one of Witkacy most colorful works. Its ancien regime is a world of operetta, picturesque in its tinsel costumes, pageantry, and intrigue, complete with hidden letters, mysterious sums of money, concealed identities, and secrets of parentage. But its overbright colors are eclipsed by the grays and blacks of the grave-digging levelers, who carry out "the anonymous work."

THE ANONYMOUS WORK

Four Acts of a Rather Nasty Nightmare
(1921)

Motto:
The Grizzloviks yelp at the sight of Black Beatus the trundler.
(From a dream in 1912)

Dedicated to
Bronisław Malinowski

CHARACTERS

DR. PLASMODEUS BLÖDESTAUG—Small gray gentleman, with a huge head of hair and a mustache. No beard. Gold glasses. Sixty–two years old.

PLASMONICK BLÖDESTAUG—His son. Dark, handsome, brown–haired with delicate features. A painter. Consumptive.

ROSA VAN DER BLAAST—Twenty-eight years old. A famous composer. A reddish blonde, very beautiful.

CLAUDESTINA DE MONTREUIL—Twenty-two years old. A light blonde, with short hair. A painter. Very soulful and pretty.

TZINGAR (known as Joseph)—Nearly forty. Broad-shouldered, dark-haired. Short mustache. Thick, somewhat curly hair. A very handsome "lomofam" (l'homme aux femmes). A social activist.

COLONEL MANFRED, COUNT GIERS—Fifty-six years old. Medium height. Graying brown hair. President of the Military Tribunal.

TWO GRAVEDIGGERS:

GRAVEDIGGER I—Old, gray, somewhat decrepit. Clean-shaven.

GRAVEDIGGER II—Young, beardless, dark-haired. Twenty-six years old. His name is JOSEPH LEON LOPAK.

TWO OFFICERS ON THE MILITARY TRIBUNAL:

DAYBELL—Old major with a mustache but no beard. Glasses.

FLOWERS—Young lieutenant with a mustache and a small Vandyke beard. Dark-haired.

PRINCE PADOVAL DE GRIFUELLHES—Twenty-seven years old. Blond hair, beardless.

OLD PRINCESS BARBARA—His mother. Descended from the royal house of Stewart. Née Countess Bambord of Cleverhaaz.

LYDIA, BARONESS RAGNOCK—*Dame de campagnie* of the Princess. Fifty-six years old.

PRISON GUARD—Navy-blue uniform with large silver buttons.

SOPHIE—Ten-year-old daughter of ROSA VAN DER BLAAST.

MAID to ROSA VAN DER BLAAST—Very beautiful. Dressed in bright green.

CROWD OF PRISONERS—Gray prison suits with large yellow circles on the front; red numbers in the circles.

SOLDIERS OF THE GUARD—Green uniforms with white facings and tricornered hats.

GENDARMES—Navy-blue uniforms with red facings. Tricornered hats with red plumes.

EIGHT GRIZZLOVIKS—Dressed like workers. Disciples of Joachim Grizzelov, the founder of a religious and social society. Grizzelov is an immensely fat old man with very long hair and a milk-white beard. His face is ruddy and robust. (He is known only through the portrait of him painted by PLASMONICK.)

OFFICER OF THE GUARD—Dressed like the guards, but with gold epaulets edged in red.

CROWD—Motley in the extreme. In the clothes worn by the crowd there is a total absence of the colors yellow and red in those shades (cadmium lemon and Chinese vermilion) which the prisoners have on their chests. Green, violet, and crimson predominate, and, less frequently, sky blue.

Act I.   A field on the outskirts of the capital of Centuria.
Act II. Rosa van der Blaast's apartment.
Act III. A prison.
Act IV. A square in front of the prison.

ACT ONE

An almost entirely flat field on the outskirts of the capital of Centuria. Day begins to break. In the background the glow of the distant city. Beyond the horizon are seen distant spires and smoking chimneys. The field is covered by bushes with dark-green leaves and fluffy, light-blue flowers. In addition, high greenish-yellow grass with bronze tufts is growing everywhere. There are no trees. In places the earth shows through, cherry-red in color. Here and there a few irregularly placed large rocks (rose-colored granite). To the right, TWO GRAVEDIGGERS *in gray-blue blouses and trousers of the same color are working, waist-deep in a freshly dug grave. They toss out dirt of the color indicated above. They wear small, round, black caps on their heads. In the middle of the stage, near one of the rocks, stands* MANFRED, COUNT GIERS. *He has long hair and quite a long beard and mustache. No hat. He is wearing the same kind of blouse as the* GRAVEDIGGERS, *fastened around the waist by a black belt with a large gold buckle. Wide crimson pants, but in a color a bit more brick-red than the earth. Black patent-leather shoes with violet pompons. His face is turned toward the audience. He is leaning on a tall black cane with a gold knob.*

GRAVEDIGGER I (*stops digging*):   Look here, sir. Tell the truth now; what's this grave all about?

GIERS: I'm paying you twice as much as you usually get for cemetery work, aren't I? What's the rest of it to you?

GRAVEDIGGER I: All right—but what about this land? Is it yours or isn't it? We don't want no trouble over it later on.

GIERS: I can tell you who I am, my fine conscientious fellow. The land is mine, and so is most of the land on the outskirts of the city.

GRAVEDIGGER I: Hold on there, sir! You're an honest-to-god madman. Maybe you're even the Prince himself, our gracious sovereign?

GIERS: Stop bothering me and dig.

GRAVEDIGGER II *keeps on digging, not paying any attention to this conversation.*

GRAVEDIGGER I: Listen, the times are past when even a genuine great lord could get a common man to stop bothering him so easily. Tell us, or we don't dig no more.

GIERS (*grudgingly pulls a piece of paper from under his blouse, goes over to the grave and hands it to the* GRAVEDIGGER *to read*):   Here, you— take this! Read it, if you know how.

GRAVEDIGGER I (*puts on round glasses and reads with difficulty in the dusk*):   "Manfred, Count Giers, Colonel, chief military judge." (*Gives the paper back to* GIERS *indifferently.*)   If it's like you say, OK. (*He goes back to his digging.*)

GRAVEDIGGER II (LOPAK) (*digging*): I understand you, Colonel, sir. I write poems. Actually they write themselves. (*Stops digging.*) You know, it's strange, but I'm totally unable to figure out how those poems pop into my head. Take this one, for example. (*Recites.*)
>   Oh you, imperceptibly little facts,
>   In the Infinity of black desire,
>   Oh, how paltry are all the acts,
>   Of those who swagger, necks buried in the mire . . .

GIERS: Keep on digging!   Nobody asked you for any of your poems! (*Violently.*) Dig! Dig faster! It's going to be dawn any minute now, and that'll be the end of it anyhow.

LOPAK: All right, all right. Just tell me; what do you want this grave for, Colonel, sir?

GIERS (*impatiently*): I've told you a thousand times—I'm an old man with one foot in the grave. I want to have a grave so I can put one foot in it and meditate. That's all.

LOPAK: Yes, but . . .

GIERS (*menacingly, hitting the rock with his cane*):   That's enough stupid questions! I said: dig, and quit shooting off your mouth. Leave me alone.

GRAVEDIGGER I: Leave him alone. There's nothing you can do with him.

He's a madman and that's all there is to it.

LOPAK: Or he's pretending to be a madman, so as to get his own way easier. I know the type.

GRAVEDIGGER I: Quiet! I tell you . . .

They both dig. A pause. From the left two SOLDIERS *of the guard carry in* PLASMONICK BLÖDESTAUG *on a stretcher; he is wearing a long yellowish-gray coat.*

PLASMONICK: Good morning, Colonel. Any new developments?

The SOLDIERS *set the stretcher on the ground to the left and stand at attention. They have their rifles slung over their shoulders.*

GIERS: At ease!

The SOLDIERS *go limp.*

PLASMONICK: Colonel, why don't you answer? Why do you torment an innocent human being?

GIERS (*ironically*): Human being! You are an officer in the reserves and on top of that you're suspected of spying. That's called a human being! Ha!

PLASMONICK: I'm an ex-officer in the Guards. I'm a true nobleman exempted from military service because of consumption. I'm going to die soon. And you still keep on torturing me so in the last hours of my life!

GIERS: If you've got TB, stay home, and don't have them cart you around the countryside at night.

PLASMONICK: I can't, I can't stay home doing nothing. I have visions and I'm not able to work. You won't even let me finish my last paintings before I die!

GIERS (*ironically*): What a great pity! I should say so! So much the better if there's less of that garbage.

PLASMONICK: It's cruel and inhuman treatment of an innocent person! That letter can be explained in a totally different way . . .

GIERS: Shut up! Or I'll lock you up tight till the end of the investigation! No exercise or workshop—just a dank hole—understand?

A pause. PLASMONICK *sighs. The* GRAVEDIGGERS *dig in silence.*

PLASMONICK: If that were my only misfortune! But I'm also involved in an unhappy love affair, I've got TB, I'm suspected of spying, and I can't complete my latest paintings. Oh—it's all too much !

GIERS (*banging his cane on the ground*): Are you going to keep on whining?

He stands silently and looks threateningly at PLASMONICK. *From the right, between the grave and the footlights, enter* CLAUDESTINA DE MONTREUIL, *wearing a gray suit and a little gray cap. A paint box in her hand.*

CLAUDESTINA (*to* GRAVEDIGGER II): Is this where it is, Mr. Lopak? It really is a lovely place.

LOPAK: This way, Miss. The only bright spot in this cursed boring landscape of ours.

GIERS: Who are you?

CLAUDESTINA: I am Claudestina de Montreuil. I'm a painter. (PLASMONICK *raises himself a little on the stretcher, with interest.*) I was looking for a place to paint the dew on cobwebs. You see, I stylize it a little metaphysically, and then . . .

GIERS (*impatiently*): All right, all right—paint anything you like. I don't give a hoot about that. Only don't say anything to anyone about this grave or about any of this. (*Makes a sweeping motion with his hand.*) I don't want all the idiots and good-for-nothings in town spreading gossip about my supposed mental derangement. Do you understand?

CLAUDESTINA: Yes—I think I do. Oh—those pale blue flowers are wonderful! Oh—this earth, the color of clotted blood . . . (*She spreads out her paint box on the rock to the right.*)

GIERS (*to the* GRAVEDIGGERS): Lopak, I told you not to tell anyone, but that fool still couldn't keep his big mouth shut.

LOPAK: Won't happen again. Now I know who you are, and I won't breathe a word to nobody.

GIERS (*with a smile*): In love with that paint slinger? Huh?

LOPAK *starts digging again, without answering.* GIERS *sits down and looks at his watch.*

CLAUDESTINA (*to* PLASMONICK): And what do you do?

PLASMONICK: I'm a painter like you. The only difference is that I'm incapable of doing anything. They're torturing me in the last moments of my life with some hideous business about spying.

GIERS: Oh—now that whining's going to start again! (*To* CLAUDESTINA.) Do all these weak-kneed artists always carry on like this?

CLAUDESTINA (*to* PLASMONICK): Go on. Talking doesn't disturb me in the least.

She begins to paint a bush with light-blue flowers which is growing between PLASMONICK *and her. It becomes lighter and lighter. The glow over the city dies out.*

PLASMONICK: Just imagine. I wrote to my friend, Rosa van der Blaast—you know? the composer—and I've got to confess to you that I've been in love with her for two year, and unhappily at that—as I was saying, I wrote a letter thanking her for the money she gave me for doing certain sketches. I didn't think that for artists there was anything at all wrong in accepting such a slight amount, some ten thousand gryblers . . .

GIERS: That's hideous! I can't listen to this! Spy money! Ha!

CLAUDESTINA (*to* PLASMONICK): Go on—I'm listening.

PLASMONICK: But—just imagine, Rosa is suspected of spying. My letter was intercepted—I haven't been out of the house, I've been sick . . .

GIERS: At least if he were healthy! But he's sick!! I can't stand sick people. If I could, I'd tear down all the hospitals. Let the bastards all die off!

CLAUDESTINA (*to* GIERS): Don't interrupt. (*To* PLASMONICK.) Well, what happened then?

PLASMONICK: So now I'm suspected of belonging to a spy ring, and what's worse, they say Rosa's lover is the chief spy . . .

GIERS (*jumping up*): Shut up! Or off to the hole with you! (*A pause.*)

CLAUDESTINA (*pointing at* GIERS): Who is that gentleman?

PLASMONICK (*in a weak voice*): That's Colonel Giers—president of the Military Tribunal.

CLAUDESTINA: Aha—well, let's talk about something else. I'm very sorry for you. And what about your paintings?

PLASMONICK: They were sketches. You know—I created a certain theory; actually I didn't, my father did. But I'm the one who's putting it into practice . . .

GIERS (*keeps pulling at his beard*): A little discussion about art is about to begin. Oh—to hell with you and your art! (*To the* SOLDIERS.) You can sit down.

The SOLDIERS *sit down on the left.* GIERS *lights his pipe.*

PLASMONICK: You see, it's a question of expressing the metaphysical strangeness of Existence in purely formal constructions directly through the harmony of colors utilized in certain compositions . . .

CLAUDESTINA (*jumping up*): So you're Blödestaug! Plasmonick Blödestaug! I know your father's theory. It's brilliant in its own way. But I don't agree with it.

PLASMONICK: And what are you trying to accomplish?

CLAUDESTINA: I paint the wonders of nature, from the point of view of insects, frogs, and other little creatures. Still, I don't paint them as they really are, but in the light of my metaphysical spiritual outlook. For me *form*, in your father's sense of the word, doesn't exist.

PLASMONICK: It's strange, I haven't heard anything about you. Let's talk some more. Then I can forget at least for a moment the frightful situation I'm in. Physical pain and theoretical discussions are my only pleasures—then I don't think about the reality of my life . . .

GIERS: Stop that whining! I can't stand it . . .

CLAUDESTINA: You see, I understand it, but it's impossible in actual practice. I don't believe that metaphysical feelings can be expressed in pure constructions. That would only be another kind of sensual pleasure. I'm concerned with the spiritual . . .

PLASMONICK: Just how do you bring it out? I don't see any place for the spiritual in a painting. In a painting conceived formally.

CLAUDESTINA: It's *there!* It's in the conception of things seen from a certain standpoint. It comes out in an absolutely down-to-earth way.

PLASMONICK: Why, for instance, should the point of view of a field bug give it? Besides, they're such tiny little creatures, we don't know how they see nature.

CLAUDESTINA: You don't understand me. You can paint anything this way, even a spider web from the fly's point of view, from a purely hypothetical point of view. What counts is the inner approach whereby everything becomes transformed and I bring out this transformation in the finished painting.

PLASMONICK: So it's a kind of trance? A kind of metaphysical ecstasy?

CLAUDESTINA: Yes—something like that. Now I have to stop talking; I feel *it* coming on. (*She starts to paint.*)

GIERS (*gets up and stretches*): Oh—how boring all this is—how deadly boring!

PLASMONICK: That's not true, Colonel! Basically it's over these things, and not just over trade and industry, that people chop one another to pieces. At the bottom of everything there are only two values: art and religion, which for us nowadays means philosophy.

GIERS (*shaking the ash out of his pipe*): Don't get excited. That's a lot of bunk. (*Listens intently.*) I think someone's coming on horseback. Who in hell can it be now?

The sound of a horse's hooves. CLAUDESTINA *paints in a trance. The* GRAVEDIGGERS *keep on working, furiously. It grows lighter and lighter.*

PLASMONICK: Oh! When will my tortures end!

GIERS *motions to him to be quiet. Enter from the left* PRINCE PADOVAL DE GRIFUELLHES. *He is dressed in a riding costume, a long coat, and a sports cap. He has a whip in his hand.* GIERS *turns his back to him.*

PADOVAL: Hullo! What a large gathering. Aha—the gravediggers are here. Fine. You're the famous Plasmonick, aren't you? Very glad to meet you, but for the moment let's keep our distance. That lady's in a trance—I won't disturb her. But that one! Who can that be? Hey! My good man, turn around!

GIERS *turns around.*

GIERS: Yes, Your Highness.

PADOVAL: What's this? Then it's true, Colonel, you're the one they're digging this grave for way out here?

GIERS: That's right, Your Highness.

PADOVAL: You picked a fine spot. I've been wandering around in circles for an hour and couldn't find it.

GIERS: But who told you it was here, Prince?

PADOVAL: Who but your former love, Baroness Ragnock. And I found out something else even more interesting from her.

GIERS: Could that be it? (*He points to the old* GRAVEDIGGER.)

PADOVAL: It could indeed. (*He goes over to* GRAVEDIGGER I.)

GIERS (*raising both fists on high. A pipe clenched in his right hand*): Oh, these women, these women! Wretched busybodies! (*Sits down helplessly.*) The last place for significant reflections on death has been forever defiled.

PADOVAL (*to* GRAVEDIGGER I, *in a totally indifferent tone of voice*): Listen, my good man: do you know who you are?

GRAVEDIGGER I: Are you kidding?! I've been a gravedigger for forty years, and my name is Virieux.

PADOVAL: Well, of course, that's who you are and who you've always been. Still, life is full of such strange coincidences that without changing at all, you can become someone entirely different. It happened to me two hours ago. I did a small service for a certain elderly lady. She wanted to return the favor. "I'm bored, hellishly bored," I tell her, "I'd like to be someone entirely different." "You really want to?" she asks me. "Yes." "Swear it." "Fine," I say, "just as long as it's quick." Then, just imagine, she told me that one of the men digging the grave for that gentleman (*points to* GIERS) is my father.

GRAVEDIGGER I: Well, so what? Think I don't have more than my share of sons like that all over the world? I don't even know for sure if they *are* mine.

PADOVAL (*with a certain impatience*): Well, all right, but for me it's a very important event. It radically changes my attitude toward life: it's exactly what I was waiting for.

GRAVEDIGGER I: And just who are you, sir, that it's changed you so much, my son? I'll bet you spend your days behind the counter in a shop somewhere or in some branch post office. What of it?

GIERS: He's sized him up. A shrewd customer. (*To* GRAVEDIGGER I.) You don't know who you're talking to, pop. If the crown prince dies, he's next in line for the throne: that's the Prince himself in person.

GRAVEDIGGER I. Well, what of it? I ask you. He can be my son if he wants to so bad. He won't make me king; a cabinet minister's probably the most I'll be.

GIERS: It's a waste of breath talking to people like that. Nothing makes any impression on scum like that, not even finding out they were descended from the Titans or gave birth to all the stars in the Milky Way.
(GRAVEDIGGER I *crawls out of the grave.*)

PADOVAL (*who has been standing biting the knob of his whip*): You know what, Colonel, I'm really furious at that old hag for telling me that. Last night I thought it was amusing, but now it's completely spoiled my good humor.

GRAVEDIGGER I: Well, Mr. Jeers—our work's done for today. Crawl out, Lopak; we're going to go get some sleep. The sun's going to rise any minute. (GRAVEDIGGER II *crawls out of the grave.*)

PADOVAL: Listen, old boy: did you know that the woman you treated so nicely at the cemetery then was my mother? You know—by my father's grave. My father hadn't had any children for twelve years, and then . . .

GRAVEDIGGER I (*angrily*): Will you quit pestering me, Prince! I don't know, and I don't remember.

PADOVAL: But I was told so by that woman who heard it all herself from behind the wall. Only she was so frightened she fainted and . . .

GRAVEDIGGER I: I'm telling you, Highness: don't lower yourself just for the fun of it. The time will come for all of us at the last judgment or even right here. But for the time being, Prince, if you want to, well, give me some money to square things, but why stir up the past? Right?

PADOVAL (*embarrassed*): But I don't have any money with me.

GRAVEDIGGER I: When you set out to find your long-lost father, you should at least have thought about having something to give him.

GIERS: How much, Your Highness? I'll lend it to you.

PADOVAL: Well, about ten thousand gryblers.

PLASMONICK. The exact amount I'm atoning for with my whole life . . .

GIERS (*motions to him to be quiet*): Quiet! Someone's coming. (*On the horizon, which is slightly elevated in a gentle slope, the silhouette of an approaching carriage drawn by two black horses is seen. The carriage passes from right to left.*) Here, Prince. (*Gives* PADOVAL *a roll of bills.*) Who in holy hell could be coming here now? A regular human avalanche is crashing down on my poor grave.

PADOVAL *takes the bills and gives them to the* GRAVEDIGGER.

PADOVAL: Here, take this, my good man, and now let's forget about this unfortunate incident. (*To* GIERS.) All this has left me feeling horribly disgusted.

GIERS: But, my Prince, I've known about this for years and years, but I didn't say anything, since I knew nothing good could come of it. You've got to forget about it.

They listen intently. The carriage turns and goes behind the mound. The creaking of the wheels grows louder and louder.

PADOVAL: My former direction in life has been destroyed, but I haven't been given a new one. I don't know how to start all over again.

GRAVEDIGGER I: My son, I'm going to give you a bit of advice: get to work starting right now. Think I'm going to stop digging graves? (*The sun rises from the left and bathes the stage in orange light. CLAUDESTINA awakes from her trance and stops painting. She sits totally still.*) No— I'll be what I am till the end of my days. You won't get away from yourself, even if you happened to find out you're the son of Beelzebub himself.

PADOVAL (*lost in thought, bites the knob of his whip. The creaking of the carriage wheels can be heard nearby, to the left*): Yes—that's what's really disastrous. I found that out today. (*Shakes hands with the* GRAVEDIGGER.) Thanks, father, and we won't see each other anymore.

GRAVEDIGGER I: That's not even necessary. Why don't we get drunk together today—and to hell with everything.

From the left the following characters rush in: the PRINCESS, *wearing black, with a lace scarf over her gray hair, and the* BARONESS, *wearing violet and a black hat.*

PRINCESS: My Padoval! At last! Oh, that awful Baroness! This is terrible! Those awful rumors! (*Points to the* GRAVEDIGGER.) He's the one! He's the one!!

GRAVEDIGGER I *goes out to the right without saying a word. First he tries to pull* LOPAK *by the sleeve, but* LOPAK *resists and stays where he is.*

PADOVAL: Well, what of it, mother? No need to get carried away. Nothing bad has happened. I must say, all in all, I'm even glad. Sometimes something happens that seems completely senseless at the time, but then, years later, we see that it all had a hidden meaning, and that it's all very deep.

PRINCESS (*calmed down*): Is that really so, my son? You haven't suffered a nervous shock, have you?

PADOVAL (*gloomily*): When you're the son of a tough old bird like my father, it's not so easy to have your nerves shocked. He's old as a boot, and just look at that hole he's dug. And at night too. At *night!* It's incredible!

BARONESS (*to the* PRINCESS): He was bored, Your Highness, bored to death. I had to think up something to entertain him.

PRINCESS: It's all right now, my dear. As long as Padoval is happy, I don't ask for anything more. (*To her son.*) But you won't think badly of me?

PADOVAL: Oh, you know me, mother. "Never let anything surprise you"— that's my motto. Although I was a bit surprised today. Oh—now I see that if I ever go crazy, it'll come from your side of the family, mother. (*He hugs and kisses her.*)

PRINCESS: Oh, that Giers—what a character. Still thinking about death, Colonel?

GIERS: Yes, Your Highness. I'm an old man with one foot in the grave; please don't forget that.

PRINCESS: Yes, yes. I know about your obsession and I respect it.

GIERS: I'm attempting to become so familiar with death that the thought of it won't keep me from carrying out last things as the end of life approaches.

PRINCESS (*not listening*): And just who is that young lady? (*Points to* CLAUDESTINA; *to* PLASMONICK.) I've heard about you. It's your fault that my poor Rosa is suspected of spying.

PLASMONICK (*suddenly jumping up from the stretcher*): Yes, yes—dear Rosa! So dear that Your Highness refused to give her a modest grant for the construction of her new instruments. The devil only knows how she was supposed to get the money to do it, and now she's suspected of spying, because she can't explain the source of her income. And *I'm* suspected too, since I took that stupid ten thousand from her.

GIERS: That's just the point. Not another word! (*Trying to change the subject.*) That young lady is a painter. She creates metaphysical mysteries from the point of view of field bugs

They all go over to CLAUDESTINA, *who gets up. The* PRINCESS *and the* BARONESS *look through their face-à-main.*

PRINCESS: Everyone has his little faults. I know I'm stingy, but . . . (*Glances at* CLAUDESTINA's *picture.*) Why, that's just marvelous . . .

Two GRIZZLOVIKS *appear from the right.* LOPAK *motions to them to sit down. They sit on the grass.*

GIERS (*looking at the picture*): It certainly is. I don't know much about painting, but that's just magnificent.

BARONESS: Oh—that spider web! And those drops of morning dew! It's lovely!

PLASMONICK (*coming over*): It's a sentimental interpretation of nature without any value whatsoever.

PADOVAL: I don't agree with you. You're obviously the product of your father's theory: metaphysical construction of forms or something of that sort. Ha! Ha!

CLAUDESTINA: Don't laugh, Prince. Doctor Blödestaug is right too, but in a completely different dimension.

PADOVAL: Forget about all those Blödestaugs! Perhaps you'd like to come back with us in our carriage and have breakfast at the palace? I think mother is going to make you court painter. (*To the* PRINCESS.) Right, mother?

PRINCESS: Yes—it's lovely. But don't you see: we've got to consider the costs. But please come along with us.

Three more GRIZZLOVIKS *appear at the left.* LOPAK *motions to them. They sit down on the grass.*

PLASMONICK: Lucky people! They ride, they walk, they paint. But what about me? All because of that accursed letter! (*To* PADOVAL.) Prince, I hope Your Highness believes me: I am innocent. Please intercede for me.

PADOVAL (*reluctantly*): Possibly. Possibly. I'm not committing myself to anything. The investigation will clear it up. (*To the ladies.*) Well, let's go. Nothing else significant is going to happen now. (*Notices the* GRIZZLOVIKS.) And just who are those people?

LOPAK: They're the workers laying pipes to drain the swamps, Your Highness.

PADOVAL: Aha. (*To* GIERS.) Well, what are you planning to do, Colonel?

GIERS: I'm staying. A moment for meditation, and then I'm going to walk home.

PRINCESS: The ghosts of those he condemned to death are tormenting him, the way they did Richard III. Right, Colonel? Good-bye, good-bye!

The BARONESS *offers her arm to the* PRINCESS; PADOVAL *offers his to*

CLAUDESTINA. *They go out to the left.*   PLASMONICK *gets back on the stretcher; the soldiers carry him out, following the others.*

GIERS: *Dis donc,* Lopak: what are those people sitting there for? I don't want to be bothered.

LOPAK *comes quickly over to him.*

LOPAK (*mysteriously*):   Colonel, sir: they're *Grizzloviks.* I arranged to meet them in secret, here by the grave, since it's the only clearly marked spot in this wasteland. I thought everyone would have gone off home before the sun came up.

GIERS (*amazed*):   Grizzloviks?! So you're one too?! . . .

LOPAK: That's right. Colonel, pretend to be somebody else. I'm taking a chance, but I believe you'll come over to our side, Colonel.

GIERS: Oh—this is interesting! You want to convert me? I don't know if I'll stay, but thanks anyhow. (*Grasps him by the shoulder.*)   This is a very significant moment in my life. Now I can stop meditating on death, but I'm not guaranteeing anything. I might become your real enemy.

LOPAK: For the time being, pretend to be somebody else. The situation's very complicated. We'll clear it up later on. Oh—here comes our president, Baron Buffadero. (*From the left enter* TZINGAR, *disguised as a worker, with three* GRIZZLOVIKS. TZINGAR *stops.*)

TZINGAR (*pointing to* GIERS): Who's that?

LOPAK: A new member, Baron. A candidate for conversion.

The five remaining GRIZZLOVIKS *encircle them as they talk and close in on them.*

TZINGAR: Fine. (*To* GIERS.) Do you know what our goals are? But—but where do I know you from? I have the impression I've seen you somewhere before in uniform.

GIERS: It's possible we met somewhere. But I don't think I was in uniform. You've got it mixed up.

TZINGAR: Quite possibly. It doesn't matter. Our goal is the replacement of temporal power by ecclesiastical power. We'll be the priests, in keeping with the system of beliefs devised by Joachim Grizzelov, our prophet. The only difference is that he believed in some kind of crypto-pantheism, whereas we won't believe in anything. A certain form of mealy-mouthed democracy under the guise of a cult. Something along the line of the Egyptian priests. The people howl for a new religion—the fact that theosophical nonsense has so many followers proves it. We've got to get it all under our control and spread it throughout society. Understand?

GIERS: Yes, but what's the new system of government going to be? The form of worship itself doesn't much concern me, even though in a certain sense I'm a mystic.

TZINGAR: The system of government? What the present brand of pseudo-mealy-mouthed democracy does unintentionally, we'll do systematically, in full consciousness, without getting carried away, and the trial-and-error method will show us what further stages of development there should be. Point number one: no extrapolations. All that's needed is to create a new kind of state run by priests. What other churches weren't successful in doing because of their real faith and the compromises made with that faith, we'll do consciously as a pragmatic and systematic hoax . . .

GIERS: Well, all right, but what about the system of government?

TZINGAR: What a thick skull you've got, Mister Unknown. I keep telling you: a pseudo-democratic system of government without any parliamentary bluffing. We've got to give the labor unions a true fictitious religion, not a substitute like the myth of a general strike. Believe me, people today are far more inclined to adopt any old belief than the totem worshipers in New Guinea. There must be belief—even if we have to resort to spiritualism and table-tipping.

GIERS: I think I'm beginning to understand.

TZINGAR: Well—heaven be praised. Sit down. (*To the others.*) And you too, gentlemen! In the name of Joachim Grizzelov, *we are about to begin.* I declare the meeting open.

ACT TWO

ROSA VAN DER BLAAST's *salon. Dim, spectrally pure green light from above. A grand piano in the left-hand corner. A harp next to it. Lots of musical instruments on the walls. Portraits of great musicians. Sofas to the left and right. A single small sofa in the middle of the stage. Lots of pillows. The prevailing colors are ultramarine blue and black. Occasional patches of violet and dark red. Doors to the left and center, the latter hung with an emerald curtain. To the right, next to the sofa, a black cabinet. In the right-hand corner a green canopy over a large black sofa. Near the small sofa in the middle of the room a little table with equipment for tea.* ROSA, *wearing a light green dress, sits on the small sofa in the middle of the room holding* SOPHIE *in her arms;* SOPHIE *is wearing a blue dress with dark-violet sashes. A pause. From the left enter a* MAID, *dressed in green.*

MAID: The Baron de Buffadero.

ROSA (*jumping up*): Show him in. (*To* SOPHIE.) Sophie, go and play in the Cavern of Evil. (SOPHIE *runs over to the sofa to the right and plays with her dolls there, not paying attention to anything else until further notice. Enter* TZINGAR *wearing a black frock coat.*) Why are you so late? Don't you realize I can't live without you? (*She throws herself into his arms.*)

TZINGAR: Now, don't get so excited, my dear.

ROSA: I was so upset I tore my last prelude into pieces out of sheer nervousness—you know, the one in A-sharp that I dedicated to you. I'll have to write it all over again. And on top of that, there's that accusation about spying! That conspiracy! Couldn't you at least take those papers away? I'm so afraid.

TZINGAR: I'll take it all away today. But first sit down and listen to me carefully. This is the ultimate test of your attachment to me. In the first place. I had a talk with Giers yesterday; he's joined the Grizzloviks.

ROSA: How did you persuade him?

They sit down at the little table in the middle of the room.

TZINGAR: Only because I didn't know who I was talking to. It all came out later. The next piece of news is worse. The suspicions about your belonging to a spy ring are all the more justified since I'm the chief spy for the land of the Macerbators. I had to do it to get money for higher goals.

ROSA *listens to him stupefied; then she covers her face with her hands and bends her head down to her knees.*

ROSA: You're cruel to wait till now to tell me. Now that you've got me so completely in your clutches I'm ready to commit any crime for you. Oh, you horrid man!

TZINGAR: That means you haven't stopped loving me?

ROSA: No—even if it means damnation, I'll be yours till death. You and music. Oh—and those new instruments of mine, and the possibility of having my Fifth Symphony performed—does it all come from the same sources?

TZINGAR: Exactly the same. No escaping it. Do you love me or don't you?

ROSA: Yes, yes—only now I'm so terribly torn . . . I don't know anything anymore . . . Oh—what a terrible man you are, Joseph! But maybe that's why I love you so.

TZINGAR *strokes her head.*

TZINGAR: I'll tell you something to console you: I sold them documents that are practically worthless, but in hopes of getting better things in the future, they paid me handsomely. From now on—now that Giers has come over to our side and I'm more sure of myself—I want to stop being a spy. That's why I'm telling you this. I couldn't bear to have this lie constantly between us. Understand: there's swinishness and there's swinishness. Telling lies to you all my life isn't the sort I could commit.

The MAID *runs in.*

MAID: Her Highness has arrived, ma'am. The whole house is surrounded by the police. They're not letting anyone out. You can get in, but not out.

TZINGAR *gets up suddenly, but doesn't lose his presence of mind. The* MAID *goes out.*

ROSA: Oh, God, God! What'll we do?!

TZINGAR *runs quickly toward the center door. Voices are heard to the left.*

TZINGAR (*at the door, halfway through the green curtain*): Where are those papers?

ROSA: I just put them in that cabinet today. (*Points to the right.* TZINGAR *looks out from behind the curtain and nods toward the cabinet;* ROSA *does likewise. The* PRINCESS, *the* BARONESS, *and* GIERS *appear at the door to the left.*)   Too late!! (TZINGAR *disappears behind the curtain without being seen.* GIERS *has his beard shaved off and his hair cut. A dark-blue uniform with red facings.*)

PRINCESS (*who has heard the last exclamation*): What's too late, my child?

ROSA: Oh—it's nothing . . . I'm so nervous.   Excuse me, Your Highness. (*She greets them all.*)

PRINCESS: Don't be afraid, my dearest. I succeeded in persuading Giers to search your house today. Everything will be brought out into the open and finished with once and for all. (*To* GIERS.) Colonel, I always told you that Rosa's secret lover was just a myth. (*To* ROSA.) He didn't want to search your house now, "to give the trap a bigger snap," as he put it. Today he finally decided to act like a human being.

GIERS: But I've already been informed that someone came in here and he hasn't left yet. We'll see, we'll see! It's not known what he looks like, since his face was hidden by his coat collar. Quite tall, with broad shoulders. Heh, heh!

ROSA: But, Colonel . . .

GIERS: All right, we'll see.

The PRINCESS *sits down at the little table with her right profile to the audience.*

PRINCESS: Please, sit down, all of you. I'm so sure of my Rosa I'm not afraid of anything. I came along for the search to make you feel more secure, dearest.

They sit down.

ROSA (*vaguely*): Yes . . . That is . . . I thank you with all my heart, Your Highness. (*To* SOPHIE *at the right*.) Sophie! Come here and kiss her Highness's hand. (SOPHIE *runs over quickly, kisses the* PRINCESS*'s hand, and immediately goes back to her toys*.) Your Highness will excuse me, I've got to take care of something over here. (*She goes to the right, toward the cabinet*.)

GIERS (*getting up*): Perhaps her Highness will excuse you, but I won't. Please take a seat.

ROSA: Sophie, get those things out of that cabinet and take them into the bedroom.

SOPHIE *abandons her toys reluctantly.*

GIERS: Sophie! Keep on playing! (*Sophie goes back to her dolls*.) Ho! Ho! Suspicious things are starting to happen here! Please sit down. Mr. Plasmonick will be coming here right away for the confrontation. (*He rings. The* MAID *runs in*.) Ask Lieutenant Flowers and the two gendarmes to come in.

The MAID *goes out.* ROSA *sits down at the little table, showing signs of extreme nervousness.*

PRINCESS (*sipping her tea*): Don't be afraid, dear. Nothing bad's going to happen. Everything's still going to turn out all right.

GIERS: We'll see, we'll see. (*Enter* FLOWERS *and the* TWO GENDARMES, *their hats on.* FLOWERS *in the same uniform as* GIERS. *Only their epaulets are different. They are followed by* TWO GUARDS *who lead in* PLASMONICK.) Make a search of all the rooms.

The LIEUTENANT *and the* GENDARMES *begin their search in the living room.*

ROSA (*getting up*):   Look what's happening, Mr. Plasmonick; isn't this just horrible—they're searching *my* house.

PLASMONICK (*coldly, ironically*):   I don't see anything strange about that. We're both very suspicious characters. But what about your secret lover? Has he been found yet? (*To* GIERS.) I assume I can talk about everything now?

GIERS: Why, go ahead, talk all you want. (*He lights a cigarette and looks at the men conducting the search.*)

ROSA   (*to* PLASMONICK, *while watching the men searching, out of the corner of her eye, with terrible anxiety*):   So you're against me too! Everyone and everything has conspired against me! (*She falls into the armchair.*)

PLASMONICK (*speaks coldly and ironically, still standing between the* TWO GUARDS *to the left*): Unhappy love either changes to tender feelings or it grows more and more violent until it finally turns to hatred. The latter case applies to me. I don't know what will happen—I don't even have the slightest inkling—but I feel such terrible tension in my unconscious will that I think I could blow this house sky-high.

GIERS: Don't be ridiculous, Mr. Blödestaug. This isn't the proper moment.

ROSA: Oh, God, God!

The PRINCESS *starts to watch with cool curiosity, without a trace of her former sympathetic attitude.*

PRINCESS: Really—This is beginning to get interesting.

PLASMONICK: I feel the denouement's about to take place. I'm going to act the way the secret voice of higher consciousness tells me to.

At this moment LIEUTENANT FLOWERS *breaks open the black cabinet on the right and pulls out a bundle of papers.*

FLOWERS: *Ça y est, mon Colonel.* I found them. The secret documents of the Grizzlovik conspiracy.

GIERS *goes over to him.*

GIERS (*taking the papers*): This is interesting. (*Skims through them.*) Signed Baron de Buffadero. (*To* FLOWERS.) Is that all?

FLOWERS (*rummaging through the cabinet*): Oh—there's another packet.

He gives it to GIERS, *who feverishly undoes the packet and becomes deeply engrossed in reading.*

ROSA (*jumping up*): Colonel! Those are my love letters! You have no right to look at them.

GIERS: Stay where you are. (*A* GENDARME *goes over to* ROSA.)   Nice love letters! Between you and the northern fortress of Centuria? (*Waving a map at her.*)   Between you and the fortress in Croissantia on the Kamur Delta?   At last!   Flowers, you hold onto this, and give me the Grizzlovites' papers to look over.

They exchange papers. ROSA *sits inertly on the couch.* SOPHIE *keeps on playing.* *The* PRINCESS *observes the situation through her* face-à-main. PLASMONICK *suddenly changes into a completely different person. With a firm step, his head held high, he goes over to the* COLONEL *and stands at attention, even though he's dressed as a civilian, in a gray suit.*

PLASMONICK: Colonel, sir, reporting for duty. Reserve Lieutenant Blödestaug, of the grenadiers bodyguard to His Highness, Prince Peter. Conclusive evidence, but on one condition.

Without realizing it, GIERS *stands at attention too.*

GIERS: What is it?

PLASMONICK: When you put us in prison, me and her (*he points to* ROSA), I must have a guarantee that we'll be put in the same cell.

A pause. The PRINCESS *bursts out in screeches of laughter. The* BARONESS *accompanies her with a high-pitched squeal.*

GIERS: What a wild idea! And how can that be arranged?

PLASMONICK: Colonel, I'm warning you, although all weapons have been taken away from me, I still have this (*takes a small object out of his vest pocket*), a nicely mounted razor blade. Colonel, if you don't promise me this minute, I'll slit my throat on the spot and you won't find out anything. *Ever!* The thread that could unravel this mystery breaks with me. Come to a quick decision.

GIERS (*hesitating*):   All right—I agree. As long as it doesn't involve your personal freedom.

PLASMONICK: It doesn't. Your word as an officer?

GIERS: My word as an officer.

PLASMONICK: All right. (*Solemnly.*) *I* am the chief spy for the land of the Macerbators. Those papers belong to me. Rosa van der Blaast is my accomplice.

ROSA *sits dumbfounded on the couch.*

GIERS: Hullo! Oh, that's marvelous! Now I understand! But why didn't you do this earlier?

PLASMONICK (*breathing heavily*): I couldn't make up my mind to. Now it's all over. I'm on the other side.

GIERS   (*to* FLOWERS):   Lieutenant, telephone for Major Daybell immediately!

FLOWERS: At your orders, sir. (*He goes out to the left.*)

ROSA (*who until now has been sitting as if turned to stone, staring wide-eyed straight ahead, jumps up and cries out*): It's not true!

GIERS (*coolly*):   Please keep calm. The principal defendant has admitted his guilt.

ROSA *goes limp again after a terrible struggle with herself and falls on the couch. The curtain over the center door is raised, and* TZINGAR *comes out from behind it, completely self-possessed.*

GIERS   (*turning around. The others turn around too*): Hullo! Still more surprises! Baron de Buffadero. What are you doing here?

Heading for the COLONEL, TZINGAR *squeezes* ROSA*'s arm as he passes by her.* ROSA *cries out in pain.*

ROSA: Oh!!!

TZINGAR   (*hypnotizing her by looking her directly in the face*): Shut up, you wretch!! You don't have the right to breathe a single word. I didn't know what kind of house I'd been visiting. My good name was jeopardized at every moment. (*Goes over to the* COLONEL; PLASMONICK *stands petrified.*) Good evening, Colonel. (*He offers* GIERS *his hand;* GIERS *shakes it mechanically.* ROSA *sits, completely reduced to jelly.*)

GIERS: But how did you get in here, Mr. Buffadero?

TZINGAR: I came in the back way.

GIERS: But why the back way?

TZINGAR: Because I felt like it.

GIERS: That's no answer. We're conducting a search here in this nest of spies. Please be more precise in your testimony. I'm here in my official capacity.

PLASMONICK: He's the one! She had a lover! She's been deceiving me for two years, for two long years! But now I've got her. Oh—now she'll be mine, only mine. In hell or in prison—what does it matter? You will keep your word, won't you, Colonel?

GIERS   (*impatiently, turning toward him*): I will, I will. (*To* TZINGAR.) All right—go on, Baron. Your life is at stake—and something else too, you know? Heh, heh!

TZINGAR   (*turns toward* ROSA *and looks at her for a moment*): You slut! (*To the* COLONEL.) I still can't get hold of myself. I was here—Colonel, I can't bring myself to say it. Who is this lady?

He indicates the PRINCESS, *who has been observing the situation continually through her glasses. Completely shattered,* ROSA *goes over to* GIERS *and speaks.*

ROSA: Colonel, he fell in love with my maid. Such a great man to fall so low. She is the personification of everything that's perverse. It's horrible.

GIERS (*to* TZINGAR): Is that true?

TZINGAR (*lugubriously*): Unfortunately—yes, it is. (*He bows his head low.*)

PLASMONICK (*falling on his knees before* ROSA): Then he wasn't your lover? Rosa! This is the most beautiful day of my life. When we're together—you'll have to love me. I'm a different person now. I have tremendous strength within me. I'll even get the best of my sickness.

ROSA (*utterly distracted*): Maybe, maybe. I don't know anything now.

She sits down and covers her face with her hands. Kneeling, PLASMONICK *kisses her limp hand.* TZINGAR *talks in a whisper with the* COLONEL. *Enter old* BLÖDESTAUG, *accompanied by* MAJOR DAYBELL.

BLÖDESTAUG: Plazy, what are you doing here? I've been looking for you all week. I didn't know you were acquainted with this lady. They just told me now. I've been looking for you at all your friends.

PLASMONICK *gets up and rushes over to his father.*

PLASMONICK: Father! Don't judge me. Awful things have been happening. But someday you'll understand me and then you'll forgive me. Someday I'll be completely vindicated.

BLÖDESTAUG (*taking him in his arms*): But what is it? What really happened?

PLASMONICK: I'm a spy. I was a suspect. Now I've confessed. My life is over. Now I'll work exclusively on putting your theory into practice.

BLÖDESTAUG: Oh, God! How horrible!

PLASMONICK: Father, greet Her Highness.

BLÖDESTAUG *turns around, goes over to the* PRINCESS *and kisses her hand.*

PRINCESS (*stroking his hair*):   God is sending you a difficult trial, Mr. Blödestaug.   And me as well.   My darling Rosa is a spy, an espionagette. Yes, that's right—it's frightful!

PLASMONICK: And now everybody listen to me: an artist's life is pure chance. In acting as I have up until now, I have followed the voice of my artistic intuition.   There are artists who by creating produce positive values in life, and there are those who create most significantly by destroying their own lives, and even those of others.

PRINCESS: What a cynical attitude! I'll help you get through this, Mr. Blödestaug.

BLÖDESTAUG *sinks down at her knees. She clasps his head in her hands.*

PLASMONICK: Listen! I've been living in a dreadful state of anguish, but I haven't been able to find any artistic justification for it, I couldn't change it into significant values. Now it's over. My father's theory will truly be put into practice and that's how I'll make amends for this horrible wrong I've done him. If they locked me up all alone, I'd go mad and I wouldn't create anything. With her (*points to* ROSA) I'll accomplish downright diabolical things.   So will she.   I'll metaphysicalize her music. I know I have the strength for it now. I owe it all to Colonel Giers.

GIERS: Maybe something will come of it. I'm not an expert in such matters. For me you're a loathsome reserve officer and a spy—a combination that physically I simply can't stand. The very thought of it makes me sick. (*To* ROSA.)   What have you got to say about that?

ROSA: Oh, Colonel, art before everything. If he accomplishes what he says he's going to, then even prison holds no terrors for me. But by the way, will I be allowed to have a piano?

GIERS: No—certainly not. Absolutely no racket. Any kind of noise in prison is out of the question. Besides, can't you compose without a piano?

ROSA: I can, but I'd rather . . .

GIERS (*suddenly tapping his finger against his forehead*): But, but— Mr.Plasmonick, why write to this lady for money? As a spy you must have had piles of it.

PLASMONICK: That particular day I absolutely had to have ten thousand gryblers. My contact told me that if I didn't give it to him that very day— he'd squeal on me. And the package from the Macerbators was late.

GIERS: Perhaps you'd squeal on your accomplices too? Huh?

PLASMONICK: Don't force me to new heights of swinishness. Isn't it enough as it is?

GIERS: Just one thing more: the papers are signed by a certain Tzingar. What does that mean?

PLASMONICK: Oh, God! How he tortures me! My pseudonym. Tzingar— that's me.

GIERS: Fine—nothing more is needed now. With this one thread we'll be able to unravel the whole mystery. (*To* DAYBELL.) Major, let's get to work.

PLASMONICK: Don't despair, Father—I'm going to do wonderful things. I feel healthy as a bull. (*To* GIERS.) By the way, Colonel, how many years will I get?

GIERS: At least fifteen.

PLASMONICK: That's quite a bit.

GIERS: Yes—but in return for your quick confession I'll see that you get equipment for Swedish gymnastics, even though the regulations make absolutely no such provisions. Still . . .

PRINCE PADOVAL DE GRIFUELLHES *rushes in accompanied by* CLAUDESTINA DE MONTREUIL *and the* TWO GRAVEDIGGERS. *He is wearing a guard's uniform, green with white facings. Except for* CLAUDESTINA, *they are all very drunk.*

GIERS: Attention!! (*All the military stand at attention;* GIERS *goes over to the* PRINCE.)   Your Highness, the spies have been caught. I've saved the state from infamous treason. Plasmonick Blödestaug has freely confessed his guilt himself.

PADOVAL: Very good, very good, old boy. At ease!

GIERS: At ease!!

The military go limp.

PADOVAL (*to the* PRINCESS, *who does not let go of* BLÖDESTAUG): Mother! Mother! Forget that old puppet. Have you fallen in love with that old dodderer in your old age, mother?   But you know what, Mother? Knowing the true facts about one's birth still does count for something. I wonder what kind of look our aristocrats would have on their faces if they knew all the secrets about their origins. As for me—I've started a New Life. My father's a wonderful man! He's a sage! Maybe I'll become a gravedigger too. It'd be worth being one to have such a philosophy of life.

GRAVEDIGGER I: You're getting carried away, my son. I'm an ordinary drunken bum—that's all I am. To you that's a novelty.

PADOVAL: And what's more I've fallen head over heels in love with that lady. (*He points to* CLAUDESTINA.) Mother, she's got to be our court painter and be given a title. Then—I'll marry her.

PRINCESS: Fine, fine, dear boy. Just as long as you're not bored.

BLÖDESTAUG *gets up.*

CLAUDESTINA (*to* BLÖDESTAUG): You're distressed by your son's behavior, aren't you? Professor, I too paint, a little differently perhaps than you'd like, but still there's something to it. Don't lose heart. I'll take your son's place.

BLÖDESTAUG: Fifteen years!! Oh, God, God! And besides, it's all so hideous. He'll be locked up with *her!* (*He points to* ROSA.)

CLAUDESTINA: Fifteen years is nothing.   When he gets out, he'll be forty—five. An ideal age. In the meantime, consider me your daughter, Professor. And anyhow it'll be better for him with her.

BLÖDESTAUG *embraces her.*

PLASMONICK: You can all rest assured that I won't waste my time.

ROSA: But Sophie! I completely forgot about her.

CLAUDESTINA: Your little girl? I'm taking her home with me. I'll have an artificial father and an artificial daughter. I've been so alone the last few years!

PADOVAL: And take me as your artificial husband, Miss Claudestina. I can't live without you.

CLAUDESTINA: I don't know yet. You have too violent a nature, Prince.

PADOVAL: I'll tone it down. Still, I'm very grateful to the Baroness for these revelations. Would it ever have occurred to me before to marry a lady painter? Freedom! What a wonderful thing!! Lopak, old pal, you'll forgive me for taking your love away from you. No matter—you'll find somebody else more suitable.

LOPAK: Right now I'm not concerned with problems of that sort. I have something more important on my mind, Your Highness.

PADOVAL: Most likely poetic nonsense. Well, my friends, let's go—everyone to his proper place.

GIERS: Yes—take the defendants. The trial is tomorrow. (*To the* OFFICERS.) Since there's been a confession, it'll be a mere formality. Let's go.

TZINGAR: Colonel, one more favor, please. I want to say a few words of farewell to Miss van der Blaast.

GIERS: Certainly. (*Laughs.*) Just don't break any of her bones with your conversation. (*To the others.*) All right, my friends—let's get out of this den of horrors.

CLAUDESTINA: Sophie, you're coming with me. Mama's very busy today.

SOPHIE *runs over to her.* CLAUDESTINA *takes her by the hand. The* PRINCESS *leads out* BLÖDESTAUG, *who is unsteady on his feet. They are followed by* CLAUDESTINA *with* SOPHIE, *and then by* PLASMONICK *between the two guards.*

PLASMONICK (*on his way out, to* ROSA): We begin, starting tomorrow night.

ROSA *is silent.* TZINGAR *stands next to her. Both betray frantic impatience.* GIERS *goes out last with the officers and gendarmes. The door closes.* ROSA *and* TZINGAR *talk hurriedly in choked whispers.*

ROSA: Do you love me? Do you understand what I've done for you?

TZINGAR (*embraces her and kisses her on the lips*): I know. You are truly great. Besides, this won't last long. I'll get you out in no time. Once our conspiracy has proved successful.

ROSA: I'll never be his. Do you believe me?

TZINGAR: I'd like to believe you. No matter what. We've got to sacrifice everything for things on a higher plane.

ROSA: I love you. I'll torture him to death in that prison. The low-down snake.

TZINGAR: I enjoy this kind of life. Think how everything hung by a thread. If I hadn't met Giers yesterday, and if he hadn't joined the Grizzloviks, and if that idiot Plasmonick hadn't been in love with you—we'd both have rotted away in prison. What a series of coincidences! Two weeks ago the death penalty was abolished. Ugh—I could have been hanged. And if the death penalty had still existed, that blockhead would never have taken the blame on himself. You know, life is ruled by chance far more than we think it is under normal conditions.

ROSA: But not the life of artists. You'll see what diabolical things I'll compose in *there*. But I don't think you're upset enough by the fact that they're locking me up with him. You don't love me. Remember, if I didn't love you as much as I do, you wouldn't have got out of this either. You don't take that into account at all.

TZINGAR: But I do—believe me, I do. I resign myself to the inevitable, what else can I do? Once our conspiracy has proved successful, the world will be groveling at your feet: new instruments, new music, everything! (*He kisses her.*)

GIERS'S VOICE (*from behind the door*): Come on—hurry up, Baron. (*Opens the door halfway—*GIERS, *that is, not his voice.*)

TZINGAR (*grabs* ROSA *by the arm*): Get going! You goddam dirty swine! Rot in a dank cell!! (*Shoves her brutally toward the door, which* GIERS *opens.*) Because of you I almost lost my good name!

ACT THREE

A large prison cell. Gray walls. A window, with bars facing the audience. Through it can be seen flowering fruit trees, bathed in sunlight, outlined against the blue sky. In the corners two beds covered with gray blankets with yellow stripes. A bolted door to the left. Three plain wooden chairs. To the right an easel with a picture on it, the back turned toward the audience. PLASMONICK *in a gray prison uniform, sits at the easel. On his chest he has a large yellow circle with the number 117 in red. To the right, nearer the audience, about ten canvases turned with their faces to the wall, and still nearer the audience an iron wash basin, over which hangs a huge tank. Beneath the window a table piled high with papers and books To the left, between the footlights and the door, a small table, at which* ROSA *sits, also in a prison uniform. She has the number 118 in red on a yellow circle. She hums something, then writes it down on music paper.* PLASMONICK *paints. A pause.*)

PLASMONICK (*putting down his painting materials and moving away from the easel*):   Rosa, this can't go on any longer. It's three in the afternoon—Tuesday. A week's gone by, and you haven't said a single word to me. Don't you realize I've got enough troubles as it is? I've got to do this cursed portrait of Grizzelov, or else I won't earn enough for extra food for the two of us. Do you understand what it means for me to paint from a photograph, when I want to do something entirely different: finish that composition with those intersecting lines. (ROSA *remains silent.*) Rosa, I beg you, just say one little word. Don't torture me any more. (*Silence.*) Well, damn it all to hell, this has got to stop once and for all! When will you finally understand that I love you to distraction, to the point of utter madness? I've metaphysicalized your music, haven't I? If it hadn't been for me and my theory of art, or rather my father's theory of art, if I hadn't explained it to you—because you've got to admit that with that poor little bird brain of yours you didn't understand a single phrase in my father's books—you'd still be wallowing in disgusting shallow sentimentality. New instruments and new scales wouldn't help in the least—it would be simply a question of musical notation. (ROSA *remains silent and hums.*) Will you say something, or won't you?

ROSA (*without turning around*): Do you want the guards to pour cold water on us again the way they did in March? (*Points to a scar on her forehead.*) Look at that and shut up. Keep on slinging paint at your stupid pictures. Painting is not art. (*She goes on writing.*)

PLASMONICK: Rosa, don't start theoretical discussions, when you know it's really about something totally different.

ROSA (*cynically*): I know—for you all it's really about is tonight, and after that, all the other nights to come.

PLASMONICK: What a horrible cynic you are, Rosa! You absolutely fail to understand what dimension my attachment to you assumes . . .

ROSA: The third undoubtedly. At any rate not the second or the fourth. Ha! Ha! Ha! (*She hums and writes.*)

PLASMONICK: I beg you, this has to end once and for all. I can't stand these secrets coming between us any longer. They're poisoning our life.

ROSA (*gets up, after having drawn two perpendicular lines*): Remember what we swore to each other: never to speak about that. Only on that condition is our life together somehow possible.

PLASMONICK: I can't go on living this way—I simply *can't*.

ROSA: Remember what I told you: that resolving certain things will turn our life into pure hell and we'll have to live apart.

PLASMONICK: But I'm suffering. I can't live without you. The more I'm with you, the more attached I become. You're like Cleopatra: one can never tire of you or get enough of you.

ROSA: Then just be glad you've got me. Remember, if you had been locked up without me for fifteen years, you'd undoubtedly have gone mad and wouldn't even have painted half those blobs. In fourteen years you'll leave here the greatest painter in the country, maybe even in the world. Oh, what a low art painting is! If it weren't for the publicity all this imprisonment is bringing you, you wouldn't even be what you are now.

PLASMONICK: Rosa, please, don't insult my profession. I don't meddle in music at all, except for having metaphysicalized *your* music.

Theoretically I recognize that music has a right to exist.

ROSA (*mimicking him*): "Metaphysicalized," "theoretically!" I can't stand those expressions of yours. There's something about you that reminds me of a pedantic German professor. I'd have come to the same conclusions all by myself even without you. You know what Beethoven said? "Musik ist höhere Offenbarung als jede Religion und Philosophie."

PLASMONICK: Read the introduction to Cennini's treatise on painting, and you'll learn something totally different.

ROSA: No wonder—a painter wrote that.

PLASMONICK: And a musician said that.

ROSA: Oh—it's impossible to discuss anything with you.   In any case, painting is at best nature deformed—nothing more. All those attempts to musicalize painting are nothing but a big lie—you painters will never free yourselves from the objects you paint.

PLASMONICK: Just as music, even the most abstract, will never free itself from human emotions. But neither music nor painting is important— the only important thing is Pure Form . . .

ROSA: "Pure Form!" If you mention that Pure Form of yours one more time, I'll go stark raving mad. I can't stand hearing that expression anymore.

PLASMONICK: But you're concerned with form in music.

ROSA: No—all that's just a means for expressing metaphysical feelings. Music creates feelings that don't exist in real life.

PLASMONICK: A delusion—all feelings can be reduced to a combination of simple qualities.

ROSA: Oh—"qualities!" Another word I hate. You repeat your father's drivel like a parrot. Got an answer for everything—like an automaton.

PLASMONICK: You don't like to discuss things purely dialectically, like women in general and unintelligent men . . .

ROSA: You're not in the least intelligent; you have clever little formulas for everything. You say something and then you start to think it's really so. That's "dried-up drivel," as the old Princess used to say.

PLASMONICK: Yes—your drivel is moist. Some Greek sage claimed that moisture is the essence of Existence. You can use that as your starting point and create a new wet theory. Bergson and other mythomaniacs will help you.

ROSA: Say what you like—I know, because I feel it myself. I feel how what I compose, but don't actually hear, creates another world within me, and that's without even having the work played.

PLASMONICK: You don't have any self-knowledge. That's just faulty introspection.

ROSA: Will you drop that pseudo-scientific jargon of yours once and for all? You paint one of your blobs and at least get more or less what you had in mind, but I only put little circles and dots down on paper. You don't know what torture it is not to be able to hear one's own works.

PLASMONICK (*going over to her*): I know you're miserable. Rosa, don't get so upset. You know how I love you. I took the whole blame on myself . . .

ROSA: Don't say it, don't say anything! It's all petty, hideous, disgusting. Don't come near me. You got me by a trick.

PLASMONICK: But did I really get you? I don't know. Sometimes I think I did, but other times I'm horribly tormented. Rosa—it *can't* go on like this any longer. We quarrel about art, but really an abyss is opening between us because of those secrets. We've got to put an end to that.

ROSA: If you want to put an end to everything with me, then go ahead—just ask me about it!

PLASMONICK. It's not quite so easy to end everything with me. The court sentenced us to prison together. It's not just a question of moving to another room, like in a hotel. It would take a retrial. But what if I go back on my previous testimony? Then your secrets will have to come out in the open.

ROSA: I implore you, be quiet! You torture me more than the executioner could. I want to forget about it. It won't be long now . . . (*She gets hold of herself.*)

PLASMONICK (*suddenly uneasy*): Are you planning to kill yourself?

ROSA: Kill myself? Ha, ha, ha! Why, you idiot . . . (*Gets hold of herself.*) Let's not talk about it.

PLASMONICK: I'd *prefer* not to talk about it. But don't you see it's always there, lurking at the back of all our conversations, of everything that happens to us? It's monstrous!

ROSA: Yes—it *is* monstrous.

PLASMONICK: I keep asking myself the same hellish questions: why didn't you defend yourself after I confessed, and who was the chief spy, and were you his lover?

ROSA: I implore you once more, for God's sake: keep quiet and don't ask any more questions.

PLASMONICK: I've got to tell you something: sometimes—this is comical— I think it was that damned Buffadero, or whatever his name was. That thought haunts me too. (ROSA *remains silent.*) Do you know, the fact that you were perhaps an espionagette yourself doesn't make you any less attractive to me?

ROSA: All of this is so revolting, so disgusting, so petty, that I'm simply suffocated by it all! If you could see how loathsome you are! If you were at least a musician! But a painter! A *painter!* That word alone is capable of poisoning everything.

PLASMONICK (*speaks morosely, sitting down in the chair in the center*): If that's the case, my position is really becoming terrible. Those secrets have created a hatred in you which didn't exist before.

ROSA: There wasn't any hatred, because I wasn't your mistress. I even had a favorable opinion of you, before we became close. Now I hate you, hate you, hate you. Understand? Forever and ever.

PLASMONICK: Then it's all over between us?

ROSA: Why, no, not at all. I can still be your mistress. Your *lover!* Or even your wife. We can have a wedding if you like. I don't care. Just so you know I hate you. Worse still, I despise you.

PLASMONICK (*jumping up*):   No—that I can't bear. I've got to know everything!

ROSA (*laughing*):   And the fourteen years that are still ahead of us? Doesn't that terrify you? Will you be able to endure living with me after what I'm going to tell you?

PLASMONICK: Now I've got to know. If you don't tell me, I'll strangle you. You've got to. Understand?

ROSA: Remember today is visiting day.   Someone may come at any moment. Wouldn't it be better if we didn't get so excited?

PLASMONICK: No, no, no! Answer my questions! Why did you come here with me and not even try to save yourself? Quickly! Answer me!!

ROSA: Because I loved HIM and I still love him and only him, and I wanted to save him.

PLASMONICK (*through clenched teeth*): Who is he?!

ROSA: Joseph Tzingar, the chief spy for the Macerbators.

PLASMONICK (*insanely curious*): Which one was he? Was he the one who . . . ?

ROSA: The one who came out of my bedroom then. He was acting as a Grizzlovik, under the name of Buffadero.

PLASMONICK: That slob! That bastard! And it was for him. . . ! Oh—this has got to come to an end once and for all! It was for him I went to prison, for that scoundrel!

ROSA: Not for him, but for me. You got what you wanted. I was your lover.

PLASMONICK (*hissing*): So he was the one you were getting the money from and *I* was in *his* debt for that ten thousand? Oh—how hideous!

ROSA: Never accept anything from women, remember that and you won't get into such messes.

PLASMONICK: Aaaaaah! What monstrous swinishness! I've plunged from the loftiest heights to the very bottom. I'm completely destroyed.

ROSA: You never were on any heights. He painted a couple of puny pictures and thinks that entitles him to be rotten. You are a miserable, weak little wet noodle. He thought he was a hero!

PLASMONICK: So you never loved me the least little bit? So you didn't even like me? Oh, you . . . !

ROSA: Don't despair too much. I liked you well enough to be your lover when he wasn't around.

PLASMONICK: Oh—and so if I wasn't around, you'd be capable of being the mistress of the guard there who's keeping an eye on us. What kind of a morass have I sunk into!

ROSA: One of your own making. You brought it all on yourself.

PLASMONICK: Now for the first time I see who you are: a hideous espionagette, mistress to a scoundrel.

ROSA: Only now? But just a minute ago you said it didn't make me any less attractive to you—the first of those things, not the second. He wasn't a scoundrel—he had to have money for higher goals. He brought the ideas of Joachim Grizzelov back to life, the man whose portrait you're smearing away at there.

PLASMONICK: So that's what such a noble ideal is based on? A new religion made a reality by an ordinary scoundrel and *rastaquouère!* I'm sinking lower and lower. It's horrible!

ROSA: He is strong, he is *great*. From that day on he stopped being a spy.

PLASMONICK: Stopped being a spy! Do you understand what you're saying? It's not the same as stopping drinking or playing cards. An out-and-out rogue from start to finish, right down to the innermost fiber of his being, that's what he was and still is. He stopped being a spy—that's preposterous!

ROSA: He's a strong man. I prefer evil to a jellyfish like you. A painter, an artist! Ugh.

PLASMONICK: Shut up! For the sake of art one has the right to do swinish things. But even for art, *I* didn't do anything wrong . . .

ROSA: Because you don't have either the strength or the courage. If you were stronger, you'd be a hundred times worse than he is. Maybe I'd fall in love with you then.

PLASMONICK: Oh—don't talk about us! There's an abyss between us. Now you're as repulsive to me as a bedbug.

ROSA (*coquettishly*): Now—but in six hours it may be a bit different. Just think . . .

PLASMONICK (*inwardly shaken*): Don't talk that way . . . I'm not reproaching you because you took spy money for your music, only because you could love him so much that to save him you'd go to prison and deceive me for such a long time. When I loved you so . . .

ROSA: That wasn't love, just weakness.

PLASMONICK: I can't understand how lying can make a social prophet seem great to you. He's got to personify his cause in his own life, or else he won't create anything. You're judging it by standards you'd apply to art, not to life. You'll see that that Tzingar of yours . . .

ROSA: Don't talk about him. You've said enough already. What happened, happened.

PLASMONICK: But how are we going to go on living? Fourteen years! No—I've got to get out of here. I simply can't—I can't love you anymore. Oh, God, God! No—there has to be a retrial. It's all a stupid, hideous dream. It's got to come to an end.

ROSA: Just stop and think, Plazy, what proof have you got? They'll take you for a madman and it's all over. The court isn't a tool for psycho-physiological experiments—the court has got to have evidence.

PLASMONICK: Aha—so you're afraid of staying here, are you? I'll persuade them by the power of the truth itself. By the power of suggestion which enabled me to persuade them when I was lying, plus the fact that in this case it'll be the truth.

ROSA: Don't you dare! You may ruin everything and go from here straight into the insane asylum. And this time without me! Ha, ha!

PLASMONICK (*indecisive*): Then what are we to do?

ROSA: I'll tell you: Tzingar's organizing the great Grizzlovik revolution. It's going to start any day now and then we'll get out of here for sure. I'll ask him to let you out too, after all you're *someone* . . . I got a letter from him. (*Pulls a piece of paper from her bosom and reads.*) "Dearest Rosa: The day when we'll meet again is near. It's quite likely I'll now be able to run the risk of visiting you. I'm already far enough along in my work not to have to fear arousing suspicions. But what will your victim, poor Plazy, have to say . . ."

PLASMONICK (*rushing at her*):   Stop it! . . . I can't stand any more. . . How vile you are, Rosa!

Knocking at the door to the left.

ROSA: Quiet! Someone's coming. Don't you dare let on by as much as a wink there's been anything between us. (*In the direction of the door.*) Come in!

The doors are unbolted. Enter LOPAK *in a black shirt, red tie, pointed black cap, and* GIERS's *pants from Act One.*

LOPAK (*without removing his cap*): Morning. Got the portrait ready?

PLASMONICK: It will be soon. Tomorrow perhaps.

LOPAK: Let's see!

PLASMONICK *turns the easel around so that it faces the audience, and we see the portrait of an old man, done completely naturalistically, with a certain stylization using "hard contours"* (*pseudo-cubism*). *The old man is fat; both his hair and beard are fabulously long and milk-white.*

PLASMONICK: Here it is. Sinking as low as an artist possibly can to make money.

LOPAK: Terrific. You got that monkey just right. He won't be running things for long—not even in that portrait. Ho, ho! You don't know what's brewing. But here in this hole, what do you care? Strange, strange things are going on. (*Recites.*)

> Cattle, grown human, have begun to integrate
> Their lack of power into monstrous might.
> With stealth these cattle thoughts set out to wind
> The ribbon of louse feelings in a spring coiled tight.
> Leaven of Marx's works, poured into cattle skulls,
> Creates a most strange mixture with the brain.
> Some thug jams all this in a fire hose
> To squirt it on the world out through the drain.
> Someday in a picture the little man of the future
> Will look at these events and whine with rapture,
> History in shiny helmet of pure gold
> Will portray the splendid moment beyond recapture.
> But once again *that* moment will never return—
> It's passed, and after it the abyss gapes still
> With the boredom of waiting it sates the dark force
> Of the masses who never once gulped down their fill.
> (*Knocking to the left.*) Ssh—not a word about what I just said.

The door is unbolted. Enter GIERS, *the* PRINCESS, *and* PADOVAL DE GRIFUELLHES. *All of them are dressed as in Act Two.* LYDIA RAGNOCK *follows them.*

PRINCESS: Good morning, dearest. I can come here only if the colonel escorts me. They're afraid I'll become an espionagette too. (ROSA *kisses her hand. The men behave quite icily and don't greet anyone.*) For me you're first and foremost a great artist.

PLASMONICK: To the extent that it's possible for a woman to be a great artist. A woman's feelings always get the upper hand to the detriment of form, that is, of Pure Form.

PRINCESS (*icily*): I didn't come here to see *him*, only Rosa. *Allez–vous* out of my way, *per favore*. (*She talks with* ROSA.)

GIERS: Yes—you'd better pretend you're not here. (*Notices the picture.*) Oh! Grizzelov! He came out perfectly. Perfectly.

PLASMONICK: Someday you'll find out the truth, Colonel. I don't have any proof, but I *am* innocent.

GIERS: Yes, yes. But doesn't your official confession count for anything? Just as if it didn't exist? You're starting to get hard to handle, Mr. Plasmonick. Control yourself, or there'll be trouble. (*Knocking.*)

ROSA: Come in.

The door is unbolted. Enter DR. BLÖDESTAUG *with* CLAUDESTINA.

BLÖDESTAUG: Your Highness will excuse me, but he is my son after all. And besides, Miss Claudestina wanted to look at his paintings. (*To* PLASMONICK.) How are you feeling, Plazy?

PLASMONICK: I'm in a state of great inner transformation, Father. For me the world has turned round one hundred and eighty degrees at the very least.

CLAUDESTINA *silently indicates the pictures to the right.* PLASMONICK *shows her two canvases covered with incredibly pure Pure Form, leaning them against the easel with Grizzelov.*

GIERS: It will turn even more, but in dead earnest. Since Prince Padoval is on our side, I'll tell you frankly: I have become a Grizzlovik. Under other circumstances I would have stuck with the old system to the very end. But present circumstances have convinced me. We're changing the form of power, but not its real nature.

LOPAK: Ha, ha, ha, ha, ha, ha!!!

The men all look at the paintings in silence.

GIERS: What's that poetnik laughing at? Power will continue to be power. I was always something of a mystic, but I didn't know how to relate it to my guiding principle about the supremacy of the state. He's the one (*points to the portrait*) who convinced me. I'm a Grizzlovik *faute de mieux.* No telling where it will lead later on.

LOPAK: I know, but I'm not going to tell. Anyhow, it's got to be put to the test.

BLÖDESTAUG: I have my own set of beliefs too. The Mystery of Existence is unfathomable, regardless of what system of ideas we're working with. The calculated nationalization of this mystery, while preserving diversity in the expression of different ideas, is the sole idea which can save mankind from total decline and fall.

LOPAK: That's utter rubbish, Professor, but even so the post of minister of health and art in the new government is yours. Ha! Ha!

Knocking to the left.

ROSA: Come in.

The door is unbolted. Enter TZINGAR *in a white flannel suit. He has a blue necktie, and on his head a white, soft hat, which he immediately takes off.*

PRINCESS: Greetings, Mr. Buffadero. (TZINGAR *greets the ladies and* ROSA, *who jumps right out of her skin. Every muscle tensed,* PLASMONICK *comes out into the middle of the stage, leaving* CLAUDESTINA *with the paintings.*)

PLASMONICK: I never asked that man to visit *us.*

TZINGAR: I didn't need your permission, young fellow. Keep still and behave yourself. (*To all of them.*) Today is the decisive day: the *coup d'état* takes place tonight. (*To* GIERS.) General—since I can call you that now—you'll see to it that our garrison is put on alert for ten tonight. I had to speed up events. (*To* PLASMONICK.) And as for you, young man, don't you get too frisky, since it's in my power to keep you in this hole for fourteen years or let you go free tomorrow.

GIERS: Mr. President! A spy can't be set free, even in a state based on the principles of Joachim Grizzelov. The state remains the state.

TZINGAR: Don't forget that you are *my* minister of war and that's all you are—*my* minister of war! You're being watched by *my* agents. Your function is only to execute *my* will.

ROSA *looks at him adoringly.*

GIERS: I've got involved in some hideous moral compromise. Making certain kinds of concessions exacts its own vengeance. Remember I can always refuse at the last minute.

TZINGAR: You're forgetting that the propaganda among the officers has been carried out quite effectively. At the most, maybe two or three people from the Prince's immediate entourage support you. Let's not talk about that. I have certain obligations to that gentleman. (*He points to* PLASMONICK.)

GIERS: The President has obligations to a spy. A fine state of affairs!

TZINGAR: From my earliest youth. It's a family secret.

GIERS: Your origins are quite suspicious. At a certain point the thread breaks off and from there on absolutely nothing more is known.

TZINGAR (*emphatically*): *General*, I don't advise you to become too absorbed in investigating those secrets before ten o'clock tonight. You could easily find yourself in that gentleman's place. (*He points to* PLASMONICK.)

GIERS: That's how it is. "Trust a slob," as someone once said. The moral compromise I made is exacting its vengeance on me with fatal consequences. What's done is done—I can only sink in deeper.

TZINGAR: That's the best thing for you to do. You'll find yourself on heights you never even dreamed of.

ROSA. Talk all you want: although I refuse to acknowledge painting as an art, Plazy is our only painter. He must be saved.

TZINGAR *bows.*

GIERS: There's something suspicious going on here. (*To* TZINGAR.) What did you actually come here for?

TZINGAR (*insolently*):   To meet you and give you your final orders. That's what. Ha, ha!

GIERS *shrivels up.*

CLAUDESTINA (*moving away from the paintings*): Excuse me everyone, but *I'll* take care of Mr. Plasmonick. I'm clairvoyant. (*To* ROSA.) You want to destroy him by playing on his lowest level, on his instinct for life. I'll protect him from you. I know that now we're going to create something significant in painting together.

ROSA: I don't want to destroy him or to put him on a pedestal either. I want to get him out of here and never see him again.

GIERS: To make matters worse, they're starting to rave about art. Shall we go, Your Highnesses?

PADOVAL (*who until now has been standing like a mummy behind the* PRINCESS's *chair*):   Miss Claudestina, you're forgetting that I'm your fiancé.

CLAUDESTINA: I'm breaking off my relations with you from this moment on, Prince. I must keep his spirit from giving way to despair. That's the truly significant task in my life. Prince, you can find consolation with anyone, even with women of that person's ilk.

She points to ROSA. *The* PRINCE *draws back toward his mother, very displeased.*

PLASMONICK: Do you really believe in me? I'm at the very bottom.

CLAUDESTINA: You wanted to destroy yourself violently and systematically. You wanted to speed it up, the way Mr. Buffadero wants to speed up his revolution. I'll destroy you too, but in a far more creative way. I won't let you sink to the bottom of life. You're going to play yourself out in Pure Form, without sinking to swinishness in reality.

PLASMONICK *shakes his head incredulously. The* PRINCESS *gets ready to leave.*

GIERS: That's enough of that nonsense. Let's go. What awaits me is the simply hellish task of overcoming my own nature.

ROSA: Yes. That's enough. You'll all be able to deal with those practical matters tomorrow—on the outside.

CLAUDESTINA *silently crosses over to the left and without saying good-bye to anyone* (*even to* PLASMONICK) *leaves at the same time as the* PRINCE, GIERS, *and* PADOVAL.

BLÖDESTAUG: Take care of yourself, Plazy. Tomorrow you'll be free. I'm minister of art and public health. On the day of the *coup d'état* I don't imagine I'll be very busy—we'll have a chance to talk about everything.

TZINGAR (*toward the door*): Don't close the door there! I'm just about to leave. (*The door closes, but is left unbolted.*) All right—now we can talk frankly. Only no long faces, my friends. Mr. Plasmonick, I turned your love for Rosa to my own advantage and I owe my life to you. From the looks on your faces I realized that Rosa wasn't able to keep it to herself and blurted out everything.

PLASMONICK: You're forgetting that I can tell all and you'll go from the presidency to a gray uniform with a yellow circle on it.

TZINGAR: Nobody will believe you now. My technique for covering my tracks is infallible. None of my accomplices is alive anymore. What happened to them—the devil himself couldn't figure out. Contagious diseases—you understand? Better try to reach an understanding and you'll be director of the Academy of Fine Arts. We don't need those naturalistic old fogies anymore.

PLASMONICK: Never. I don't believe that any remaking of society, based on individuals like you, can ever succeed. If Joachim Grizzelov could see the kind of people who are carrying out his idea of the priesthood— he'd die a second death from shame and despair. I am alone and shall remain alone.

TZINGAR: As you like. Tomorrow you'll be free or we'll all die. Still, you've got to admit that I was discreet. I didn't see my Rosa for almost a year. I didn't want to bother the two of you until I was sure of victory.

PLASMONICK. I'd prefer that it never got started than to have it end like *this*. Still, I've got to admit you're a monstrous scoundrel, Mr. Tzingar.

TZINGAR: You're wrong. The position I now occupy has ennobled me. Napoleon was an ordinary crook at the start of his career. But leading France to glory made him truly great—the way he was at Waterloo. Now I would be utterly incapable of being a spy.

PLASMONICK: What megalomania! Rosa, can't you see he's a disgusting clown, that darling Tzingar of yours?

ROSA: Can't *you* see what a clown *you* are? No, Plazy, he has true greatness in him. We can't evaluate him properly; we're seeing him too close up. Only history can judge him.

TZINGAR: All right—that's enough babbling. Rosa—a great future lies ahead of us. With your permission, Mr. Plasmonick, I must kiss the future Mrs. President just once. (*He kisses her.*)

PLASMONICK (*rushing at him*): Don't you dare! You—low comedian! You *scoundrel!*

TZINGAR *slips off quickly to the left.* PLASMONICK *stands still, breathing heavily. His fists are tightly clenched. The* GUARD *appears at the door.*

GUARD: Hey, you—number hundred and seventeen! Gonna be quiet? Want to go back to solitary again, like when you beat up number hundred and eighteen? (*He glares threateningly for a moment.* PLASMONICK *goes limp. The* GUARD *withdraws and bolts the door.*)

PLASMONICK: Oh! If only I could get out of here right now. (*Suddenly changes his tone.*) Rosa! The last day. That scoundrel is capable of not letting me out. It was a mistake for me to lose my temper. Rosa! Try to love me the way you used to. Maybe I can convince you I'm the only one who really loves you.

ROSA: You'll find consolation with your Claudestina. She'll destroy you in an incredibly subtle way. Ha, ha!

PLASMONICK: Rosa, stop joking. This may be the last day of my life.

ROSA: All right, my darling. After all, I am indebted to you for saving Joseph Tzingar's life and for the fact that I'm going to be the President's wife. Come here! Kiss me.

PLASMONICK: You don't know how monstrously you're torturing me . . .

ROSA: I do know—I know perfectly well. (*They kiss.*) Torture is the absolute essence of love . . .

ACT FOUR

IN THE SHAPE OF AN EPILOGUE

A square in front of the prison. The prison wall, a pale ocher color with white stripes, goes at a sharp angle to a line parallel to the line of the footlights, in the right corner of the stage. Gate with bars. To the left the corner of a house, in the shadows right next to the footlights. Dawn. The sky cannot be seen. It is only reflected in the prison windows. Distant bursts of machine-gun fire and the very distant but continual rumble of artillery are heard. To the left a crowd is waiting in front of the prison. To the right there are also a few people. The most diverse clothes, all mixed together. Very bright colors, green, carmine red, and violet predominate. Less frequently, sky blue. A complete absence of yellow and light red—colors that indicate the prisoners. In the middle of the square there stands a lamppost and lantern, which burns with a yellowish-greenish glow. At the gates two members of the guard push back those who come too close. In the first row of the crowd to the left: the PRINCESS, *the* BARONESS, BLÖDESTAUG, CLAUDESTINA *and* SOPHIE, ROSA'S MAID, GRAVEDIGGER I *and* LOPAK, *who is dressed as in Act Three.*

FIRST WOMAN: Oh, my God! When will they let them out!

FIRST MAN.   They say the palace's already been captured by the Grizzlovites. Giers led the attack himself.

SECOND WOMAN: The palace has been taken, but even Prince Padoval got locked up for Grizzlovism. Look—you can see old Princess Barbara—over there. (*Points to the left.*) She's waiting for her son, just like us.

SECOND MAN: He just got put in the clink yesterday. They say the papers still haven't come yet.

FIRST WOMAN: Always the same old story in this country. The papers come very slowly, sometimes slower than a person's life.

The OFFICER OF THE GUARD *comes through the prison gates.*

OFFICER: The papers have come. The prisoners will be coming out in two or three minutes. I can inform you that the palace has been taken. Our army is fighting victoriously beyond the Eastern Gate against the forces of Count Münsterberg who came to the rescue of Prince Peter. Victory is certain. Long live the memory of Joachim Grizzelov! Long live the New Theocracy!! Hurrah!!!!!

Rather feeble cheers from the CROWD.

BLÖDESTAUG: I'm terribly alarmed. As minister of health and art, I don't have anything to do today—as is usually the case with people in this profession during a *coup d'état,* but I have the worst forebodings.

LOPAK: With good reason, Professor—there's a tiny little cloud on the horizon. You're going to see some strange things yet.

BLÖDESTAUG: I don't like the way the lowest elements are behaving. That's the basic material for a revolution.

LOPAK: And I'm just delighted with how they're behaving. The Grizzlovites won't last long.

BLÖDESTAUG: Not so loud! Just who are you, anyhow?

The crowd listens closely to what they are saying.

LOPAK (*in a loud voice*): Ho, ho, Professor! These things can't be settled just "between ourselves," just in passing. I am the creator of *The Anonymous Work!*

BLÖDESTAUG: Just don't go too far, Mr. Lopak. You could easily find yourself hanging *there.*

He points to the lantern, which at this very moment goes out. The light of dawn can be seen more distinctly on the wall of the prison.

LOPAK: No telling yet who's going to be hanging there today, me or Mr. Tzingar!

BLÖDESTAUG: Tzingar was the pseudonym my son used as a spy. Plazy will be free today—Buffadero promised.

LOPAK: Oh, that's just it—Buffadero! I was talking about a completely different Tzingar, not about your Plazy. He's about as much of a spy as I am, or maybe even less.

BLÖDESTAUG: What's that you're saying? Then he was imprisoned for almost a year even though he was innocent? That's horrible!

LOPAK: A lot of other horrible things are going to come out in the open. As soon as *my* little trick works.

BLÖDESTAUG: You're devilishly sure of yourself, Mr. Lopak.

LOPAK: Just don't you be too sure of yourself. Oh—look: here come the prisoners.

The CROWD *of prisoners starts to come through the gates. All of them are dressed like* ROSA *and* PLASMONICK; *only they have small, round, gray caps without visors.*

OFFICER (*from the window*): From now on, prison dress will be the uniform of the Grizzlovik guards. All prisoners automatically become guards— common criminals as well as political prisoners, and even women. Long live the Grizzlovite national guard!!

No one cheers. The prisoners and the "prisoneresses" run to their families and friends. Greetings and exclamations. General happiness.

LOPAK: Those were the common criminals. Now they're going to let the political prisoners out.

PRINCE PADOVAL *comes out wearing prison clothes and throws his arms around the* PRINCESS's *neck.*

PADOVAL: Mother! See how nice I look in my new uniform. I'm an officer in the Grizzlovite guard. At any rate I'm not one bit bored.

PRINCESS: My child, as long as you're not bored, I'm happy, utterly happy.

PADOVAL: And you know, Mother, Uncle's in the clink. The officer of the day just told me. They got a phone call. Münsterberg's been crushed— he's retreating.

PRINCESS: Are you glad?

PADOVAL: Of course I am, Mother.

PRINCESS: In that case, I am too. (*They kiss.*)

PADOVAL: There's only one thing that bothers me: that's my unhappy love for Claudestina.

CLAUDESTINA: Don't say anything more about that, Prince. *I'm* waiting for Plasmonick.

PADOVAL: Oh, that Plasmonick of yours is actually plasma, not a human being. Mother, your Rosa made total psycho-physiological mincemeat out of him.

ROSA *comes out of prison in the same costume she wore in Act Three.*

ROSA (*in a loud voice*): Isn't Baron de Buffadero here?!

FIRST MAN: Buffadero is at the castle. But he's not a baron any more; all titles have been abolished.

ROSA: Oh, reeeeeally? That's too bad!

LOPAK: Ha, ha, ha, ha, ha! You won't be a baroness!

PRINCESS: You can take comfort, my dear. I'm just plain Mrs. Grifuellhes too.

ROSA *greets the* PRINCESS.

BLÖDESTAUG: And how's my Plazy doing?

ROSA: He's having some kind of complications with his papers. But they say he'll be coming any minute now.

BLÖDESTAUG: Oh, those papers, those papers! In my ministry there won't be any kind of paper except the "perfectly pure article: water–closet paper," as the English call it. Poor Plazy! Lopak claims he never was a spy at all.

ROSA (*turning to* LOPAK): Whaaaat?! How dare you?!!!

LOPAK: Careful, Miss Rosa! You're not Mrs. President yet, and maybe you never will be.

ROSA *becomes flustered and quiets down. It grows lighter and lighter. A rosy glow begins to light the wall of the prison. PLASMONICK comes out through the gates in prison clothes. The crowd made up of the relatives, friends, and mentors of the criminals breaks up slowly, as they take the prisoners home. Only those waiting for the political prisoners, who come out one by one, remain.*

PLASMONICK: Good morning, everyone! How are you, Father? I'm a bit dazed and don't have any direction or any clear-cut line of action for the future. I'm waiting for my secret inner voice to tell me something.

CLAUDESTINA: I'll help you, Mr. Plazy. I know what you've got to do. I made a sketch of it yesterday.

PLASMONICK: You know—I'm not happy to be free. (*They talk.*)

ROSA (*notices* SOPHIE, *whom* CLAUDESTINA *is holding by the hand*): Oh— my Sophie! How you've grown! How lovely you are! I'd completely forgotten about her.

Caresses and endearments Suddenly there's an uproar to the left. The clatter of many horsemen can be heard. Enter TZINGAR, *dressed in a riding outfit. He has a light-blue sash across his chest and a whip in his hand. The crowd grows larger again.*

TZINGAR (*with forced gaiety*): Good morning, Rosa! How are you, Madam President? (*Kisses her hand.* ROSA *forgets about* SOPHIE.) Oh—we're here in full force. Mr. Grifuellhes, you'll excuse me for not having you released until now. Your uncle has already been disposed of. He was surprised half out of his wits. By the way, Mr. Plasmonick, is the portrait of Grizzelov done? (*He offers him his hand.*)

PLASMONICK: The portrait's done, but keep your distance. Would you mind paying me right now? I want to settle a debt with Miss Rosa. (TZINGAR *gives him a bundle of banknotes, which* PLASMONICK *hands over to* ROSA.) Here's that cursed ten thousand. Take it and may I never set eyes on you again.

TZINGAR: Friends, I must tell you in strictest confidence that the situation is far from clear. I left the palace on purpose, so that—how can I put it— so that things would settle down by themselves. Rioting has broken out among the lowest segments of the rabble. The fifth regiment began plundering the northern district. It's all being stirred up by some totally unknown people in pointed black caps.

LOPAK (*laughing*): Caps like mine maybe? Eh?

TZINGAR (*flustered*): That's right. How'd you get here? You're supposed to be at a meeting of the Committee for the Protection of Incapacitated Civilians now! What are you doing here?

LOPAK: I'm doing what I think is best, and I'm where *I am* most needed.

TZINGAR: What? How dare you?! If that's how my subordinates are going to follow my orders, there's no hope of keeping the rabble under control.

LOPAK: I knew you'd come here to get your Rosa, Mister—*Tzingar!*

BLÖDESTAUG: Tzingar?

TZINGAR: (*Roars*) Whaaat?!!!

LOPAK (*taking two steps backward*): I'm that agent of yours you saw only once, and then I was wearing a mask. I'm the only one you didn't know personally, Mr. Tzingar! But I played that game so as to be able to put the blame on you once you weren't useful to us anymore—to *us!*—the people in the pointed black caps! The second regiment is ours!

TZINGAR (*roars*): Seize him!!

LOPAK (*roars to the soldiers standing guard at the gates, pointing at* TZINGAR): Seize that scoundrel! That's Tzingar—chief spy for the Macerbators. (*The sentry grabs* TZINGAR, *who seems more dead than alive, and holds him.* ROSA *cuddles* SOPHIE *in her arms. To everyone.*)

Fellow citizens!   Men like this aren't our leaders; they're garbage waiting to be carted off! We—the real people—have made use of them for our own purposes! They made the first breach! We don't need a priest-run government masquerading as a mealy-mouthed democracy. We're going to create our own true self-government. We're going to get along without any parliament by organizing trade unions of true loafers. We're going to create a true paradise on earth without any leaders and without any work! That's what we're going to do! The uniform, gray, sticky, stinking, monstrous mass: a new Separate Being, defying all metaphysics based on the concept of the individual and the hierarchy! There are no individuals!! Down with the personality! Long live the uniform MASS, one and indivisible!!! Hurrah!!!

THE CROWD: Hurrah!! Long live the uniform MASS!!! Down with the individual!!! Down with the personality!!!

(GIERS *rushes in from the left accompanied by the* OFFICERS. *The first ranks of the army can be seen behind them.*)

GIERS: Where is Buffadero?!! (*Because of the dense crowd, he cannot see that* TZINGAR *is being held, and he shouts, pushing his way through the crowd*) Mr. Buffadero! The fifth regiment, along with the mob, is coming at us full tilt. The second has revolted too. Münsterberg's forces are supporting the rabble, not Prince Peter! (*Notices that* TZINGAR *is being held by members of the guard.*) What the devil is going on? What are they holding you for?

TZINGAR (*in a trembling voice*): Sir . . . General . . . we're . . . lost. . . .

LOPAK (*to* TZINGAR): Shut up! Scum! (*To* GIERS.) Ho, ho, General, here's some good news for you. Do you know who this Buffadero of yours is? He's Tzingar! The chief spy!!

GIERS: That's impossible! (*Grabs his head in his hands.*) Oh—what an idiot I've been! It was so obvious all along, and I, like an utter ass, couldn't figure it out!!

LOPAK (*to the crowd*): String that mangy bum up to the lamppost.

THE CROWD: String him up to the lamppost! Hang him! Hang him! *Hang both of them!* String the whole government up to the lamppost! Down with the priests! String Giers up to the lamppost! (*They rush at them both.*)

GIERS (*draws his sword and tries to run* TZINGAR *through*): Let me go! I'm going to kill that scoundrel!

They get his sword away from him and drag them both to the lamppost. At this point the following must take place. At the prison gates dummies, with sacks over their heads, must be ready, dressed exactly like GIERS *and* TZINGAR. *The crowd swarms around the two live characters and conceals them from the audience. Meanwhile the dummies must be put in their places, and the live actors who play* TZINGAR *and* GIERS *must crawl off unnoticed, concealed by the* CROWD, *through the prison gates into the wings. Sorry—it's indispensable.*

THE CROWD: String the rascals up to the lamppost. Hurrah!!!

GIERS (*as he is dragged off*): Mr. Plasmonick! Forgive me! Oh! How cruelly the compromise I made has exacted its vengeance!!!

They are completely engulfed. Both the hanged figures are pulled up on the lamppost, over which ropes have been thrown. From the left the sun floods the square, the lamppost, and the wall of the prison with a glaring orange light.

LOPAK (*whose black cap falls off his head*): And now on to the palace! Hang the whole government!! Hurrah!!!!

He goes out, surrounded by the crowd, to the left. There remain only the PRINCESS, *the* BARONESS, ROSA *and* SOPHIE, PADOVAL, CLAUDESTINA, *and* PLASMONICK—*and, of course, the two false corpses on the lamppost.*

BLÖDESTAUG (*rubbing his hands with satisfaction*): They forgot about me. That's marvelous! Well, Plazy—we're starting a new kind of underground existence.

ROSA: Plazy, I'm yours—*only* yours. I've woken up from a horrible nightmare. I don't love him any more.

PLASMONICK: It's too late, Miss Rosa, it's too late. I love Miss Claudestina de Montreuil. I've finally woken up from a dreadful nightmare too—the nightmare of loving you. I'm starting to paint in a completely different way.

BLÖDESTAUG: Then let's go home for morning coffee. I'm inviting all of you.

PLASMONICK: No, papa, I *cannot* live in a society run by Mr. Lopak and the mob from across the tracks. I've come to like my room in that building very much. (*Indicates the prison.*) Art has come to an end, and no one is going to produce an artificial religion—not even the late Tzingar with the help of Grizzelov, or even of Lopak *himself.* I'm going back to prison. And in order not to be tempted to get out again, I must do something suitably monstrous. I assume that even in a new state based on the Lopakian rabble and the myth about cattle-brained worklessness, certain crimes will have to be punished. (*He pulls out from inside his jacket his razor blade in a wooden holder, from which he is inseparable, and shows it to the assembled group.*)

BLÖDESTAUG: Plazy! Don't kill yourself! Art!!

He tries to grab him. PLASMONICK *pushes him away.*

PLASMONICK: Wouldn't think of it, Father. (*To* ROSA.) Miss Rosa—your turn now. (*Rushes at her and slits her throat with lightning speed.* ROSA *falls dead. Calmly.*) My secret inner voice told me to. She already had composed herself out anyway. She told me so in her moments of sincerity, so it's no loss to art. In our times there are only two places for metaphysical individuals: prison or the insane asylum. (*They are all petrified, including* SOPHIE.) Are you coming with me, Miss Claudestina?

CLAUDESTINA: Anywhere you want. We're still going to get out of here: to another world, which I see dimly somewhere in the future. What exists now cannot last.

PLASMONICK: No, thanks. I won't get out, since I don't believe in any of that. Social phenomena are *ir-re-vers-i-ble.* (*He syllabifies the last word.*) Good-bye, father. You can come visit me tonight.

He goes in through the prison gates. CLAUDESTINA *goes in after him, closing the gates with a bang. In the distance the rattle of machine guns can be heard again.*

PADOVAL (*picking up* LOPAK's *pointed cap off the ground*): Well—if that's the way it is, I'll become "the unknown man in the pointed cap." I'm leaving now to incite my regiment of grenadier guards to go all the way. (*Puts the cap on his head.*) Compared to me, Philippe-Egalité will be just a harmless little joke. Is that all right, Mother?

PRINCESS: As long as you're not bored, dear boy. Do whatever you want, whatever you think is best.

BLÖDESTAUG: That Plazy really *is* a madman. Did you ever hear of slitting a woman's throat that way like a chicken, and in the *morning* at that? In the *morning*! And that Claudestina—she's a real demonic fairy godmother. They're not normal types. (*Takes* SOPHIE *by the hand.*) Come along, Sophie! I'm inviting all of you for coffee and nice fresh rolls.

27 November 1921

Stanisław Ignacy Witkiewicz
The Lower Depths
circa 1910

THE CUTTLEFISH

or

THE HYRCANIAN WORLD VIEW

A Play in One Act
(1922)

Foreword

Witkacy wrote *The Cuttlefish, or The Hyrcanian World View*, "A Play in One Act," in April 1922 and published it the following year in a Cracow Expressionist journal. The play did not reach the stage until December 1933 when it was presented by the Cracow artists' theatre Cricot. Of all the productions of Witkacy's plays given during his lifetime, this legendary performance was the most distinguished artistically. A brilliant visual spectacle almost in the style of a puppet show, the play became the occasion for a timely warning about the rise of fascism. The costume and design were the work of the sculptor Henryk Wiciński, who dressed the characters as ideograms. Pope Julius II, divided down the middle in yellow and white, resembled a cross. The prostitute mother, minus arms, had the shape of a cat; the uncles looked and moved like penguins. Hyrcan was dressed as a Nazi. The performance, which was given twice, proved to be the next to last production of any of Witkacy's plays until after World War II.

Tadeusz Kantor chose *The Cuttlefish* to open his new theatre Cricot 2 in May 1956 in the same space as in 1933 in order to stress continuity with the traditions of the Cracow pre-war avant-garde. This production also became a legend; as the first post-World-War-II performance of Witkacy, it created a sensation by its flamboyant break with the canons of socialist realism, which had been mandatory in the Polish professional theatre during the Stalinist years.

For Kantor's *Cuttlefish*, the audience was seated as if at a café listening to a jazz concert; the spectators surrounded the small stage on which the show took place. The painter, Paul Rockoffer, was chained to a column, out of the top of which his head appeared. The vivified statue Alice d'Or lay on an operating table in the pose of a sphinx. The most important prop on stage was a coffin, an object connected to the other world, which was accompanied by Paul's two dead wives. All the characters wore colored tights, differentiated only in the details, so that every one appeared to be a clown. The Pope was wrapped like a mummy, with only scraps of papal garments attached to the sleeves. All the actors wore half-masks, except for Hyrcan, who had a helmet that came down over his face, with holes cut out for the eyes. The would-be dictator in Kantor's version was as much a commentary on Stalinism as a satire of Hitler.

These two productions of *The Cuttlefish* in 1933 and 1956 served to define the ways in which Witkacy's plays would be interpreted on stage in the post-war Polish theatre for the next twenty years. Largely disregarding

Witkacy's detailed stage directions, Polish directors, who were often also artists and designers, used the plays to create striking visual effects and to draw topical political parallels to the repression of artistic and intellectual life under communism. *The Cuttlefish* has remained one of Witkacy's most popular plays in Poland, lending itself to a variety of modes of production: as puppet theatre, as student cabaret, and as radio drama.

The play's enduring success is due to its kinetic imagery that animates a fast-moving debate about creativity in art and politics. The ideas flow in profusion, but are constantly reconfigured in surprising shapes and colors that make *The Cuttlefish* an outstanding example of Pure Form in the theatre.

Paul Rockoffer, a cockeyed avant-garde painter without family, isolated and alienated from society, exists nowhere, in a limbo of the consciousness outside time or space, where he carries on a dialogue of the dead with his sometime muse, the shapely statue Alice d'Or, and Pope Julius II, Renaissance patron of the arts. The recent destruction of his paintings by governmental decree has plunged the artist into despair and taken away his sense of who he is. Rockoffer, who cannot create without recourse to drugs, finds that talking with ghosts allows him to justify his own lack of artistic authenticity and identity. But his hideaway is invaded by visitors from other realities. The first comers are his clinging, pragmatic fiancée (the many-tentacled "cuttlefish" of the play's title) and her ex-whore mother, who hope to tie him down to practical domesticity.

When Paul's old schoolmate arrives, dressed in a purple cloak and red-plumed helmet, sword in hand, claiming to be Hyrcan IV, strongman and creator of the imaginary kingdom of Hyrcania, the battle is joined between two opposing archetypes: the artist and the tyrant. Upon learning from the would-be dictator that the Hyrcanian world view is a linguistic ploy to forge a reality that does not exist, Rockoffer asks, "But how does all this differ from theatre?" Power for power's sake is the real goal.

In *The Cuttlefish* Witkacy considers the advent of twentieth-century dictatorship through scrutiny of the performance aspects of totalitarian regimes: the histrionics and scenography. The modern tyrant fashions himself out of nothing by manipulating costume, staging, gesture, and language; he is a creative artist making himself and his realm into a work of art that appeals to both the masses and the elite.

Artists share the dictator's creative ambitions and envy his absolute power to impose his vision on all of society. In *The Origins of Totalitarianism*, Hanna Arendt notes the intellectuals' fascination with the strongmen of the 1920s and 30s. Otherwise bereft of influence or status, artists and writers, by adopting the violent social activism of extreme parties, find a ready-made identity in a group that wields power.

Hyrcanian desires are a seductive temptation: the power to transform life (the word prefiguring the thing). Rockoffer, a self-doubting artist who believes that all his art has been fraudulent, toys with the idea establishing a new reality in life, not art. But he sees that Hyrcania is only a virtual reality, or artificial realm in the old style, based on a vulgar understanding of Nietzsche's superman, which can only result in "an ordinary theatrical hoax." It is the theatre critics who write about Hyrcania

The Cuttlefish presents three possible stances, from past, present, and future times, that the artist can take toward the world—as protégé of a Maecenas like Pope Julius, as unaffiliated but marginalized individualist like Rockoffer, or as mouthpiece for state ideology like those who preach the Hyrcanian world view.

Like all Witkacy's heroes, Rockoffer seeks to transform himself and become someone else. The appeal of Hyrcania for an artist like Rockoffer is that it will enable him to re-invent himself.

In *The Cuttlefish*, three dialecticians, embracing different world views, debate the situation of art in the modern world where a crisis of values prevails. With the demise of philosophy and religion, only art is left to represent the absolute.   But art is also a way of being recognized as someone and of asserting one's identity, and Hyrcan uses it for self-aggrandizement.

Ridiculing Hyrcan's linguistic fabrications and manipulations of appearances, Rockoffer murders the self-fashioned dictator and becomes Hyrcan V. Renouncing art for life, Rockoffer has assumed the identity and power of the dictator, proclaiming a state based on the principles of avant-garde art, not avant-garde politics.   As Paul and his entourage depart for the imaginary kingdom on the Hyrcania Express, the new ruler declares, "Together, we will create pure nonsense in life, not art." Rockoffer fancies that he can transform himself into a philosopher king by traveling to the imaginary kingdom of Hyrcania, which is nowhere.

THE CUTTLEFISH

or

The Hyrcanian World View

A Play in One Act
(1922)

Motto:
Don't give in even to yourself.

Dedicated to
Zofia Żeleński

THE CHARACTERS

PAUL ROCKOFFER—Forty-six years old, but looks younger (his age becomes clear during the course of the action). Fair-haired. In deep mourning.

THE STATUE ALICE D'OR—Twenty-eight years old. A blonde. Dressed in a tight-fitting dress resembling alligator skin.

THE KING OF HYRCANIA—Hyrcan IV. Tall, thin. Vandyke beard, large mustache. A bit snub-nosed. Large eyebrows and longish hair. Purple cloak and helmet with a red plume. A sword in his hand. Under his cloak a golden garment. (What he has on under that will be revealed later on.)

ELLA—Eighteen years old. Chestnut hair. Pretty.

TWO OLD GENTLEMEN—In frock coats and top hats. They can be dressed in the style of the thirties.

TWO MATRONS—Dressed in violet. One of them is Ella's mother.

GRUMPUS—The Footman. Gray livery coat with large silver buttons and gray top hat.

JULIUS—Sixteenth-century Pope. Dressed as in the portrait by Titian.

The stage represents a room with black walls with narrow emerald–green designs. A little to the right on the wall in the center of the stage is a window covered with a red curtain. In places marked (x) a light behind the curtain goes on with a bloody glow, in places marked (+) it goes out. A little to the left a black rectangular pedestal without ornamentation. ALICE D'OR *lies on her stomach on the pedestal, leaning on her arms.* PAUL ROCKOFFER *paces back and forth, clutching his head in his hands. An armchair to the left of the pedestal. Another one closer to the center of the stage. Doors to the right and to the left.*

ROCKOFFER: Oh, God, God—in vain I call Your name, since I really don't believe in You. But I've got to call someone. I've wasted my life. Two wives, working like a madman—who knows why—after all, my ideas aren't officially recognized, and what's left of my paintings were destroyed yesterday, by order of the head of the Council for the Production of Handmade Crap. I'm totally alone.

STATUE (*without moving; her head in her hands*): You have me.

ROCKOFFER: So what? I wish I hadn't. All you do is remind me there's something else. But you—you're just a poor substitute for what's really important.

STATUE: I remind you of the long, long road ahead of you in the wilderness. All the fortune-tellers have predicted you'll devote yourself to Occult Knowledge in your old age.

ROCKOFFER (*with a contemptuous wave of his hand*): Pooh! I'm absolutely incorrigible in maintaining a perpetual grudge against poor humanity, and I can't find a single drop of healing medicine. I'm like a futile, barren pang of conscience, from which not even the meagerest bud of hope for improvement can blossom.

STATUE: You're a far cry from real tragedy!

ROCKOFFER: That's because my passions aren't very strong. The life I've wasted fades hopelessly into the gray distance of my past. Is there anything more horrible than the gray past which we have to keep on digesting over and over again?

STATUE: Think how many women you could still have, how many unknown mornings, softly gliding through to the mysteries of noontime, then finally how many evenings you could spend in strange conversations with women marveling at your downfall.

ROCKOFFER: Don't tell me about that. Don't try to pry open the innermost core of strangeness. It's all locked up—forever closed, because of boredom: raging irrepressible boredom.

STATUE (*with pity*): How trite you are . . .

ROCKOFFER: Show me someone who isn't trite, and I'll let my throat be cut as a sacrifice on that person's altar.

STATUE: Me.

ROCKOFFER: A woman—or rather the personification of everything impossible about women. Life's unrealizable promises in the flesh.

STATUE: At least be glad you exist at all. Just think—even prisoners serving life sentences are glad of the gift of life.

ROCKOFFER: What's that got to do with *me?* Should I be happy just because right now I'm not impaled on a lonely mound in the middle of the steppes or because I'm not a sewer cleaner? Don't you know who I am?

STATUE: I know you're ridiculous. You wouldn't be, if you could fall in love with me. Then you'd grasp your mission here on *this* planet, you'd be unique, true to yourself and utterly incomparable—who you are, and no one else . . .

ROCKOFFER (*uneasily*): So you do recognize that there's an absolute, I repeat, an absolute hierarchy of Beings, do you?

STATUE (*laughing*): Yes and no—it depends.

ROCKOFFER: Tell me what your criteria are, I humbly beseech you.

STATUE: You've given yourself away. You're neither a philosopher nor an artist.

ROCKOFFER: Oh, so you have had your doubts about that at least. No, I'm not.

STATUE (*laughing*): Then you're just an ambitious nobody, aren't you? For the world at large, despite everything, you're *the* genius of new metaphysical shocks.

ROCKOFFER: I'm pretending—just pretending because I'm bored. I know it's not even decent to pretend.

STATUE: Still, you've got something in you that goes way beyond anything my other lovers had. But unless you love me you won't get one step further.

ROCKOFFER: Stop talking about those eternal lovers of yours you're always bragging about. I know you have influence in real life and that through you I could become the devil knows what. But somebody real, not just somebody in my own eyes . . .

STATUE: You're exaggerating: greatness is relative.

ROCKOFFER: Now I'm going to tell you something: you're trite, worse— you're thoughtful; worse, a hundred times worse—you're basically good.

STATUE (*upset*): You're wrong . . . I'm not good at all. (*Suddenly in another tone.*) But I love you! (*She stretches out toward him.*)

ROCKOFFER (*staring at her*): What? (*Pause.*) That's true, and that's why it doesn't matter to me in the least. The light of the Sole Mystery has been extinguished for me . . . (x) (*A knock at the right; the* STATUE *assumes her former pose.*) and its unfathomableness . . .

STATUE (*impatiently*): Quiet—the Pope's coming.

ROCKOFFER (*in another tone*): I beg you, introduce me to the Pope. He's the only ghost I still feel like talking to . . . (*Enter the* POPE.)

JULIUS II: Greetings, daughter, and you too, my unknown son . . . (PAUL *kneels. The* POPE *gives him his slipper to kiss.*) Only let's not talk about

Heaven. Alighieri was one hundred per cent right. Even a child knows that, but I still have to say that the human imagination cannot conceive such happiness. That's why it was hell that our son Dante portrayed with so much talent. I'll even go so far as to say that Doré's illustrations express quite well the inadequacy of human concepts and the human imagination to portray this kind of, as it were . . .

STATUE: Boredom . . .

JULIUS II: Quiet, daughter. You don't know what you're talking about. (*Emphatically.*) This kind of happiness. (*Jokingly.*) Well, my son: get up and come over here and tell me who you are . . .

STATUE: Holy Father, he's the great artist and philosopher, Paul Rockoffer.

JULIUS II (*raising both hands up in horror*): So it's you, is it? You, wretched infidel, who dared reach out for the fruit of the Highest Mysteries?

ROCKOFFER (*proudly, rising*): It is I!

JULIUS II (*with humility, his hands on his stomach*): I'm not talking about you as an artist. You're great. Oh, I was a fierce patron of the arts. (+) That's all over now! Yes, I've learned to appreciate decadence in art. They don't understand it, and yet that's how they live themselves. I'm talking about the people of your time. (*Indignantly.*) What a terrible thing—all your paintings burned. My son, eternal reward awaits you in Heaven.

STATUE: In Heaven? Ha, ha, ha.

JULIUS II (*good-naturedly*): Don't laugh, daughter. Heaven has its good sides too. Nobody suffers there, and that counts for something.

ROCKOFFER: I'm a philosopher, Holy Father, but I've continued to be a good Catholic too. I can't stand that lie any more.

JULIUS II: Yes—you're a Catholic, *maître* Paul, but you're not a Christian. There's a great difference, a very great difference. And what lies can't you stand any more, my son?

ROCKOFFER: That I'm pretending as an artist, that is, that I've been pretending up to now. All my art is a hoax, a deliberate carefully planned hoax.

JULIUS II: I'm disregarding the fact that there can be no question of Truth once we start discussing Beauty in the abstract. But that's what's so awful, that your art and the art of people like you is the sole Truth. You've discovered the last possible consolation, but I've got to take it away from you. (*Solemnly.*) Your art is the sole Truth on earth. I didn't know you personally, but I do know your paintings very well, in marvelous divine reproductions. (*Gloomily.*) That's the sole Truth.

STATUE: And what about the dogmas of faith?

JULIUS II (*hurriedly*): They're Truth too, but in another dimension. In earthly terms they're the Truth that our poor understanding can grasp. Only there (*he points to the ceiling with his finger*) does their mystery blaze forth in all its fullness before the dazzled intellect of the liberated.

ROCKOFFER (*impatiently*): Holy Father, theology isn't my specialty, and I'd prefer not to talk about philosophy. With Your Holiness's kind permission, let's talk about Art. I know I lie, and that's good enough for me. No one will make me believe that my Art is genuine, not even you, a guest from genuine Heaven.

JULIUS II (*with his finger pointing toward the ceiling*): Up there, where I come from, they know about that better than you do, you miserable speck of dust. But after all an artist's worth comes from either rebellion or success. What would Michelangelo have been if it weren't for me or other patrons of the arts (may God punish them for it). A few madmen eager for new poisons raise up the man who concocts them to the apex of humanity, and then a crowd of non-entities adore him, gaping at the agony and ecstasy of the ones who've been poisoned. Isn't the fact that the Council for the Production of Handmade Crap burned your works a proof of your greatness?

STATUE: You're beaten, Paul baby. Bow down before His Holiness's connoisseurship. (ROCKOFFER *kneels.*)

ROCKOFFER: Something terrible's happened. I don't know any more whether I'm lying or not. And I was the one who knew everything about myself. Holy Father, you've taken away my last hope. I'd finally found one thing I was *absolutely* sure of, and you, you cruel old man, you've destroyed even that.

JULIUS II (*to the* STATUE, *pointing at* ROCKOFFER): That's what comes from pursuing the absolute in life. (*To* ROCKOFFER.) My son, in life as in philosophy, relativity is the only wisdom. I was a believer in the absolute myself. My God, what respectable person hasn't been. But those times are over. Now, what all of you fail to realize is that not every biped who's read Marx or Sorel is highest in the earthly hierarchy of Beings, nor do you realize that I, for example, and the rest of you are two different kinds of Beings, and not just varieties of the human species. Only Art, despite its decadence, has remained on a high plane.

ROCKOFFER (*getting up, in despair*): She tells me the same thing. I'm surrounded by treachery on all sides. I don't have any enemies. I look for them night and day in all the back alleys and only find some sickening mush, but no opponents worthy of me. Can Your Holiness understand that?

JULIUS II (*placing his hand on* ROCKOFFER's *head*): Who could understand you better, my son? Do you think history has given me full satisfaction in that respect? Who do you take me for? Can you suppose that I, Julius Della Rovere, was content having as my chief foe that mediocrity Louis XII? (*With deep emotion.*) Oh! Like God without Satan and Satan without God is he who has not acquired an enemy worthy of him.

STATUE: It's dangerous to base one's greatness on the negative value of one's foes. It's worse than admitting the relativity of Truth.

JULIUS II (*drawing near her and stroking her under the chin*): Oh, you adorable little dialectician! Who educated you so well, my nice little woman?

STATUE (*sadly*): An unhappy love affair, Holy Father, and with somebody I despise. Nothing can teach us women dialectics so well as the combination I just mentioned.

JULIUS II (*to* ROCKOFFER): Poor *maître* Paul, how you must have suffered with that *précieuse*. In my day that type of woman was a little different. They were real titanesses. I myself, my God, even I . . .

ELLA *runs in from the left. Dressed in a sky-blue dress. A man's straw hat with sky-blue ribbons. She has gray gloves and a whole pile of different colored packages in her arms.* GRUMPUS *follows after her in a gray servant's coat and a gray top hat, carrying twice as many packages in each hand as she is. Both of them pay absolutely no attention to* ALICE D'OR.

ROCKOFFER: Help! I forgot, I have a fiancée.

ELLA (*throwing the packages on* GRUMPUS *and running up to* ROCKOFFER): My dearest! But you're happy you have one, now that you've remembered her. My one and only: look at *me.* (*She cuddles up to him.* GRUMPUS, *laden down, stays where he is.* JULIUS II *crosses over to the left and stands leaning against the base of the* STATUE.)

ROCKOFFER (*embraces her gently with his right arm and stares straight ahead with a mad look*): Wait, I have the impression that I've fallen down three flights of stairs. I don't understand myself very well. You know, Mr. Della Rovere has just proved to me that my Art is the Truth. I've lost the last prop for my carefully planned hoax.

ELLA (*chattering away*): I'll do everything for you. Just rely on me. I've fixed up our little apartment divinely. The sofas have already been covered— you know, the golden material with the tiny rose stripes. And the sideboard is just the most beautiful thing. All the furniture for the dining room is really pretty, but there's something strange about the sideboard. There's some sort of dreadful mystery lurking in those faces made of iron-gray wood. They were done by Zamoyski himself. You can keep all your drugs in there. I won't bother you, I'll let you do everything you want, only in moderation. (ROCKOFFER *smiles vacantly.*) Aren't you happy? (ELLA *suddenly grows sad.*) Mother furnished my boudoir for me herself. Everything's covered in pink silk with little sky-blue flowers.

ROCKOFFER (*embraces her with sudden tenderness*): But of course—I am happy. My poor little thing . . . (*He kisses her on the forehead.*)

JULIUS II (*to the* STATUE): Look, daughter, see how this little bird's chattering is lulling our good docile snake to sleep.

ELLA (*looking around*): Who's that old man?

ROCKOFFER: Don't you know? It's Pope Julius II: he's come straight from Heaven to bless us.

ELLA (*turning to* JULIUS II): Holy Father . . . (*She kneels and kisses his slipper.* GRUMPUS *puts the packages on the ground, also kneels and kisses the* POPE*'s other slipper.*) Oh, how happy I am!

JULIUS II (*to the* STATUE):   Well, what can you do with such innocence and goodness? (*To all those present.*) I bless you, my children. I wish you a swift and unexpected death, my dear little daughter. You'll be the most beautiful of all the angels whose garlands twine about the throne of the Almighty.

ROCKOFFER (*falling on his knees*):   Oh, how beautiful this is! I feel from now on I could start painting like Fra Angelico. All decadence has vanished without a trace. Thank you, Holy Father.

JULIUS II (*to the* STATUE): See how it's possible to be a sower of good in this world without even meaning to be. Look at the blissful faces on those two children. *Maître* Paul has grown at least ten years younger.

STATUE: Not for long, Your Holiness. You don't realize how quickly time passes for us. Time is relative. You know Einstein's theory, Holy Father. Transferring the concept of psychological time to physics has produced a wonderful flowering of knowledge about the world, an indestructible construction of absolute Truth.

ELLA *gets up and goes over to* PAUL, *who also gets up. They kiss in ecstasy.* GRUMPUS *gets up likewise and looks at them, deeply moved.*

JULIUS II: My, my, my! In Heaven, none of us believes in physics, my child. It's only a simplified system for all of you to understand mathematical phenomena since your brains stopped short at the boundary beyond which the creation of metaphysics is possible. Every step in the hierarchy of Beings has its own boundary. Human philosophy reached a dead end. The co-efficient of all knowledge is infinite only within each boundary. But what's happening on the planets of Aldebaran! Ho, ho! They recognize their own "Einstein" there too, but they've been able to place him in his proper sphere.

STATUE (*anxiously*): And so the world really has no bounds?

JULIUS II: Of course not, my child.

STATUE: Then even you, Holy Father, won't live eternally? But what about Heaven?

JULIUS II: Heaven is only a symbol. You people must accept the theory of diverse bodies united in a single individual. But the number of these bodies is limited. Eventually we'll all die for good. The sole mystery is God. (*He points to the ceiling.*) (x)

STATUE: Ah! (*She collapses on the pedestal.* JULIUS II *sits on the chair on the left side.*)

ELLA (*drawing away from* ROCKOFFER): What's that? I heard a voice inside me saying something about eternal death. (+)

ROCKOFFER (*pointing to the prone* ALICE d'OR): That statue said it. It just passed out. It's a symbol of the past I sacrificed for you.

ELLA (*astounded*):   But there's nobody there!

ROCKOFFER: Didn't you hear how His Holiness was philosophizing with it?

ELLA: Paul, stop joking. The Holy Father was talking to himself. Don't stare so blankly: you're frightening me. Tell me the truth.

ROCKOFFER: You wouldn't understand anyhow, my child. Let's not talk about it.

JULIUS II. Yes, daughter, *maître* Paul is right. A good wife shouldn't know too much about her husband. Within certain limits, a husband should be a mystery.

ELLA: I have to know everything. You're torturing me, Paul. Our little apartment, which made me so happy, is beginning to terrify me in this vision of the future you and the Pope have created together. It's as though a shadow has fallen across my heart. I want go home to mother.

ROCKOFFER (*taking her in his arms*): Quiet, little girl. *I've* begun to believe in my future. I'm going to return to Art and I'll be happy. We'll both be happy. I'll start painting again calmly, without any orgies with form, and I'll end my life as a good Catholic.

JULIUS II (*bursts out laughing*): Ha, Ha, Ha!

ELLA: End your life? But I'm just beginning it with you.

ROCKOFFER: I'm old—you must understand that once and for all.

ELLA: You're forty-six—I know. But why does your face say something different? Can the soul really be so different from the face?

ROCKOFFER (*impatiently*): Oh, quit bothering me about my soul. It's an essence so complicated I've never been able to see myself as a whole. It was only an illusion. Stop thinking about me and accept me as I am.

ELLA: Paul, tell me who you really are. I want to know you.

ROCKOFFER: I'm unknowable even to myself. Look at the paintings I've already done and you'll see who I used to be. But if you look at what I'm going to do now, you'll see what I want to be. The rest is a delusion.

ELLA: And is that what love is?

ROCKOFFER: Love? Shall I tell you what love is? In the morning I'll wake you with a kiss. After a morning bath, we'll drink coffee. Then I'll paint, while you read books, which I'll select for you. Then dinner. After dinner, we'll go for a walk. Then work again. Tea, supper, a little serious discussion, and finally not too fatigued by sensual pleasures, you'll fall asleep to replenish your strength for the following day.

ELLA: And so, on and on, without end?

ROCKOFFER: You mean: to the very end. Such is life for those devoid of absolute desires. We are limited, and Infinity surrounds us. It's too trite even to talk about.

ELLA: But *I* want to live! With that hope in mind I've fixed up our dear little apartment, I've taken care of everything. I must live really.

ROCKOFFER: Tell me, please, what is life "really"?

ELLA: Now I don't know anything any more and that terrifies me.

ROCKOFFER: Don't force me to make speeches. I could tell you things, beautiful and horrible, deep and infinitely distant, but it would be just one more lie.

STATUE (*waking up*) (x): An intimate drama is beginning. Our little Paul has decided to become sincere.

ELLA: I'm hearing that strange evil voice of an alien being inside me again. (*Looking around.*) That's funny—I feel there's somebody here, but I don't see anyone except you and the Pope. (+)

STATUE: I am the lady Pope for fallen titans. I teach them the gray wisdom of daily existence.

ELLA (*in fear*): Paul—stop hypnotizing me. I'm afraid.

ROCKOFFER: Don't say another word. I'm beginning to be afraid myself. I don't even know how I know that person.

ELLA: What person? Oh, my God, my God—I'll die of fright. I'm afraid of *you*. Holy Father—save me. You've come from Heaven.

JULIUS II (*getting up, speaking with cruelty*): How do you know that Heaven isn't a symbol for the most awful renunciation? Renouncing one's real personality? I'm a shadow, just as she is. (*He points to the* STATUE.)

ELLA: But there isn't anyone there, is there? Take pity on me, Holy Father. All this affects me like a bad dream.

JULIUS II: Dream on, my child. Maybe this moment of terror is the most beautiful in your whole life. Oh, how I envy all of you. (ELLA *covers her face with her hands.*)

ROCKOFFER: A strange force is taking possession of me again. Ella—I can't conquer decadence with you.

ELLA (*without uncovering her face*):   Now I understand you at last. I've either got to die for you or stop loving you. (*Uncovers her face.*) I love you now I see you descending into the abyss. This is my real life.

STATUE: That little virgin's making progress like crazy. Now I'll never get you back again, Paul love.

ELLA: That voice again. But I'm not afraid of anything now. It's happened. My fate's already sealed somewhere. And the sooner the better. Paul, I won't go back to mother. I'll stay with you.

JULIUS II: Don't be in such a hurry, daughter. You're already on the right path. But it doesn't mean you've got to be in quite such a hurry.

ROCKOFFER: Holy Father, the speed of my transformations terrifies me too. In a moment I may become a statesman, an inventor, who the hell knows what. Whole new layers have shifted in my head like an avalanche.

JULIUS II: Wait—I hear footsteps in the hallway downstairs. I have a rendezvous with the King of Hyrcania today.

ROCKOFFER: What? Hyrcan IV? Is he still alive? You know, he was a classmate of mine at school. He was always dreaming about an artificial kingdom in the old style.

JULIUS II: And he created it. I guess you never read the newspapers. (*He listens.*) That's him—I recognize his powerful, commanding footsteps. (*Suspense.*)

ELLA: But is he real or is he something like Your Highness?

JULIUS II (*outraged*): Something like! You're taking too many liberties, my daughter.

ELLA: I'm not afraid of anything now.

JULIUS II: You've already died—you've nothing to fear.

ELLA: Nonsense. I'm alive and I'll create a completely normal life for Paul. He'll fall to pieces slowly, creating wonderful things. I'm not at all as innocent and stupid as you all think. I've got a little venom in me too . . . (x)

From the right enter HYRCAN IV *in a purple coat which comes down to the ground. He has a helmet on his head with a red plume. A huge sword in his hand.*

HYRCAN IV: Good evening. How are you doing, Rockoffer? You weren't expecting me today. I've heard you're getting married—won't work. (*Kneels quickly in front of the* POPE *and kisses his slipper; getting up.*) Glad to see His Holiness is in good health. Heaven agrees with him very well. (*Approaches the* STATUE.) How are you doing, Alice—Alice d'Or, isn't it? Remember our orgies in that marvelous dive—what was it called? (*He squeezes the* STATUE's *hand.*)

STATUE: Perdition Gardens.

ELLA *turns around at the sound of her voice.*

HYRCAN IV: Exactly.

ELLA (*pointing at the* STATUE): She was the one who was here! It was her voice I kept hearing as though it was inside me. It's not nice to eavesdrop on our conversation that way!

STATUE: It's not my fault you didn't see me, Ella . . .

ELLA: Please don't address me by my first name. I'm asking you to leave this house. I'm staying here with Paul now. (*To* ROCKOFFER.) Who is that woman?

ROCKOFFER: My former mistress. I'm letting her live in this room. I was a little afraid in such a big house and that's why . . .

ELLA: You don't have to justify yourself. From now on I'm going to be here and I'm asking you to get rid of that lady immediately.

JULIUS II: Not so fast, my daughter. You may overreach yourself.

ELLA: I don't want her here and that's the end of it. Paul, did you hear what I said? (*She sits down in the armchair to the left.*)

ROCKOFFER: Certainly, my dear. That's no problem. (*Goes toward the* STATUE.) Alice my girl, we must part. Get off that pedestal and clear out. This is the end. You'll get money from my bank. (*He pulls out a check book and begins to write.*) (x)

HYRCAN IV (*to* ROCKOFFER):   If I may be permitted to ask—who's that broad? (*He indicates* ELLA.) Is she your new mistress, or is she the fiancée I've been hearing about?

ROCKOFFER (*he stops writing and remains indecisive*):   My fiancée.

HYRCAN IV (*to* ELLA): Oh—in that case perhaps you'll allow me to introduce myself: I'm Hyrcan IV, king of the artificial kingdom of Hyrcania. Be good enough not to order my friend about, or you'll find I make short work of things.

STATUE: You talk marvelously, Hyrcan.

HYRCAN IV: I don't need your advice either, Alice. I'll settle things with you too at the proper time. The situation—apart from my kingdom, which is the only really unusual thing—is the tritest in the world: a friend decided to liberate his friend from women—from the ordinary bags, masculettes, and battle–axes who've infested him.

ROCKOFFER: To prove what? Isn't your kingdom only a badly disguised form of insanity, my friend?

HYRCAN IV: You'll find out soon enough. You're already suffering from a prison psychosis living in freedom. Over-intellectualized sex combined with fluctuation between decadence and classicism in art. First of all, to hell with art! There's no such thing as art.

JULIUS II: Excuse me, sire. I won't allow *maître* Paul to be made an ordinary pawn in the hands of Your Royal Highness. He's got to go to pieces in a creative way.

ELLA: That's just what I've been saying . . .

HYRCAN IV (*speaks to the* POPE *without paying any attention to what she has just said*): He doesn't *have* to go to pieces at all. That's just the way perverse young girls jabber when they sniff carrion or the way depraved patrons of the arts think. Paul won't go to pieces: he'll make himself into someone new and different. None of you has any idea what conditions are like in my country. It's the sole oasis left in the whole world.

JULIUS II: The world is by no means limited to our planet . . .

HYRCAN IV: Holy Father, I don't have time to plumb the depths of Your Holiness's posthumous knowledge. I am a real man, or rather a real superman. I create reality by embodying Hyrcanian desires.

STATUE: There are no such things as Hyrcanian desires . . .

JULIUS II (*politely to the* STATUE): That's just what I wanted to say. (*To* HYRCAN.) That word doesn't even exist, it's just an empty sound without meaning.

HYRCAN IV: Once I give it a definition, that empty sound will become a concept, and from then on it will exist in the world of ideas for all eternity.

JULIUS II (*laughing*): But only ahead, not behind, sire.

HYRCAN IV: That's just the point. No behinds for me. I reverse events, and life too only goes ahead, not behind.

ROCKOFFER: You know, Hyrcan, you're beginning to interest me.

HYRCAN IV: Experience it—it's wonderful. Once you experience it, you'll be so thrilled and have such a sense of power, you'll go out of your mind. (*To the* POPE.) You see—I call Hyrcanian desire the desire for the absolute in life. Only by believing in the absolute and in its realization can we create something in life.

JULIUS II: And what good will that be to anyone? What will come of it?

HYRCAN IV: That's senile skepticism or rather senile doddering. Oh, that's right—I forgot that Your Holiness is practically 600 years old. What'll come of it is that we'll experience our life on the heights of what's possible on this damned small globe of ours, and not waste away in a constant compromise with the ever-growing power of social togetherness and regimentation. Some consider me an anarchist. I spit on their rancid opinions. I'm creating supermen. Two, or three—that's enough. The rest is pulp—cheese for worms. "Notre société est aussi pourrie qu'un fromage." Who said that our society is as rotten as a cheese?

JULIUS II: Never mind about that, sire. I came here for a serious discussion on saving art from total decadence. The fight against so-called *purblaguism*. It's got to be proved that Pure Blague is impossible. Even God, although he's all-powerful, wouldn't really be able to blague anything perfectly and completely.

HYRCAN IV: Humbug. Coming here, I gave some thought to the problem of Art. Art has come to an end and nothing will ever revive it. There isn't any sense to our discussion.

JULIUS II: But, sire, as I see it, Your Royal Highness is a follower of Nietzsche, at least in social questions. Nietzsche himself recognized Art as the most important stimulus for personal power.

HYRCAN V (*threateningly*): What? Me a follower of Nietzsche? Please don't insult me. He was the philosopher of life for a bunch of dunderheads willing to drug themselves with absolutely anything. I don't accept any drugs and therefore I don't accept art either. My ideas came about completely independently. I didn't read any of that trash until after I'd created my country. That's enough. Our conversation is over.

JULIUS II: All right. But just one more thing: isn't formulating the question that way, with the end already in view, pure pragmatism? You can believe in the absolute in life or not, but to believe in it as a preconceived theory for experiencing on the heights, as Your Royal Highness put it, this wretched life of ours on our small globe—likewise your expression, my son—is a self-contradiction and a devaluation of Hyrcanian—yes, I repeat *Hyrcanian* desires themselves! Ha, ha!

HYRCAN IV: That's pure dialectics. Maybe in Heaven it's worth something. I'm a creator of re-al-i-ty. Understand, Holy Father. And now that's enough—don't get me upset.

JULIUS II: Sire, I beg you, just one more question.

HYRCAN IV: Well?

JULIUS II: How's religion doing in your country?

HYRCAN IV: Everyone believes whatever he wants. Religion is done for too.

JULIUS II: Ho, ho! That's a good one. And he wants to create old-time power without religion. Really, sire, that strikes me as a stupid farce. Look at the most savage tribes, at the aboriginal Arunta or whoever they are. Even they have a religion. Without religion there are no countries in the old sense of the word. There can only be an ant hill.

HYRCAN IV: No, no—not an organized ant hill, only a great herd of straggling cattle, over which I and my friends wield power.

JULIUS II: But what do *you* believe in, my son?

HYRCAN IV: In myself and that's good enough for me. But if I ever need to, I'll believe in anything, in any old fetish, in a crocodile, in the Unity of Being, in you, Holy Father, in my own navel, what difference does it make! Is that clear?

JULIUS II: You, sir, are a very clever but ordinary bandit and the worst kind of pragmatist. You're not a king at all, at least not for me. From now on we won't have anything more to do with each other. (*He goes to the left and sinks exhausted into his armchair.* HYRCAN *remains standing looking angry, leaning on his sword.*)

STATUE: Well, you got taken down a peg or two, my petty chieftain. The Holy Father is really a first-class dialectician.

ROCKOFFER: You know, Hyrcan, actually His Holiness is partly right in all this. Besides, I must point out that the tone of our group deteriorated as soon as you came in. The conversation became downright crude.

JULIUS II: You're quite right, my son; to talk to slobs you've got to talk like a slob.

ROCKOFFER (*to* HYRCAN): I don't entirely agree with you on fundamental principles either.

ELLA: Oh, Paul, then all's not lost yet.

HYRCAN IV (*waking up from his meditation*): Yes—I'm a slob, but I'm what I am and there's no one else like me. Listen to me. I'm talking to all of you as equals for the last time. Paul—make up your mind. Alexander the Great was a slob too. And anyhow, we have a sovereign here with us. You can read about Mr. Della Rovere and his doings in any outline of history.

JULIUS II (*getting up*): Shut up! Shut up!

ROCKOFFER (*quietly to* HYRCAN): Leave him alone. (*Aloud.*) I won't allow anyone to insult the Holy Father in my house, not even the King of Hyrcania.

JULIUS II: Thank you, my son. (*Sitting down.*) A pragmatist on the throne! No—this is absolutely unheard of. It's actually funny. Ha, ha, ha!

HYRCAN IV: Well, Paul, go ahead say something. Maybe your objections will be somewhat more to the point. Believe me, I only want your happiness. If you don't leave with me now for Hyrcania on the eleven o'clock express, you're through. I won't come back here again. I'll break off diplomatic relations and start a series of wars. Digging up and burning down ant hills, molehills, and dolthills. A lovely business.

ROCKOFFER: You've already done one thing for me. All the little problems I used to be concerned with seem completely insignificant to me now.

ELLA (*seated in the armchair to the left; suddenly wakes up from her stupefied condition*): Does that include the problem of love too?

ROCKOFFER: Wait a minute, Ella, I'm in a different dimension right now. (*To* HYRCAN.) But I must confess I don't see greatness on your side either.

HYRCAN IV: What do you mean?

ROCKOFFER: His Holiness used a word that I can't get out of my head—but you won't be offended, will you, Hyrcan?

HYRCAN IV: At you—never. Go ahead. What word?

ROCKOFFER: Bandit. You're actually a petty robber baron, not a true sovereign. You're only great given the extremely low level of civilization in your country. Nowadays, Nietzsche's superman can't be anything more than a small-time thug. And those who would have been rulers in the past are the artists of our own times. Breeding the superman is the biggest joke I've ever heard of.

HYRCAN IV: You're talking like a moron. You don't understand the first thing about my concept of Hyrcanian desires. You're living your life as an absolutist—that's a fact. You're too much either for yourself or for so-called society. You're a perfect specimen of "moral insanity," but you've got the strength of at least four normal people, according to the standards of our times.

ROCKOFFER: Yes, that's a fact. That's why I've decided to end it all right now by committing suicide.

ELLA (*getting up*): Paul, what's happening to you? Am I dreaming?

STATUE: He's right. I never dared tell him that, but it's the only solution, and the tritest.

HYRCAN IV: Shut up, you sluts! One's worse than the other. (*To* ROCKOFFER.) You fool, did I come all the way from my Hyrcania to see my only friend go under? I've already got two of the right sort of people. I've absolutely got to have a third. You're the only one who can fill the bill.

ROCKOFFER: But what's a regular work day like in this Hyrcania of yours? What do you really occupy yourselves with there?

HYRCAN IV: Power—we get drunk on power in all its many forms from morning till night. And then we feast in an absolutely devastatingly glorious fashion, discussing everything and viewing everything from the unattainable heights of our reign.

ROCKOFFER: A reign over a heap of idiots incapable of organizing themselves. An ordinary military dictatorship. Under favorable conditions really radical state socialism can do the same thing.

HYRCAN IV: But what was humanity in the past but a heap of beings, a formless pulpy mass without any organization? Pseudo-titans evolved by socialism have to lie in order to hold on to their power. We don't. Our life is Truth.

ROCKOFFER: So it's a question of Truth. Is Truth also an integral part of the Hyrcanian world view?

HYRCAN IV: Of course. But once all humanity wears a mask, the problem of Truth will disappear all by itself. I and my two friends, Count de Plignac and Rupprecht von Blasen, are creating just such a mask. Society masked and we alone know everything.

ROCKOFFER: But how does all this differ from theatre? You know what put me off the most? Your costume.

HYRCAN IV: But that's a trifle. I thought you were more impressed by the scenery and that's why I dressed up this way. I can take off these glad rags. (*He goes on talking as he takes his clothes off. Under his coat he reveals a golden garment. He throws it off and stands in a well-tailored, normal cutaway. He takes off his helmet as well. He piles the clothes in the middle of the stage. He continues to hold his sword in his hand.*) Know what greatness consists of? Attaining isolation. To create such an island of brutalized, bestial spirits amidst a sea of regimentation engulfing everything, now that takes a little more strength than Mr. Della Rovere had in the sixteenth century. Not to mention the Borgias— they were just common clowns.

GRUMPUS: Most gracious lord—I'll go to Hyrcania too. If you're going to serve, you might as well serve real masters.

HYRCAN IV (*to* ROCKOFFER): See? That dolt's recognized my true worth, but you won't even try to understand me.

ROCKOFFER: Wait; my daemon has split in two. It's an unheard of event in the history of mankind. I hear two secret voices telling me two parallel truths that will never come together. The contradiction between them is of an infinite order.

HYRCAN IV: I keep a certain philosopher at my court, one Chwistek by name. On the basis of his concept of "the plurality of realities," he's establishing the systematic relativization of all Truth. He'll explain the rest to you. He's a great sage. I'm telling you, Rockoffer, come with me.

ROCKOFFER: My conscience as a *former artist* is growing to the dimensions of an all-consuming tumor. A new monster feeds on itself. Monsters, till now tormented in cages, have conquered unknown areas of my disintegrating brain.

ELLA (*getting up*): He's simply gone mad. Most Gracious Lord, ask whatever you will, but don't take him away from me. Now that he's a madman, he'll create wonderful things as long as he's with me.

ROCKOFFER: You're mistaken, little girl. I'm clear-headed as never before. Long ago I recognized my madness—for me it was much less interesting than my icy self-possession.

ELLA *sits down, stunned.*

STATUE: That's the truth. Once, when I was with him, he overcame a fit of madness. It was metaphysical madness, of course, but my life was also hanging by a thread. He's a psychic athlete, and a physical one too—sometimes.

HYRCAN IV: Alice, believe me, for him you were only a sort of vinegar in which he preserved himself until my arrival. I'm grateful to you for that. You can come with me to Hyrcania.

STATUE (*climbing down from the pedestal*): All right—you can make me into a priestess of whatever cult you want. I'm ready for anything.

JULIUS II: So you've also become a pragmatist, my daughter. I didn't expect that.

STATUE: But Holy Father, in the depths of your soul aren't you really a pragmatist, too?

JULIUS II (*getting up*): Perhaps, perhaps. Who's to say? My world view is subject to constant transformations.

HYRCAN IV: In return for recognition of my concept, I'm even willing not to let Art disappear from my realm for good and all. I appoint you patron of the dying arts, Holy Father, on condition that you won't tempt Paul Rockoffer. He can be an absolutist only in life, not in art.

JULIUS II: All right, all right. I give in. In any case, you've opened up new perspectives for me. Just between you and me, you have no idea how madly, hopelessly bored I've been in Heaven. Starting today I'm extending my leave for at least three hundred years.

HYRCAN *and* ROCKOFFER *whisper.*

STATUE: Julius Della Rovere, you can count on me: with my dialectics, I'll make twenty of those three hundred years a delight for you. In the evening, after a tiring day's work, you'll tell me all about it and have a really serious talk with a woman who's both wise and moderately perverse.

JULIUS II: Thanks, daughter. I'm going to Hyrcania.

ELLA (*getting up*):   I can't take it any more! This is some ghastly nightmare, all these discussions of yours. I'm not at all good and noble, and I feel as though I've been asphyxiated by some hideous poison gas. And besides, all this is boring. You're tearing my heart apart as a game, a stupid, boring game. I want to go to Hyrcania too. When Paul feels unhappy, at least he'll have me and I'll save him. Sire, will Your Royal Highness take me with him?

HYRCAN IV: Out of the question. Paul must forget his former life. You'll start tempting him right away to make artistic excuses for why he fell or who the hell knows what. All his creative impulses must be nipped in the bud.

ELLA: And how's this finally going to end? What happens afterwards?

HYRCAN IV: Then, as usual, death takes over, but along with it the feeling that life has been experienced on the heights, and not in the fetid quagmire of society, where there's art instead of morphine.

ROCKOFFER: So you're opposed to drugs? I can't get along without them.

HYRCAN IV: I approve of alkaloids, but I have the greatest contempt for all psychic drugs. Aside from the fact that you won't create anything, you can do whatever you want.

ELLA *approaches* PAUL *and whispers to him.*

JULIUS II: Your Hyrcania, Sire, strikes me as a kind of sanitarium for people sick of society. The way you describe it, of course. Actually it's the lowest kind of whorehouse for the playboys of life . . .

HYRCAN IV: But they're absolutists every one of them—if they don't manage to get through a wall, at least they leave the bloody marks of their smashed skull on it. There lies my greatness.

JULIUS II: But after all, you could just as well have been a pickpocket, Sire, like the Prince Manolescu.

HYRCAN IV: I could have been, but I'm not. I'm the king of the last real kingdom on earth. Greatness lies only in what succeeds. If I'd been completely inept, I'd have been ridiculous from the very start.

JULIUS II: You can still fall. And then what?

HYRCAN IV: I'll fall from a certain height. After all, there's never been a tyrant who didn't fall.

JULIUS II: That's just where the pettiness lies: in the idea of a *certain* height.

HYRCAN IV: I can't fall through Infinity. Even in the world of physics we have finite speed, the speed of light. Practically speaking, it's infinite.

JULIUS II (*ironically*): Practically speaking! Pragmatism's at the bottom of everything. But it doesn't matter. For the time being, I prefer it to Heaven.

HYRCAN IV: Rockoffer, did you hear that? No one has ever received a greater compliment. The Holy Father is with us.

ELLA (*clinging to* PAUL): Answer me, at least make up your mind.

ROCKOFFER: I'm going. It's always worth abandoning the foreseeable for the unknown. Besides, it's the basis for the New Art, the Art of outrageous surprises.

HYRCAN IV: Thanks, but don't even compare Hyrcanianness and Art. Hyrcania must be experienced.

ROCKOFFER: The Dadaists said the same thing about Dadaism, until they were all hanged. No—that's enough. I'm yours. Everything's so disgusting that there isn't any folly colossal enough not to be worth sacrificing everything in life for. I'm ready to die, but not in all this pettiness. I had intended to go die in Borneo or Sumatra. But I prefer the mystery of becoming to the mystery of staying the same. I'm coming.

ELLA: Paul, I beg you. I won't bother you. Take me with you.

ROCKOFFER: No, child. Let's not say any more about it. I know your spiritual ambushes. As a woman, you don't exist for me at all.

ELLA: Paul, Paul—how cruelly you're tearing my insides apart! I'll die. Think of our poor, lonely little apartment, and my poor unhappy mother.

ROCKOFFER: I'm terribly sorry for you. Now I really love you for the first time . . .

ELLA: Paul! Wake up from this hallucination. If you can't stay, at least let me go to my death and destruction!

HYRCAN IV (*pushing her away from* ROCKOFFER): Lay off him. She's a cuttlefish, not a woman. Did you hear me? This is the last time I'm telling you.

ELLA (*flaring up*): Then kill me—I won't leave him of my own accord.

From the right enter TWO MATRONS *and* TWO OLD GENTLEMEN *elegantly dressed in black.*

MOTHER: Ellie, let me introduce you to two of your uncles you don't know. They're financing your marriage with Paul. Mr. Ropner and Mr. Stolz—

my daughter and my daughter's fiancé, the well-known painter Mr. Paul Rockoffer.

The TWO OLD GENTLEMEN *greet* ELLA.

ROCKOFFER: First of all, I'm no longer her fiancée, and secondly, in introductions a person's first name and occupation should never be mentioned, particularly since I've changed my occupation. You'll have to pardon me, but unknown perspectives are opening up before me. I'll be something along the line of a cabinet minister in Hyrcania. The gratification of Hyrcanian desires. It would take too much time to try to explain so many things all at once. I hardly understand it myself.

MOTHER: I can see that. You must be drunk, Paul. Ella, what does this mean?

ELLA: Mama, it's all come to nothing. He's not drunk, and he hasn't gone mad. It's the most obvious, cold, cruel truth. The King of Hyrcania is taking him with him. He's stopped being an artist.

The MOTHER *is dumbfounded.*

HYRCAN IV: Yes, Ma'am, and we'll settle things amicably. I don't like big scenes in the grand manner when I'm not on my own home ground. I'll pay you whatever damages you ask.

MOTHER: I'm not concerned about money, but about my daughter's heart.

HYRCAN IV: Don't be trite, please. And besides, I'm not just any lord or master, I'm a king.

MOTHER: I've read about that Hyrcania of *yours* in the newspapers. It's the theatre critics who write about it. Not one decent politician even wants to hear it mentioned. That Hyrcania of yours is a cheap theatrical spoof. A depraved and degenerate band of madmen and drunkards took it into their heads to simulate a regime in the old style! You ought to be ashamed, Mister! Hyrcania! It's simply a disgrace, "bezobrazie" *à la manière russe.*

HYRCAN IV (*throwing his sword on the pile of clothes*): The old lady's gone crazy. Be quiet. Rockoffer's agreed and I'm not going to let any mummified battle-axes get him in their clutches. Let's go. (PAUL *remains undecided.*)

ELLA: Mama, I won't survive this. I want to go too.

MOTHER: What? So you're against me too? Aren't you ashamed in front of the uncles you've just met? If you keep behaving this way, we won't get a penny. Ella, come to your senses.

ELLA (*clutching her head*): I don't want to live! I can't! Only I don't have the courage to die. (*To the* KING.) Hyrcan, most poisonous of civilized reptiles, crowned slob, kill me. I want pain and death—I've already suffered too much today.

MOTHER: Ella, what a way to talk! Who taught you such dreadful expressions?

ELLA: I don't even know myself. I'm playing a role—I know that—but I'm suffering so terribly. (*To the* KING.) I beg you—kill me.

HYRCAN IV: You want me to? That won't cost me anything. In Hyrcania everything is possible. The absolute in life—can you understand that, you vile dishwashers of plates others licked clean long ago?

ROCKOFFER: Wait—maybe there's a way it can all be settled amicably. I can't stand scenes and rows. Ella will go back quietly to her mother, and I'll at least leave with a clear conscience.

ELLA: No, no, no—I want to die.

MOTHER: Do you want to poison the last days of my old age? And what about our little apartment, and our lovely evenings together, just the three of us, and later surrounded by the children: yours and Paul's, my darling grandchildren.

ELLA: Mama, don't torture me. I'll poison your life more if I stay with you than if I die right now at the hands of the king.

MOTHER (*in despair*): What difference does it make who kills you? You die only once, but my old age will be poisoned to the very end.

ELLA: No—I must die right away. Every minute of life is unbearable anguish.

HYRCAN IV: Do you mean that seriously, Miss Ella? (x)

ELLA: Yes. I've never been so serious.

HYRCAN IV: Well, all right, then. (*He picks up his sword, which has been lying on the pile of royal robes, and strikes* ELLA *on the head with it.* ELLA *falls without a groan.*)

MOTHER: Oh!!! (*She falls on* ELLA*'s corpse and remains there until almost the end of the play.* HYRCAN *stands leaning on his sword. The* TWO OLD GENTLEMEN *whisper vehemently among themselves.* MATRON II *remains calm.*) (+)

ROCKOFFER: I'm just beginning to understand what the Hyrcanianness of Hyrcanian desires actually is. Now at last I know what absolutism in real life is. (*He clasps* HYRCAN*'s hands in his.*)

JULIUS II: I've committed many atrocities, but this pragmatic crime has moved me deeply. I bless you, poor mother, and you also, spirit of a maiden pure and lofty beyond all earthly measure. (*He blesses the group on the left; to* HYRCAN.) Well, sire, she lived her life as an absolutist too—you've got to admit that.

HYRCAN IV: Her death has moved me too. I've discovered a new kind of beauty. I didn't know there could be anything quite so unexpected outside of Hyrcania.

ONE OF THE OLD MEN (*drawing near*): Well all right, gentlemen, but what now? How are we going to settle all this? We understand, or rather we can guess what it's all about. Actually it's a trite story, but how can it all be explained and justified?

JULIUS II: Well, gentlemen. I'm a tolerant person, but I can't stand your company any longer. You understand—I was the Pope. Kiss me quickly on the slipper and clear out, while you're still in one piece. I can't stand dull, trite thinking masquerading as phony good nature. (*The* TWO OLD GENTLEMEN *kiss his slipper and, crumpling their hats in their hands, go out to the right with astonished faces. Meanwhile, the others continue talking.*)

HYRCAN IV: Paul—go with this flunky right now and get ready for the trip. The Hyrcania express leaves in an hour. I'm here incognito and don't have my special train with me.

ROCKOFFER: All right—Grumpus, leave those ladies behind and come along.

He and GRUMPUS *cross over to the right.* MATRON II *comes up to* HYRCAN. ROCKOFFER *and* GRUMPUS *stop by the exit.*

MATRON II: Hyrcan—don't you recognize me? I'm your mother.

HYRCAN IV: I recognized you instantly, Mama, but you're the one hidden shame in my life. I'd prefer not to apply the Hyrcanian world view to my own mother. My mother, mother to a king—an ordinary whore! How hideous!

JULIUS II: And so even you have saintliness hidden in the depths of your pragmatically criminal heart? I didn't expect that.

HYRCAN IV: Holy Father—don't meddle in what's none of your business. (*To* MATRON II.) Mama, I advise you, get out of here and don't ever cross my path again. You know, I inherited a bloody and violent disposition from my father.

MATRON II: But couldn't I be a priestess of love in your country? In olden times the daughters of Syrian princes voluntarily offered up their virginity to unknown strangers for a couple of copper pieces.

HYRCAN IV: That was in olden times and that's what made it beautiful. You didn't get started that way. You were the mistress of our idiot aristocrats and obese Semitic bankers. I don't even know whose son I am—me, a king. Nasty mess.

MATRON II: Why should you care? All the more credit to you that starting from nothing you've raised yourself up to the height of a throne. A ridiculous one, but a throne all the same.

HYRCAN IV: Still, I'd prefer to know my genealogy and not get lost in guess work.

MATRON II: You're ridiculous. What difference does it make to you whether you're Aryan or Semitic or Mongolian? Prince Tseng, ambassador of the Celestial Empire, was one of my lovers too. Nowadays . . .

HYRCAN IV: Shut up—don't get me in a rage!

JULIUS II: Common pragmatic snobbery. So even in Hyrcania there are irrelevant issues. Yes—Napoleon was right: *recherche de paternité interdite.*

STATUE: Ha, ha, ha! Hyrcan and the mother problem, that's a good one!

HYRCAN IV: I'm leaving. I don't want to have a new row. If I weren't here incognito, it would all end quite differently. (*He goes to the door and leaves at the same time as* ROCKOFFER *and* GRUMPUS.)

MATRON II (*running towards the door*): Hyrcan, Hyrcan! My son! (*She runs out.*)

JULIUS II (*to the* STATUE): That's a fine kettle of fish! And what do you say to that, my daughter!

STATUE: I knew we wouldn't get off without a few discordant notes.

Behind the scenes, a shot is heard, and then a dreadful roar from HYRCAN IV.

JULIUS II: What's that now? Some fiendish surprise. My stay in Heaven has made my once nerves-of-steel too sensitive. I've grown unaccustomed to shooting.

ELLA'*s mother hasn't even batted an eyelash.*

STATUE: Quiet. With Paul, anything is possible. Let's wait: this is a really strange moment. I feel an extraordinary, non–Euclidean tension throughout all space. The whole world has shrunk to the dimensions of an orange.

JULIUS II: Quiet—they're coming.

ROCKOFFER *runs in with a revolver in his hand, followed by* MATRON II.

ROCKOFFER: I've killed him. I've avenged poor Ella's death.

JULIUS II: Who? Hyrcan?

ROCKOFFER (*embracing* MATRON II): Yes. And you know what turned me against him most? It was that scene with his mother. I don't remember my mother, but I feel sure I wouldn't have treated her that way. If you want absolutism in life, there's absolutism for you. He drove me to it himself, the brute.

JULIUS II: Well, fine—that's very nice of you, my son. But what's going to come of it?

ROCKOFFER (*to* MATRON II): Just a minute. First of all, I ask you, in memory of your son and my friend, to consider me as your second son. He was unworthy of you. A matron—a whore—where could I find a better mother?

MATRON I (*kissing him on the head*): Thank you, Paul—my son, my true, dear son!

ROCKOFFER: That's enough. Let's go.

JULIUS II: But where? What are we going to do without that thug Hyrcan? Worse still—what'll we do without Hyrcania? Now that our Hyrcanian desires have reached their peak and, so to speak, run absolutely wild?

ROCKOFFER: Oh—I see Your Holiness has really lost all his wits. Is there anyone who deserves to be King of Hyrcania more than I do? Who is more of an absolutist in life than I am? Give me the whole world and I'll smother it with kisses. Now we'll create something diabolical. I feel the strength of a hundred Hyrcans in me. I, Paul Hyrcan V. I won't be a joker the way he was. Clear out this junk. (*He kicks the royal robes and sword on the floor.*) I'll create a really cozy little nook in the Infinity of the world. Art, philosophy, love, science, society—one huge mishmash. And not like groveling worms, but like whales spouting with sheer delight, we'll swim in it all up to our ears. The world is not a rotten cheese. Existence is always beautiful if you can only grasp the uniqueness of everything in the universe. Down with the relativity of truth! Chwistek's the first one I'll bump off! We'll forge on in the raging gale, in the very guts of absolute Nothingness. We'll go on burning like new stars in the bottomless void. Long live finiteness and limitations. God isn't tragic; he doesn't become—he is. Only we are tragic, we, limited Beings. (*In a different tone.*) I'm saying this as a good Catholic and I hope I won't offend Your Holiness's feelings by doing so. (*In his former tone.*) Together, we'll create pure nonsense in life, not in Art. (*Again in a different tone.*) Hm—it's possible that by defining Dadaism properly . . . Oh, no—it's revolting! They're all different names for the same gigantic, disgusting weakness. Completely new—everything new. (*Clutches his breast.*) I'm getting tired. Poor Ella! Why couldn't she have lived till now. (*He falls into deep thought.*)

STATUE: Didn't I say that with good old Paul you can expect anything?

JULIUS II: But you won't leave me for him, my daughter?

STATUE: Never. Paul is too intense for me—and too young. (*She kisses* JULIUS II's *hand.*)

JULIUS II: I'm only afraid the actual results may not live up to such a promise. I'm afraid of humbug.

STATUE: I am, too—a little. But it's always worth trying.

ROCKOFFER (*waking up from his meditation*): And you, Holy Father, will you come with us? In Heaven, will they grant you an extension of your leave?

JULIUS II: To tell the truth—in Heaven they think I really belong in Hell. But you see, as the Pope they can't decently do . . . that to me . . . you know? That's why I can get a leave to go to any planet I want without any difficulty whatever.

ROCKOFFER: That's great. Without you, infernal old man, I wouldn't be able to take any more. You appealed to me because your inner transformations were sincere. But poor Ella—if it were only possible to bring her back from the dead! What wouldn't I give for that right now! That damned Hyrcan made me do it. (ELLA *suddenly springs up, pushing her* MOTHER *aside.*)

ELLA: I'm alive! I was only knocked out. I'm going with you! I'll be queen of Hyrcania!

ROCKOFFER (*embracing her*):   What happiness, what endless bliss! My most dearly beloved, forgive me. (*He kisses her.*) Without you, even Hyrcania would be only a ghastly dream.

MOTHER (*getting up in tears*):   You're a good man, Paul. I knew you wouldn't abandon poor Ella. (PAUL *goes over to her and kisses her hand.*)

ROCKOFFER: Adopted mother and mother-in-law, I'll take both of you with us to Hyrcania. I know how to appreciate the advice of older women who've experienced a great deal.   Even the uncles—those two old idiots, we'll take them with us too.   Let's go—whatever he's done, Hyrcan opened a new way for us. May his memory be sacred to us.

JULIUS II: What generosity, what generosity!   This is one of the most beautiful days of my posthumous life.   In any case, God is an inscrutable mystery. (x) Come, my daughter.

ROCKOFFER: Matrons, let's get a move on—the Hyrcania express leaves in ten minutes—we've got to hurry.

The MATRONS *leave, passing by* GRUMPUS.

GRUMPUS: His Royal Highness just breathed his last in my arms.

ROCKOFFER (*offering his arm to* ELLA): Well, may he rest in peace. Now I am king of Hyrcania. And even if I have to stand on my head and turn my own and other people's guts upside down, I'll carry out my mission on this planet. Understand?

GRUMPUS: Yes, Your Royal Highness.

ROCKOFFER *goes out with* ELLA. JULIUS II *goes out after them with the* STATUE. (+)

JULIUS II (*as he leaves*):   Even the worst hoax that scoundrel perpetrates on society has the strange charm of a finished work of art. I wonder if

I'll be able to create a new artistic center in this infernal Hyrcania.

STATUE: In artistic matters, you're the almighty power, Holy Father . . .

They go out, followed by GRUMPUS. *The packages and the clothing of the* KING *remain in the middle of the stage.*

April 1922

Stanisław Ignacy Witkiewicz
Multiple self-portrait, St. Petersburg
1914-17

DAINTY SHAPES AND HAIRY APES

or

THE GREEN PILL

A Comedy with Corpses in Two Acts
and Three Scenes
(1922)

Foreword

Written in 1922 and originally projected for production in Torun the following year, *Dainty Shapes and Hairy Apes, or The Green Pill,* "A Comedy with Corpses in Two Acts," did not actually reach the stage until 1967 in a student theatre production in Warsaw after the lost manuscript was recovered and printed in 1962.

In 1973 Tadeusz Kantor presented *Dainty Shapes* at Cricot II in his Cracow basement art gallery as a manifestation of his theory of Impossible Theatre, in which text and performance are disconnected and spectators must not seek meaning, but submit to hypnotic action. The drama took place in the cloakroom where two twin attendants—part circus clowns, part silent film comedians—bullied both the spectators and actors, giving orders, arranging the seating, and managing the entrances and exits. They forcibly enlisted audience members to play the Forty Mandelbaums, who gestured helplessly, while their cries, "What about us?" were piped through loudspeakers.

In 1977 Krystian Lupa presented *Dainty Shapes and Hairy Apes* for his diploma project as both director and designer at the Cracow Theatre School. This landmark production, repeated professionally in 1978, broke with the existing traditions of staging Witkacy and proposed a new approach. Lupa treated the text seriously, eliminating or toning down the parody and sarcasm, and refusing to look for political meanings or allusions to the present. For Lupa the play was a psychodrama about thwarted longings for brotherhood and human closeness; the characters' psychological problems were not treated as grotesque caricatures but as tragic dilemmas worthy of pity

The sources of *Dainty Shapes* are to be found in the decadent literature of the 1890s that Witkacy had absorbed as an adolescent. This "comedy with corpses" owes its erotic *fin-de-siècle* atmosphere to Oscar Wilde's *Picture of Dorian Gray*. The initiation into the higher mysteries, hatred of real life, and renunciation of the base world of contingency through a retreat to an isolated tower are motifs found in Villiers de l'Isle-Adam's *Axel*.

But these symbolist-era mysteries are interrupted by the arrival of discordant visitors who come from different time frames and dramatic genres and sensibilities. Six bumptious lechers out of a sex farce and a seething mass of forty salivating males all named Mandelbaum are jarring elements that do not fit easily within the decadent enclave.

Characters consumed by desire to create give Witkacy's plays an atmosphere of mounting expectation and tension. In *The Cuttlefish*, for example, Rockoffer and Hyrcan are consumed by desire to create a new artistic or social reality. But promises outrun possibilities of delivery, schemes prove defective or fraudulent, human creativity fails and must fall back on pills, or other pragmatic compromises. Frustration of desire—thwarting of the creative urge—brings a violent backlash leading to murder and suicide.

Dainty Shapes and Hairy Apes is a study of sexual desire in its different varieties, manifestations, and configurations. No play of Witkacy's is as obsessively erotic. In Pandeus's palace, desire is ubiquitous, voracious, and omnipotent. But it is above all desire to create a new sexual reality—to extend the boundaries of the erotic. Pandeus promises a transcendent form of desire, a meta-desire that will encompass all other desires. Thus the failure of Pandeus's erotic ideal (revealed to be a cheap seduction) is a bitter disillusionment for Tarquinius, leading him to seek death in his duel with Sophia.

At the heart of *Dainty Shapes* lies an erotic triangle composed of two men—Pandeus and Tarquinius—and one woman—Sophia. The three possible pairings of these lovers constitute the innermost tragic circle of the drama. What is unusual is that each loves both the other two. For these hyper-attractive young people (the "dainty shapes" of the title) totally consumed by eros, desire is something deeply personal, at the center of existence, lodged in the deepest parts of their bodies and psyches. Their sexual natures, incapable of single definition, drive them and torment them without hope of resolution.

These quintessential lovers are surrounded by two concentric circles of lesser lovers, or rather males in heat (the "hairy apes" of the title): the first, Sophia's General Staff, the second, the forty Mandelbaums. Stereotypical figures from farce, defined by race, nationality, wealth, social station, and profession, the six members of the General Staff are colorful but ludicrous middle-aged males, who try to use their power and position to buy sexual gratification. Incapable of satiation, they need pills to sustain their desire. Capitalist, consumer sexuality is totally dependent on affluence, luxury goods, and motor cars.

While six obstreperous middle-aged buffoons trying to barter their power and prestige for sexual favors are comic caricatures, a horde of sullen, angrily muttering sex-starved men can only be disconcerting or frightening. The forty Mandelbaums are sex on the most basic level, monotonously insistent and impersonal, without the least touch of glamour or individuality.

The third concentric circle in *Dainty Shapes* is the thing-in-itself, male desire *per se*, which serves as the background (or subtext) of the entire drama—but it is a background that is constantly pressing to the fore. The outermost circle finally closes in on their tormentor and literally consumes her. The libidinal chorus with a Jewish family name suggests that, like outcast and persecuted Jews, lowly desire has been ghettoized, discriminated against, and viewed as a threat to society.

Witkacy employs the forty Mandelbaums as a partially abstract element of mass, movement, and sound, similar to experiments in the modern painting of his time. In Witkacy's theatre, mob is used as mass in the pictorial as well as the political sense. Ultimately the physical presence of the human body onstage—in all its weight and relief—is Witkacy's principal theatrical medium. The surging, pulsating crowd of Mandelbaums seems to take on the shape of a single living organism composed of many cells that expand and contract; they become a biological entity whose mating urges send ripples of movement across the stage. Synchronizing sound with movement, conjoining human and animal lust, Witkacy counterpoints the muttering of the Mandelbaums to the screeching of the Brazilian guans, the tropical birds on which the biochemist Sir Grant Blaguewell-Padlock is carrying out experiments with his new aphrodisiac: the Green Pill.

The Mandelbaums are the dispossessed biological mob in revolt; the instinctual insurrection acquires a public dimension as they protest against exclusion. As is always the case in Witkacy, the sexual become political, (and the political sexual); *Dainty Shapes and Hairy Apes* shows the evolution of herd instincts into the overt violence of rebellion.

The death of Sophia recapitulates the ritual dismemberment (*sparagmos*) and eating (*omophagia*) of a sacrificial body, as found in the myths of Osiris, Orpheus, and Pentheus (in Euripides's *Bacchae*). Like a chorus of male bacchantes, the forty Mandelbaums tear apart and then devour the heroine, leaving nothing on stage except her slippers and the bodies of her frustrated lovers who have taken the deadly green pill that gives infinite sexual desire but kills within hours.

Dainty Shapes and Hairy Apes comes to a tragic end with an apocalyptic orgy; Sophia, the last of the Abencérages, dies along with her lovers. But then comedy arises from amidst the corpses in the marriage announced by Teerbroom between his daughter Liza and one of the forty Mandelbaums, which will give rise to a new race and new world.

DAINTY SHAPES AND HAIRY APES

or

THE GREEN PILL

A Comedy with Corpses in Two Acts
and Three Scenes
(1922)

CHARACTERS

SOPHIA KREMLINSKA OF THE ABENCÉRAGES—Thin, rather short, very pretty and demonic, reddish blonde. Twenty-eight years old.

NINA—Blonde, seventeen years old. Pretty and very flighty. Daughter of the late St. Edwards, Duke of Passmore.

LIZA—Pretty brunette, seventeen years old, of a distinctly Semitic type.

TARQUINIUS FLIRTIUS-UMBILICUS—Very beautiful young man, eighteen years old. Dark chestnut hair, soulful and at the same time passionate. Rather long hair. Aquiline nose.

PANDEUS CLAVERCOURSE—His friend. Very beautiful and blasé young person, twenty-eight years old. Dark hair. Straight nose. Completely clean-shaven.

SIR THOMAS BLAZO DE LIZA—English Baronet. Thirty-eight years old. Nina's uncle. Dark hair. Clean-shaven. Tall.

SIR GRANT BLAGUEWELL-PADLOCK—Eminent biochemist, knighted for his discoveries, fifty years old. Rather tall and fat, balding on the crown of his head. Gray-haired. Aquiline nose.

OLIPHANT BEEDLE—American billionaire. Heavyset, sixty years old. Short gray hair. Tremendous power in his every gesture.

GOLDMAN BARUCH TEERBROOM—Semite, forty years old. Liza's father. Dark-haired, graying at the temples, fat, but nonetheless, very sure of himself and of his people.

DR. DON NINO DE GEVACH—Cardinal. Dressed in red, in a cardinal's hat, fifty-two years old. Gray-haired, completely clean-shaven. Doctor of Theology. Absolute insatiability is apparent in his every gesture.

GRAF ANDREI VLADIMIROVICH TCHIRPIN-KOKETAYEV—Thirty-eight years old, Captain of the Cavalry in the Cuirassiers Regiment of His Imperial Excellency's Bodyguard. Azure blue uniform, cuirass. White trousers, long cuirassier's boots. Carries his helmet emblazoned with an eagle. Mustache.

FORTY MANDELBAUMS—Small, large, old and young. Very large aquiline noses. Large mustaches and small beards. Long hair. Dark-haired and gray-haired. Dressed in normal suits, quite varied as to color.
In case of a lack of supernumeraries, the number of Mandelbaums may be reduced to fifteen. However, it must never fall below this limit.

YOUNG FOOTMAN—In a red frock coat.

OLD FOOTMAN—In a normal black frock coat.

ACT ONE

Salon in PANDEUS CLAVERCOURSE'*s palace. Totally fantastic furnishings in dark blue colors. An occasion for the most uninhibited scene designer to show what he can do. Facing the audience, a fireplace projecting out very far. A door in a recess to the right. Facing the stage, to the right and the left,* CLAVERCOURSE *and* UMBILICUS *in white tropical outfits sit sprawled in Ceylonese deck chairs in front of the fireplace and smoke gigantic red cheroots.* NINA *sits in an armchair to the left, dressed in a light red dress and red stockings. Her shoes are Veronese green. She is completely indifferent. The gentlemen do not pay the slightest attention to her. It is white hot day. Nevertheless a green fire is burning in the fireplace. Offstage every so often there can be heard the singing of canaries, the cackling of hens, and the crowing of roosters. In designated places the glare becomes simply blinding. No windows. It is ruled out to have any modernistic paintings whatsoever hanging on stage, my own included, unless it is specifically called for in the stage directions. It is likewise ruled out to use a stage setting made out of old properties, such as, for example, some "cozy little nook" from a Bałucki comedy, and so is the combination of this possibility with the preceding one. These last requirements apply not only to this play, but to all those I have written up until now or still may write.*

PANDEUS (*speaks with growing grandiloquence*): I tell you, Quinnie, there aren't any problems any more in the real sense of the word, in the old sense of the word. In philosophy there are only the so-called *Scheinprobleme*, make-believe problems, while in life everything is defined, clarified, resolved. We are just one step away from complete social inertia, worse than what will take place after the extinction of the sun. Death during one's lifetime, almost unattainable for individuals, is actually becoming a reality in our present-day social systems. I say "almost" unattainable, because we do have creeping paralysis and drugs. But I cannot consider that the full equivalent of humanity's self-cannibalizing in the form of growing specialization. Even belief in a catastrophic ending to this entire story is the last illusion on the part of degenerates from the *ancien régime*. Catastrophe is something too beautiful to have happen to our species of Individual Beings. Everything that was more or less known is over now. And yet it seems to me I've discovered something totally new, something that can be tested only by the two of us . . .

TARQUINIUS: There'll always be love. (*Points to* NINA, *who does not bat an eyelash.*) That, Pandy, is the dilemma from which you isolated me by a wall of premature doubt.

PANDEUS: I want to protect you from all those monstrosities I've been through; I've been in love with innocent young ladies and with demonic ones, running the gamut from the highest class down to the very lowest. I've been a victim, a tiny little fly in the clutches of frightful spiders, I've been a demon myself and crushed hearts like strawberries, and then devoured them like jam made of pure anguish. I have experienced both sadism and masochism, not to mention love affairs exalted and harrowing to the point of madness through their inability to satisfy even the simplest expectations. I am young and beautiful, and yet I am closing my life as casually and nonchalantly as if I were slamming the lid of my strong box after having removed all the items of essential value. (*Emphatically.*) We must return to Greek times: revive friendship which is in danger of dying out. In our times friendship has become something repulsive, since the feeling of basic enmity has disappeared. But we won't go astray in a wilderness of hideous sexuality: our friendship will be a renunciation of all sensual shocks. Sublimation of homogeneous feelings in the highest sphere of knowledge of life. I shall lead you along a steep path to the absolute unity of male souls . . .

TARQUINIUS (*leaping up*): That's perversion in disguise. I beg you: allow me at least this once to fall in love really and truly. A man is beautiful only when he is all alone or when he attains his highest dream in the form of a woman who is more than a chance encounter. Homogeneously united, the male elements are—I should say—too hairy psychically. Strength must be solitary, and the prey cannot become one with its conqueror.

PANDEUS (*striking the arm of his chair with the palm of his hand*): No, no, no. I won't allow you to defile yourself. Oh, what I wouldn't give at this moment to be able to rid myself of everything I've been through. You are pure, you've been given what I must try to attain by slogging through the frightful deserts of the past, overcoming phantoms and ghosts at every turn. I love you and I cannot allow you to destroy what is most beautiful in you: your lack of memories. And besides, you won't possess all the women in the world in any case. That is the most atrocious thing about this whole problem.

TARQUINIUS (*sitting down*): Yes, that's right. Oh, my God, my God. How frightfully I am suffering! At least permit me to take some drugs, Pandy. Otherwise I won't be able to stand your training.

PANDEUS: At the very most, you may smoke. I have triumphed over morphine, C_2H_5OH, *et tu dois savoir, mon cher*, alcoholism is the hardest to cure, since the majority of drunkards—*ne cesseront pas de boire*—will not stop their drinking. I went on to conquer hashish and cocaine, to say nothing of all Sir Grant's latest discoveries, his incomparable cerebro-spinaline and his infernal aphrodisiacs of the family trinitrobenzoaminophends. You are familiar with his epoch-making experiments on Brazilian guans. I have been to all the laboratories in the world where they are fighting poisons. I too have been fighting them, in the deserts of Australia and the jungles of Peru and Borneo. No—I won't give you one single drop of anything. I am the incarnation of will power in its most formidable, deluxe edition. You, as someone pure and innocent, will infinitely surpass me.

TARQUINIUS: But, I say, Pandy. Aren't you so powerful precisely because you already have all that behind you? Will I ever be able to achieve that perfection without first having known the dangers: both my own and those that are called external. Now isn't it renunciation that produces the most intractable desire? And then it all attacks the brain and gains control of more and more of its areas.

PANDEUS: *Der Mensch ist ein sich selbst betrügendes Tier.* Man is a self-deceiving animal. I forgive you on this occasion, but you must promise me that it's the last time. Promise?

TARQUINIUS (*getting up*): I promise. I feel I'm going to explode from such constant insatiability, but I'll hold out. Even if I have to go mad, or just plain nuts, I'll hold out.

PANDEUS: That won't happen. I know your nature better than you yourself can. Thanks to my own experiences, I see you as a tiny little piece of transparent crystal under the deadliest Rutherford and Bohr rays. Given my methods, I shall make you into an athlete of the most basic unsatisfied longings, which only then will open for you the gates of the highest mystery: the principle of INTRINSIC INDIVIDUAL IDENTITY. This mystery has two levels, which are mutually impenetrable, like Einstein's two possible Worlds. Even the dumbest moron knows that a thing is what it is and not something else. And yet in a higher understanding of this principle, we can resolve the most diabolical dilemma facing all potential and actually existing Beings. (*An old servant in a frock coat runs in from the right.*)

OLD FOOTMAN: Pandy! Sophia Kremlinska of the Abencérages is about to descend upon us in six autos with her whole staff. The Forty Mandelbaums! And God knows who else! I got the news by telephone from the station at the grange on Antares. They've already passed the embankment at Honed Fish River. (*He runs out.*)

TARQUINIUS (*uncertainly*): Well, what now?

PANDEUS (*slightly dampened in his former grandiloquence*): Don't worry— we'll hold out.

TARQUINIUS: But when will you introduce me to the higher sphere of your thoughts?

PANDEUS: Tonight—perhaps tomorrow—I don't know. The presence here of that whole disreputable mob will be just the perfect test for you. You'll see the negative side of life in its most elegant edition. I am going to the tower to watch the show created by the arrival of that band of metaphysical snobs. (*He starts to leave to the right.*)

TARQUINIUS: Do you know that Kremlinska personally?

PANDEUS (*stopping*): I once did. But she was a bit different then than she is now. (*He goes out to the right.*)

NINA (*raising her head for the first time*): Aren't you bored by all that high-flown talk our host indulges in so freely? (TARQUINIUS *remains silent.*) Look here, Mr. Quinnie, you can be as frank and open with me as with anyone—including even your own master.

TARQUINIUS: Yes—I'm bored. You see, I know a great deal, but only theoretically. I've read far more than he suspects. I know the Kamasutra and Weininger, Freud and the Babylonian sexologists. I know all the first-rate novels that were ever written and almost the entire body of world poetry. All that lumped together already bores me in advance. Still, what Pandy sketched out for me in its general outlines does contain something new and unknown.

NINA (*getting up*): Do you believe in those ultimate initiations? (TARQUINIUS *keeps obstinately silent.*) I have the impression it won't ever happen, that at the bottom of it all there's only an artistic cliché counterfeiting reality. Why can't Mr. Clavercourse do it himself? Why are you so absolutely necessary to him, why precisely you, and not any one else?

TARQUINIUS: I don't know. (*In a different tone.*) You know, I'm not even really so innocent? (*Mysteriously.*) Just imagine, I once kissed Liza here—behind the ear. (*With his finger he points to his neck behind the ear.*)

NINA (*sharply*): Oh—no intimate confessions, please. Liza never said anything to me about it and I don't in the least wish to accidentally pry into her secrets. (*In a different tone.*) Do you know what the arrival of that whole band means to me? My uncle, Sir Thomas Blazo de Lizo, is one of Madame Sophia's closest friends. He's sure to be coming here with her. That means: the end of my freedom.

TARQUINIUS: Oh, bosh—your freedom! You'll get married, have lovers, do whatever you want. But what about me! I am the slave of a tumor that diabolical Pandy has grafted into my brain. I'm a complete automaton in his hands. (*Suddenly.*) Tell me, was there ever anything between the two of you?

NINA: Nothing, I give you my word. In his relations with me he never overstepped the bounds of the most proper guardian.

TARQUINIUS (*clenching his fists*): Actually, I'm not jealous of his past—I've already gotten over that, but, you know, if I were to find out now that he's doing something he shouldn't, believe me, I would kill him like a dog.

NINA (*looking him in the eye*): You're jealous of him. You love him.

TARQUINIUS (*dementedly*): I don't know. I don't know if it's love. (*Forcefully.*) I only know that if it's going to go on like this, if he really isn't going to introduce me into another world that can take the place of life for me, I'll become a monster such as has never existed before until now.

NINA: Come, come—don't get carried away. You're a poor little child, not a monster. (*She strokes his head*.)

TARQUINIUS (*pulling away from her angrily*): Don't pity me! That's insulting. I'd rather that you tell me what you think of him.

NINA: I'll tell you quite frankly: I'm in love with him too.

TARQUINIUS (*terrified*): What? . . .

NINA (*laughing*): Calm down, nothing can ever come of it. (*Seriously*.) When he was your age, he was my late mother's lover. My mother was a bad woman. I read her diary. I can't think about it without feeling disgusted.

TARQUINIUS (*threateningly*): About what, about what?

NINA (*laughing*): About his kisses, only about his kisses. And besides, he's finished, destroyed forever. (*Ironically*.) Oh—he's invincible, his front horns almost came off because of his love for Madame Kremlinska—she's invincible too. Perhaps you'll conquer him, Mr. Quinnie. You're so pretty.

TARQUINIUS: So you do love him after all! You hope to provoke him by feigning indifference. What treachery!

NINA (*ironically*): Oh, what theoretical understanding of life. Oh, what loftiness of soul. (*In a different tone*.) And besides I love you too. You're a lovely, innocent little boy. You're like a tiny little star in the Milky Way. (*She kisses him suddenly on the mouth and runs out to the left*. TARQUINIUS *remains motionless for a moment*.)

TARQUINIUS: Oh, the mouth is a diabolical thing. Now I don't know anything about anything.

Through the center door, at the back of the stage, to the right of the fireplace, enter SOPHIA KREMLINSKA OF THE ABENCÉRAGES, *dressed in a motoring outfit, holding a horsewhip in her hand. She is followed by* SIR THOMAS, TEERBROOM, *and* OLIPHANT BEEDLE, *likewise dressed in motoring outfits. Next come* DR. DON NINO DE GEVACH *in a cardinal's robes and* GRAF TCHIRPIN-KOKETAYEV *in the full dress uniform of the Cuirassiers Guard.* FORTY (*unequivocally forty*) MANDELBAUMS *come crowding in last.* TARQUINIUS *is thunderstruck at the sight of* SOPHIA.

SOPHIA: Why are you so dumbfounded, my good man? What's your name? Where is the proprietor of the chateau?

TARQUINIUS: He went to change his clothes. My name is Umbilicus.

SOPHIA: A lovely name. I am Sophia of the Abencérages, etcetera etcetera. And why didn't you go change your clothes for my arrival?

TARQUINIUS: I was engaged in an important conversation with Nina St. Edwards, Duchess of Passmore. My head is in an indescribable fog, and for some time now . . .

SIR THOMAS: Hullo! So she's here, just as I thought. Don't you know . . .

TARQUINIUS: You can rest quite easy, Sir Thomas. My friend loves me and only me. He has created a new order of absolute, purely spiritual friendship. Tomorrow or perhaps even tonight I am to be admitted into the ultimate mysteries.

SOPHIA: Then I came in time. (*Points to* TARQUINIUS.) See how lovely he is. With such a rival I shall have a hard struggle. (*A threatening murmur in the crowd of* MANDELBAUMS *and a yell or two from the general staff.*) Quiet, Mandelbaums, and you too, idolaters of the first class.

TARQUINIUS: You are insulting my friend. With that tiny little female brain of yours, you cannot grasp the greatness of his soul. You seem to think you have some rights to him. You'd better get over any such illusions once and for all.

SOPHIA (*to the staff*): Did you hear that? It's quite unprecedented! For such a delicate little flower to survive in the house of this monster! And he still believes in him. (*To* TARQUINIUS.) Dreadful moments await you, sad youth. You still have no idea what psychic crimes are. Look at me;

am I not young and beautiful? And yet there's nothing inside me, I am a mummy, I am thousands of years old, and my cruelty is boundless. It was that Pandeus of yours who made a spider woman out of me—after eating my fill of bodies I devour souls. Look at that mob. (*Points to the staff and the* MANDELBAUMS.) Nothing but the sheaths of chrysalises from which the butterflies have flown away. And those butterflies, their souls, I hold in my net and I play with them when I wish and as I wish, you young idiot. Would you like to be a specimen in my collection?

The mob is silent.

TARQUINIUS: You are a silly, common goose. Those gentlemen have already signed their own death warrants, if what you say about them is true. I am above the vulgar appetite for life thanks to him, the one man on this earth who exists for me and whom you insult here in his own home.

SOPHIA: Silly little braggart. You will be talking differently in a few days. I shall reveal his intentions to you in all their horror. You don't know . . .

TARQUINIUS: I know all I need to know. Please leave me alone. (*He goes quickly towards the door to the right.*)

TEERBROOM: Young man! Young man! Is my Liza here?

TARQUINIUS: Yes, she is. Yesterday I kissed her on the ear. I'll atone for it however you wish—not only out of respect for your age and for her sake, but also for my own self-respect. (*To* SIR THOMAS.) And today your niece kissed me on the mouth, thereby defiling my sacred love for Pandeus. (*To* SOPHIA.) I detest all you women and I will never be yours. Your posthumous memoirs and stupid little poems will let the world know how thoroughly I could have enjoyed your so-called "love," if only I had wanted to. (*Pulls a bundle of papers out of his pocket and gives it to* TEERBROOM.) Here are the poems your daughter wrote to me. (TEERBROOM *puts the poems in his pocket.*) I am sacrificing all that in order to attain the ultimate truths of existence, far from your vile snares and machinations. Good-bye. (*He storms out to the right.*)

SOPHIA: That boy is a real gem. I'll make bloody mincemeat out of him. I'll eat his nerves sautéed over a slow flame. I feel the blood of all the

Abencérages boiling inside me.

TEERBROOM: But I say, Madame Sophia! This very day I'll give you the automobile that belonged to the last czar of Illisia.

SIR THOMAS: I'll buy St. Patrick's abbey for you. Whatever the consequences. Only not that, not that, or I'll go mad.

OLIPHANT BEEDLE (*to* SIR THOMAS): Only not what? You've already gone mad, Sir Thomas. (*To* SOPHIA.) Madame: the yacht belonging to the Duke of York is, as of today, your own personal property.

SIR GRANT: The pills! The green pills! Today I'll write out for you on the finest parchment my most closely guarded secret formula.

KOKETAYEV: Madame Sophia, (*accented on the second syllable*) I'll put all the platinum from the Ural mountains into your sweet little predatory hands. As we say in Russian, we'll "blow up a tornado."

CARDINAL NINO: Madame, you have no idea what sensual pleasure and gratification of ambitious desires come with seducing the Church's highest dignitaries. In the old days it didn't count for anything, but at present . . . And besides, the Villa Calafoutrini with all its priceless treasures is yours. May God protect me. (*He prays.*)

MANDELBAUMS: What about us? What about us? What about us?

SOPHIA (*silences the commotion with a snap of her hand and a stamp of her foot*): Don't talk to me as you would to a girl of the streets. I can't be had that way now.

SIR GRANT: Since when, since when?

SOPHIA: Since right now, since right now (*looking at the watch she wears on her ankle*), since two o'clock this afternoon when I became a saint. I can be had only by a complicated psyche plus maximum of strength.

SIR THOMAS: Who has shown such qualities, emboldening you to talk about them like that, as though they actually co-existed in one person. Who is that aberration?

SOPHIA: The little boy who was here a moment ago, young Umbilicus. (*The* MANDELBAUMS' *roar grows louder and louder each moment.*)

OLDEST OF THE MANDELBAUMS: We have those qualities—we Mandelbaums. I protest in the name of us all!!

SOPHIA (*threatening to strike him with her whip*): Silence!! (*The roar subsides. The* OLDEST MANDELBAUM *draws back.*) Service!! Service!!! (*A* YOUNG FOOTMAN *in red livery runs in from the right.*)

YOUNG FOOTMAN: Yes, Your Ladyship.

SOPHIA (*indicating the crowd of* MANDELBAUMS *with her whip*): Show that horde of riffraff out, give them something to feed their faces, and put them in their rooms.

YOUNG FOOTMAN: Yes, Your Ladyship. (*To the* MANDELBAUMS.) This way, gentlemen. This way. (*He pushes them towards the center door.*)

SOPHIA: Mark my words, Mandelbaums, for me you are nothing but a confused background of impersonal and intermittent masculinity, *un fond de masculinité impersonelle et intermittente.* Get out!! (*They leave.* SOPHIA *flings herself into a chair.*) I'll make that big baby into an antidote to Pandy. Now I feel strong, today is my day.

From the left side enter PANDEUS. *The two young girls hold onto him, one on each side.* NINA *to the right,* LIZA *to the left.* NINA *wears a black dress.* LIZA *the dress that* NINA *wore previously.* PANDEUS *in a black frock coat.*

PANDEUS: Excuse me for having kept you all waiting so long. I had to change my clothes and prepare Liza for what awaits her. (*To* TEERBROOM.) Mr. Teerbroom, you don't know how to bring up your daughter. She will stay with me as long as is necessary; when I know the time has come, I'll return her to you a superior and accomplished woman.

TEERBROOM: I am ready even for that—out of snobbery. But what you do not know is that my Liza and your friend have already been kissing. I have here in my pocket a whole bundle of poems she wrote to that Umbilicus. I have complete confidence in you, but not in those . . . ugh . . . wards of yours . . .

PANDEUS: That's impossible! How dare you!

TEERBROOM: He said so himself a moment ago. Isn't that right, gentlemen?

SOPHIA: Yes, Pandeus—I can vouch for that. You have been powerfully shaken in your . . . hmm . . . designs. But I shall console you with Sir Grant's new pills .

PANDEUS: This is frightful! Today was the day I wanted to begin revealing to him the ultimate mysteries of the highest understanding of life.

SIR THOMAS: And that is not all: as your pupil himself confessed, my niece Nina kissed him on the lips today. He seemed to be quite mortified by the fact, but I believe he was pretending because he was afraid of me.

PANDEUS: By Aldebaran, Sir Thomas! Mr. Teerbroom! I am innocent. Simply, quite simply the earth is slipping from under my feet. I feel faint. (*The young ladies hold him up.*)

SOPHIA: Pandeus, your initiations are a fraud. I know how it will end. You want to recapture your youth by conjuring up memories of your days at Harvard College. Remember, you disappeared from the horizon at that point. We know what happened: a year in the house of correction on Crippen Heath.

PANDEUS: Yes—I admit it. And from then on I have lived according to the laws of nature, although there are people who dare to maintain that the periods of the highest civilization are always closely tied to flouting those laws. What I'm dreaming of now is beyond your base suspicions. You judge it by your own standards, Sophie. Oh, yes—you are capable of the most atrocious things! I know you. But nothing will come of it. You will be the last temptation for Quinnie, a temptation he will overcome. And if he conquers you—there are no more temptations left for him in this world.

SOPHIA: Thanks for recognizing my abilities. At least you are fair. But a bit of advice: be on your guard against yourself. The subconscious always works like that. You do not know yourself. I am the only one who knows you. You still have satanic possibilities ahead of you.

PANDEUS: For example, the possibility of falling in love with you again!!! Ha, ha, ha!

SOPHIA: You never can tell. Pills—that's the last word of the mystery. But as for me, I have not yet sunk so low as to be the object of your idiotic experiments with your mediums.

NINA: A point of order: couldn't the two of you postpone that conversation until later? Liza, go pay your respects to your father. (LIZA *falls into* TEERBROOM*'s arms; to* PANDEUS.) These people are tired after their journey. Perhaps you could see about showing the guests to their rooms. I'll take care of the flowers for dinner.

PANDEUS: Of course, you're quite right, Miss Nina. Please come with me. (*He goes towards the center door, from the right side* TARQINIUS *runs in, dressed as before*.)

TARQUINIUS: Pandy! I've been looking for you all over the palace. I have horrible forebodings. That lady (*points to* SOPHIA) doesn't appeal to me at all, but she upsets me terribly. (SOPHIA *angrily strikes her whip against her coat*.) I'm in a state of total divergence of my quintessential directional tensions.

PANDEUS (*gloomily*): You have betrayed me. Now I don't know if I shall succeed in saving you from life. You have ceased to be a pure spirit without memories.

TARQUINIUS: Oh, those girls have betrayed me! No—the men must have told you. (*With tremendous ardor.*) It was nothing: those were grazing touches I no longer remember. You must initiate me immediately. I'm in a state of frightful inner tension. I could explode: I could crash to one side or the other with all the force of a volcano. But I swear to you: at heart, I am pure. Take me to your slothroom.

PANDEUS: No—let's put it off until tomorrow. I'm not in the right frame of mind today, I am not sufficiently concentrated. First withstand temptation, prove yourself worthy. Have a little talk with Madame Sophia first of all.

TARQUINIUS (*very disappointed*): Oh, so that's it. Now I'll tell you something dreadful: you don't believe in yourself, you don't believe in the truth of your own system. You're afraid, you don't have the strength. You mask the pettiness of your desires behind a false little theory. Why can't you be alone with yourself? Why am I absolutely necessary to you? Admit you still don't know what you are going to tell me. You're trying to find inspiration in me, inspiration to make you believe in yourself, to fill the horrible void that keeps you from living. But you don't even have the courage to regret it any more.

PANDEUS (*with bitterness*): See what frightful havoc those supposedly superficial grazing touches have wreaked in your soul. I have been betrayed, hideously deceived and betrayed.

SOPHIA: Yes—Pandy has been unmasked. I said the same thing.

PANDEUS: You have no right to say a word on this subject, Sophie. I ceased to exist for you from the moment I could no longer be a man in my relations with you. You too are being unmasked.

TARQUINIUS: But what will happen to me? Life is rushing into my frenzied brain through all my pores.

SOPHIA: Poor boy! Say no more. It will all be resolved by itself. We shall finally be freed from this cursed Pandeus Clavercourse problem. He is either a vulgar charlatan, or the greatest metaphysical brute I have ever known. Let's go bathe, and then eat. (*She goes towards the center door, and the others follow her. The* CARDINAL *prays as he goes.*)

TARQUINIUS (*to* NINA): Miss Nina, I have to tell you something. My ganglions are bursting with inexpressible thoughts. (*He grabs* NINA *by the hand and drags her off to the left.*)

PANDEUS (*shouts after him*): You may live to regret it! Watch out. (SOPHIA *bursts out laughing and leaves. She is followed out by* PANDEUS, TARQINIUS *and the others.* SIR GRANT BLAGUEWELL-PADLOCK *remains behind and holds back* OLIPHANT BEEDLE.)

SIR GRANT: Do you understand? It's all in my hands. (*Takes a little box out of his vest pocket and taps it with his finger.*) The green pills. Still, when you think about it, life nowadays would be something dreadful if it weren't for drugs. I am the last benefactor of mankind in its declining days, unless, of course, my pill proves fatal in its aftereffects. I've not had the courage to try it on human beings.

OLIPHANT BEEDLE: Fine—but actually, what's all that to us? You are all manufacturing artificial problems.

SIR GRANT: But she must be mine, today, straight away, when I want her. (OLIPHANT *makes a threatening gesture.*) Don't get excited, I'm saving the next pill for the two of you. It's an old, old story: instead of a potion—now we have pills. And as for the Pandeus problem, it is not as insignificant as you think. On the basis of this example, I shall demonstrate certain eternal truths.

YOUNG FOOTMAN (*entering through the center door*): This way to the baths, Your Lordships. (*They go out quickly, passing in front of the* FOOTMAN *who holds the door open.*)

ACT TWO

Scene One

*The same room. Half past nine in the evening. Through the center door
enter* SOPHIA, *dressed in a black ball gown, accompanied by the two young
ladies.* NINA *dressed in green,* LIZA *in yellow.* SOPHIA *sits down on the sofa
which is now to the right of the fireplace, opposite the door* (*the green fire
continues to burn in the fireplace*), *and puts something which she has been
clutching tightly in her hand into a small powder box.* NINA *sits down on her
right,* LIZA *on her left. Off-stage, protracted, dismal roars can be heard from
time to time.*

NINA: What are you doing there, Madame Sophia?

SOPHIA: That is the mystery of the evening. I've never been as strong as I
      am now. I have found a counterweight to Pandeus's psychic perversity
      in the person of that little boy. But that is only negative strength. I
      have something else, ha, ha, I have something else!

NINA: A woman's strength is always negative, even without that having the
      connotation of something bad.

LIZA: Yes—I think so too. Women's strength is concave—their strength is
      convex . . .

NINA: Wait a minute, Liza: Madame Sophia says she has something more,
      something positive. What do you have in that little box?

SOPHIA (*getting up*): I have Sir Grant's green pill. A new drug that creates
      such monstrous insatiability that, compared to those who take it,
      Messalina would be a perfect angel. The old rascal dropped the pill
      into my wine glass. But I noticed and held it between my teeth. And
      then afterwards, I took it out without anyone seeing. Whoever I give it
      to will love me as no one has ever loved since the world began.

NINA: Only please spare Tarquinius. I love him.

SOPHIA: You won't have the strength to counteract Pandeus's influence.
      You don't know with whom you're fighting. I am the only one who can

overcome the fiction of a higher knowledge of life without love that Clavercourse implanted in him.

NINA: Yes, but while you're at it, you'll take him for yourself. I don't want that to happen.

SOPHIA: And just how are you going to stop me, silly little goose? You don't realize how well I know them. I know every fiber of their seemingly complicated souls. There's never been one of them who could resist me.

NINA (*ironically*): Except for Pandeus, against whom your negative strength no longer suffices.

SOPHIA: But it seems you love Clavercourse too. At least that's what I'm told.

NINA: If it weren't for the fact that he was my late mother's lover, I would love him just as he is—without Sir Grant's green pills. (*Imploringly.*) Please, don't take Tarquinius away from me. I beg you.

SOPHIA: All right: I shall simply prepare him for you. Only as much as I'll need to overcome the temptations posed by Pandy. And not that much more. (*She shows the very tip of her forefinger with her thumb.*)

NINA: Thank you. (*She kisses her hand.*)

LIZA: How beautiful Madame Sophia is in everything she says and does! (*To* NINA.) If anyone else talked the way she does, it would be revolting.

NINA: Unfortunately, men's actions have an absolute value. What a woman does is overly dependent on her face, her figure, and her clothes, and above all on whether or not she has pretty arms and legs. (*Through the door to the right enter* TARQUINIUS *in a frock coat,* SOPHIA *arches.*)

TARQUINIUS: I've come for that test of my strength. But I warn you, I am concentrated as never before. Everything hangs by a single thread that has the holding power of steel cable.

SOPHIA: So much the better for me, Mr. Umbilicus. Do sit down.

TARQUINIUS (*sitting down between the girls*): You don't understand me, I was talking about essential things. I feel a loathing for you that almost borders on physical pain. In every word you utter, you are cynical and repulsive. In every statement you make, even of the most indifferent kind, some lecherous thought lies hidden. Your voice doesn't seem to come from your throat, but from the devil only knows where . . .

SOPHIA: That's the basis of my strength. Things said that way sink deep into the innermost recesses of your bodies and then it becomes as difficult for you to root them out as it is memories of sensual pleasure.

TARQUINIUS (*shuddering*): Oh, how disgusting! I detest you. (*He gets up.*)

SOPHIA: But all the while you felt that mysterious shiver you've never known till now. You know what I mean.

TARQUINIUS: How did you know? You're clairvoyant. (*The young girls lean towards each other and look at* SOPHIA *adoringly.*)

SOPHIA: Actually, I am dimvoyant, but I see with perfect certainty. My secret eyes circulate along with the red corpuscles of your young blood and look into the hidden recesses of your being.

TARQUINIUS: You slipped up there! That statement doesn't make me feel the slightest shiver. Artistically it's a flop. Your voice quavered and cracked. Don't try to fake things beyond your abilities, or you could take a spill.

SOPHIA: Oh—don't talk so crudely. Look at me—don't avoid my gaze. Now don't you feel monstrous despair at the thought of what never, *never* will be? At this moment the entire world has ceased to exist for you. All its colors have paled somewhere far in the distance, and the forms of the most beautiful landscapes have shriveled into the hideous wrinkles of withered senility, as though a mysterious flame from the bottomless void had consumed them from within. All your feelings have become the expression of the most terrifying inner boredom and the coming day seems to you an infinite desert, to get through which is an impossibility lasting for all eternity. Look at me: isn't that true?

TARQUINIUS: It's true—you see right through me. My head is spinning.

SOPHIA (*pointing to* NINA): Just what is that poor little, pure little feeling you have for her, compared to the insatiability of all the desires you now experience? I can turn all that into a reality or walk out of here this very instant with a cruel smile and leave you, reduced to ashes, paralyzed, rigormortized by the unspeakable suffering caused by the enormity of your never satiated longing. Look into my eyes. You appeal to me.

TARQUINIUS (*drawing closer to her*): It's frightful—I can't resist. (*He looks around at the young girls.*)

NINA (*springing up*): I won't give him up! I love him—you only want to amuse yourself with him. Let go of him immediately.

SOPHIA (*gently*): Run along this instant, my child. Take Liza and off to bed with you both. But before you fall asleep, talk all this over.

Dejected, NINA *takes* LIZA *by the hand and they both go out slowly to the left.* SOPHIA *and* TARQUINIUS *look one another over. The moment the door slams shut,* TARQUINIUS *throws himself at* SOPHIA *who envelops him in a snake-like embrace. Kissing, they both fall on the sofa. At this precise moment enter* SIR GRANT *through the center door.* TARQUINIUS *and* SOPHIA *spring apart.*

SIR GRANT: Madame Sophia! I confess to everything, I put the green pill in your wine. You promised me once . . . It's starting to have its effect already . . . Prematurely, unfortunately . . . According to my experiments on my guans, it shouldn't start working until four hours later at the earliest. I beg you . . . You gave your word . . . We are the only ones who can test it.

SOPHIA (*getting up;* TARQUINIUS *remains seated*): You are a consummate ass! I have your pill here—look. (*Shows him the small powder box.*) I held it with my tongue against my teeth. Go back to your guans. (*Roars, louder than before, are heard.*) Well—can't you hear them roaring? I'll take the pill when I feel like it, or I'll give it to whomever I want. That's better still. Do you understand, Mr. Poisoner? You can go now! (*She shows him the door.* SIR GRANT *leaves, crestfallen, without a word.*)

TARQUINIUS (*pulling* SOPHIA *towards him on the sofa*): More . . . Give me your lips.

SOPHIA (*sitting down next to him*): No, my little one, now we are going to have a serious talk. I crave not only your lips, no matter how exquisitely you can kiss. You instinctively possess what it takes others years to learn. But I love you, I want your soul. You must be truly mine before you satiate your desires. Otherwise you will be poisoned by me the way the others were.

TARQUINIUS: Then you really love me?

SOPHIA: Yes—you must believe in your good fortune: I am yours. Learn to know me now so that later on you won't regret not having appreciated my true worth. I can be everything. All I need is to be loved very, very much. Perhaps I'll relive my girlhood days when I was truly happy.

TARQUINIUS (*starting to make advances to her*): Then let me kiss you. Why are you pushing me away?

SOPHIA: No, no—not now. I want only your soul now.

TARQUINIUS (*gloomily*): You know—at this moment I don't feel I have any soul at all. (*In the voice of a child who begs for candy.*) I want your lips.

SOPHIA: You only think so. Sit down here quietly next to me, lean your little head against me, and talk. Talk to me the way you would to Nina, or to him . . . to Pandy.

TARQUINIUS (*settling down next to her*): I don't have anything to say. I've forgotten everything. Come with me right now, to my room.

SOPHIA: No, no, I won't come. You're not in the least mine. You're only attracted to me. All the time you're thinking about him, about that cursed Pandeus.

TARQUINIUS (*getting up*): That's just what's so awful, I've forgotten about him. I feel horrible pangs of conscience. Not only towards him, but towards myself as well. I have betrayed myself. I am a fallen man.

SOPHIA (*getting up*): You child! You don't know who that Pandeus of yours is. He is the incarnation of the most sordid appetites in the service of the worst perversion. Today for the first time you will see for yourself that all his theories about the higher life are a complete fraud. There really is no higher mode of existence. Those are only fabrications invented by socialized cattle like us. At the bottom of Pandy's soul there's nothing but a masked desire for the commonest pleasure-seeking.

TARQUINIUS (*getting up*): You're in error. You didn't know with whom you were dealing. I am stronger than you think. And besides, I know more than you suppose. Give me concrete proof. I have not yet been initiated into the ultimate mysteries, but what I do know is enough to convince me that it's not a hoax. Give me concrete proof.

SOPHIA: I know—the principle of Intrinsic Individual Identity. Everything that exists is what it is and not something else. But we all know that. It's a barren truth and it's no accident that the greatest sages in the world have disregarded it. What's strange about that?

TARQUINIUS: The principle is simple—I admit that. But its actual consequences can be remarkable.

SOPHIA: I know that too. Each moment for its own sake, surmounting life not through Nirvana, but by concentrating one's individuality—of course, another person is needed for that. Just let Pandeus manage to experience that all by himself. I'd prostrate myself in front of him. But this is a doctrine that exists solely because it's being indoctrinated. (*Angrily.*) It's all a hoax! Either there's one definite course of action, this particular one, and not any other—no matter whether it's creative work in art or in life—or else there's Nirvana. The rest is a sham concocted by puny weaklings incapable of living.

TARQUINIUS: That's not true! I feel that beyond that there is something else I cannot grasp. Not in words, but in the actual execution. That's what has to be carried out. It cannot be defined before it has been created.

SOPHIA: Bergsonian balderdash! You are both idiots. One deludes the other, and each deceives himself into the bargain. You'll see what the carrying out will be like. You'll see tonight. Remember what I have told you. Remember!

TARQUINIUS: All right. We'll see. If it turns out to be untrue, you can consider me your own personal property. In that case my life won't be worth a single stinking dead guan.

SOPHIA: But I don't want you in the least. Not any more. That was a moment of delusion. For me you are only an antidote: a means of controlling myself so I can conquer him. I care only for him, for that stupid, deceitful master of yours. What am I saying: not for him, but only for his tangible outer shell—his soul I've already had and I vomited it up a long time ago, it was so petty and disgusting.

TARQUINIUS: Now you have mortally offended both him and me. I no longer know what is true in me. Only chance—or rather destiny—can decide that.

SOPHIA: In whom do you wish to embody your chance destiny?

TARQUINIUS: In you. The idea is not as foolish as you think. That's exactly what life is: chance destiny. That expresses the initial contradiction inherent in existence. Those two viewpoints are irreconcilable, and yet life constantly reconciles them at every moment. By consciously creating the potential for chance, we challenge the workings of the universal law that everything is predetermined. (*He grows lost in thought.*)

SOPHIA: Come to the point, boy. You really do display some signs of strength, and that is beginning to intrigue me.

TARQUINIUS: I have grasped an idea that has been wandering lost in the unconscious depths of my ego. I know you won third prize in fencing at the international competition in Melbourne. I'm not a bad fencer myself. We shall fight over him and over me, and perhaps even over you as well. That depends on you.

SOPHIA: You know, that is a splendid idea! At two, tonight, immediately after the initiation, provided, of course, you don't lose faith once you've heard it all.

TARQUINIUS: Even then I shall be fighting over myself and over that something in you that I cannot fathom. I won't manage to seduce you just like that.

SOPHIA (*with irony*): Seduce me . . . ? And some warped little nobody like you dares say something like that to me . . . ?

TARQUINIUS: Shut up! First I must get to know the higher law of my life, not the petty everyday rules and regulations. For me you are only a means now, a piece of litmus paper, with which I can test the reactions of my soul. But you must promise me one thing: you will fight me without showing any mercy. (*He holds out his hand to her.*)

SOPHIA (*giving him her hand*): But of course I promise. What conceit! I'm not in the least concerned with you. It's the idea that appeals to me as a totally new motif added to the tangled skein of all these sexual disorders. (TARQUINIUS *pulls his hand away from her.*)

TARQUINIUS: Horrid vixen! But all the same, here are certain conditions: if you wound me, and I have lost faith in Pandeus, I shall consider myself your property; if I wound you, you shall never cross my path again unless I expressly desire it. If one of us dies, the problems between us will, of course, be resolved all by themselves.

SOPHIA: Very well, my pet. You're starting to appeal to me again.

TARQUINIUS: Good-bye, until two, here in this room.

He goes out to the left. At the same time the entire company of men with PANDEUS *at their head enters trough the center door. The staff in frock coats. The* MANDELBAUMS *as previously.*

SOPHIA (*to herself*): I'm afraid I've taken an overdose of the antidote. That boy appeals to me a bit too much.

PANDEUS: How did the temptations go? Too bad I didn't see any of it. But Sir Grant got roaring drunk and told us such marvelous things about those concoctions of his that I simply could not tear myself away. But where is Tarquinius?

SOPHIA (*vexed*): He went to get ready for the ultimate initiations. Really, you do have diabolical power over him. Only torture can part you.

PANDEUS (*triumphantly*): So you see. I knew that Quinnie wouldn't betray me. Today I shall initiate him definitively.

SIR THOMAS: Our chances are increasing. I think that instead of squabbling among ourselves, we'll form an association of the worshipers of this new Astarte.

CARDINAL NINO: May God protect us. I have the feeling that something frightful is going to happen.

Uneasy murmuring from the MANDELBAUMS. *From the left the two young girls enter in dressing gowns.*

SOPHIA (*suddenly brightens up*): Mr. Teerbroom and you, Sir Thomas, allow my little girl friends to enjoy themselves for one last time today. You can be sure of my favor in return. (*Hesitation on the part of* TEERBROOM *and* SIR THOMAS.) Fine—then it's settled. Let us begin the orgy. Pandy, have them serve the very best you have. I'm not specifying the things I crave lest I be suspected by you of trivial snobbery or bad taste.

PANDEUS *goes out through the center door.* LIZA *goes over to her father. The men remain at the back of the stage.* SOPHIA *and* NINA *in the foreground.*

NINA: Well, what happened? Did you seduce him?

SOPHIA: What an idea! We're fighting with swords at two in the morning. Don't be afraid, Nina. Nothing bad will happen to him.

NINA: You've given me your word. But what are you going to fight about?

SOPHIA: A mere trifle. He has to retrieve his lost—what does he call it?— honor. He has to look into his innermost depths or something of that sort. Such subtleties are beyond my understanding. What amuses me is the fact itself.

NINA: You always amuse yourself, but what about me?

SOPHIA: Rest assured I shan't do him any harm. I'll return him to you even nobler than he was.

NINA: I was sure you'd give him that pill—I was so afraid! But Liza and I didn't dare come in.

SOPHIA: Tarquinius doesn't need any pills. He's a wonderful boy. If it weren't for the fact that I really do love Pandeus and only him, I'd take Tarquinius away from you in an instant. But now listen to me, and then watch closely. I don't have anyone to confide in. I'll give Pandy the green pill today. In that way we'll discredit him in Tarquinius's eyes; as it is, the boy's faith in him has already been shaken. And then, free of delusions about the higher life, Tarquinius will be entirely yours.

NINA: How noble and beautiful you are in all you do! I thank you for everything!

She kisses her hand. Enter PANDEUS *with a footman bearing wine and wine glasses. Wine is poured and drunk. The* MANDELBAUMS *stand sullenly in the background.*

SOPHIA (*dropping the pill into her own glass*): Pandy, take this glass from me and empty it to the health of your disciple and to his successful initiation into the doctrine of the higher consciousness in life, life without women. You are doing this not to attain Nirvana—we all know that—but only to intensify even to the bursting point our wretched, filthy, socialized individuality. Hurrah!

PANDEUS (*taking the wine glass*): Now we shall finally live as friends. Who knows—perhaps even you, Sophia, will come around to my belief, once you have exhausted all the pleasures of the senses. But in the meantime, I drink to the greatness of the principle of Intrinsic Individual Identity, which until now I alone of all the philosophers in the world have understood. Among the rare specimens of our species long live the supreme, asexual happiness offered by the higher consciousness of life, without belief in the other world, without theosophy, without any hoaxes whatsoever! Hurrah!

They all drink.

SIR GRANT (*to* PANDEUS): Don't drink that: it may contain the green pill. She . . .

PANDEUS *stops and looks around with a questioning glance.*

SOPHIA: Shut up! The old man has gone crazy! Drink up, Pandy—I have never betrayed you.

SIR GRANT *staggers back.*

PANDEUS: Yes—I totally believe you, our souls never parted. (*Drains the cup to the bottom.*) And now let us go to the round chamber for the wildest of orgies. I must fortify myself by the sight of real-life swinishness before revealing the ultimate truths to Tarquinius.

TARQUINIUS *runs in from the left.*

TARQUINIUS: Pandy! I cannot stand it any longer. Let us go this instant. Initiate me, or I shall crash all the way over to the other side.

PANDEUS: All right—it may as well be now. I feel a strange force taking possession of all the layers in my brain, and mysterious shudders run through my torpid marrow. I think there still may be some new revelations even for me. I shan't attend that orgy. (*To the guests.*) Go ahead without me. If you'll excuse me. (*To* SOPHIA.) Sophia, take them to the round chamber where we have experienced so many moments of fleeting sensual pleasure. Tarquinius and I will rejoin you in an hour or two. By then we shall be on the inaccessible heights of friendship and absolute knowledge. Like two parabolic mirrors turned towards each other, we shall reflect each other in ourselves, in closed Infinity.

SOPHIA: Ha, ha, ha, ha, ha!

PANDEUS (*coldly*): What are you laughing for, Sophia?

SOPHIA: For no reason at all—just like that—for the sheer joy of it. (*To the staff and the* MANDELBAUMS.) Come, gentlemen, and you too, my dear young ladies. (*Embraces* NINA *who has been standing next to her until now.*) We shall amuse ourselves as never before, while awaiting further developments. (*She goes toward the center door with* NINA. *The crowd follows her. The* MANDELBAUMS *mutter under their breath. Meanwhile* PANDEUS *speaks.*)

PANDEUS: Come, Tarquinius, only now will the ultimate knowledge penetrate you. You won't lose your individuality, you will simply create yourself anew above the chance realm of day and night. You will be one and indivisible, unique for yourself and for me. Only as two can we accomplish this. Solitude kills the essence of the self and brings us closer to Nirvana. Only what I call hermetism of a higher order opens the gates of the mystery for those suffering from a raging thirst for the absolute. Neither art, nor any real deed, nor any faith can be higher than what we are going to create. The world will give way to Nothingness, leaving us in the cold, crystal sphere of the truth about ourselves. We are unique.

TARQUINIUS: I must tell you something. I do not feel worthy—I've been kissing your Sophia.

PANDEUS (*interested*): So you've been kissing. I don't know why, but today even that gives you added charm. I love your soul. (*He embraces him.*)

TARQUINIUS (*with a slight shudder*): She told me exactly the same thing.

PANDEUS: She's lying. Come, let us go to my slothroom in the north tower. I can feel my mind like a cold dagger ripping into the blazing womb of the Eternal Mystery. The solution lies neither in concepts, nor in systems of concepts, nor in the intuitive flight from reality. Nor is it to be found in the renunciation of life. It lies in life itself, in the dual comprehension of the uniqueness and identity of each moment of duration in and of itself.

They head towards the door to the right and go out. Off-stage can be heard SOPHIA*'s wild laughter and the far-off muttering of the* MANDELBAUMS— *then the roar of the guans.* SIR GRANT *rushes in through the center door and looks all around.*

SIR GRANT (*screams*): They're not here! (*He runs to the door at the right. The* YOUNG FOOTMAN *appears at the door, with the* OLD FOOTMAN *right behind him, revolvers in their hands.*)

YOUNG FOOTMAN: Not one step further, Sir Grant! His Lordship gave us orders to put a bullet through the head of anyone trying to break into the north tower.

SIR GRANT: Too late, too late. (*He runs out through the center door*.)

Scene Two

The same room, in almost total darkness. The stage is empty for a moment. From the right someone can be heard running down the stairs at breakneck speed. TARQUINIUS *dashes in, wearing bright pajamas, and turns on the light. Then he falls on the sofa and hides his face with his hands.*

TARQUINIUS. Oh, what a filthy beast! How dared he? It was all a lie. A cheap seduction on the part of a cynical, perverted *roué*. Oh . . . (*Looks at his wrist-watch.*) Three minutes to two. She should be here any minute now. Everything's become so mixed up I no longer understand anything at all. I have to fight a duel. I have the feeling that will decide everything. The truth will come out all by itself. I don't even know who she is or who I am. All I know—and I don't even know that for certain—is that he's a monster. But his monstrosity is such a frightfully complex mystery for me that I don't know what facts could serve to explain it. (*Calling for her as he lies helplessly on the sofa.*) Madame Sophia, Madame Sophia!

From the left SOPHIA *enters, dressed in red tights. She is holding two swords in her hand.*

SOPHIA (*calmly and quietly*): Easy, Mr. Quinnie. Easy. I'm here. I'm ready.

TARQUINIUS (*getting up*): Madame Sophia, if you only knew what I've been through! It's the ruin of all my dreams, of my whole higher life.

SOPHIA: Calm down, baby. (*Strokes his head.*) Tell me all about it.

TARQUINIUS (*in a different tone*): Oh—if only I could. But I loathe you too.

SOPHIA: Why? It never is possible to unite absolute truth with life in a single living whole. What do you want from me? Simply love me.

TARQUINIUS: You're lying. You're thinking only of him. I know your principle of antidotes: the system of two essential lovers—not counting all the others.

SOPHIA: That's Pandeus's system: the principle of two mistresses. I was the only one he wasn't unfaithful to—nor did I betray him. I was the last.

TARQUINIUS: He wanted to be unfaithful to you, but he couldn't, because I didn't want him to. Give me a sword.

SOPHIA (*gives him his choice of swords, he takes one*): Why, certainly, certainly. If this duel is absolutely necessary for you to gain self-knowledge, then go ahead and fight. I should prefer you to kill yourself. I could hurt you badly. I promise you I shall fight in earnest.

TARQUINIUS: Yes—and if I detect the slightest trace of pity in your eyes, I shall shoot you down like a rabid bitch. And then myself, and him, I'll kill everybody and those cursed girls too. I have a revolver in my pocket.

SOPHIA (*coldly*): I imagine you'll kill all the others first, and then yourself— it will be simpler that way. I need a shock to my nerves after all those abortive perversities and initiations. Pandeus must be mine.

They position themselves: TARQUINIUS *to the left,* SOPHIA *to the right, and begin to fight.*

SOPHIA (*after a moment; coldly*): Watch out, I'm starting to get hot.

TARQUINIUS (*enraged*): Get hot and burn up, you slut! Once I've run you through, there'll be nothing left of you but a pool of liquid putrefaction. Take that, and that!

SOPHIA: Ho, ho. His attack is not half bad. But now it's my turn. Back two steps; (*a couple of thrusts*) back three steps. Oh, that's it, oh, that's it! That's it, that's it, that's it. (*She pins him to the wall, to the left.* TARQUINIUS *falls in front of the door.*)

TARQUINIUS: I'm dying. My heart . . . all these insatiable longings . . . oh, how I wish I could live . . . (*Attempts to get up and lunge at her;* SOPHIA *knocks the sword out of his hand; he falls again.*) I detest you!

He dies. SOPHIA *stands motionless. Then she wipes off the sword on her right thigh, throws it down and lights a cigarette. A tremendous racket is heard, someone running down the stairs, to the right.* PANDEUS *rushes in, wearing bright pajamas.*

PANDEUS: Sophia, it's you! I am young and healthy as a bull on the pampas. All those revelations are sheer rubbish. Truth exists only in life, without any philosophy, without any metaphysical friendship, without any self-identity. All that's impossible! Absolute truth is one and indivisible, beyond life—there it is pure. But here in real life everything exists only in division, in multiplicity, in plurality itself, in total disorder. Only chaos and the absurd are beautiful. Sophie, do you agree with me?

SOPHIA (*pointing to* TARQUINIUS's *corpse with her cigarette*): I was just saying the same thing to that disciple of yours. He didn't want to believe me. I had to fight with him in earnest, since he insisted on my promising him I would. And there he lies insatiable, defiled by his last thought about his unfulfilled life, run straight through the heart by me.

PANDEUS (*without paying any attention to* TARQUINIUS): Sophie, forgive me for everything. But how could I ever have supposed that I would grow normal and healthy again. I love you and only you and I shall never abandon you.

SOPHIA: I have killed my sole antidote to you. I am yours and yours alone. Now for the first time I truly love you. Come.

PANDEUS: Wait, in a moment I'll lose the power to speak from sheer excess of strength. An entire lifetime turned in the wrong direction has been stacked in my head as a pyramid of absurdity dancing bottoms up. My marrow rears up like a giant anaconda. Now for the first time I see what misery it was: the higher consciousness of life and other lofty delicacies. Hoaxes perpetrated by bunglers—that's all they are. My bones are made of India rubber, and my muscles bulge with savage power. Down with deeds that are purposeful or resolute. Only one thing counts—pleasure. Greatness nowhere to be found, neither wealth, nor art. Those are only symbols of the great misery that is existence, and he alone lives who experiences pleasure, and that in the most bestial way. Everything else is a social mask worn by the weak and exploited.

SOPHIA: Enough of that speechifying. I've had it up to here with people too. For once in our lives let's behave like two dumb beasts, like two May flies.

PANDEUS: Yes, yes.   But I had to grow conscious of it.   Higher consciousness of one's own animality is the highest form of life. It's quite another thing if one is totally unaware of it: then it's just plain, ordinary swinishness.

SOPHIA *leads him off to the left.* PANDEUS *pushes* TARQUINIUS's *corpse out of the way, lets* SOPHIA *go ahead, and they both disappear through the door which they lock behind them.* SIR GRANT, *in pajamas, dashes in through the center door. He rushes off to the left and rams against the door as he tries to open it.*

SIR GRANT (*not seeing the corpse*): Too late! Too late! Help! I gave her my pill! And she gave it to Clavercourse!

He goes limp and collapses by the door. The whole pack rushes in: the staff in pajamas, and the MANDELBAUMS *in clothes thrown hurriedly over their naked bodies, their shirts not buttoned or tucked in, and their hair disheveled.* TCHIRPIN-KOKETAYEV *in an unbuttoned uniform,* CARDINAL NINO *in his unfastened cardinal's robes, but with his hat on.*

TCHIRPIN-KOKETAYEV: What! Where?!!

CARDINAL NINO: Who did what to whom?!!!

SIR GRANT: They went in there together! And he has the pill dissolved in his blood stream. She promised me. I shall go stark raving mad.

SIR THOMAS: Look! Tarquinius Umbilicus is lying dead over there by the door. There are swords. A duel took place here.

OLIPHANT BEEDLE: Clavercourse killed Umbilicus! How horrible! And all because he was jealous of our fetish.

Muttering in the crowd of MANDELBAUMS, *who surge forward. Off-stage roars of the awakened guans.*

SIR GRANT (*barely conscious*): Those are my guans roaring! Help me break down the door!

The CARDINAL *and* KOKETAYEV *rush to the door and help* SIR GRANT *break it open.* SOPHIA *appears in the doorway with her hair down, wearing a green dressing gown; she comes out onstage.* KOKETAYEV *and the* CARDINAL *let her pass and dash into the room, to the left.*

SOPHIA: He's dead. He died at the height of sexual pleasure.

SIR GRANT (*horrified*): What are you saying?

SOPHIA: Your pills kill, Sir Grant. Their effect is wonderful, but fatal for whoever takes them.

SIR GRANT: So the guans could take it, but not the human beings! That's the finishing touch. My invention is good for nothing. (*With passion.*) But for you, I'll even take three!

SOPHIA: Well, take them, you doddering old fool, and go die with your guans. I have no such intention, and without the pill, I'm incapable of loving you.

SIR GRANT: So that's how it is? Very well.

He goes off to the right and blows his brains out. No one pays the slightest attention to him. KOKETAYEV *and the* CARDINAL *carry in* PANDEUS'*s corpse through the door to the left and put it in the sofa.*

SOPHIA: Look, there is the greatest man of us all and of many others too. He died like a dumb beast, like an insect, conscious of the fact that nowadays it's not worth it to be a human being. I regret I cannot devour him the way the female scorpion does her mate. (*The* MANDELBAUMS *mutter in the background.*)

TEERBROOM: But who killed that other chap? Did *he* do it? Oh! These puny weaklings nowadays really do devour one another like insects.

SOPHIA: I killed that other chap in a perfectly correctly conducted duel. But he disgraced himself by begging for life at the last moment . . . while Pandeus died as he lived. . .

TEERBROOM: That is to say, like the worst swine.

SOPHIA: You are mistaken, Mr. Teerbroom. He lived a lie, but he died with the truth on his lips like a true beast: he said he loved me. And I believed him, but I still don't believe any of you. You are all deluding yourselves, but if I should feel like it, rest assured that the same thing will happen to you, provided fate allows you such bliss.

TEERBROOM: Yes, but then one can only live for one short moment . . .

TCHIRPIN-KOKETAYEV (*his Russian accent and syntax becoming more pronounced*): What does matter? Short moment, not short moment! Madame Sophia (*accented on the second syllable*), you are marvelous woman! Yei-bogu!

CARDINAL NINO: My villa! This hat . . . Everything! ! (*He takes off his cardinal's hat and flings it to her.*)

SOPHIA: For shame, Your Eminence. You're showing your true colors as a disgusting, vulgar old reprobate. (*The* MANDELBAUMS *mutter more and more vociferously.*) What I ask of you, gentlemen, is a little more sublimity—of the beastly, not the human sort. In all of you there is still too much of the human, on which you so pride yourself, but which I so despise.

SIR THOMAS: That may well be, but if it hadn't been for the green pill, even that Pandeus of yours wouldn't have died like a beast; he would have rotted away in his former lie. After all, those pills are the highest expression of human civilization. We're just a step away from being able to bring the dead back to life in order to kill them off still more cruelly.

SOPHIA: How can you talk such utter rubbish at a moment like this?

SIR THOMAS: Perhaps for you the moment is extraordinary. For us, it's an ordinary everyday sort of day. There only exist these two principles: preservation of the individual and preservation of the species. In the proper balance between these two elements lies the highest point in the development of humanity. The limit points are: the solitary beast, human or non-human, at the one extreme; and the human ant hill at the other. The relativity of ethics results from the possibility of a differing balance between these elements . . .

SOPHIA: Don't poison my sole moment of happiness with doubt, wretched old man. I'd give a great deal to die the way he did, a beast conscious of his own beastliness, consciously surmounting human lies. That is something totally new. And besides, Sir Grant still has a whole box full of pills. All right—any volunteers! Who wants to experience the supreme happiness of conscious beastification? Search the corpse and swallow the poison. And then drop dead! Die, the sooner the better, so that I won't ever have to set eyes on you again. (*With the exception of the* MANDELBAUMS, *they all throw themselves at* SIR GRANT's *corpse.*) And who knows, perhaps what was too strong for him will be just right for you?

Having found the little box (SIR THOMAS *finds it first*), *they hurriedly divide its contents. Only* TEERBROOM *does not swallow his pill, but ostentatiously puts it in his vest pocket. The* MANDELBAUMS *form a tight circle and approach* SOPHIA, *who, busy observing the above scene, does not notice what they are doing. As soon as the others have finished, the tight circle of* MANDELBAUMS *surrounds* SOPHIA. *With a wild roar, the* MANDELBAUMS *throw themselves on* SOPHIA *and cover her completely. (At this point, the actress, having quickly thrown off her dressing gown, must crawl out behind the fireplace without being seen, or disappear through the floor by means of a trap door.) The roar dies down. Only panting can be heard. A single frightful cry from* SOPHIA *rends the air, then silence and panting.*

TCHIRPIN-KOKETAYEV: Why, zey will smother her to dying!

CARDINAL NINO: So much the better, my last temptation is over. Oh, God! My thanks to Thee! And the Villa Calafoutrini with all its priceless treasures will continue to be mine! (*He kneels and prays.*)

SIR THOMAS: Perhaps it is better that way. She tortured herself too by the life she led, as well as torturing you. Let her perish once and for all. I tell you, gentlemen, at last we shall breathe freely.

OLIPHANT BEEDLE: Gentlemen, you forget that we have taken the pills. Their effect may prove fatal not only for degenerates of the Clavercourse variety.

CARDINAL NINO (*interrupts his prayer*): What does it matter, gentlemen. We are all old men. Perhaps God will take pity on us. We have four hours left, either to make our peace with God or to enjoy life to the very end.

From the left, NINA *and* LIZA *rush in, wearing dressing gowns:* NINA *in blue,* LIZA *in red.*

NINA: What happened? They're both dead!

LIZA: How horrible! Oh, God!

TEERBROOM: Liza! Come here this minute! For a moment, I had forgotten I have a daughter.

LIZA *runs to her father and nestles up to him. The* MANDELBAUMS *get up and move to one side. There is not a single trace of* SOPHIA. *Only her green dressing gown lies on the floor. And, optionally, her stockings and slippers may also be lying there.*

OLDEST MANDELBAUM: She is dead. That is what we call a lynching, carried out in the name of vengeance by the confused masculine background.

NINA: She does not exist, nor do I really. I shall take her place for you! I know everything already. I shall create a new type of Cybele or Astarte—it doesn't matter which. Follow me, gentlemen, for the final initiation without any self-identity or fraud.

SIR THOMAS: Nina dearest, you do not know that we all have taken the pills.

NINA: So much the better for them and for you, uncle. Doesn't anyone have a pill for me?

TEERBROOM (*obligingly*): Here you are, Duchess. There's nothing I could refuse a friend of my daughter's. (*He takes the pill out of his vest pocket and ostentatiously hands it to* NINA.)

NINA (*takes the pill*): Thanks. (*Swallows it.*) An abyss has opened within me. I shall fill it with our corpses. Now I know how life should be lived. (*She goes toward the center door*, SIR THOMAS, OLIPHANT BEEDLE, CARDINAL NINO, *and* KOKETAYEV *follow her. The* MANDELBAUMS *try to follow them.* TEERBROOM *stops them.*)

TEERBROOM: Mandelbaums! Not one step further. We are going to create the new race of the future. I give you Liza. She will be the mother of the new line. But I shall give her to the one I choose, to the one who will be the most authentic incarnation of the race. After what she has seen here, she will be the best mother. Follow me.

He takes LIZA*'s arm and goes to the left. The* MANDELBAUMS *follow them. On stage there remain only the corpses of* TARQUINIUS, PANDEUS *and* SIR GRANT, *and on the ground, in the middle of the stage, a small heap of clothes that belonged to* SOPHIA KREMLINSKA OF THE ABENCÉRAGES.

28 July 1922

Stanisław Ignacy Witkiewicz
*The Prince of Darkness Tempts Saint Theresa
with the Aid of a Waiter from Budapest*
circa 1913

THE BEELZEBUB SONATA

or

WHAT REALLY HAPPENED
IN MORDOVAR

(1925)

Foreword

Written in 1925, published in 1938, and first performed in 1966 (and subsequently made into an opera), *The Beelzebub Sonata* is the last surviving drama from Witkacy's most creative period of playwriting when from 1918 to 1925 he wrote over thirty works for the stage. In one sense, all Witkacy's plays are about the act of creation and all his heroes are would-be or actual creators, but *The Beelzebub Sonata* in particular deals with artistic creation, and its hero, the composer Istvan, embodies the dilemma of the modern artist.

Like Thomas Mann in his novel *Doctor Faustus* (1947), whose composer-hero makes a pact with the devil in order to create a new type of music, Witkacy has gone to the legend of Faust to illustrate the modern artist's inevitable alliance with evil. Also like Mann, Witkacy has made use of Arnold Schoenberg as his model for a modern creative genius. Schoenberg developed his radical twelve-tone music, which rejected the nineteenth-century musical heritage and the old system of tonal relationships, in the period just before, during, and after the First World War, although he first published works in this style in 1923. *The Beelzebub Sonata* was completed only two years after this revolution in modern music had taken place, and Witkacy, himself a brilliant amateur pianist and close friend of Karol Szymanowski and Artur Rubinstein, was aware of this major upheaval in the art of music, with its parallels to cubism, the breakthrough in painting which Witkacy discusses in *New Forms*.

A proponent of a similar revolt against tradition in theatre, Witkacy dramatizes in the character of Istvan his own plight and that of all modern artists who are caught between interrelated but contradictory revolutions that pull in different directions and leave the creative genius no place in either art or life. On the one hand, the revolution in art drives the creator to further extremes, away from all known paths and accepted values; on the other, inevitable changes taking place in early twentieth-century society offer the artist only the impossible choice between a crumbling old order that has become obsolete or an emergent new one for the gray masses with no use for individuals. In such circumstances, the artist is utterly isolated, and creation is possible only through destruction—by destroying the old while at the same time destroying oneself. There is no place for the creative artist to turn but to the satanic forces within oneself and within the universe. To create, the artist must give up life and cease to exist as a human being. The artist must become the Devil's own.

The Beelzebub Sonata reflects the Nietzschean view, shared by

Mann, that the artist must stand outside the framework of existing culture and reject tradition and conventionality; inevitably, the creative genius is lonely and alone. However, Witkacy dramatizes the unavoidable conflict between art and life, the artist and society, in a highly ironic, rather than solemn manner, and he shows the preposterousness and impossibility of all positions. The Nietzschean artist becomes a clown, and selling one's soul to the Devil becomes a cabaret act. Precisely because the themes are deadly serious and painful for Witkacy, his treatment becomes ferociously sardonic and grotesque.

Istvan is unable to create what he regards as true music because he is mired in real life and its banal, petty concerns of love, romance, and the routine of daily existence. Mordovar with its mountains and moods (undoubtedly patterned after Zakopane) is a provincial backwater where old-fashioned notions of honor still prevail. Confronted with the new vulgar people who appear on the other side of the lake and threaten to bring mechanization and the disappearance of individuality, the Mordovar social circle attempts to preserve the past and cling to its traditions of peace and quiet. This old order that once might have stood for individuality is now no more than a parody of former aristocratic greatness, represented by the ludicrous Baron Jackals and his snobbish mother.

Plebeian in origins and without the others' prejudices, Grandmother Julia sees further with her fortune-telling and offers Istvan the choice of yielding to his fate, that is, the inner forces of his psyche and the compulsion of historic necessity, or of lapsing into mediocrity as the local piano player who contributes to the charm of cozy Mordovar evenings. Istvan can be either a normal member of his society with his own personal life, or he can be an artist. If he is to be the latter, he must give up all feelings and desires of his own, all attempts to control his destiny, and all use of his conscious mind in order to become simply an instrument through which the dark forces can create.

Writing in 1912, Schoenberg described the creative process as self-abnegation in similar terms of yielding to a superior force: "Let it be remembered that the creative urge continues, the greatest works are conceived, carried through, and born, but the creator who brings them forth does not feel the bliss of generation, he feels himself merely the slave of a higher ordinance under whose compulsion he ceaselessly does his work."

Schoenberg also talks of the work being "dictated" and of "obeying an inner compulsion," much as Istvan feels himself simply a medium being used by another. It is perhaps no accident that as Istvan starts to conceive "The Beelzebub Sonata" at the end of Act Two, he tells us that it is in F sharp minor, the key of Schoenberg's *Second String Quartet* of 1907, his first atonal work, and the connection between Istvan's infernal composition and demonism and fortune-telling has its counterpart in parallels drawn between Schoenberg's art and astrology. Like Schoenberg, Istvan is seeking a form for music that will be its own *raison d'être*; rejecting the concept of music as a direct expression of feelings and reflection of life, he wishes the sounds themselves to be self-sufficient and autonomous.

Istvan's temptation occurs when the mysterious Brazilian planter Baleastadar appears and becomes transformed into Beelzebub, the embodiment of evil, incapable of creativity himself, but a source of it in others. He is aided by the singer Hilda (counterpart of Margarete in *Faust*), who is not a victim of the devil, but his partner. Contact with her demonic sexuality transforms Istvan into a creator. Belonging to neither the past nor the future, Istvan as artist exists outside of time. But since the artist must always serve someone, he agrees to serve the forces of darkness and pure evil, even in their contemporary debased guise as a cabaret act. He chooses his fate, or rather is chosen by it. The loneliness, alienation, and isolation of the artist—no longer dignified and sublime, but absurd—constitutes a form of social and personal death. By the time Istvan begins to play the sonata that has been dictated to him by the dark, destructive forces, he is completely finished as a human being. Since the work of creation has been accomplished, the artist is absolutely unnecessary in life.

After Istvan commits suicide, Beelzebub the pianist appropriates the dead composer's work and takes the sonata on a world tour, introducing it to the masses in a final flare-up of metaphysical feelings before the final extinction of creativity. Although as a suprapersonal medium he is able to produce "The Beelzebub Sonata," Istvan fails both in life and in art, since he is not even able to consider that he himself has created the works that will bear his name. Such is Istvan's tragedy, but the tragedy goes awry since the hero ceases to be tragic and becomes a puppet or automaton even before the institution of mass, mechanized society, which will turn all its members into cogs in the machine.

Out of these conflicts, incapable of resolution, that revolve around the position of the modern artist in society and in the universe, Witkacy has created *The Beelzebub Sonata*, his final statement on the problem of art and his last full-scale portrait of the artist in his writings for the theatre.

THE BEELZEBUB SONATA

or

WHAT REALLY HAPPENED IN MORDOVAR

1925

Motto:
Musik ist höhere Offenbarung als jede Religion und Philosophie.
Beethoven

Dedicated to
Marceli Staroniewicz

CHARACTERS

GRANDMOTHER JULIA—Sixty-seven years old. In a brown dress and glasses.

CHRISTINA CERES—Her granddaughter. Eighteen years old. Dark brunette, very pretty.

ISTVAN SAINT-MICHAEL—A composer. Twenty-one years old. Light chestnut hair.

HIERONYMUS BARON JACKALS—An elegant young man-about-town. Twenty-two years old. Brown hair, very fiery.

BARONESS JACKALS—His mother. Small, thin matron. Fifty-eight years old.

TEOBALD RIO BAMBA—A bearded individual, dark hair. Fifty-seven years old.

JOACHIM BALTAZAR DE CAMPOS DE BALEASTADAR—About fifty years old. Huge, broad-shouldered. Brown hair. Long black beard. Slightly graying hair around the temples. Bald. Planter.

HILDA HAJCZY [pronounced "Hisee"]—Twenty-nine and a half years old. Red haired. Demonic. Opera singer in Budapest.

ISTVAN'S AUNT—A little old woman, rather commonish.

DON JOSÉ INTRIGUEZ DE ESTRADA—Forty-five years old. Vandyke beard. Brown hair. Spanish ambassador to Brazil.

SIX FOOTMEN—Big strapping guys with Vandyke beards, in red livery. Black stockings and braid.

BARONESS JACKALS's FIRST FOOTMAN—Navy-blue livery with red facings. Silver buttons.

(The action takes place in the twentieth century in Mordovar, Hungary.)

ACT ONE

The drawing room in GRANDMOTHER JULIA*'s apartment.   Modest old-fashioned furnishings.   Whitewashed walls.   A dark-brown ceiling supported by cross beams.   Pictures and miniatures on the walls.   Wide French windows upstage open out onto a verandah overgrown with grapevines turning red. In the distance, mountains covered with fresh snow are visible. A lamp with a green shade is burning.* GRANDMOTHER JULIA, *in a white bonnet and a brown dress, is sitting at a round table. To the left on the other side of the table,* ISTVAN SAINT-MICHAEL, *dressed in a sports outfit, rocking back and forth in a rocking chair. A pause. Dusk is falling. Later on, a moonlit night.*

ISTVAN: Grandmother, couldn't you tell me a scary story before Christina gets back—waiting's such a bore. What I'd like most is to hear the one about the Beelzebub sonata that you've been promising me for such a long time now. You remember, grandmother, Christina wouldn't let you finish—she can't stand hearing the same story twice.

GRANDMOTHER: Well, all right then. Now here's what happened: once here in Mordovar there lived a young musician who was exactly like you, only for those times a bit more abnormal. Some people even considered him a moron, but that probably wasn't fair. When I was a child, I knew people who had seen him. Now then, from the time he was a little child, he was always dreaming about writing the Beelzebub sonata, as he called it—he meant the kind of sonata that would outdo all others hands down.   And not only Mozart's and Beethoven's sonatas, but absolutely anything that had ever been or could ever be created in music—the kind of sonata that Beelzebub himself would write if he were a composer.   Then he went mad: he claimed he knew Beelzebub personally and had traveled through hell with him. He was supposed to have been—Beelzebub, that is—a perfectly ordinary gentleman with a black beard, dressed somewhat old-fashionedly, a little like our Brazilian-Portuguese hidalgo, de Campos de Baleastadar.

ISTVAN: Who is he, grandmother? And why did you have to compare him to someone real? I so like fantasy that's not contaminated by the slightest trace of real-life justification.

GRANDMOTHER: You'd better not go in for things like that, Istvan, or you might go crazy too—the same way he did. I'm old, I'm going to speak to you frankly—it'll make things simpler. Remember, you're not to wrong my Christina—that I won't forgive; dead or alive—I'll avenge her.

ISTVAN (*shuddering*): Oh—not dead I hope. (*Seriously.*) Believe me, grandmother, it all just depends on money.

GRANDMOTHER (*severely*): I'd rather it depended solely on your conscience.

ISTVAN: Oh—let's not talk about that now; well then, what happened to that Beelzebub? And who is this hidalgo?

GRANDMOTHER: The foremost planter of vineyards in Mordovar. It's obvious you haven't been here very long if you don't know who de Campos is. Now then, the two of them—Beelzebub and the musician— kept on going around everywhere together looking for the entrance to hell, which, according to an old Mordovar chronicle, was said to be in the vicinity of Mount Czikla. Supposedly that bearded fellow told the young man everything in great detail—he described what hell looks like just as though he'd been there himself any number of times or even lived there. Only he couldn't remember where the entrance was, poor fellow. Ha! ha! They both went mad—as a matter of fact, no one actually knew who that fellow was. They said many different things about him. And then the young man was found hanging by his own belt at the entrance to an abandoned copper mine shaft on the slopes of Mount Czikla. They say he had the makings of a musical genius.

ISTVAN: That's not a very interesting story, and besides it's too short, grandmother dear—I expected something better. If no one knows who that gentleman was, where he came from and where he disappeared to—I must say I'm not at all taken by any of it. You can make up a dozen stories like that every hour.

GRANDMOTHER: You can make up quantities of them, and much more interesting ones at that. Mordovar's a place expressly created for extraordinary happenings. The mountains are strange and so are the people. And even the people who come here from the outside have to be the same way and not any other—strange too.

ISTVAN: I'm not at all strange. I'm an artist—I'm aware of that. Perhaps I don't fully realize what it means to be an artist—but there's nothing at all strange about being one. I compose because I have to—the same way another person is a bank clerk or a merchant. I write notes the same way I'd write figures in a ledger.

GRANDMOTHER: That's just what you think, Istvan. You don't seem strange to yourself, because you're totally immersed in the strangeness you create all around you—you swim in it like a fish in water; only the fish doesn't create what it swims in. But others feel this strangeness: I do, Christina does, and even all those people on the other shore of the lake—I mean the permanent residents of course.

ISTVAN: I can't stand them. They sit in judgment on me. They think I'm a sponger, a loafer who's squandering his old aunt's fortune. If I were the piano player in some pub on the other side of the lake, they'd worship me. But since I'm studying in town, they're jealous of me and that's the only reason they turn up their noses at me. Our side of the lake is better.

GRANDMOTHER: Perhaps that's why it's worse for you. Nowadays it's better to be from the other side.

ISTVAN: Oh—that's quite enough of that Norwegian-style symbolism. Chance would have it that a bunch of disgusting parvenus live on that side, whereas on this side there are a few individuals who have retained a touch of the old traditions. I'm not saying this out of snobbery—what matters to me is the tradition of truly important things.

GRANDMOTHER: Yes, yes—that's what they all say, but the fact is it's really something quite different. Only I don't know which group to put de Campos in. He's a person who doesn't fit into any known category.

ISTVAN: I'd like to meet him. Although . . . (*He waves his hand contemptuously.*)

GRANDMOTHER: Undoubtedly he'll be coming here to see us today—as he usually does on Saturdays. I always tell his fortune for the entire week. But I wouldn't advise you to get overly friendly with him. They say that his relations with young people have not always been devoid of what could be called—if one wanted to—something in the nature of . . .

ISTVAN (*impatiently*): Oh—I'm absolutely sure nothing will happen to me. I'm completely immune in that respect. Whatever isn't aesthetically beautiful doesn't even exist for me.

GRANDMOTHER: Alas—human nature is so constructed that what fills us with disgust in our youth later on becomes a passion that drags us down as low as we can sink. It's calm here in Mordovar the way it is before a storm—and I'm afraid that future events are gathering like threatening banks of clouds on the horizon of our destiny.

ISTVAN: Grandmother, you're the one who always urged me to be courageous and today you're saying that! Today when I so need peace and quiet.

GRANDMOTHER: What for?

ISTVAN: I don't precisely know.

GRANDMOTHER: Then why are you saying it?

ISTVAN: Perhaps it's because of my undefined attitude towards Christina. I feel within me an audio-spatial vision of sounds that I cannot capture in duration. It's as if I held a closed fan in my powerless hands and could not open it and discover the picture that is already present in sections on each of its parts. I see the absurd shreds of something, as though on the haphazardly jumbled blocks of a puzzle, but the whole of it is hidden from me by some mysterious shadow. Perhaps it's the Beelzebub sonata that the piano player was dreaming about. Because really something within me seems to take the form of a sonata and is somehow almost beyond the human. I'm no megalomaniac, but . . .

From the right side enter, without knocking, BARON HIERONYMUS JACKALS, *dressed in a riding outfit with a whip in his hand.*

JACKALS: Grandmother: your fortune-telling cards—and be quick about it. (*Kisses* GRANDMOTHER *on the cheek and nods his head from a distance to* ISTVAN *who bows without getting up.*) I am, as they say, in the clutches of a demonic woman. It's all so disgustingly trite—as in the trashiest romantic novel. Well, what's new, Maestro? How are your masterpieces coming?

ISTVAN (*in an offended tone of voice*):   First of all, I'm not a Maestro, and secondly I haven't created any masterpieces yet . . .

JACKALS (*not at all taken aback*):   Excessive modesty, Maestro. How about dropping in on us for dinner sometime—my mother loves music with a passion—even yours: Futuristic as it is. (*Shuffles the cards while he is talking.*) I wonder what our legendary Mordovar Beelzebub sonata would sound like in a Futuristic transposition. All right, Grandmother, you can begin. (*He gives the cards to* GRANDMOTHER *who begins to lay them out for fortune-telling.   Behind the French windows to the verandah* RIO BAMBA *stands unnoticed, with a glowing cigar in his mouth. He is dressed in a long black Spanish cape.*)

ISTVAN (*belatedly*): Thank you, Baron, but I always eat dinner at home . . .

JACKALS: Oh, how depressing . . . Well, what about it, grandmother? That queen of spades is undoubtedly my demon, next to the nine of hearts—for my sexual feelings. (*Hums and then recites.*)
    A thousand loves I've had from different spheres,
    A thousand loves—is that beyond your reach,
    You guttersnipes with just one woman each?
    A thousand loves—that's why there now appears
    A heart forever, when my fortune's told,
    Surrounded always by those spades so bold.
    Each one of them was a betrayal to be
    Of her, the one and only, the true she,
    Who's non-existent, but just the one for me.

ISTVAN: Aren't you ashamed to recite such doggerel? No doubt it's your own handiwork.

GRANDMOTHER: Istvan, be polite. The Baron isn't accustomed to being treated that way. Anyhow, the thought behind that poem is quite nice.

ISTVAN: Poetry is not the expression of thoughts in rhyme, but the creation of a synthesis of images, sounds and semantic meanings in a certain form. But if the form is nauseating, then even the finest thought can make us sick.

GRANDMOTHER (*threateningly*): Istvan!

JACKALS: No cause for alarm—the Maestro's in a foul mood—that's why he's talking so pedantically, but in such bad taste.

ISTVAN (*rising*): If you call me Maestro once more . . .

JACKALS: Then tomorrow you'll probably be a corpse, Mr. Saint-Michael. I've hit an ace on a pendulum at a distance of thirty-five paces, and with a saber I don't have an equal in the whole district. All right, grandmother, go ahead.

ISTVAN *sits down. From the left side* CHRISTINA *runs in, in a green dress and an orange and black shawl.*

GRANDMOTHER: Get these young men to make up, Chris. They were almost at each other's throats.

CHRISTINA: How can I get them to make up when I know that *I* am actually the cause of their quarrel?

GRANDMOTHER: Chris!

CHRISTINA *becomes embarrassed.*

JACKALS: You're mistaken, Christina, I am in the power of a demonic woman. I came to ask your grandmother for advice.

CHRISTINA (*very embarrassed*): What's that? Oh—anyhow I don't believe it. It's revolting.

ISTVAN (*getting up precipitously*): I can't stand this any longer. I've got to leave. Baron, tomorrow we duel with pistols. The meeting place–the old mine shaft at the foot of Mount Czikla. Seconds are unnecessary.

JACKALS: At your service. However, I'll bring a second: my gamekeeper.

ISTVAN: As you wish—I don't care in the least. After all, I'm only doing this for my own personal artistic goals. You're nothing but a totally accidental pretext.

JACKALS: Pointless confessions.

CHRISTINA: They've gone mad! Hieronymus, how can a cipher like you, such a well-dressed, straight-shooting and impeccably-mannered cipher, dare deprive Hungary of her future glory!

JACKALS: But Christina, I only came here to have my fortune told. I had no intention of offending the Maestro. I swear I'm not in competition with him for you. Still, I am compelled to shoot it out with him.

CHRISTINA: You see, Istvan, you're the one who's making all the trouble. You've got to stay—we'll play the piano, we'll improvise four hands the way we did last Sunday at your aunt's.

ISTVAN: I was drunk then. All in all that was an unlucky day for me, let's say no more about it. That's when I fell in love with you. (*Suddenly in another tone of voice, with sudden decisiveness.*) Well, all right—I'm staying. But on condition that you don't ask Jackals to stay. It's not fitting for me to be seen with him socially.

JACKALS: Oh—what excessive tact. But there's no need for it: I'm occupied this evening. Well, how about it, grandmother, am I ever going to find out what's going to happen to me and whether I'll succeed in taming my demon?

GRANDMOTHER: Frightful things are in store for you, young man. Tonight you'll murder a woman with flaming red hair, at daybreak you'll shoot yourself, and towards evening the following day your mother will take her own life. Unless you stay with us—then perhaps you'll be able to save all these people and yourself as well. The fates are busy tonight.

CHRISTINA: I'll keep you company, Hieronymus—even till morning.

GRANDMOTHER: How can you . . .

CHRISTINA: To save this young man from certain death, I think I can sit up with him till eight in the morning—at eight-thirty I have to go to the Lycée. I see nothing wrong in that. As it is, I wouldn't be able to sleep tonight. Somehow I'm abnormally excited. You won't hold it against me, Istvan.

ISTVAN (*gloomily*): I don't know about that.

JACKALS: I don't want any new misunderstandings to arise because of me. As a rule I am too frank with the wrong people. So be it. I must make clear to all of you that I am not in love with Christina and even if I were, I would never marry her—I am a snob conscious of his own snobbery.

CHRISTINA: Yes, but at any moment you might marry Miss Hajczy, a singer from the Budapest opera, since that would be scandalous enough for you.

JACKALS: Why mention names right away—it's so vulgar.

GRANDMOTHER: Unfortunately, all Mordovar knows about it.

CHRISTINA: Once you've divorced her and surrounded yourself with an aura of scandalous legend, you'll give your weary heart to some young lady from a good family for purposes of propagating the race and transmitting property.

JACKALS: Given the constant threat of revolution and the expropriation of property that will follow, those questions play less and less of a role in the marriages of our social sphere.

ISTVAN: All that's so boring.

JACKALS: Oh, yes—I can shoot myself at any moment: I'm distracted to the point of madness. (*Pulls out a revolver.*) No one understands me. Oh, if you only knew! (*He points the revolver at his temple.* ISTVAN *springs at him and tries to take it away from him. A struggle.*)

ISTVAN: Don't deprive me of the possibility of getting satisfaction. And don't twist my arm: I'm a musician. Anyhow, none of that will do any good.

ISTVAN *wrests the revolver away from him and puts it in his pocket. At that same moment enter through the French window* RIO BAMBA, *wrapped in a cape, with a cigar in his mouth.*

RIO BAMBA (*without taking off his black hat with its gigantic brim, the cigar constantly clenched between his teeth*): It's agreeable to relax a bit in this Mordovar of yours after adventures on the south seas and in tropical jungles—but only then. Life here on a permanent basis must have a deadly effect: simply debilitating. Istvan, I must inform you that I am your uncle. Rio Bamba is my name now and anyone who calls me anything else will pay dearly for it. I count on the discretion of everyone here.

ISTVAN: Oh, uncle, I remember that night on board the *Sylvia* as though it were yesterday—it was an old war hulk converted into a merchant ship; I was five years old then. We were going to Rio and you, the prodigal uncle, were puffing away on your everlasting cigar, just like now.

RIO BAMBA: I am a character from a forgotten dream. But Mordovar has always been alive in me. I had to come back here. I owe this opportunity to my partner, Joachim Baltazar de Campos, who'll be arriving at any moment.

ISTVAN: Our poor Mordovar invaded by Brazilian planters. But what do we care about the experiences of ordinary people?   With artists experiences are transformed into something else and transposed into another dimension, and that's why every detail of an artist's life has such tremendous value and why their biographers are concerned with these details to such a ridiculous extent.

JACKALS: He's already dreaming of his future biographer who will do research on the mystery of this evening as it relates to his musical compositions. Art is a plaything no better or worse than any other. The way we put artists on a pedestal is a proof of our decadence.

ISTVAN: I'm not answering you since for the moment we are enemies, according to the silliest of social conventions that has ever existed. Honor is a relic of the past—nowadays no one can give an exact definition of the concept.

JACKALS: Yet you're still talking to me. And despite what you say about honor, you're going to fight me.

ISTVAN: Solely and exclusively for my artistic goals. I need some kind of shock to release what I have to write. I'm a terrible coward—that's why I choose fear sent me by chance. If I were a sex-fiend, I'd choose to give up my one and only love.

JACKALS: And if you were a gourmet, you'd decide to go on a hunger-strike. Fear, sex and hunger—these are the three sources to which materialistic and pseudo-scientific bird-brains would like to reduce religion.

ISTVAN: They'll never succeed. Religion, along with philosophy, is an intellectually inspired working out of certain feelings which I call metaphysical.

RIO BAMBA: That's all well and good—but, gentlemen, consider if you will the fact that I have returned to Mordovar.

JACKALS: What's that got to do with what we're talking about?

RIO BAMBA: Perhaps more than you think. But I don't have any idiotic notions about sticking to the subject. Now then: to all appearances, I was better off in Brazil. Yet I couldn't stay there; I took advantage of Joachim's mania for Hungarian wine and these local mountains and I came here. Besides, I must tell you an important secret: the person who ruined my life was grandmother Julia. Even though I was ten years younger than she, I embezzled funds for her, and I am still doing penance for it.

GRANDMOTHER: Yes, alas—I was his mistress and he was the father of my late daughter. In my youth I was a moral monster, but I was so physically attractive that people slashed their wrists because of me.

RIO BAMBA: That's right—she's telling the truth.

GRANDMOTHER: Your father was one of them, Baron. (*Deep twilight; the snow-covered mountains shine in the evening's orange glow, and later in the cold moonlight.*) So now we live through this night of memories, leaning over a well from which we can draw forth whatever we wish: bane and gall, or nectar and ambrosia, or even a cure for the pain in our souls, for our longing and the torment of our conscience.

ISTVAN: Yes—it's a typical Mordovar evening: the mountains are ablaze with the glow of twilight and the earth truly seems a strange planet, not a place of everyday triviality.

RIO BAMBA: That's it exactly: you expressed it wonderfully, my dear nephew. I wanted to interest all of you in a fact without general significance: to have you all share the strangeness of my personal sensations—by making you feel the magical enchantment of my own memories. But that can't be done. Each one of us lives enclosed in his own world as in a prison and thinks that the same evening cloud he sees *as he meditates on eternity* is also floating across someone else's sky—yet for that other person it may be a starless night filled with debauchery, or a disgustingly bright noon, in which a business deal has just been concluded.

JACKALS: Rio Bamba, old boy—you have expressed quite simply and somewhat imprecisely a very important but nonetheless banal fact: the absolute isolation of every single individual in the universe.

ISTVAN: Oh—if only I could capture that in musical sounds. But I jot down notes on the staves the way a book-keeper jots down figures in his ledgers, and my work is dead for me, despite the fact that it pleases others. It's well-made music all right, but it's not art. Oh, now I understand that fellow who wanted to compose a sonata that Beelzebub himself might have written! I've suddenly grasped it in a flash. (*Enter through the French window upstage* BALEASTADAR *in a black cape and black pointed hat with a broad brim; following him, momentarily hidden from the others' view by his imposing figure, comes* HILDA HAJCZY *in a black fur coat without a hat.*) I don't want life to be expressed by sounds, I want the musical notes themselves to live and fight among themselves over something unknown. Oh, that's something no one will ever understand!!

BALEASTADAR: But suppose I understand it already? Suppose what you're thinking of actually happens because of me? (*They all turn towards him.*) Good evening. Please, don't disturb yourselves. I don't want to spoil this truly Mordovar atmosphere, possible only here in these mountains.

GRANDMOTHER: There's your Beelzebub, Istvan. (*Catches sight of* HILDA *whom no one yet has noticed.*) What sort of alien presence has found its way into our little gathering? But perhaps she will actually help fulfill my prophecies.

ISTVAN: Don't play the innocent, Grandmother. That's Jackals's demon. A marvelous woman, Miss Hajczy—I only know her from the opera. She has a phenomenal voice.

JACKALS: Hilda! Why have you come here? The one place where I could stop thinking about you, and you poison it for me with your presence, reminding me of the total reality of my downfall. I'd just begun to think I'd been successful in transposing it into an artistic Mordovar mood.

HILDA: Shut up—there are strangers here. No one's asking you what you feel. There are more important things.

ISTVAN: Her voice is so different when she's not singing . . .

HILDA (*to* JACKALS, *pointing to* CHRISTINA): What do I see here—some innocent little lambikins that you're going to seduce with the poison I injected you with. Apparently you need women like that, you good-for-nothing. Oh—how unhappy I am! That's how this clown consoles himself instead of conquering my soul that cannot be had by petty spirits.

JACKALS: Hilda! You're forgetting yourself. Now it's my turn to tell you: there are strangers present.

HILDA: Not to be able to humble oneself before the man who arouses one's wildest passions—is there anything more abominable for a woman like me?

BALEASTADAR (*puts his hand on her shoulder*): But Hilda, you were already on the right track. Remember our first conversation in the vineyard by the light of the afternoon sun?

JACKALS: Have you already bought this wretch? (*Points to* HILDA.) Because, make no mistake about it, I'm the only one she finds attractive.

BALEASTADAR: No, I have not bought her and I don't intend to, although I could outbid you easily enough, Mr. Jackals. There's something far more interesting in the wind. Even the stupidest legend contains some particle of truth; it's based on some form of reality, no matter how symbolic.

ISTVAN: Tell us frankly, why did you come here all the way from Brazil?

CHRISTINA (*bursting out laughing*): Ha! ha! ha! In other words: who knows whether you're not Beelzebub—that's a good one!

BALEASTADAR: Don't laugh, my child: there are many, many strange things in the world which city dwellers have long since forgotten. Sometimes, in the depths of the mountains, or on the boundless prairies, something comes rolling by and, catching hold of something else, creates a tangled web of new ultrasurreal possibilities. To unwind such a web . . .

ISTVAN (*impatiently*): Then who are you actually?

BALEASTADAR: I am Joachim Baltazar de Campos de Baleastadar, breeder of bulls in Brazil, but here—in this country of yours—a planter of vineyards. I am also an unsuccessful pianist—unsuccessful because of a certain love-affair that has nevertheless created something within me that all the fame and all the concerts in the world could never have given me.

ISTVAN: Well—is that all?

BALEASTADAR: Don't think I want to mislead you. But I've been strengthened in my belief by meeting this woman here, today of all days, three days after your arrival, Mr. Saint-Michael. It's time to break off this Mordovar magic and its peaceful moods; otherwise until the end of your life you'll go on jotting down your little musical notations which others will admire, but you will never realize yourself as an artist.

ISTVAN: Could you really be the Beelzebub that Grandmother has been promising? I don't believe in that dimension of strangeness. Art is the strangest thing.

BALEASTADAR: But not the kind you're creating. That's common, ordinary strangeness, the kind so many artists delude themselves with nowadays. They're successful—that goes without saying, but in two hundred years no one will want to play their music, or read their books, or look at their pictures. They exist only to make people thoroughly sick of both art and life. Nothing will remain of them.

ISTVAN: I don't want to be one of them. I'd rather stop creating. Even though that would be frightful torture.

BALEASTADAR: You don't have to give up anything yet. Rather risk everything—all, or nothing . . .

ISTVAN: But how? Risk what? I'm totally helpless, I don't know where to begin. Should I climb a cliff somewhere on Mount Czikla and hurl myself over the edge like an idiot or run out in front of the Kosice express racing at top speed or drink five liters of Czech brandy— those are the risks at my disposal.

BALEASTADAR: So you're a coward? Is that it?

ISTVAN: Yes, I am—so what? Stop trying to embarrass me.

JACKALS: I'm beginning to take a new interest in life. Even though I'm suffering atrociously on account of that copper-haired beast, for the moment I'm not thinking about it so virulently.

RIO BAMBA: Why not try beating her, Baron? That works in novels sometimes—perhaps it will in real life too.

JACKALS: I've tried it—a cold-blooded beating doesn't do any good. You don't understand me, my good Rio Bamba. She is mine and refuses me nothing. And yet I still can't rule her. I have no idea what her soul is like, I don't even know if she has one. So how can you rule something that doesn't exist?

ISTVAN: Gentlemen, couldn't we talk about these matters later on? There are really far more interesting things in the foreground that may indirectly affect you too. *Everything* may be transformed in a way no one has ever seen before.

BALEASTADAR: Yes—I'm not lying, I'm not speaking symbolically, and I don't believe in anything, even though here in this world, I feel, hmm— how can I put it—quite strange—but not so much as to start believing . . .

CHRISTINA: In what? That you're Beelzebub?

BALEASTADAR: Let's leave it at that—for lack of anything better.

CHRISTINA: These are the hopeless ravings of a maniac.

BALEASTADAR: Just a minute, just a minute! There's no need to be excessively realistic about life. When Rio Bamba, Istvan's uncle, first told me that whole so-called Mordovar legend of yours, I only laughed at it. But then I began to think it over again and again, without ever stopping, until something finally clicked inside me, something I knew about unconsciously as though in a dream. My wife stopped existing for me, even though—but that's another story . . .

GRANDMOTHER: That's it—exactly!

BALEASTADAR: Don't interrupt! I felt something strange inside me, a kind of conviction that somehow I had known all this from before and that I had to see this part of the country. I immediately had my agents buy me a vineyard here, and for three weeks now I've been waiting here for Istvan.

CHRISTINA: Here's your Beelzebub, Istvan. There's no getting around it.

BALEASTADAR (*without paying any attention to her*): In the final analysis it doesn't matter whether I'm Beelzebub or not, the question that so preoccupies Christina. The only thing that matters is that sonata. Actually, I am a pianist, only I missed my calling in life. But I always dreamed of someone who would incarnate my ideas—which ones I don't even know myself—I feel them inside me like a huge charge of explosives for which there's no fuse or match.

CHRISTINA: Exactly, there's no match, and yet he comes here all the way from Brazil!

ISTVAN: Just you wait, Christina.

CHRISTINA: A new candidate for the loonybin . . .

BALEASTADAR (*finishing his thought*): And when I found out there was a musician in the neighborhood and that he was the nephew of my old friend Rio Bamba to boot, I knew all there was to know. Because why did his uncle become my steward, why did Istvan, a little boy of seven, run away from Rio to Budapest right after he got there? Eh? Those aren't accidents. You only have to have the courage to try.

CHRISTINA: To try whether you can't accidentally manage to go crazy—for lack of anything better to do.

BALEASTADAR: We can call it that. But if we all go crazy that way and everything turns into something else, even though our relative positions remain the same, that is, if we simply change the center of the coordinates . . .

CHRISTINA: I've just taken analytical geometry and your comparisons don't impress me. Changing the center of the coordinates used simply to be called going nuts . . .

BALEASTADAR (*threateningly, losing patience*): That's enough of that girlish prattle! This evening is no accident. I was waiting for all this down there in Brazil. During the sweltering nights in town, when the hot wind carried the sounds of the guitar from the street, or in the quiet of the pampas when my family had long since gone to bed, I dreamed about these wretched mountains of yours and the caved-in mine, and about you, Istvan.

ISTVAN: But if this comes true, I mean: if I write the real Beelzebub sonata, perhaps we'll all come out in some other dimension?

BALEASTADAR: If I succeed in instilling in you the strangeness of the music that I have within me, then perhaps you will create what you've been dreaming about. I can't: I don't have the talent. That's why in the legend they talk about the sonata that Beelzebub would (*the stress is on "would"*) have composed if and so on and so forth . . . It's not a lack of belief in the possibility of his really existing, only in the possibility of his composing the sonata—even given the strongest inclinations in that direction.

CHRISTINA: It seems to me Beelzebub couldn't possibly be a person of real talent; he could do everything, but it would all be counterfeit.

BALEASTADAR: A person! But he was able to attain the truth of evil through others, at the cost of destroying their lives. On the other hand, in art he should be able to create greatness—but only in our times, in an era of artistic perversity. *Until now* there was no greatness in that dimension.

CHRISTINA: You talk so convincingly about this Beelzebub that at times I'm really starting to believe in his existence.

A violent gale suddenly starts to rage. A pause.

GRANDMOTHER: You've ruined my prediction, Mr. Baleastadar, and the cards have never failed me before.

BALEASTADAR: You see, Grandmother, whenever I've had my fortune told, it's never come true.

JACKALS: Some of it must come true. I won't stand for any more of this humiliation. If I don't do it, I'll die in a state of moral decay a hundred times worse than anything that might happen later.

He pulls the revolver out of ISTVAN*'s pocket, while* ISTVAN *is lost in thought, and shoots* HILDA, *who falls to the floor.* JACKALS *runs out through the door to the right in the midst of blasts of wind from the intensifying autumn mountain storm.*

GRANDMOTHER: And the word became flesh! In the name of the Father, the Son, and the Holy Ghost—give grandmother a kummel toast!

CHRISTINA: My God—Grandmother has gone crazy!

RIO BAMBA: Look after that person, Chris. I'll bring Grandmother back to her senses with memories of the past.

He strokes GRANDMOTHER*'s hair and whispers something to her, his cigar clenched between his teeth.*

HILDA (*sitting on the floor*): My God, he'll kill himself. I love him so. What does he want from me? He's got it into his head he doesn't know my soul. Who'll cure him of that madness if I die?

She suddenly falls over backwards. CHRISTINA *feels her pulse and checks to see if she's still breathing.*

CHRISTINA: I think she's dead—I don't hear her breathing. Lovely as an angel! It can't be that what they say about her is true.

BALEASTADAR: And so the evening has begun. Come along, Istvan, let's go to the mine in Mount Czikla. And even if we don't find hell there, we'll find more than enough of it within ourselves to outdo all the Beelzebubs in the world with our sonata. I don't believe in it myself, but some mysterious force superior to me and to everything else forces me to talk this way.

ISTVAN: Oh, what happiness to live and suffer in Mordovar! I feel something joining previously isolated sounds into a theme that I still cannot hear. I should like to plunge to the very depths of moral wretchedness and from down there look at my work piling up on top of me like a gigantic tower in the rays of the spectral setting sun. Then dusk could fall in the valleys of my life.

BALEASTADAR: Come—this is precisely the right moment. But remember: if we cannot find hell either there or within ourselves, and it turns out that I'm purely and simply an ordinary Brazilian planter and would-be pianist, then neither of us will breathe a single word of complaint. We'll drink our morning coffee at the railroad station at Uj-Mordovar and go home to bed. And then ordinary life will resume again as though nothing had ever happened. Promise?

ISTVAN: Promise.

They go out into the midst of the gale through the center door. ISTVAN *takes his black overcoat and gray sports cap from the coatrack by the door.*

CHRISTINA: Things have got off to a nice start. The only good thing about it is that Jackals has totally lost his appeal for me.

RIO BAMBA (*solemnly*): Let's not put a stop to this evening, this truly Mordovar evening in which the strange and the commonplace are intertwined in a marvelous garland of moments, eternal in their beauty. Oh, praised be the commonplace—without you there would be nothing strange in this world! Chris, pour some wine!

The wind blows more and more powerfully. CHRISTINA *gets up and goes to the left.*

ACT TWO

A subterranean vault in an abandoned mine in Czikla, fixed up like a comparatively fantastic hell. Facing the audience, a recess between pillars. A door behind the left pillar on the left side. Bizarre chairs and sofas. Everything in black and red. The dominant tone is that of the demonic frippery found in public places of amusement, plus something really unpleasant in the highest degree and even menacing. A piano on a small platform in the recess between pillars. Through the door to the left, enter BALEASTADAR *and* ISTVAN: *The former dressed as in Act One, and the latter has on a black overcoat with the collar turned up and a gray sports cap.*

BALEASTADAR: Well, you see, Istvan, even though it's not quite all we could ask for—there is *something* to all this. To be sure, this hell does suggest a bit too strongly some Parisian cabaret or even the latest refurbishings in the Salon di Gioja in Rio, but there is *something* to it— no doubt about that. As far as I can make out, we're in the chamber for psychological tortures.

ISTVAN: It reminds me of one of those so-called demonic chambers in Osz-Buda-Var in Pest.

BALEASTADAR: Yes, that's right: it isn't a first-class establishment. But I think that the kind of hell we dreamed about is not only unattainable in reality, it's even unimaginable. But just think: to enter a buried mine shaft in the depths of Mount Czikla on the outskirts of Mordovar and to find a Parisian or Budapest-style cabaret there—that too might be considered a kind of miracle. Don't you agree?

ISTVAN (*reluctantly, hiding his fear*): Yes, of course. Still I do feel a bit different. That evening seems to be at least some five years ago. We left at eight, and now it's midnight—four hours: time has dragged terribly for me.

BALEASTADAR: For me too—but that's not it. Quite simply you're afraid, aren't you?

ISTVAN (*evasively*): Something is swirling around at the very bottom of my being. I've turned into a cave full of crooked passageways where ghosts lie in wait. But it still doesn't have any connection to music.

Infinity separates my own form from what it's to be filled with . . .

BALEASTADAR. Can't you keep your mouth shut for a while—we'll soon see what's going to happen next.

From behind the fantastic purple sofa to the right there appear two FOOTMEN *in red livery, with Vandyke beards. Mephistophelean appearance. They go over to* BALEASTADAR *and speak in unison, bowing.*

FOOTMEN: Monseigneur! (*They remain bowed over.*)

BALEASTADAR (*to* ISTVAN): That's how the proprietors of some cabaret in Paris—"le Chat Noir" if I'm not mistaken—address every customer. Can it really be that hell, even one located inside the Mordovar mountains, is nothing but some stupid sort of fun house? That would really be something too idiotic for words. Too bad we didn't go instead to the Magas Cafehaz on the other side of the lake for a quiet talk. I don't feel the slightest bit like Beelzebub.

FIRST FOOTMAN: Your Highness, look at yourself from behind. (*He places a mirror appropriately.* BALEASTADAR *twists about, feels himself from behind under his cape and looks at himself. The* SECOND FOOTMAN *removes his cape for him.* BALEASTADAR *is revealed to be holding his own thick devil's tail in his hand, a tail like a rat's, but ending in a triangular metal hook.*)

BALEASTADAR: What the devil! I never noticed that before. (*He examines his tail carefully.*)

SECOND FOOTMAN: The Prince of Darkness has to have a tail. And that kind of swearing is considered bad form here.

BALEASTADAR: This is incredible! But this tail is dead, even though it's growing out of me. And you both have tails—are yours dead too?

FIRST FOOTMAN: Even with today's technical advances hell has to be shown as it really is. In the old days it was better. But we don't tolerate any trickery, even though if we wanted to . . .

BALEASTADAR (*suddenly in a completely different tone: imperious, Beelzebubian, growing more so every minute*): Enough! Supper for nine—there'll be more of us any minute. But first of all: an ax and a chopping block! Look lively! Get a move on.

FOOTMEN: Yes, Your Highness! At your orders, Your Highness! (*They run behind the pillars to the left.*)

ISTVAN (*through his tears*): You're beginning to enter into your role, Mr. Baltazar.

BALEASTADAR: What else can I do—we shall see what comes of it. A wild strength is pulsating in my entrails. I'm growing hard as steel. I'm bursting with a furious hatred totally without any object. That, it would seem, is pure evil. (*The* FOOTMEN *bring in the chopping block and ax and place them in the middle of the stage.*) And now, Istvan, you're going to chop off my tail—I can't stand third-rate demonic effects out of keeping with the general situation. Chop away—I wonder if it's going to hurt.

ISTVAN *puts* BALEASTADAR's *tail on the chopping block and takes aim.*

FIRST FOOTMAN (*to the* SECOND): Chebnazel, there's something suspicious about this.

ISTVAN *chops. The tail falls off.* BALEASTADAR *screams with pain. Blood pours out of the chopped-off part and from the stump.* BALEASTADAR *sits down on the sofa sideways.*

SECOND FOOTMAN (*to the* FIRST): I'm telling you, Azdrubot, it's the first sign of his authenticity. Who else but the Prince of Darkness himself would dare to try something like that? (*To* BALEASTADAR.) Sir, say those four words again: you know the ones I mean?

BALEASTADAR (*getting up*): Banabiel, Abiel, Chamon, Azababrol!! I don't know what I'm saying myself. But it all has some sinister meaning. I am already on *the other side*!

SECOND FOOTMAN (*to the* FIRST): Azdrubot, hadn't we better fall down on our faces. It's him. At last hell has its Beelzebub.

They both fall down on their faces in front of BALEASTADAR.

FIRST FOOTMAN (*lying on the ground*):   It isn't always this way. Sometimes we have to wait a long time for such a one to be born among men. You alone, Sir, have had the courage to believe what others think is total nonsense. You are the one, you are the one! By that very fact you raise us, poor flunkies in a cabaret, to the dignity of true devils.

BALEASTADAR: Azdrubot is right. Stand over here by the chopping block, boys, and put your tails on it, side by side. (*The* FOOTMEN *execute the order immediately.*)   Chop away, Istvan—let's finish this disgusting comedy once and for all. Underground cabaret or modern hell—what's the difference—but it's got to be in good taste. Down with ignorance, obscurantism, and superstition! Chop away! (ISTVAN *chops, the tails fall off. The* FOOTMEN *make terrible faces due to the pain, but remain in place.*) And now take away that ax and chopping block and if there's anyone else in your crew with a tail—chop it off immediately. Understand? And see that supper is ready in ten minutes. Forward, march!

FOOTMEN: Yes, Sir, Your Highness! At your orders! (*They run off with the chopping block and ax behind the pillar to the left.*)

ISTVAN: This hell is way behind the times. I don't know whether you'll be able to fit in here with your flamboyant temperament.

BALEASTADAR: All that's going to change right now.   We still have impenetrable sloughs of psychological horrors ahead of us. Naturally, we'll simplify because of lack of time.

Through the door on the left four other FOOTMEN (*without tails*) *carry in three dark red coffins and place them in a row along the left side. While this is going on,* BALEASTADAR *speaks.*

BALEASTADAR: Most likely those are yesterday's corpses.   You know, Istvan, it's already the next day. Everything's going faster and faster. At first you won't be able to keep up with events, but then you'll get used to it. Life here depends on constantly catching up with and then outdistancing oneself. (*To the* FOOTMEN.) Open the coffins!

The FOOTMEN *began to pry the coffins open.*

ISTVAN: How I wish I could relive that last Mordovar evening! I wasn't ready for it then.

BALEASTADAR: You prematurely crossed a certain dividing line which great politicians, artists, or thinkers sometimes reach only in their sixties or seventies. But you're a musician—music first shows itself in childhood and doesn't demand maturity.

ISTVAN: Oh—so many people react to music with what I'd call "the howling dog reaction." A dog howls exactly the same way whether you play him Beethoven or Richard Strauss—he howls because his feelings are stirred up by the sheer noise of the sounds, by their emotional but artistically irrelevant element. That's why I must go all the way to pure music.

BALEASTADAR: You'll get there, but first you have to give vent to all your feelings in musical form. It's by working them over, pursuing them relentlessly, that you'll acquire your own style and Pure Form. *Here* this can happen through an inner process, without having to put useless little notations on staves to excite adolescent girls and hysterical women. Hell—even one like this—is a marvelous incubator for a fledgling musician.

ISTVAN: When will it happen, and how? Am I supposed to earn my living as a wretched piano player in this cabaret hell, throwing to the diabolical rabble what I hold most precious in life: my feelings?

BALEASTADAR: He doesn't understand a thing, the dim-wit! What's happened to your ambition to create the Beelzebub sonata that would beat the world-wide record for musical monstrosity? Have you forgotten about that already? You'll understand it all once I show you an example. (*To the* FOOTMEN.) Hurry up there, you satans. (*The corpses of* HILDA *and the* BARON JACKALS *appear in the coffins. The* FOOTMEN *start to pry open the third coffin.*) Possibilities are all I can give you. I'll never write my sonata myself even though I know all there is to know about it. You will write it inspired by me, but it will be your own. The spirit of evil, barren in its essence, can never be satiated: it must have mediums—interpreters of its murky conceptions and that's why its work will never be what it ought to have been.

ISTVAN: Then must I choose between life and art? For the voluptuous pleasure of creating musical values must I give up the immediate experience of life? Will it all be dead for me even before it's born?

BALEASTADAR: That's what all great artists have always done, appearances sometimes quite to the contrary. That's why the madness of artists, so fascinating to ordinary people and arousing such envy, is nothing but the bitter aftertaste left by the true events in their inner world of imaginary greatness—a pure construction of the mind. In the past this happened within the sphere of good; now that art is coming to an end, it has to take place in the realm of evil and darkness.

ISTVAN: I'd still like to get my fill of happiness in the world of feelings.

BALEASTADAR: Too late. Unless you want to continue being a would-be artist, the vilest thing in the world. And what's more, a would-be artist in your own eyes, not for the pack of howling dogs.

ISTVAN: I don't want that—not for anything. Let the sacrifice be made once and for all. The only thing that concerns me at this moment is how it's going to happen.

BALEASTADAR: Quite simply, like everything in hell. Here, we don't stand on ceremony with feelings. It will only be a kind of abridgment of life, not something qualitatively different from it. Not even Beelzebub himself can create that.

ISTVAN: Perhaps I won't miss that other world so much after all? Perhaps I'm just pretending to myself? Why is it impossible to experience any feeling all the way, why are states of feeling so contradictory? Everything has always seemed the past even before it's taken shape as the present. And to suffer such remorse about those I've vilely cheated, repaying their truth with the falsehood of my defective—oh, they're not even feelings—but rather psychic states.

BALEASTADAR (*suddenly menacing*): Enough of that gushing! (*Claps his hands; two* FOOTMEN *come dashing in*.) Get those corpses out! Get them ready for me at once! (*The* FOOTMEN *have just pried open the coffin in which the* BARONESS JACKALS *is lying dressed in black and violet.*)

FOOTMEN: At your orders, Your Highness!

The six FOOTMEN *take the corpses out and place them in chairs. The corpses are stiff and have their eyes closed.*

ISTVAN (*in a trembling voice*):   Mr. Baltazar, I'm afraid of you. You're so strange and frightening—let me out of here.

BALEASTADAR: Shut up, you clown! Do you want to hang by your own suspenders at the entrance to the mine shaft. like that other musician? Even before creating the works which would justify your miserable existence? Afterwards you can hang yourself to your heart's content. If you run away now, you'll never be able to lead a normal existence again.

ISTVAN: I don't want anything, Mr. Baltazar. I only want to go home to my aunt. I just want one more nice Mordovar evening, with everything calm and peaceful . . . I want to play those old preludes of mine, read a novel, and fall asleep. And to dream of our beloved Mordovar, heightened, the way it was in the past. I won't ever do it again. Forgive me, Sir.

BALEASTADAR (*glaring at* ISTVAN *with a devastating look*): I am not Sir, I am Beelzebub, Prince of Darkness. Address me as "Your Highness." Understand, you might-have-been?

ISTVAN (*falling to his knees*): It's frightening here . . . I don't want . . . Except to get out of here . . .

BALEASTADAR (*in a terrifying voice*):   In you I render mortal original sin through the artistic creativity that I arouse in you. Through art alone humanity remembers that everything in Existence contradicts itself. Without art I'd have no life any more. In the mire of mechanized cattle there's no work for me to do. But as long as art exists, I exist, and I satiate myself with existence on this planet by creating metaphysical evil. On the moons of Jupiter they have their own Beelzebubs.

ISTVAN: Oh, God! Save me! Mercy, Your Highness! (*The corpses sit stiffly in their chairs. Standing very straight, the* FOOTMEN *wait rigidly for orders.*)

BALEASTADAR: Don't you dare mention that Name here. For me it's only the symbol of nothingness, *my own* nothingness—but I want to live and I shall live. Yet I must live through someone else. Artists are the only material for me now. To create by destroying! The last form of strength left capable of blowing things up, since the death of religions, which once created the evil spirit's ghost. I personify all that—do you understand? What have you got a brain for? Think, but don't feel anything.

ISTVAN (*falling into a state of catalepsy*): Something monstrous is turning my blood to ice. I feel the evil fang of an amorphous ghost ploughing my brain into the zigzags of a lightning-quick, inexpressible thought.

BALEASTADAR: What do you see?

ISTVAN: I see Mordovar the way it used to be, as in a dream, taken to the limits of inhuman, bestial beauty. Masks are falling from the trees, the mountains, and the clouds. I see a merciless black sky and a small stray globe which you, Prince of Darkness, envelop with your bat-like wings. And I am a worm, a little caterpillar, crawling along the leaves, irradiated by the sinister glow of the suns bursting in the Milky Way.

BALEASTADAR: Come down lower, to the level of your own feelings. Dig deep into yourself one last time.

ISTVAN: My feelings are pills prepared by some hideous interplanetary pharmacist who hurls them into nothingness to be devoured by frozen, starving space.

BALEASTADAR: Lower still

ISTVAN (*suddenly waking up from his cataleptic state*): I want to go back to Mordovar, to my aunt! (*In a final attempt at labored irony.*) You've entered into the role of Beelzebub wonderfully well, but I've had enough of this comedy.

BALEASTADAR *smacks him on the head with his fist.* ISTVAN *stays on his feet and falls into the previous state all over again.*

ISTVAN: This is the end. The very core of my being has gone numb in an icy blast from the center of Non-Being.

BALEASTADAR: Do you understand now? There's just one thing I can't do, just one: create art. And yet I was born an artist. In the past I was told to create life, now I am unemployed in a world growing ever more perfectly mechanized. Don't ask who told me to, don't think about it. Certain secrets must be kept.   Know that I alone am the sole superreality, the sole evil. If it weren't for evil, nothing would exist, not even your aunt, even though she's a notoriously saintly person.

ISTVAN (*with a final effort*):   And yet I can see you, a cursed planter from Rio. Oh, look—horns are growing on your forehead—oh, that's very funny! I know how it's done. He had his tail cut off because having a tail is ridiculous. But he kept the horns for effect. Or perhaps those are the horns which your wife Clara di Formio y Santos bestowed on you . . .

BALEASTADAR *smacks him another one on the head with his fist.*   ISTVAN *falls down. While* ISTVAN *has been talking, small horns about four inches long have been growing on* BALEASTADAR's *forehead. (On his wig he has two rubber fingers connected to a bifurcated tube with a bulb at the end in his pocket with which he can blow them up.) The* FOOTMEN *upstage burst out laughing.* BALEASTADAR *doesn't notice this.*

BALEASTADAR: Well—that takes care of him. Put him with the corpses. That clown doesn't understand that potentially he's the greatest musical genius in the world. What he'll accomplish—no one else will. (*To* HILDA *who suddenly opens her eyes wide and stares at him*, *sitting stiffly in her chair; the other corpses sit with their eyes closed.*)   What are you giving me the eye for, Hilda? He's your true lover. Through him we'll create the music of Pure Evil distilled into Pure Form. Oh—if only I could be an artist myself! (*Sobs wildly for a moment*, *then gets control of himself and says:*)   The Beelzebub Sonata must be created. And you (*addresses* HILDA) will sing the songs of Beelzebub, and through my inspiration that clown will also write a string concerto—for cello or violin—what does it matter—and some violinist will perform it without understanding the first thing about what he is playing; the piano works I'll perform myself, suffering the torments of the damned, because I didn't create them myself, and they'll all howl in ecstasy like a pack of jackals.

HILDA: But why do all this here, tonight, instead of gradually out there on the surface of the earth?

BALEASTADAR: To condense evil—out there, it would ooze away into the rotten jellyish mass of Mordovar or even Budapest moods. (*In a different tone.*) It's all so petty: miserably squeezed out of the last recesses of the very depths. (*In the previous tone, passionately.*) But unique of its own kind—do you understand, Hilda? There's nothing else to start with in this grand finale of the world. Thus art must be the synthesis of evil and for the sake of art it's still worth attempting something, despite all the anguish and repulsion, because art is the only thing that has come down to us from the good old days, even though it's going to the devil too and quite rapidly at that. I'll begin with music, and then later perhaps I'll work on the other arts in the same way, although I doubt much can be done with them. But first of all, the sonata, a school exercise like the your first sonata at the conservatory. All right—wake up, you mannequin of a genius.

ISTVAN (*suddenly wakes up from his stupefaction and gets up; all at once he becomes a completely different person: self-controlled, joyful and almost demonically evil*): At your orders, Your Highness. Where do we begin?

BALEASTADAR: Here's a woman for you, Istvan. You must love her and lose everything you have treasured until this moment. You won't find anything like her on this earth. She is the incarnation of woman's strangeness in the wildest transformation of the center of coordinates for pure evil.

ISTVAN: I understand. You're exaggerating a bit, Prince. Hilda, I never really understood you until the present moment. I was a child.

HILDA: And you're still a child now, despite all your musical demonism. Come to me—I'll teach you to be yourself. You'll be mine and you'll die because of it, like all the others, but in a different way; together we'll create hellish works which lonely satans will long for during sleepless nights, as they dream of satanesses such as never existed. The inner hell of my unsatisfied desires will drag every love down into the mire of destructive sensuality. But die you must in a frightful state of moral collapse such as you have never even imagined until this moment.

ISTVAN: I've heard of men destroying themselves like that over women, but I never believed it. But I'll convince you. Beneath the mask I wear, there's nothing real. I'm not afraid of anything. A whirling mass of dark sounds conceals from me the mystery of your body. Dagger-like, I'll rip it open with a kiss on your guilty lips. (*Kisses her.*) Now I know who I am. My strength knows no limits. I'll enclose it all in a pyramid of diabolical music, in a construction of pure metaphysical evil, of frozen Dionysian frenzy.

HILDA: I am yours in the unattainable depths of my innermost being, which is insatiability in crime and lying. Nothing can satiate me. You're a monstrous, horrid little boy. I love you. You are transforming me into those sounds of yours, I can feel it.

BALEASTADAR: And to think how low I've fallen! I, who centuries ago battled against the holiness of art, now only dream of being able to compose a mere eight measures of good music. I'm being torn apart by that contradiction. Oh—what hell to be Beelzebub and not be able, even nowadays, to be an artist! (*To* ISTVAN.) But you, you idiot, without me you wouldn't be anything either. That's the only thing that consoles me. I can't express it in these cursed human concepts. But what's going to happen will speak for itself. (*Through the door to the left enter* RIO BAMBA, *leading in* ISTVAN's AUNT *and* GRANDMOTHER.) Rio Bamba, bring those matrons over here closer. Let them watch and see. I'm glad you've all come, you'll be the backdrop for my ideas.

RIO BAMBA: So now we see clearly that this whole Mordovar legend was not such nonsense as it might have seemed at first. (*Embraces* GRANDMOTHER.) You see, Julia, how old sins can become a splendid setting for new monstrosities.

GRANDMOTHER: Oh, I feel so good with you, Teobald.

AUNT (*to* BALEASTADAR): I'm grateful to you, Your Highness, for totally transforming my nephew. The Prince of Darkness could not have acted more graciously.

She kisses BALEASTADAR's *hand.*

BALEASTADAR (*to the corpses*): Baroness, wake up, please. And you too, Hieronymus.

The corpses of the BARONESS *and* JACKALS *open their eyes.*

BARONESS: But Your Highness, please arrange it all nicely, so that nothing bad happens to my little boy Rony. That murder's already worn him out so! But I think a Jackals might be allowed to kill some little Budapest floozy who has dared to snub him.

JACKALS (*suddenly springing up*): Hilda! What are you doing here with that vile piano player? How dare you in my presence? Do you want me to kill you all over again?

BALEASTADAR: Baron, you don't yet know that Istvan is a count. We found out about it at the Bureau of Records here, by the entrance. I looked over the papers when I first came in. Everything's in order. They show that Istvan is a descendant of the Count Palatine Clapary, who was the lord of the Orava castles. Istvan's grandfather, implicated in the War of 1848 in a not very commendable fashion—as an Austrian spy out of pure conviction—escaped to Mordovar, and lived under an assumed name. He had a son, who died, leaving Istvan in the world. Rio Bamba is a Count too—but that's beside the point.

JACKALS: Oh, this is disastrous! I've lost my last trump. What a tiresome complication. Since that's the case, Count, we're fighting.

ISTVAN: I could disqualify you, but I don't want to. If you'd known I was some idiotic Count last night, you wouldn't have dared commit suicide once you'd been challenged. Snobbery is killing all other feelings in you except for jealousy over her, and now she is mine.

He points to HILDA. *The* FOOTMEN *provide them with swords.*

BARONESS: Don't let that good-for-nothing get the better of you. Even though he's spared us from the question of marriage with that (*points to* HILDA) lady, still you must avenge yourself for his daring to take a woman away from you in the first place.

The young men fight.

JACKALS: My arm is going numb. I've forgotten all my best lunges. I, who defeated Count Sturz and Trampolini. Enough of this. It's frightful. Where did he ever learn to do all that?

He falls, hit. The BARONESS *and the* FOOTMEN *rush over to him, give him first aid, and bandage his wound.*

HILDA: Oh, Istvan, how I adore you! (*She throws her arms around* ISTVAN. CHRISTINA, *wrapped in a black shawl, runs in through the door to the left.*)

CHRISTINA: What's going on here? Oh, I'm so tired. A tremendous gale has blown down half the forest on the slopes of Czikla. I was barely able to get here. Oh, it's so frightening here! A strange man in an old Spanish costume brought me here. (*Enter* DON JOSÉ INTRIGUEZ DE ESTRADA *in the costume of a seventeenth-century Grandee.*)   Don't be angry, Grandmother, but he said you sent him to get me.

DE ESTRADA: Greetings, Baltazar. I couldn't keep myself from coming to see you. I arrived from Rio tonight. I'm on leave for two months.

BALEASTADAR: Ladies and gentlemen, may I present to you: my wife's lover, Don José Intriguez de Estrada, ambassador of the King of Spain to Rio.

DE ESTRADA (*disconcerted*): You must be joking, Baltazar.

BALEASTADAR: Don't Baltazar me, I am Beelzebub, Prince of Darkness! Can't you see these horns? (*Points to his head.*) You're the one who put them on me. But now they have become the symbol of my devilishness. Sit down. (DE ESTRADA *sits down, but it is obvious he feels very ill-at-ease.*) The only thing that matters here is for this young musician to write a sonata worthy of Beelzebub himself—that is to say, worthy of me.

DE ESTRADA: All this makes me feel very ill-at-ease. Very well, if you want to play the madman, I'm not going to stop you. I remember you once told me something similar when you were drunk. I'm in a peculiar situation; instead of returning to Madrid I came by way of Fiume-Budapest directly to Mordovar. Now I see that none of this makes any sense. Once in Mordovar, as soon as I left the station, I went straight to a house totally unknown to me, and then with this young lady here, whom I saw for the first time in my life, I came here to this cabaret in an abandoned mine. On the way, our horses dropped from under us and we came on foot, amidst falling trees—you have no idea what a gale . . .

BALEASTADAR: Shut up! I'll give you a cabaret! (DE ESTRADA *faints and falls over backwards in his chair. His hat falls off his head.*)

CHRISTINA: Now I see it clearly for the first time. But it's already too late! I loved only Istvan.

GRANDMOTHER: And besides it turns out Istvan's a Count. With the help of the Prince of Darkness, he's going to be the greatest musician in the world.

CHRISTINA: Everything's collapsing. He can be whoever he wants—I don't care in the least! (*Weeps.*) I love him so terribly, so hopelessly.

JACKALS: My last hope of salvation gone. Christina, I ran away from you because I was afraid of Mother and a misalliance.

HILDA: You can all see how vile he is!

ISTVAN: Don't interrupt me. Something creative is starting to take shape in me. The first theme of the sonata . . . In F sharp minor . . . (*Becoming absorbed in thought.*) It's all lurking inside me like a big, murky bomb.

BALEASTADAR: Oh—at last! Sometimes I really feel like laughing when I think that the ultimate goal of all this is some idiotic sonata. That shows to what extent the very idea of Beelzebub has in recent times, how shall I put it—*passez-moi l'expression*—gone to the dogs. In order to truly experience his own existence, even Beelzebub himself has to become some half-ass patron of the arts and a virtuoso because that's the only place an individual can still assert himself in a tolerably perverse manner. Everything else is mechanized pulp, not worth a glance from even the lowest of the devils. Isn't that right, Chebnazel? And you, blockhead, Azdrubot, would you like to tinker around with the mechanism of our ideally planned social systems?

SECOND FOOTMAN (*laughing*): Never, Your Highness. I prefer working in this cabaret.

FIRST FOOTMAN: At any rate it's better than the Enfer or the Cabaret du Néant at Place Pigalle.

BALEASTADAR: And now let's get to work! Get the piano ready. Bechstein or Steinway?

FIRST FOOTMAN: Bechstein, Your Highness. (*They run to the back of the stage and open the magnificent Bechstein.*)

CHRISTINA: Istvan, you're the one I really . . . Get rid of that slut from Budapest. Remember how we played four hands together. Back there in our dear, peaceful Mordovar—those evenings of ours.

ISTVAN: There weren't so many of them, and they were all poisoned by my cursed unrequited love for you. I shudder in disgust at the very thought of it. If I had married you, I never would have become an artist. For me you're only the theme for a macabre minuet which will be the second part of my sonata, the true Beelzebub sonata. I can already see it published in a Universal-Edition, and it will be dedicated to the Prince of Darkness: *Dem Geiste der Finsterniss gewidmet*—just like on those sonatas of Beethoven that amused me when I was seven years old.

BALEASTADAR: Go on, go on—I hope something more is going to happen. All this is still not enough.

ISTVAN: Is that so? Then out of my way, last and most miserable pang of conscience! May nothing else ever remind me of those Mordovar baubles. (*He pulls a knife out of his pocket and slits* CHRISTINA's *throat.*)

BARONESS: Serves her right—for having the nerve not to love my only son. I never would have approved of that marriage anyhow.

HILDA (*to* ISTVAN): Now you are truly mine. That young calf would never have been enough for you anyhow. (*They whisper together.* RIO BAMBA *starts to dance with* GRANDMOTHER.)

RIO BAMBA: I'll become a devil in my old age. Together with that witch. I'll create a stupendous house of psychic ill repute for the ruggedest individuals of our times.

BALEASTADAR: If only such people existed. I'm afraid it will be nothing but a cooperative society for the last remnants of lonely lost artists.

GRANDMOTHER (*hopping about*): Really—to be able to stop playing the matron and gorge myself on life once more—that was something I never expected. To be a sorceress for so long and have to play the respectable little matron: that was torture.

She dances with RIO BAMBA. *One of the* FOOTMEN *plays a shimmy very softly.*

BALEASTADAR: It's all so hopelessly night club-and-cabaret, so tasteless. But without the setting nothing would get done. And now—listen, Istvan, you shouldn't throw yourself into life with such abandon—our joint work: the initial sonata, the germ of all Beelzebubian music, will suffer for it. Give you a little foretaste and then totally cut off the possibility of satisfaction—that's what I had in mind.

ISTVAN: I don't understand—then what am I . . . ?

BALEASTADAR: Leave that lady alone. She's my quarry. For you she's a momentary plaything, for me—she's the last love of an old man who has nothing more to look forward to, even if he is Beelzebub himself.

ISTVAN: And Your Highness dares say that to me? For the first time I've come to understand what existence really is, and Your Highness wants to take it away from me. No, I'd rather have life than any conceivable musical composition *à la* Beelzebub. In my art I will be pure without any evil, even metaphysical evil.

They glare at one another, locked in a staring duel until instructions to the contrary.

BARONESS: That's all very well, but why does it have to happen just like this? There isn't the slightest necessity for it: *c'est contingent tout cela*—pure chance. Somewhere in Mordovar in Hungary—why not in Mexico?—a handful of people happened to meet by chance. But why precisely must *this* gentleman be Beelzebub and why must that Saint-Michael fellow use him for his own artistic goals—that I do not understand and I never shall.

AUNT: So that my nephew, who is like a son to me, can become a great musician.

BARONESS: That's not a sufficient reason for something as grand as the appearance of the true Beelzebub. And why here, and not somewhere else?

BALEASTADAR (*to the* BARONESS): It had to happen somewhere. It doesn't matter where, does it, given the infinity of worlds? There are scores of planets, Baroness. It's the same as with the speed of light: it has to be some speed, and a finite one at that—does it matter whether it's 300 or 500 thousand kilometers a second?

ISTVAN *lowers his head and stands more dead than alive.*

BARONESS: Yes, but I don't like that anthropocentric world view. I am an enlightened woman, *un bas bleu,* if you want, but *au fond* a pantheist.

BALEASTADAR: I can't, at a moment's notice, give a lecture on the necessity of chance for *précieuse*ish matrons. Hilda, you are mine, come to my arms. This evening is in a class of its own.

HILDA (*falling on her knees in front of him*): Oh, my one and only! So it's true? I'm to have the inhuman happiness of being mistress to the true Beelzebub? I think I'll go mad, I shan't live through it! (*She grovels at* BALEASTADAR's *feet.*)

ISTVAN: Ha—I'm not going to live through it so calmly either. He takes my only love away from me. He only gave her to me in order to rob me cruelly.

He throws himself at BALEASTADAR, *but stops as though hypnotized.*

GRANDMOTHER: Quiet, for Satan's sake! The Ambassador will wake up and be an unwanted witness. He's not one of ours yet.

DE ESTRADA (*getting up*): Oh, but I am, Grandmother dear. I'm one of yours. I regret that all this isn't taking place in Spain. I'd be proud if it were. You can all count on my discretion. Baltazar, old boy, I believe you are the true Prince of Darkness. To be on a first name basis with Beelzebub, that's a great honor even for a Grandee of Spain and ambassador of His Royal Highness.

ISTVAN: I'll kill that scoundrel. (*He throws himself at* BALEASTADAR *who deliberately falls over backwards on the ground just as* ISTVAN *gets to him, spreading out his arms, and laughing demonically.*)

BALEASTADAR (*falling*): Hit me, shoot me, slit my throat, stab me. You'll never kill me . . . I am eternal. Here's a revolver! (BALEASTADAR *offers him a revolver. ISTVAN stabs him several times with a knife in a wild fury. BALEASTADAR keeps on laughing. ISTVAN, blinded by hopeless rage, grabs the revolver and shoots him six times. BEELZEBUB gets up laughing, and raises* HILDA *up, taking her in his arms.*) And now to the piano, you non-entity! Now at last life will be transformed within you into that hellish melange of form and content called art. Enough of this perversity in life. It's miserable, miserable, indeed, like all art, but unique and evil—that's what's most important.

ISTVAN (*awakening from his reverie*): Come along, Hieronymus. You'll find consolation with me after those women. I still need something more myself, some little monstrosity to tip me over to the other side, the dark side of my destiny. The mystery of this transformation is unfathomable, no matter how commonplace its manifestations may be in real life. (*The* BARON *gets up*, ISTVAN *embraces him and they both move upstage.*)

BARONESS: Ronnie, don't get into that demon's power. I've been keeping something else in reserve for you: the heiress of Keszmereth castle—a ravishing little fifteen-year-old. I've dreamed about it all my life, but didn't want to tell you prematurely.

BALEASTADAR: That's enough out of you, you old prig. Can't you see he's going to play my sonata, the Beelzebub sonata—and for that he must have the final setting. Oh, boundless happiness! Now at last I am something of an artist. Through him a frightful mass is being celebrated to the unknown and unknowable evil of which you are all separate particles within me.

BARONESS: Then it's a kind of pantheism, even though transposed into Beelzebubian concepts.

BALEASTADAR (*crossing to the piano with his arms around* HILDA): Quiet over there! Here's an apparatus to record the notes you play—you can start by improvising. (*He points out the device on the right side of the piano.*)

ISTVAN (*sitting down at the piano*): Now at last I know what is meant by the formal spatial conception in music. The entire Beelzebub sonata exists within me beyond time. I shall unfold it like a fan—the greatest work since the beginning of the world.

The BARON *stands behind him, leaning on him in a state of ecstasy.* BALEASTADAR *and* HILDA *stand by the end of the piano.* ISTVAN *strikes the first notes of wild music.*   RIO BAMBA *starts a fantastic dance with* GRANDMOTHER. *Seated in her chair, the* BARONESS *falls into a trance as she listens intently. Meanwhile the curtain falls slowly.*

ACT THREE

The BARONESS JACKALS's *salon in her castle on the outskirts of Mordovar.
The whole thing is a rather narrow strip (about ten feet in width) running the
length of the footlights. The rest of the stage is separated from this visible
part by a dark-cherry colored curtain which can be pulled open from both
sides. Rococo furniture. Doors to the left and to the right. To the left the*
BARONESS *and* ISTVAN's AUNT *are seated—they are knitting. Near them* DE
ESTRADA *dressed as in Act Two. A fire is burning in the fireplace to the left.
A rosy twilight is slowly falling.*

AUNT: I'm so grateful to you, Baroness, for letting me spend the night here.
I'm terribly worried about Istvan.

BARONESS: But, dear Madam, ever since they found the papers proving
he's a count, a career beyond reproach has opened up for him. The
misalliance which Istvan's father, Mr. Saint-Michael—I mean, Count
Clapary—made when he married your sister—you'll forgive me for
speaking so frankly—is in no way an insurmountable obstacle. We'll
marry Istvan to one of those innumerable rich Americans who keep
coming here to Mordovar for the summer.

AUNT: Oh, let's not worry about that now. I'm afraid that old madman will
drag him into some scandalous affair with that Beelzebub sonata of
his.

BARONESS: Oh, I'm sure they'll come back—nothing will happen to him.
It's just what they call artistic experiences. I'm more worried about my
son.

DE ESTRADA: But look here, Madam, that ridiculous shot he took at that
Budapest strumpet—I can't describe that woman any other way—can
be totally hushed up. And the suicide wound, if I may express myself
in the Spanish manner, is light as a feather. A slight scratch on the
skull and temporary paralysis of half the body due to a cerebral
hemorrhage. I came across countless such cases during the war—the
symptoms always went away without leaving a trace.

A FOOTMAN *enters from the left.*

FOOTMAN: The Countess Clapary, Your Ladyship.

BARONESS: The Countess who? I don't understand at all.

DE ESTRADA: You're forgetting that Istvan's father's brother—alias Rio Bamba—has also turned out to be a count as part of a chain reaction. And, as befits a gentleman, he immediately married the person known as grandmother Julia, née Ceres. Petty nobility, but it doesn't really matter.   Here too we'll use our influence to hush up his youthful escapades, and everything will be all right. In our times a good many things must be overlooked to maintain order.

BARONESS: Oh, so that's it—then ask her to come in.

AUNT: How delightful—everyone's such an aristocrat—so many titles—I'm so delighted!

BARONESS: Yes—not entirely—not everyone, surely.   Let's hope for the best.

Enter GRANDMOTHER JULIA.

GRANDMOTHER: Isn't Istvan here, Baroness? (*The* BARONESS *shakes her head negatively.*) I couldn't wait at home any longer. Something simply pulled me out of the house like a cork from a bottle.

BARONESS: He hasn't come back yet, Countess.

GRANDMOTHER: I left word that I'd be here.

AUNT: So did I. The Baroness was kind enough to take us in at this difficult moment.

BARONESS: But I think tonight will have a wonderful effect on his creativity. He's a strong boy. Surely he won't let himself fall into the clutches of that *marchand-de-vin's* power. A young person must steel himself. Please sit down—we'll wait for the news together.

GRANDMOTHER (*sitting down*):   Yes, quite so—it's not worth a second thought. But I upset him needlessly with that Mordovar legend. An absolutely ridiculous story, and it had such an effect on his imagination.

BARONESS: He's an artistic soul in every inch of his spiritual being. But I've forgotten to congratulate you on your climb up the social ladder. My heartfelt felicitations.

GRANDMOTHER: Oh—a mere trifle. If only nothing bad comes of it. I won't ever tell fortunes again. I'm giving up palmistry too, and even astrology, forever.

BARONES:. Yes—in your present position, it's hardly the thing to do.

DE ESTRADA: Quite right, Baroness.

BARONESS: You see, fortune-telling comes true because people unconsciously push events so as to fulfill the predictions. Even if a person's forebodings all came true every five minutes, I'd still consider it pure chance, given the infinity of this world and the infinity of events and premonitions. *C'est tout à fait contingent,* isn't it, Don José?

DE ESTRADA: Certainly: the law of Large Numbers, a simple calculation of probabilities.   Statistics plays an increasingly important role in everything. Even the laws of physics, most likely, are only statistically true, that is, approximate, although . . . (*From the left side enter the* BARON, *half paralyzed, led in by the* FOOTMAN.)

BARONESS: Oh, what happiness! So you can walk already, Ronnie? We'll go south and everything will be just fine, as Don José says. My son, Hieronymus, Mr. Ambassador.

They greet one another. The BARON *kisses* GRANDMOTHER's *hand with profound respect and shakes hands with the* AUNT.

JACKALS (*sits down in a chair; the* FOOTMAN *exits*): I have such a desire to live, Mother. I feel as though I'd been reborn. The world has never seemed more beautiful to me. I remember I had the same feeling when I was recovering from typhus. Today, the delicate little leaves, seen through the window against a cloudy sky, looked more beautiful to me than the African wilds as I hacked my way through the underbrush hunting big game. I'll never kill another living creature—except perhaps flies—they're so frightfully annoying sometimes. And you know what? I've stopped being a snob; snobbery is a nasty thing—not worth ruining one's life for. I know I love Christina, even though I tried to free myself from her by debauchery, so as not to make a misalliance. That's why I got mixed up in that other love-affair. Now Miss Hajczy has totally stopped existing for me.

BARONESS (*taking him in her arms*):   My darling child! Just don't torture yourself with thoughts like that. There'll be time for everything. Don't make any decisions now—things may not yet be quite normal.

JACKALS (*pushes his mother away, slightly let down*):   Oh, Mother, I wish you were completely on my side at a moment like this. This is the great turning point in my life. I know what you're thinking: about Miss Keszmereth—a very nice young lady—but I love Christina.

DE ESTRADA (*who has been listening with a certain uneasiness and furrowed brow*):   Baron, in our youth we sometimes like to make great decisions, apparently great decisions which subsequently seem petty to us, and sometimes we suffer for them our whole lives. Tradition is a beautiful thing—one mustn't treat it lightly . . .

JACKALS: You don't understand me, Mr. Ambassador; I can't tell you all how beautiful everything is. But will Christina still want me after all this scandal? Will my paralysis go away?

DE ESTRADA (*insincerely*): Certainly—after the hemorrhage has cleared up. In two months you'll be well and then everything will seem different to you.

BARONESS (*to* DE ESTRADA): Why are you acting so strange, Don José? Do you suppose . . .

JACKALS: Mother, stop worrying about trifles. I'm happy for the first time in my life. Even if I remain paralyzed and Christina refuses to give me her hand—even then I'll be happy; I have found a strange peace within myself . . .

BARONESS (*in despair*): My God, My God, My God! . . . (*She covers her face with her hands.*)

DE ESTRADA: Come now, Baroness, it may disappear completely after the operation.

JACKALS: Mother suspects I've gone crazy in a benign sort of way because of the hemorrhage.

Enter RIO BAMBA *without being announced.*

DE ESTRADA: Here he is, our Count Clapary, I congratulate you with all my heart.

RIO BAMBA: I am and will continue to be Rio Bamba. I've atoned for a sin of my youth, and I trust all of you will save me from any other consequences of my past so I can mend my ways in my old age.

DE ESTRADA: But of course, Mr. Rio Bamba—I'll call you by your pseudonym if you like. The devil always looks for ways to do the maximum amount of evil in that one point in the universe where he meets the least resistance. Nowadays that point—or rather a myriad of them—is found in art. Where new forms are coming into being, that's where *he* is, make no doubt about it. I am convinced of it.

JACKALS (*vehemently*): Don't talk that way, Don José! (*Gently.*) There's something dreadful in those words that terrifies me. I don't want anything bad to happen—after all, I'm still very weak.

BARONESS: Calm down, my child. Sit here next to me. I'll rock you to sleep the way I used to when you were little. (*She sits next to him, he puts his head on her shoulder. She rocks him to sleep.*)

RIO BAMBA (*to* GRANDMOTHER): Well, what do you say, old girl? Aren't you touched by this scene? The world is marvelous! But we must be good. There's no way around that—it's straight as any line in Euclid.

GRANDMOTHER: Yes, that's right, Teobald. Our old age will be mild as an autumn morning in the mountains. And the old Mordovar evenings will return once more to this side of the lake.

RIO BAMBA (*laughing*): But just don't call up the spirits from the depths of Mount Czikla anymore. Away with ridiculous legends. Mordovar! My God—what a world of miracles lies stored in that idiotic word! It's good that now at least we're finally able to appreciate all the sweetness of life. Once those two maniacs come back, we'll make them forget all that horrible musical demonism.

JACKALS: Oh, yes—you're right. Only I'd like to get rid of my evil forebodings. Istvan seems to love Christina. But if she chooses me, Istvan and I will get along. We'll listen to Bach and Mozart, he'll compose in a new way. All that art is madness.

AUNT: I too believe he can be great without those artistic eccentricities. That takes its toll on one's life. If it were only possible nowadays to create that Pure Form of theirs without evil. I believe it is—don't you?

BARONESS: Oh, Madam, that insatiability for form; that constant acceleration of the fever for life! Even in total seclusion, even reading only the Bible and drinking milk, one cannot isolate oneself from the spirit of the times.

AUNT: You're well-educated. I don't know these things that well, but I believe . . .

CHRISTINA *runs in*.

CHRISTINA: Has Istvan come back?

DE ESTRADA: They haven't come back yet, but I believe this evening it will all end perfectly.

JACKALS: Mother, you know what you must do to assure my happiness— and not only mine: to increase happiness in the entire universe.

BARONESS (*to* GRANDMOTHER, *stiffly*):   Countess, I have the honor of asking your granddaughter's hand for my son.

GRANDMOTHER (*embarrassed*): Yes, of course it's a great honor although . . . But, if she loves him, naturally—only I have to tell you all that only my first daughter is Rio Bamba's daughter . . . The other one, Christina's mother—but that's enough on that subject; Chris, what do you think, my child?

CHRISTINA (*falling on her knees in front of the* BARONESS): Madam, it's too much happiness for me!

BARONESS (*brutally*): But he's paralyzed and doesn't seem quite right in the head since his suicide.

CHRISTINA: Madam, even if he were the most horrible cripple for the rest of his life, I would always love him.

JACKALS: Come here to me, Chris. I still can't move about. Kiss me. I've always loved you so.

CHRISTINA (*gets up, laughing*): And what about your snobbery? Have you stopped being a snob now, Hieronymus?

JACKALS: Yes—and I'm ashamed I ever was one.

BARONESS: Stop joking, I beg you. (DE ESTRADA *hems very loudly to show his dissatisfaction.*)

CHRISTINA (*chilled*): Oh, yes, I . . . I'm awfully sorry. And Miss Hajczy. . .

JACKALS (*getting up clumsily*): Oh, wait! I forgot! I'm a criminal! I shot her yesterday! Tell me whether she's alive. Quickly—where is she?

DE ESTRADA: I was afraid of this. He's forgotten as a result of nervous shock.

JACKALS: I beg you, Don José . . .

DE ESTRADA: But she's alive, healthy as a Murcia bull. Calm down, boy, for God's sake, or you could do yourself some harm. She fainted—you put a bullet through her paw—she'll be all right soon.

Deeper and deeper twilight falls.

JACKALS (*sinks back into his chair again*): What luck! But I could have been a murderer and not lived to see this happiness. All the same, they'll drag me through the courts—and suppose I get several years? Christina, will you wait for me?

CHRISTINA: Yes, yes—but that won't happen.

DE ESTRADA: Why of course not—with our connections? It'll be totally hushed up . . . Oh, what the devil!

The curtain parts in the middle and HILDA HAJCZY *enters from behind it. Black ball gown, hat. Her left arm bandaged. They all turn around in her direction.*

BARONESS: Where did you come from? In there?   Without being announced?

HILDA: Calm down or you'll cause still worse misfortune. Please don't yell that way.   The atmosphere is steeped in explosive matter. *Hochexplosiv!* There's absolutely no telling what will happen next; the problem of the Beelzebub sonata still isn't . . .

BARONESS: Don't talk about it, please.   Peace and quiet for the invalid before everything . . .

HILDA: Who gets excited if someone has a stomach ache during an earthquake? The way it seems to me, those Mordovar moods won't come back anymore. They'll all talk about it, as a piece of interesting gossip, on the other side of the lake: at the Kurhauz and the Magas Cafehaz and at the train station in Uj-Mordovar and perhaps even in Budapest. But believe me, I came here for the good of all of you, to warn you. Perhaps it's not the appropriate moment, Baroness, and a bit unexpected—but it can't be helped . . .

BARONESS (*having recovered her composure*):   Oh, Miss, since yesterday a great many things have changed. We're gradually getting used to it all . . .

JACKALS (*reproachfully*): Mother!

BARONESS: No need to call "Mother," that's the way it is. My son . . .

AUNT (*trying to change the subject*):   But, that's right, we were just saying that art can be great even without perversionalism, as the Baroness calls it . . .

Suddenly the curtain upstage is drawn and the entire hell from Act Two is visible, but without the forestage, which is taken up by the drawing room. Total dusk on the forestage. Hell is lighted deep red. In the middle stands

BALEASTADAR *in a frock-coat. A fantastic diabolical coat thrown over his frock coat. Horns on his head. Next to him stands* ISTVAN, *likewise in a frock coat. He is very pale. Upstage the infernal* FOOTMEN. *From the left side, enter the* BARONESS's FOOTMAN.

BALEASTADAR (*as the curtain is being drawn*): And I tell you all, no. (*Claps* ISTVAN *on the shoulder.*) I have the proof in Istvan. He is a genius such as the world has never seen. Evil—metaphysical, personal, hairy, fanged, bloody evil—he has piled it on and puffed it up shamelessly in the crystal form of pure music, malevolent as a sudden attack by the Huns. These are the final death throes, but they have the savor of former greatness, even if it is only in art.

DE ESTRADA (*with forced humor*): Well—here they are at last, our Beelzebub sonata cranks. That cursed going around in circles is about to begin all over again. But this setting I don't like in the least. There's an extremely unpleasant demonic "truc" in the way it's got up. They're very nasty things, these Mordovar legends of yours. I'm no coward, but I'm beginning to get a bit frightened. Ugh! . . . Baltazar, don't make silly jokes! He got all dressed up like the real Beelzebub! Don't play the fool!

BALEASTADAR (*roars with sudden fury*): I've had enough of your familiarities, you court jester! I am Beelzebub, Prince of Darkness! Address me as "Your Highness!" Understand?

Silence. In the midst of the silence the BARONESS's FOOTMAN *suddenly starts guffawing.*

FOOTMAN (*in a peasant accent*): Maybe for all you noble folks, this is some kinda comedy. I ain't scared of no Beelzebub.

He chokes with laughter.

BARONESS: What a way to talk! I don't even recognize you, Francis!

BALEASTADAR (*yells*): Stop laughing, you representative of future humanity!

The FOOTMAN *keeps on laughing.* BALEASTADAR *shoots him on the spot with a revolver. The* FOOTMAN *falls.*

HILDA: Oho—this is no joking matter. That was a Beelzebub shot which the grand masters at *tir-aux-pigeons* can dream of, the way Istvan dreams of his sonata. He knows how to shoot, but he can't compose anything himself. So you see, my friends: I'm a plebeian, like Istvan's aunt, if I'm not mistaken. But I belong to the so-called "aristocracy of the soul"— the latest swindle of our times. Ronnie, do you . . .

DE ESTRADA (*interrupts her*):   What insolent nonsense! That's all very well, but where in this Hungary of yours are the police at times like these? I mean, this is a perfectly organized gang, these three!

BALEASTADAR: At times like these, whether here or in Spain, the police don't know the first thing about diabolical metaphysics—they find out about the consequences when it's too late. Go on, Hilda! I don't have any idea what you're going to say and I'm curious.

HILDA: Now listen, Ronnie: do you think it's going to be enough for you, that turtledove and all this goodness of yours, and being infatuated with the pretty little leaves against the gray sky, and that mawkish self-satisfaction which fills me with disgust? You love only me and you're mine. You know how I keep hold of you—remember? Keep that in mind—no one else will give you that—come! Let's go to that hell of theirs. There true life and enjoyment are bubbling over to the sounds of the Beelzebub sonata, the last farewell fanfare of that dying swarm of insects once called humanity. You're healthy, you're not paralyzed. Stand up and come with me.

JACKALS (*gets up suddenly, healthy as a bull*):   You're right, Hilda. All that's an illusion. I'm yours. Let's go.

BARONESS: I prefer even this to that misalliance. Ronnie, I'm so happy you've recovered! And when you've enjoyed life, you'll marry Miss Keszmereth. I know after you've passed through that school, your wife will never be bored with you. That was the chief shortcoming of husbands in my generation, they . . .

JACKALS: I know, I know—good-bye, Mother, for now. (*He enters hell with* HILDA *in a circle of red light.*)

BALEASTADAR: Bravo, Ronnie! All right, Hilda, go on!

HILDA (*to the* BARON): And did you think I had really fallen that low? I only wanted to get you away from that silly goose . . .

CHRISTINA: I'm going with you! I love Istvan. I made a mistake too. Forgive me, infernal people. I won't ever do it again. Take me with you!

HILDA: You miserable little lapdog bitch. You go to hell? No—that's a place for tigers and hyenas only. Stay in your cozy drawing room and keep on enjoying Mordovar evenings. Get out of here!

JACKALS (*pulls out a revolver*): This time you won't get away from me, you stinking female! (*He shoots* HILDA, *who falls to the ground*.)

BALEASTADAR: Fine—now he's bumped her off for good. But Istvan and I don't need women. Pure Art will suffice. Ha, ha, ha, ha, ha! (*He laughs demonically.*)

JACKALS: Oh—so even this hasn't been spared me! Istvan, I implore you, be my only friend. Now I'm completely alone. You're a count—we can be on equal footing. I'm giving you everything. Women don't exist for me anymore.

ISTVAN: You've forgotten that we were supposed to fight, Baron. You insulted me. I love no one but my Master, the Prince of Darkness!

JACKALS: No—I won't fight. Too much unhappiness. I've had enough of all this. This is the end. (*He shoots himself in the temple. A scream in the drawing room. The* BARONESS *falls.*)

DE ESTRADA: *Me cago en la barba del Belzebubo.* I smell almonds. The Baroness has taken cyanide. Let's try to save her. But after all, what does it matter! I'm going to hell too.

BALEASTADAR: Oh, no! I'm no specialist in matrimonial triangles. You won't get away with that a second time, Joe. Seducing a man's wife is something even Beelzebub himself won't forgive.

He shoots DE ESTRADA *who collapses on the threshold of hell, his face towards the audience.*

RIO BAMBA: Too many corpses, by Beelzebub! They're toppling over like at a shooting gallery. Old Mordovarians, let's get out of here, while there's still time. This way. Come along, Julia, and you, old aunt. We're totally superfluous here.

They run out to the left.

AUNT (*running out*): Be great to the end, Istvan dear. I can't watch this any longer. I'm too old for these new directions of yours.

They disappear to the left. CHRISTINA, *as though demented, goes over to* ISTVAN.

CHRISTINA: I won't ever leave you. On the highest summits—in life or in art—I will be yours. I only want to serve you. I don't care about myself.

BALEASTADAR: Istvan doesn't need women anymore, nor anything else. He's finished. But you can get to work sorting out the manuscripts— that is, they're actually—the typescripts. All the compositions that he was destined to create, he has already created—starting with the sonata opus one and going up to the homo . . . how can I put it: the boundlessly complex hyperhomogeneous, and almost hypnogogic ultramadrigals and interlubrics—they're all here. Look, this heap of papers here, these are all his posthumous works—*oeuvres posthumes*—written on the machine for noting down improvisations. But these weren't improvisations—these are works born of spatial conceptions in another dimension.

CHRISTINA: What did you say? His posthumous works?

BALEASTADAR: Can't you see he's a corpse? Now we'll go on tour and I'll perform all of it. Because, although I'm not a creator, as a pianist I surpass Paderewski and Artur Rubinstein and all the others by one thousand degrees on the scale of greatness. No one will be able to play these pieces but me.   He couldn't come close to it himself with his technique. He only played enough to have it noted down roughly. But now we must *"le mettre à point,"* you understand, polish it up rhythmically. I believe you're rather musical, aren't you?

ISTVAN *stays where he is without moving.*

CHRISTINA: Yes—I studied a bit.

BALEASTADAR: Good. You'll be able to help me. These are mountains of explosive matter, the last glimmers of individual diabolicalness. For a moment more, if only in the dimensions of art, it's possible to disturb the slumber of mankind as it drowses off into communal well-being. Because crimes committed in the name of the working classes are not my specialty. They aren't even actually crimes—the devil knows what they are. I loathe and despise them. All right—you can get down to work. (CHRISTINA *digs into the piles of papers, scarcely conscious.*) And now I'll try out the famous Beelzebub sonata. Thus the most idiotic Mordovar legend has come true. (*He goes to the piano and begins to play what* ISTVAN *was playing at the end of Act Two; he plays magnificently with gestures typical of a frenetic pianist carried away by inspiration: during the pianissimo he speaks.*)   The height of irony, possible only in our vile times—Beelzebub, Prince of Darkness, ends up as a pianist!

ISTVAN *turns around like an automaton, moves upstage and goes out to the left.*

CHRISTINA (*uneasily*): Why did he leave? Where did he go?

BALEASTADAR (*playing softly*): He can't stand it that I play it better than he does. And then too, he's tormented because he knows that without me he wouldn't have composed anything. (*Frightful scream off-stage.* BALEASTADAR *plays furiously. The purple curtains at the back of the stage are drawn apart. Red dusk falls in hell. At the back of the stage Mount Czikla is visible: a craggy peak with streaks of snow as in Act One—but by the light of the rising sun. Woods at the foot of the mountain. In the foreground a black opening in the midst of whitish stone debris. Against the opening,* ISTVAN *can be seen hanging by his suspenders from a pine tree.* AUNT, RIO BAMBA *and* GRANDMOTHER *approach the corpse cautiously from the side and take it down.* BALEASTADAR, *getting up from the piano.*) Now you see why I said these works are posthumous. We don't have to mourn him. He couldn't have gone on living anyhow. He'd lived himself out completely, and what's most important, he'd composed himself out to the last drop—there was nothing left of him. When he hanged himself, he was already a corpse. We can leave the other arts in peace. We won't squeeze anything more demonic out of them than this. (*Points at the heap of papers—to the*

FOOTMEN.) And now, clowns, look lively! Bring in the chest. We can still make the Budapest express which stops at Uj-Mordovar at six fifteen. We're going on a final world-wide tour, and then it's the end of Beelzebub.

With mad speed, the FOOTMEN bring him the chest into which BALEASTADAR *and* CHRISTINA *begin to throw the papers.*

CHRISTINA: Oh, my Prince of Darkness! You're the only one I love. You won't drive me away now. There's some kind of a rondo here for two pianos—we'll play it together.

BALEASTADAR: All right—we'll see. Tonight you'll take an examination with me. And as for love—that still remains to be seen. For the moment, sexual matters leave me cold

CHRISTINA: Oh! Yes, yes—I agree to everything. But I couldn't stand any more of these Mordovar moods. I've got to get out of here and really start to live.

BALEASTADAR: All right then—what are you complaining about! We're going together, aren't we? (*To the group of Mordovarians at the back of the stage who are standing over* ISTVAN's *corpse.*)   Goodbye! And don't go creating any new legends. Next time they won't come true quite so easily.

He goes to the left, followed by CHRISTINA *and then the* SIX FOOTMEN *dragging the chest. The Mordovarians wave their handkerchiefs. A far-off train whistle. Ringing of distant bells.* BALEASTADAR, CHRISTINA *and the* FOOTMEN *leave by the door to hell on the left.*

26 June 1925

Studio Portrait of Witkiewicz
Photograph by J. Kępińska, Zakopane
1927-28

A FEW WORDS ABOUT THE ROLE OF THE ACTOR IN THE THEATRE OF PURE FORM

by

S.I. Witkiewicz

(1919)

A Few Words about the Role of the Actor
in the Theatre of Pure Form

In Warsaw recently there has been a revival of the art of the actor, initiated by Mieczysław Limanowski, a geologist well known throughout all of Europe. We are obliged to debate the matter with him—we being (in the *pluralis doppelgängerus*) a painter virtually unknown even in Poland. This seems farcical, but that's the way it is—there's no help for it. The theatre really must be in bad shape if people from such diverse specialties have something to say on this subject.

The theories according to which this "renaissance" is taking place are closely related to the principles set forth in Kommissarzhevsky's book *The Actor's Creativity and the Stanislavsky Theory.* Following these views, the actor is supposed to "experience" totally the inner life of his role. His words and gestures are supposed to result naturally from his feelings, just as would happen in real life to people under the influence of strong emotions. All this they call *perezhivaniya* (experiences), plus *voploshcheniya* (embodiment).

A second principle of the Stanislavsky school (in our view a correct one, as opposed to the first, which we must categorize as totally false) has as its aim the creation of an absolutely unified company in which no star tenor can hog the front of the stage and push the other actors into the role of accompanists, turning the play into a solo display piece for a particular actor or actress and destroying it as a work of art. It goes without saying that in the staging of the sort of Pure Form play which we have previously attempted to describe, this second principle is altogether indispensable. Despite the dominance or subordination of certain moments and individuals on the stage, it is impossible to think of any purely formal whole where unity in plurality in and of itself is not the most important goal. But, in our opinion, all kinds of "experiences" are totally irrelevant.

In the genre which we are proposing (and even for performances of the old masters of dramatic literature), the actor should be, in all he says and does, a part of the whole, without feeling any necessity to "create" the role in a realistic sense; that is to say, he need not enter into the real-life feelings of the hero and imitate onstage such a person's supposed gestures and tone of voice at various important moments in his life. Instead, the actor should truly *create the role,* which, in our interpretation, entails the following. First, the actor must understand the whole of the play, with particular reference to all the lines spoken by all the characters who appear in the work, as well as their gestures and also the different settings as they unfold during the course of the action; or, in other words, he must first understand the *formal conception* of the work (as distinct from its real-life mood) and its character, apart from all real-life probabilities. Next, he should build his role in such a way that—quite independently of his own frame of mind, his own inner experiences and state of nerves—he can execute with mathematical precision whatever is required by the purely formal conception of the particular work. This may mean that he is to say a given speech with special stress on certain words, at one moment emphasizing their logical content, at another their sound value, or to offer the spectator a new image in contrast to the real, changing picture of the given situation. His work will be genuinely creative only when he considers himself as an element in the given whole.

Once he is onstage, the actor does nothing but give a performance, which of course may be increasingly perfected throughout the rehearsals and during the course of the actual production, but he will continue to do nothing but give a performance, comparable to other performances, such as the actual painting of a picture which has already been composed, or the writing down of a symphony and its performance by an orchestra. However, the relationship between conception and execution is different for each of the arts; their moments of invention and technical realization are differently coordinated. In painting and poetry, the most—relatively speaking—happens while the work is actually in progress; less takes place during the physical writing of music, although even here various changes and improvements of initially foggy conceptions are also possible. In the theatre there should be a minimum of this, unless of course the theatre is to be nothing more than a servile copy of reality. If that is the case, then "experiences" can be immensely useful, although if we imagine a successful play in which a certain character commits two murders and is condemned to death, we may well ask what kind of a superman or superwoman would be able to experience all that, say three hundred times, without becoming seriously disturbed or, quite simply, going insane.

In our opinion, for the actor who does not have to imitate a character, but who can create his role according to his own creative intuition, the psychology of the hero as well as the lines which he has to speak should be only subsidiary means. Once he appears onstage, the actor must be like a painter who has so thoroughly thought out all the details of his painting and has such a sure hand that the execution of the picture requires nothing from him but the mechanical application of several coats of paint. It goes without saying that such a procedure is almost impossible in painting; in the art of the actor, however, the creative process should ideally proceed in that fashion, and it is in fact quite within the realm of possibility. Naturally, unavoidable small variations are of no concern.

The actor should keep himself firmly under control the way a musical virtuoso does. The only difference is that the actor has much greater scope for his creativity, but always within the limits of the *given work's remaining true to itself*—which is the director's responsibility. Every play, like every poem, contains only a certain limited number of interpretations, beyond which it stops being the work created by the author. However, we have no objective measure for this limit. In our opinion, Shakespeare staged with Stanislavsky's realism stops being Shakespeare, Beethoven played sentimentally stops being Beethoven, but unfortunately we have no objective criterion for any of this. There will always be the possibility of more or less emphasis on real-life content, and every work of art, even the purest, faces inevitable defilement; in the performance and the hearing or viewing in music and theatre, in the possibility of seeing the world of objects in painting.

Of course, it all depends on whether the author has stressed the formal content or the real-life content. Any play in Pure Form can be staged realistically, but a purely formal whole cannot be made out of every realistic work, even if the director were to stand on his head. But whereas in painting and sculpture there are only the works and those who view them, music and theatre are further handicapped in that they must depend on the performance, and in the case of theatre the complications arising from this reach quite colossal proportions.

Setting the *formal tone* depends, of course, on the director. Grasping the purely formal content of the work and creating a unified structural whole is an incredibly difficult task. But as a general guideline we could formulate the following purely negative principle. *Forget completely about life and pay no attention to any real-life consequences of what is happening onstage at any given moment as it relates to what is about to happen at the next moment.* It goes without saying—at the next moment onstage. Naturally we're not talking about real-life consequences beyond the stage, such as the possibility of an empty cash drawer, or the director, actors, and author being beaten up by the crowd, or other similar happenings which, in our opinion, the management of an experimental theatre should, at the present time, accept as the facts of life.

We should point out that in this kind of play the manner of speaking the lines, or the delivery, ought not to be uniformly a matter of the emotions. From time to time this sort of emotional emphasis might serve as a purely formal effect (for example, saying something sad in a joyful fashion or the reverse, which incidentally happens even in life when one gets upset over something totally insignificant or treats indifferently a real atrocity); however, compared to the roar of animal passions heard on the stage nowadays, compared to this hyperintensification of life, the delivery of the lines in the theatre of Pure Form must be very restrained, and all the same principles which we formulated when discussing the declamation of poetry must be applied to this question. Each play should have its own "tone," its upper and lower limits to be respected in accordance with the author's intentions which must be felt or understood by the director. We do not maintain that volleys of shots, roars, and groans are inadmissible on the stage, but only that everything must be interpreted and incorporated within the limits set by the tone of the whole, rather than be the expression of purely real-life associations. Whereas authors can afford to let themselves be carried away, the challenge of creative work on the stage depends on its rigorous limits.

If actors could only give up their ingrained bad habit of displaying emotions, the whole creative process of acting would consist solely in maintaining the agreed-upon tonality. On the one hand, this seems to be something so trifling that it is not worth talking about; on the other hand, it is infernally difficult—so much so as to be virtually impossible. However, we maintain that as soon as the tone is properly understood as a part of the formal conception, the details of the execution should fall into place of their own accord. Of course, actors would have to give up their long-standing practice of trying to send audiences into convulsive emotional twitchings, spasms, and fits—and that is one of the principal difficulties in the proper staging of a play in this new mode. The actor's need to direct the audience's attention to himself and to feel the satisfaction of being able to hit them in their innermost recesses and guts would have to become transformed into a genuine desire actually to create a whole in dimensions totally different from real-life ones, even though each actor's contribution would be only partial. To accomplish this, the actor would have to forgo his desire to impersonate, to pretend to be somebody real about whom someone else was tactless enough to write—which is what "experiencing" *à la* Limanowski ultimately amounts to. Despite all the lack of expertise in theatre of which we can be accused, we hold that the gist of what we have said is correct—from the formal point of view of course—and that the whole thing which we have outlined is completely feasible.

Let's assume that people at the first performance actually roar with laughter because they expect the play to make the kind of sense which they have always been accustomed to look for in the theatre and which *au fond* already bores them to death. Quite possibly sophisticated connoisseurs and professional theatregoers will make faces in disgust and use abusive language. But we are of the opinion that after a certain purely superficial getting used to the outer trappings of the thing, it should be possible to take far greater pleasure in performances of this kind than in French farces which already make people sick to their stomachs, or than in dramas with so much "truth" in them that they outdo life itself in truthfulness, sublimities hobbling on crutches, or various other tidbits under the rubric "renaissance."

Now we have absolutely no desire to depreciate the great masterpieces of past ages. But isn't it time to stop repeating what was created a long time ago in its most perfect form?

What we propose is twofold: to cultivate the classics with a proper feeling for their essence—but only those works of outstanding value which have stood the test of time—and to launch out on the (at least seemingly) boundless sea of experiment. In painting nothing more remained to be created in the realm of subject matter, from the point of view of life undeformed, except for inane naturalism which amounted to beating one's head against a brick wall—in other words, against the unattainable perfection of nature. Likewise in poetry, sense—worked over for the millionth time—became an obstacle to new formal combinations. In theatre the situation is exactly the same now. Don't anyone tell me that this will produce a private gibberish unintelligible to others, an individual language which only its creator will understand, or the actions of people suffering from schizophrenia. All these accusations may be true if we look at art from the point of view of life. In our understanding of the term, form is something higher than subject matter and real-life sense, which are only means in the purely personal process of creation.

There is need to unbind hands and feet, ungag mouths, and shake all the old bad habits out of our heads. Let's assume that nothing comes of it and that it all sinks down again into the same boredom and grayness typical of the creative work going on around us now and reverts to that endless rehashing of the same old thing to the point of nausea. Let's assume that it's the figment of the imagination of a sick brain—the brain of an individual who does not understand that the theatre can never be anything but what it has always been up to now. Still, isn't it worth trying?

The force with which we resist the temptation to try anything new and unknown is truly diabolical. Or has the temptation really grown too weak? That would prove that the mechanization of life has really gone so far that the theatre as a social institution *par excellence* can no longer resist the petrification of everything into a uniform, gray, undifferentiated pulp that is only superficially heterogeneous.

December 1919

BIBLIOGRAPHY

PLAYS

Karaluchy (*Cockroaches*), written 1893, published, 1965, produced 1966.

Komedie z życia rodzinnego (*Comedies of Family Life*), written 1893, published 1965, produced 1983.

Menażeria, czyli wybryk słonia (*Menagerie, or the Elephant Escapades*), written 1893, published 1965, produced 1966.

Księżniczka Magdalena, czyli natrętny książę (*Princess Magdalena, or the Importunate Prince*), written 1893, published 1965, produced 1966.

Odważna księżniczka (*The Courageous Princess*), written 1893, published 1947, produced 1970.

Biedny chłopiec (*The Poor Boy*), written 1893, published 1964, produced 1970.

Maciej Korbowa i Bellatrix (*Maciej Korbowa and Bellatrix*), written 1918, published 1962, produced 1986.

Pragmatyści (*The Pragmatists*), written 1919, published 1920, produced 1921.

Tumor Mózgowicz (*Tumor Brainiowicz*), written 1920, published and produced 1921.

Mister Price, czyli bzik tropikalny (*Mister Price or Tropical Madness*), written 1920, produced 1926, published 1962.

Nowe Wyzwolenie (*The New Deliverance*), written 1920, published 1922-23, produced 1925.

Oni (*They*), written 1920, published 1962, produced 1963.

Panna Tutli-Putli (*Miss Tootli-Pootli*), written 1920, published 1974, produced 1975.

W małym dworku (*In a Small Country House*), written 1921, performed 1923, published 1948.

Niepodległość trójkątów (*The Independence of Triangles*), written 1921, published 1962, produced 1985.

Metafizyka dwugłowego cielęcia (*Metaphysics of a Twoheaded Calf*), written 1921, produced 1928, published 1962.

Gyubal Wahazar, czyli na przełęczach bezsensu (*Gyubal Wahazar, or Along the Cliffs of the Absurd*), written 1921, published 1962, produced 1966.

Kurka Wodna (*The Water Hen*), written 1921, produced 1922, published 1962.

Bezimienne dzieło (*The Anonymous Work*), written 1921, published 1962, produced 1967.

Mątwa, czyli Hyrkaniczny światopogląd (*The Cuttlefish, or the Hyrcanian World View*), written 1922, published 1923, produced 1933.

Nadobnisie i koczkodany, czyli zielona pigułka (*Dainty Shapes and Hairy Apes, or the Green Pill*), written 1922, published 1962, produced 1967.

Jan Maciej Karol Wścieklica (*Jan Maciej Karol Hellcat*), written 1922, produced 1925, published 1962.

Wariat i zakonnica, czyli nie ma zlego, coby na jeszcze gorsze nie wyszło (*The Madman and the Nun, or There is Nothing Bad Which Could Not Turn into Something Worse*), written 1923, produced 1924, published 1925.

Szalona lokomotywa (*The Crazy Locomotive*), written 1923, published 1962, produced 1965.

Janulka, córka Fizdejki (*Janulka, Daughter of Fizdejko*), written 1923, published 1962, produced 1974.

Matka (*The Mother*), written 1924, published 1962, produced 1964.

Sonata Belzebuba, czyli prawdziwe zdarzenie w Mordowarze (*The

Beelzebub Sonata, or What Really Happened in Mordovar), written 1925, published 1938, produced 1966.

Szewcy (*The Shoemakers*), written 1927-1934, published 1948, produced 1957 (prevented by the censor), 1965 (student theatre), 1971.

BOOKS ABOUT WITKACY
(in English)

Chudziński, Edward, ed. *Witkacy at the End of the Century*. Cracow: Teatr STU, 1992.

Franczak, Ewa and Stefan Okołowicz. *Against Nothingness*, translated by Jadwiga Piątkowska. Cracow: Wydawnictwo Literackie, 1986.

Gerould, Daniel, *Witkacy as an Imaginative Writer*. Seattle: University of Washington Press, 1981.

_____. *The Witkiewicz Reader*. Evanston: Northwestern University Press, 1995.

Jakimowicz, Irena. *Witkacy, the painter*, translated by Ewa Krasińska. Warsaw: Auriga, 1987.

Kiebuzinska, Christine. *Revolutionaries in the Theater: Meyerhold, Brecht, and Witkiewicz*. Ann Arbor, Michigan: UMI Research Press, 1988.

Micińska, Anna. *Witkacy: Stanisław Ignacy Witkiewicz: his life and work*, translated by Bogna Piotrowska (Warsaw: Interpress, 1991).

The Theatre in Poland, Special Witkiewicz issues. No. 3 (March 1970); Nos. 6-7 (June-July 1978); Nos. 10-12 (October-December 1984).

Witkacy Metaphysical Portraits: Photographs 1910-1939 by Stanisław Ignacy Witkiewicz. New York: Robert Miller Gallery, 1999.

Witkiewicz, S.I. *Photographs, 1899-1939*. Glasgow: Third Eye Centre, 1989.

SOURCES

The newly revised translations are based on the definitive texts of the plays and theoretical essays that appeared in the three volumes of *Dramaty* and in *Teatr: inne pisma o teatrze* in the new complete edition of *Witkiewicz: Dzieła Zebrane* (Warsaw: Państwowy Instytut Wydawniczy, 1992-), edited by Janusz Degler. Earlier versions of the translations first appeared in the following journals and books.

The Anonymous Work in *Drama & Theatre*, XII, No. 1 (Fall, 1974).

"A Few Words about the Role of the Actor in the Theatre of Pure Form," in *Theatre Quarterly*, V (June-August 1975).

The Beelzebub Sonata, *Tumor Brainiowicz*, and *Dainty Shapes and Hairy Apes* in *The Beelzebub Sonata* (N.Y.: Performing Arts Journal Publications, 1980).

The Cuttlefish in Gassner/Dukore, *A Treasury of the Theatre*, Vol. 2, Fourth edition (New York: Holt, Rinehart and Winston, 1970).

Gyubal Wahazar in *Tropical Madness: Four Plays* (N.Y.: Winter House, 1972).

The Pragmatists in *Drama & Theatre*, X, No. 1 (Fall 1971).

"Theoretical Introduction" in *Avant-garde Drama: Major Plays and Documents* (N.Y.: Bantam Books, 1969).

ACKNOWLEDGEMENTS & CREDITS

Grateful acknowledgement is made to Janusz Degler for sharing his vast knowledge about Witkacy, to Elizabeth Swain for invaluable help with the translations, and to Frank Hentschker for expert advice on the book design.

The photographs and drawings in this volume came from the collections of Ewa Franczak, Stefan Okołowicz, Anna Micińska, and Konstanty Puzyna.

The cover illustration is "Composition with a Character Wearing Spurs," signed: "Witkacy 25 February 1935. After 50 years. No Drinking, No Smoking for Two Months," according to the artist's system of notation. (Witkacy was born on 24 February 1885.) This drawing is item #1908 in the Catalogue prepared by Irena Jakimowicz with Anna Żakiewicz for the Warsaw National Museum, 1990. It is part of the private collection of Daniel Gerould.

OTHER MARTIN E. SEGAL THEATRE CENTER PUBLICATIONS

The Heirs of Molière: Four French Comedies of the 17th and 18th Centuries, translated and edited by Marvin Carlson, includes *The Fashionable Prejudice* by Pierre Nivelle de La Chausée, *The Absent-Minded Lover* by Jean-Francois Regnard, *The Conceited Count* by Phillipe Nèricault Destouches, and *The Friend of the Laws* by Jean-Louis Laya. These four dramas are representative of French comedy of the period from the death of Molière to the French Revolution and are translated in a poetic form to capture the wit and spirit of the originals.

Pixérécourt: Four Melodramas, translated and edited by Daniel Gerould and Marvin Carlson, contains four of Pixérécourt's most important melodramas: *The Ruins of Babylon, The Dog of Montargis, Christopher Columbus,* and *Alice* as well as Charles Nodier's "Introduction" to the 1843 edition of the author's plays and two theoretical essays by the playwright.

Contemporary Theatre in Egypt, edited by Marvin Carlson, contains the proceedings of a Symposium on this subject held at the CUNY Graduate Center in 1999 along with the first English translations of three short plays by leading Egyptian playwrights who spoke at the Symposium, Alfred Farag, Gamal Maqsoud, and Lenin El-Ramley. It concludes with a bibliography of English translations and secondary articles on the theatre in Egypt since 1955.

Zeami and the Nô Theatre in the World, edited by Benito Ortolani and Samuel Leiter, contains the proceedings of the "Zeami and the Nô Theatre in the World Symposium" held in New York City in October 1997 in conjunction with the "Japanese Theatre in the World" exhibit at the Japan Society. The book contains an introduction and fifteen essays, organized into sections on "Zeami's Theories and Aesthetics," "Zeami and Drama," "Zeami and Acting," and "Zeami and the World."

Four Works for the Theatre **by Hugo Claus** contains translations of four plays by the foremost contemporary writer of Dutch language theatre, poetry, and prose. Flemish by birth and upbringing, Claus is the author of some ninety plays, novels, and collections of poetry. The plays collected here, edited and with an introduction by David Willinger, include *The Temptation*, *Friday*, *Serenade*, and *The Hair of the Dog*.

For further information on the Martin E. Segal Theatre Center visit:
http://web.gc.cuny.edu/mestc